HOW TO GET A JOB IN HOUSTON

**THOMAS M. CAMDEN
ROBERT SANBORN, ED.D.**

SurreyBooks
CHICAGO

HOW TO GET A JOB IN HOUSTON

Published by Surrey Books, Inc., 230 E. Ohio St., Suite 120, Chicago, IL 60611. Telephone: (312) 751-7330.

Copyright © 1993 by Surrey Books, Inc. All rights reserved, including the right to reproduce this book or portions thereof in any form, including any information storage and retrieval system, except for the inclusion of brief quotations in a review.

This book is manufactured in the United States of America.

2nd Edition.   2 3 4 5

Library of Congress Cataloging-in-Publication data:

Camden, Thomas M., 1938-
    How to get a job in Houston / Thomas M. Camden, Robert Sanborn.—
2nd ed.
      376 p.   cm.
      Includes bibliographical references and indexes.
      ISBN 0-940625-53-9 (paper): $15.95
    1. Job hunting—Texas—Houston. 2. Job vacancies—Texas—Houston. 3. Professions—Texas—Houston. 4. Occupations—Texas—Houston. 5. Houston (Tex.)—Industries—Directories. 6. Business enterprises—Texas—Houston—Directories. I. Sanborn, Robert, 1959-   . II. Title.
HF5382.75.U62T43 1993   92-42004
650.14'09764'1411—dc20   CIP

AVAILABLE IN THIS SERIES — $15.95 (*Pacific Rim* and *Europe* $17.95)

How To Get a Job in Atlanta by Diane C. Thomas, Bill Osher, Ph.D., and Thomas M. Camden.

How To Get a Job in Greater Boston by Paul S. Tanklefsky and Thomas M. Camden.

How To Get a Job in Chicago by Thomas M. Camden and Susan Schwartz.

How To Get a Job in Dallas/Fort Worth by Richard Citrin and Thomas M. Camden.

How To Get a Job in Europe by Robert Sanborn, Ed.D.

How To Get a Job in Houston by Thomas M. Camden and Robert Sanborn, Ed.D.

How To Get a Job in The New York Metropolitan Area by Thomas M. Camden and Susan Fleming-Holland.

How To Get a Job in the Pacific Rim by Robert Sanborn, Ed.D., and Anderson Brandao.

How To Get a Job in The San Francisco Bay Area by Thomas M. Camden and Evelyn Jean Pine.

How To Get a Job in Seattle/Portland by Thomas M. Camden and Robert W. Thirsk, Ed.D.

How To Get a Job in Southern California by Thomas M. Camden and Jonathan Palmer.

How To Get a Job in Washington, DC, by Thomas M. Camden and Kathy Strawser.

Single copies may be ordered directly from the publisher. Send check or money order plus $2.50 per book for postage and handling to Surrey Books at the above address. For quantity discounts, please contact the publisher.

Editorial production by Bookcrafters, Inc., Chicago.
Cover design by Hughes Design, Chicago.
Typesetting by On Track Graphics, Inc., Chicago.
"How To Get a Job Series" is distributed to the trade by Publishers Group West.

ACKNOWLEDGMENTS

The authors would like to thank Rebecca Robertson for her organizational contributions and midnight oil, and the following people for their invaluable help: Don Kindred, Linda Breed, Alan Ying, Victoria Mejia, Cheryl Matherly, Meg Simmons, Monique Forwand, Tam Truong. We would also like to thank Amy Orchard, Shelley Fuld, John Normand, Bernie Barcio, Filemon Silva, Laura Patterson, and Tom Sommers. All contributed hard work to the completion of this volume. Most of all, Bob would like to thank the staff of the Rice University Career Services Center for their strong support while he was working on the book. Finally, Bob would like to thank his pillars of support, his wife Ellen and his daughter Ginny Elisabet Sanborn.

Others deserving recognition are: Publisher Susan Schwartz, Managing Editor Gene DeRoin; Art Director Sally Hughes; and Dr. Bill Osher, editorial contributor.

Note to Our Readers

We, the authors and editors, have made every effort to supply you with the most useful, up-to-date information available to help you find the job you want. Each name, address, and phone number has been verified by our staff of fact checkers. But offices move and people change jobs, so we urge you to call before you write, and write before you visit. And if you think we should include information on companies, organizations, or people that we've missed, please let us know.

The publisher, authors, and editors make no guarantee that the employers listed in this book have jobs available.

JOB HUNTING?
THESE BOOKS, COVERING 10 MAJOR MARKETS, PLUS EUROPE & THE PACIFIC RIM, CAN HELP.

HOW...
to get the job you want: Each book gives you more than 1,500 major employers, numbers to call, and people to contact

WHERE...
to get the job you want: How to research the local job market and meet the people who hire

PLUS...
how to use: Local networks and professional organizations; advice on employment services; how to sell yourself in the interview; writing power resumes and cover letters; hundreds of names and numbers, many available nowhere else!

FOR EASIER ORDERING CALL 1-800-326-4430

Please send at $15.95 each ("PACIFIC RIM" and "EUROPE" $17.95):
- ___ HOW TO GET A JOB IN ATLANTA
- ___ HOW TO GET A JOB IN BOSTON
- ___ HOW TO GET A JOB IN CHICAGO
- ___ HOW TO GET A JOB IN DALLAS/FT. WORTH
- ___ HOW TO GET A JOB IN EUROPE
- ___ HOW TO GET A JOB IN HOUSTON
- ___ HOW TO GET A JOB IN NEW YORK
- ___ HOW TO GET A JOB IN THE PACIFIC RIM
- ___ HOW TO GET A JOB IN SAN FRANCISCO
- ___ HOW TO GET A JOB IN SEATTLE/PORTLAND
- ___ HOW TO GET A JOB IN SOUTHERN CALIFORNIA
- ___ HOW TO GET A JOB IN WASHINGTON, DC

Name_____ Address_____
City_____ State_____ Zip_____
Enclosed is my check/money order for $_____.
AmEx/Visa/MasterCard #_____
Exp. date _____ Signature_____

Send check or money order, *and include $2.50 per book* for postage and handling, to:
Surrey Books, 230 E. Ohio St., Suite 120, Chicago, IL 60611
Or call toll-free: 1-800-326-4430

Allow 4-6 weeks for delivery. Satisfaction guaranteed or money back.

CONTENTS

1 How To Get the Most from This Book
Page 1

What this book can and can not do for you. What you absolutely shouldn't skip. Outlook for Houston in the 1990s. Tips for finding your way around town. Chambers of Commerce. Hints for newcomers.

2 Establishing an Objective: How To Discover What You Want To Do
Page 9

The importance of knowing what you want to do before you set out to do it. Questions to help you clarify your job objective. Helpful books on life/career planning. Books on making a mid-life career change. Books for younger and older job hunters and those with disabilities. Books for women. Professional vocational analysis: where to find it, what it costs, how to evaluate a service. What to expect from career counselors. Advice for the trailing spouse. Tips for people thinking of starting their own small business.

3 Writing a Resume That Works
Page 20

The resume—what it is, what it can and can not do for you. The basics of a good resume. Recommended resume format. Pros and cons of hiring someone else to write your resume. Firms that prepare resumes: what they cost, how to evaluate them. What NOT to do with a resume. Cover letters. Sample resumes and cover letters.

4 Researching the Houston Area Job Market
Page 37

The importance of doing your homework. The local library business section, the best friend a job hunter ever had. Locations and phone numbers of local libraries. University libraries and career service centers. The Big Four directories and how they can help you. Dozens of other directories that might come in handy. Houston area newspapers and how to use them. Pros and cons of answering want ads. Feature and business magazines. Trade and special interest magazines—how to use them. Listing of trade magazines with editorial offices in the Houston, Austin, and Dallas areas. Job-hunt related publications with job listings.

5 Developing a Strategy: The ABCs of Networking
Page 57

The importance of having a strategy. How long will it take to find a job? Tried and true advice about nurturing your ego. Establishing a job-hunting schedule. Networking—the key to a successful job search. The exploratory interview. Developing professional contacts. How to keep yourself organized. How to identify and contact hiring authorities. Tips for landing an interview. A unique list of selected networking groups in the Houston area: professional organizations, trade groups, clubs, and societies, with descriptions, contacts, and phone numbers. Informal networking: favorite watering holes of various professions.

6 Using Professional Employment Services *Page 84*

Employment agencies—what they can and can not do for you, how they charge, where to check up on them. Listing of Houston employment agencies and their specialties. Career consultants; some words to the wise and questions to ask before retaining one. Executive search firms—how they operate, pros and cons; selected list. Social service and government employment services.

7 How To Succeed In an Interview *Page 98*

Formal and informal interviews and how to prepare for them. Mastering the five-minute resume. The interview as a sales presentation. Steps to a successful interview. What interviewers look for. Anticipating tough questions, and making sure you get your own questions answered. What to do following the interview. Books on interviewing. How to use references.

8 What To Do If Money Gets Tight *Page 110*

Reviewing your assets and liabilites. Pros and cons of part-time and temporary work. List of selected sources for part-time work. If you need further help: federal, state, and local government assistance programs. How to sign up for unemployment benefits. Additional sources of help, providing everything from money management counseling to emergency food and clothing.

9 Where To Turn If Your Confidence Wilts *Page 120*

Tips for dealing with rejection and stress. Recognizing danger signals. Guidelines for seeking professional counseling or therapy. Selected crisis lines and mental health centers. Women in transition. What to do if you get fired. Career transition issues.

10 Selecting the Right Job for You
Page 130

You don't have to jump at the first offer. What you should find out before accepting any job offer. Finding the right employment "culture." Tips and books on negotiating salary. How to compare job offers—sample checklist. What to do after you finally accept a job. Zeroing in on a great place to work.

11 Where Houston Works
Page 137

Names, addresses, and phone numbers of the Houston area's top 1,500 employers, arranged by industry. Plus names and titles of people to contact. Useful professional organizations, professional publications, and directories. Candid interviews and helpful hints.

Employers Index *Page 360*

General Index *Page 373*

How To Get the Most from This Book

So, you want to get a job in the Houston area? Well, you've picked up the right book. Whether you're a recent graduate, new in town, or an unemployed oil baron; whether or not you're currently employed; even if you're not fully convinced that you *are* employable—this book is crammed with helpful information.

It contains the combined wisdom of two top professionals: Bob Sanborn, Director of Rice University's Career Services Center and Houston area career guru, and Tom Camden, a personnel professional who currently heads the nationally known consulting firm of Camden and Associates.

Bob and Tom both contribute expert advice on basic and advanced job-search techniques, from how to write a resume to suggestions for racking up extra points in an employment interview. Bob also shares his knowledge of Houston's employment scene. Whether you're looking for a job in the city or the suburbs, his extensive listings will save you hours of research time.

Dozens of other Houston-area insiders have contributed tips, warnings, jokes, and observations in candid, behind-the-scenes interviews. We've

How to Get a Job

done our level best to pack more useful information between these covers than you'll find anywhere else. We would love to guarantee that this book is the only resource you will need to find the job of your dreams, but we are not miracle workers. This is a handbook, not a Bible. There's just no getting around the fact that finding work *takes* work. *You* are the only person who can land the job you want.

What we *can* do—and, we certainly hope, have done—is to make the work of job hunting in Houston easier and more enjoyable for you. We have racked our brains, and those of many others, to provide you with the most extensive collection of local resources in print.

To get the most from this book, first browse through the Table of Contents. Acquaint yourself with each chapter's major features, see what appeals to you, and turn to the sections that interest you the most.

It may not be necessary or useful for you to read this book from cover to cover. If you're currently employed, for example, you can probably skip Chapter 8—What To Do If Money Gets Tight. If you have no interest in using a professional employment service, you'll only need to browse through Chapter 6.

There are certain parts of this book, however, that no one should overlook. One of them is Chapter 4—Researching the Houston Area Job Market. Unless you're a professional librarian, we'd bet money that you won't be able to read this chapter without discovering at least a few resources that you never knew existed. We've tried to make it as easy as possible for you to get the inside information that can put you over the top in an employment interview.

Chapter 5 is another Don't Miss—especially our unique listing of organizations that you should know about to develop your network of professional contacts. We strongly suggest that you read Chapter 7, even if you think you already know all about how to handle an interview. And then, of course, there's Chapter 11—listings of the Houston area's top 1,500 employers of white-collar workers.

There's another thing about which you should know in order to get the most from this book. Every chapter, even the ones you don't think you need to read, contains at least one helpful hint or insider interview that is set off from the main text. Take some time to browse through them. They contain valuable nuggets of information and many tips that have never before appeared in print.

Keep in mind that no one book can do it all for you. While we've touched on the basic tasks of any job search—self-analysis, developing a resume, researching the job market, figuring out a strategy, generating leads, interviewing, and selecting the right job—we don't have space to go into great detail on each and every one of them. What we *have* done is supply suggestions for further reading. Smart users of this book will follow those suggestions when they need to know more about a particular subject.

How to get the most from this book

Houston weather

Houston is typically hot and humid in the summer. Average temperature from June through August is about 83 degrees with extremes in the upper nineties. Rainfall varies from four to four and a half inches during each of these months. The summer's high humidity can make the heat intolerable, so be prepared.

Winters are generally mild, with mean December-January temperatures of 50 degrees. Temperatures seldom drop below freezing and snow is extremely rare. Because of vacillating winter weather, it is not uncommon to see Houstonians wearing coats one day and Bermuda shorts the next. ■

Houston in the 1990s and Beyond

Since its founding in the 1800s, Houston has been a center of action that has attracted millions. From a group of log cabins in 1837 to a booming metropolis of over 3.3 million in the 1990s, Houston has experienced phenomenal growth. A city that once stood on 73 square miles in 1940 now swallows 557.

Although the oil industry spurred much of this growth, Houston is no longer just a refining center. NASA has made Houston synonymous with aerospace and technology, while the 38 medical, academic, and research institutions of the Texas Medical Center equate Houston with health-related technology. Houston is home to corporate headquarters for 23 Fortune 500 companies. According to the Fortune survey of the best cities for business in 1989, Houston's white-collar employment has grown 10.2 percent since 1983 and now comprises 66.7 percent of the total labor force.

During the 1990s, Houston's economic diversity should provide increased job opportunities in several fields. Medically related occupations such as home-health aides, nurses in all fields, medical records technicians, and medical assistants are in high demand, and the Texas Medical Center should provide expanded opportunities in these areas.

Engineering should continue to provide plentiful openings, especially in the domains of space, electrical, and environmental engineering, which are less prone to the boom-and-bust cycles of an oil-based economy.

Demand for computer programmers is projected to increase into the '90s. With many companies now updating their computer systems or automating for the first time, opportunities will abound for computer-literate office personnel.

Experts such as *Megatrends* author John Naisbitt predict a major trend toward a service, or "high-touch," economy as a counterpart to the "high-tech" society. Nationally, job trends in the '90s will be favorable to service-oriented and professional workers. Careers in the clerical fields will experience strong growth. The legal field is another high-growth area in which demand for paralegals, legal assistants, and lawyers will be high. Other professional occupations or those requiring college degrees should also be in for steady growth.

Areas that will probably experience little growth include low- or semi-skilled industrial work. These are jobs that were once the high-paying occupations for those without higher education.

How to Get a Job

Houston has recovered from the days when 80 percent of its economy was energy-based, which made the city both a boom town and bust town. As it did earlier in its history, Houston is once again expanding and diversifying. Its diversity in service areas, medical fields, and technological exploration should prepare it well for the 1990s and beyond.

Houston's international appeal

Houston's size and location have made it a major hub for international trade and investment. More than 600 foreign firms and 400 local companies with overseas office are located here. With 57 consulates, Houston boasts the largest consular corps in the Southwest. Undoubtedly this contributes to the city's bustling international trade, which has made the Port of Houston the nation's largest international port.

Houston increased its international recognition by hosting the 1990 world economic summit, giving over 4,000 government officials and journalists from Canada, France, Great Britian, Italy, Japan, Germany, and the United States a further look at this dynamic city. ■

Before Arriving in Houston

Most Chambers of Commerce offer informative and affordable publications that are helpful to newcomers to any community. They usually include a street map, a guide map of the major points of interest, area tax and utility reports, information on housing, transportation, shopping, medical facilities, leisure facilities, and cultural events. The **Greater Houston Chamber of Commerce** (1100 Milam Street, 77002, tel.: (713) 651-1313, fax: (713) 658-2429) publishes the *Houston Newcomer Packet*, which in addition to the above mentioned items, includes information on employment agencies and residential Realtors. It is available from their Publications Department for $9.00. The **Vistor's Information Center of the Greater Houston Area** (3300 Main Street, 77002, (713) 523-5050) also provides lists of hotel accommodations, along with yearly festivals and attractions in the area. Other chambers of commerce in the Houston metropolitan area include:

Alvin-Manvel Chamber of Commerce
105 West Willis
Alvin, TX 77511
Tel.: (713) 331-3944

Bellaire Southwest Houston Chamber of Commerce
P.O. Box 788
Bellaire, TX 77402
Tel.: (713) 666-1521

Chamber of Commerce Rosenberg-Richmond
4120 Avenue H
Rosenberg, TX 77471
Tel.: (713) 342-5464

Clear Lake Area Chamber of Commerce
1201 Nasa Road One
Houston, TX 77058
Tel.: (713) 488-7676

How to get the most from this book

Clear Lake Area Economic Development Foundation
2525 Bay Area Boulevard, Suite 640
Houston, TX 77058
Tel.: (713) 486-5535

Cy-Fair Houston Chamber of Commerce
11050 FM 1960 West, Suite 100
Houston, TX 77065
Tel.: (713) 955-1100

Deer Park Chamber of Commerce
110 Center Street
Deer Park, TX 77536
Tel.: (713) 479-1559
Fax: (713) 476-4041

Friendswood Chamber of Commerce
700 South Friendswood Drive
Friendswood, TX 77546
Tel.: (713) 482-3329

Galleria Area Chamber of Commerce
3050 Post Oak Boulevard, Suite 555
Houston, TX 77056
Tel.: (713) 629-5555
Fax: (713) 629-6403

Greater Heights Chamber of Commerce
545 West 19th Street
Houston, TX 77008
Tel.: (713) 861-6735
Fax: (713) 861-9310

Houston Citizen's Chamber of Commerce
2808 Wheeler Avenue
Houston, TX 77004
Tel.: (713) 522-9745

Houston Hispanic Chamber of Commerce
401 Louisiana, Suite 780
Houston, TX 77002
(713) 225-0018

Houston Northwest Chamber of Commerce
14511 Falling Creek, Suite 402
Houston, TX 77014
Tel.: (713) 440-4160
Fax: (713) 440-5229

Houston West Chamber of Commerce
10777 Westheimer, Suite 240
Houston, TX 77042
Tel.: (713) 785-4922
Fax: (713) 785-4944

Laporte-Bayshore Chamber of Commerce
P.O. Box 996
Laporte, TX 77572
Tel.: (713) 471-1123
Fax: (713) 471-1710

North Channel Area Chamber of Commerce
15035 East Freeway
Houston, TX 77530
Tel.: (713) 452-2800

Northeast Houston Chamber of Commerce
233 Benmar Suite 101
Houston, TX 77060
Tel.: (713) 872-8700

Pasadena Chamber of Commerce
4334 Fairmont Parkway
Pasadena, TX 77504
Tel.: (713) 487-7871
Fax: (713) 487-5530

Pearland-Hobby Chamber of Commerce
3501 Liberty Drive
Pearland, TX 77581
Tel.: (713) 485-3634

South Belt-Ellington Chamber of Commerce
11555 Beamer
Houston, TX 77089
Tel.: (713) 481-5516
Fax: (713) 481-5581

South Houston Chamber of Commerce
58 Spencer
South Houston, TX 77587
Tel.: (713) 943-0244

Southeast Harris County Economic Development Council
4624 Fairmont Parkway, Suite 208
Pasadena, TX 77504
Tel.: (713) 487-5716

How to Get a Job

Southwest Houston Chamber of Commerce
11444 Beechnut
Houston, TX 77072
Tel.: (713) 498-6071
Fax: (713) 498-5909

Tomball Area Chamber of Commerce
P.O. Box 516
Tomball, TX 77377-0516
Tel.: (713) 351-7222

INTERNATIONAL CHAMBERS OF COMMERCE

American-Philippine Chamber of Commerce
13231 Champion Forest Drive, Suite 311
Houston, TX 77069
(713) 580-7700

Arab U.S. Chamber of Commerce
525 East North Belt
Houston, TX 77060
Tel.: (713) 447-2563

Asian Pacific American Chamber of Commerce
P.O. Box 34718
Houston, TX 77235-5718
Tel.: (713) 779-1188

Houston Chinese Chamber of Commerce
9108 Bellaire Boulevard
Houston, TX 77036
Tel.: (713) 568-5872

Finnish American Chamber of Commerce
1300 Post Oak Boulevard, Suite 1990
Houston, TX 77056
Tel.: (713) 627-9700

French American Chamber of Commerce
2727 Kirby Drive, Suite 501
Houston, TX 77098
Tel.: (713) 529-9578
Fax: (713) 529-2059

German American Chamber of Commerce
5555 San Felipe, Suite 1030
Houston, TX 77056
Tel.: (713) 877-1114

Houston Interamerican Chamber of Commerce
510 Bering Drive Suite 300
Houston, TX 77057
Tel.: (713) 975-6171

Houston Mexican-American Chamber of Commerce
7923 Barberton
P.O. Box 9058
Houston, TX 77261
Tel.: (713) 748-8620

Houston World Trade Association
510 Bering Drive, Suite 300
Houston, TX 77057
Tel.: (713) 975-6171

Japan Business Association
14133 Memorial Drive, Suite 3
Houston, TX 77079
Tel.: (713) 493-1512

Netherlands Texas Business Association
2200 Post Oak Boulevard, Suite 610
Houston, TX 77056
Tel.: (713) 622-8000
Fax: (713) 622-3581

Norwegian American Chamber of Commerce
2777 Allen Parkway, #1185
Houston, TX 77019
Tel.: (713) 526-6222

Swedish-American Chamber of Commerce
6900 South Rice Avenue
P.O. Box 243
Bellaire, TX 77402
Tel.: (713) 660-8700

Swiss American Chamber of Commerce
P.O. Box 61342
Houston, TX 77208-1342
(713) 682-8047

How to get the most from this book

**Venezuelan-North American
Chamber of Commerce**
2303 Nance
Houston, TX 77020
(mailing: P.O. Box 2882, Houston,
TX 77252)
Tel.: (713) 222-8886

Arriving in Houston

Two major airports service the Houston area. **Houston Intercontinental Airport** (713-230-3000) is an international airport handling national and international flights. **Hobby Airport** (713-643-4597) is served by regional and national airlines. Several shuttles can transport you from either airport to major hubs within the city. These shuttles include:

Texas Bus Lines (Airport Express: (713) 523-8888; Charter Information: (713) 523-5694) provides shuttle service between Intercontinental and various locations throughout the city. Fares are $9.70 for adults and $4.85 for children under 12. Travel time is approximately 45 minutes to 1 hour, so travelers should plan to board a shuttle accordingly. Shuttles arrive and depart regularly every day from the lower-level baggage area.

Hobby Limousine Service (713-644-8359) provides shuttle service from Hobby Airport to various locations and also runs a shuttle between Hobby and Intercontinental airports. Fares start at $5.00.

Town & Country Airport Shuttle (Schedule Information: (713) 589-0515) runs a shuttle to hotels along the Katy Freeway for $12 one way. Shuttles leave every 15 minutes from both Hobby and Intercontinental.

METRO (713-635-4000), the city bus, provides regular transportation from a number of locations to Hobby for $.70.

With all of these shuttles, it is best to call for exact times and drop-off points before traveling.

Taxi service is available from: **Yellow Cab** (713-236-1111), **American Liberty** (713-999-0088), **United Taxicab Company** (713-699-0000), and **Fiesta Cab Company** (bilingual; 713-225-2666).

Greyhound Bus Lines (2121 Main, (713) 222-6589) and **Kerrville Bus Company,** (812 Delano, (713) 236-1887) operate bus lines from Houston. **Amtrak** (800-872-7245) operates passenger rail service in and out of Houston.

Choosing a day-care center

Affordable, safe day-care is a number one priority for working parents. It sets the parameters for where they work and the kinds of jobs they hold.

When choosing a day-care center, remember that the way your child is cared for has a major influence on the way in which he or she will grow and mature. Be sure to consider these questions: What is the center's primary function—to aid in the development of the children or simply to maintain them? Does the center have a current state license and educational

How to Get a Job

credentials? What is the child/worker ratio? What is the educational level of the workers?

Before making a final decision, try to consult the parents of children who have previously attended the day-care center. Their advise and opinions are probably the most valuable information you can receive.

For a list of day-care centers in Houston, call the United Way Referral Service at 692-3236. ■

Finding Your Way around Houston

The Houston metropolitan area encompasses more than 557 square miles and is extremely spread out, so having a car is almost a necessity. Using public transportation alleviates the high cost of parking in the city, but the system (consisting of only one bus line) is not comprehensive. Houston operates the **Metropolitan Transit Authority,** or **METRO,** for $0.70 with free transfers. In general, service radiates in spokes outward from downtown. For more information on routes, fares, and schedules, call (713) 635-4000. **METRO** will send you a general route map plus schedules for routes of specific interest.

Should you need to rent or lease an automobile, major rental car outlets are listed in the Yellow Pages under "Automobile Rental" and are available at Hobby and Intercontinental airports, as well as around the Houston metropolitan area. Car rental outlets include: **AAA Auto Rentals** (713-879-0099), **Sears** (713-944-6662), **Avis** (800-331-1212; Intercontinental: 713-443-5800; Hobby: 713-641-9300), **Hertz** (800-654-3131; Intercontinental: 713-443-0800; Hobby: 713-941-6821), and **Budget** (800-527-0700 or 713-944-1888). Economy rental outlets include: **Acorn's Used Car Rentals** (713-896-8005) and **All Save Rent a Wreck** (713-472-1660).

Deciphering Houston's highways

People seldom refer to Houston's highways by their proper numbers. To help you get around, remember:

I-610: The Loop
I-45 North: North Freeway (leads to Intercontinental Airport)
I-45 South: Gulf Freeway (leads to Hobby Airport)
I-10 West: Katy Freeway (leads to Austin, San Antonio)
I-10 East: East Freeway (leads to New Orleans)
U.S. 59: Southwest Freeway (to Sharpstown and north)
Hwy. 290: Northwest Freeway
Hwy. 288: South Freeway ■

Establishing an Objective: How To Discover What You Want To Do

One of the most common mistakes job seekers make is not establishing an *objective* before beginning the job search. Practically everyone wants a job that provides personal satisfaction, growth, good salary and benefits, prestige, and a desirable location. But unless you have a more specific idea of the kind of work you want, you probably won't find it. You wouldn't take off on your big annual vacation without a clear destination in mind. Well, you'll be spending a lot more time on the job than at the beach. As David Campbell puts it, "If you don't know where you're headed, you'll probably wind up somewhere else."

Many of our readers already have a clear objective in mind. You may want a job as a systems analyst, paralegal, sales manager, or any of a thousand other occupations. (*The Dictionary of Occupational Titles* lists

How to Get a Job

40,000 jobs!) If you know what you're looking for, you're to be commended because *establishing an objective is a necessary first step in any successful job search.*

But even if you have an objective, you can benefit from a thorough self-appraisal. What follows is a list of highly personal questions designed to provide you with insights you may never have considered, and to help you answer the Big Question, "What do I want to do?"

To get the most from this exercise, write out your answers. This will take some time, but it will force you to give each question careful thought. The more effort you put into this exercise, the better prepared you'll be for the tough questions you'll be asked in any job interview. The exercise also can be the basis for constructing a winning resume—a subject we'll discuss in more detail in the next chapter.

When you've completed the exercise, consider sharing your answers with a trusted friend or relative. Self-analysis is a difficult task. Although we think we know ourselves, we seldom have the objectivity to see ourselves clearly, to outline our personal and professional strengths and weaknesses, to evaluate our needs, and to set realistic objectives. Someone who knows you well can help.

Questions About Me

1. Taking as much time as necessary—and understanding the purpose of this appraisal—honestly describe the kind of person you are. You must evaluate your interests, workstyle, personality, and values. Here are some questions to get you started. Are you outgoing or are you more of a loner? How well disciplined are you? Are you quick-tempered? Easygoing? Are you a leader or a follower? Do you tend to take a conventional, practical approach to problems? Or are you imaginative and experimental? How sensitive are you to others?
2. Describe the kind of person others think you are.
3. What do you want to accomplish with your life?
4. What role does your job play in achieving those accomplishments?
5. What impact do you have on other people?
6. What are your accomplishments to date? Are you satisfied with them?
7. What role does money play in your standard of values?
8. Is your career the center of your life or just a part of it? Which should it be?
9. What are your main interests?
10. What do you enjoy most?
11. What displeases you most?

Questions About My Job

1. Beginning with your most recent employment and working back toward school graduation, describe *in detail* each job you have had. Include your title, company name, responsibilities, salary, achievements and successes, failures, and reason for leaving. (If you're a recent college graduate and have little or no career-related work experience, you may find it helpful to consider your collegiate experience, both curricular and extracurricular, as your work history for questions 1, 2, 3, 8, 9, and 11.)

Establishing an objective

2. How would you change anything in your job history if you could?
3. In your career thus far, what responsibilities have you enjoyed most? Why?
4. What kind of job do you think would be a perfect match for your talents and interests?
5. What responsibilities do you want to avoid?
6. How hard are you really prepared to work?
7. If you want the top job in your field, are you prepared to pay the price?
8. What have your subordinates thought about you as a boss? As a person?
9. What have your superiors thought about you as an employee? As a person?
10. Can your work make you happier? Should it?
11. If you have been fired from any job, what was the reason?
12. How long do you want to work before retirement?

Your answers to these highly personal questions should help you to see more clearly who you are, what you want, what your gifts are, and what you realistically have to offer. They should also reveal what you *don't* want and what you *can't* do. It's important to evaluate any objective you're considering in light of your answers to these questions. If a prospective employer knew nothing about you except your answers to these questions, would he think your career objective were realistic?

A banker's story

We asked a vice-president at a national bank for her job-hunting philosophy.

"Use the occasion of a job change to do some real self-searching about your beliefs and goals," she suggests. "I went to a 'career shrink,' a person trained in the techniques that Richard Bolles outlines in *What Color Is Your Parachute?* That's a book, by the way, that I can't recommend highly enough. Anyway, my career shrink assigned me to write an autobiography. It took me a month to finish, and it was 80 pages long. But it made me take a good, hard look at myself.

"I would advise every job hunter to do the same thing. Read over what you've written, figure out what you've said and what it means. Based on that thoughtful process, be willing to take a risk. That's what I did, and it certainly was a good investment. Women tend to take fewer risks than they ought to for their own self-interest." ■

People who are entering the job market for the first time, those who have been working for one company for many years, and those who are considering a career change need more help in determining their objectives. If you're still in college, be sure to take advantage of the free counseling and career planning services that are available on most campuses. Vocational analysis, also known as career planning or life planning,

How to Get a Job

is much too broad a subject to try to cover here. But we can refer you to some excellent books.

CAREER STRATEGY BOOKS

Ball, Ben. *Manage Your Own Career: A Self-Help Guide to Career Choice Change.* Oakland, CA: Beckman Publishers, 1989.

Baxter, Rogene, and Marcelle Brashear. *Do-It-Yourself Career Kit: A Career Planning Tool.* Maraga, CA: Bridgewater Press, 1990.

Bolles, Richard N. *What Color Is Your Parachute?* Berkeley, CA: Ten Speed Press, 1993. The Bible for job hunters and carer changers, this book is revised every year and is widely regarded as the most useful and creative manual available. Try it! We think you'll like it.

Breidenbach, Monica E. *Career Development: Taking Charge of Your Career.* Englewood Cliffs, NJ: Prentice-Hall, 1988.

Camden, Thomas M. *The Job Hunter's Final Exam.* Chicago: Surrey Books, 1990.

Clawson, James G. et al. *Self Assessment and Career Development.* Englewood Cliffs, NJ: Prentice-Hall, 1985. A very thorough guide with self-assessment worksheets and a good bibliography.

Figler, Howard. *The Complete Job-Search Handbook.* New York: H. Holt & Co., 1988.

Fink, Edward J. *Building a Career in the Business World.* New York: Vantage Press, 1984.

Haldane, Bernard. *Career Satisfaction and Success: A Guide to Job Freedom.* New York: AMACOM, 1982.

Harkavy, Michael. *One Hundred One Careers: A Guide to the Fastest Growing Opportunities.* New York: John Wiley & Sons, 1990.

Hirsch, Arlene S. *Careers Checklists.* Lincolnwood, IL: National Textbook, 1990.

Kennedy, Joyce Lain. *Joyce Lain Kennedy's Career Book.* Lincolnwood, IL: VGM Career Horizons, 1988. Extremely thorough; with a fast-paced style.

Kleiman, Carol. *The 100 Best Jobs for the 1990s & Beyond.* Chicago: Dearborn Financial Publishing, 1992.

Perkins-Reed, Marcia A. *The Career Workbook: A Tool for Self-Discovery.* Portland, OR: High Flight Press, 1989.

Schein, Edgar H. *Career Anchors: Discovering Your Real Values.* San Diego, CA: Pfeiffer & Co., 1990.

Shapiro, Michele. *Your Personal Career Consultant: A Step-By-Step Guide.* Englewood Cliffs, NJ: Prentice-Hall, 1988.

If you're **still in college or have recently graduated**, the following books will be of particular interest:

Briggs, James I. *The Berkeley Guide to Employment for New College Graduates.* Berkeley, CA: Ten Speed Press, 1984.

Osher, Bill, and Sioux Henley Campbell. *The Blue Chip Graduate: A Four Year? College Plan for Career Succcess.* Atlanta: Peachtree Publishers, Ltd., 1987.

For those involved in a **mid-life career change**, here are some books that might prove helpful:

Allen, Jeffrey G. *Fnding the Right Job at Midlife.* New York: Simon & Schuster, 1985.

Bardwick, Judith M. *The Plateauing Trap.* New York: AMACOM, 1986.

Danna, Jo. *Starting Over: You in the New Workplace.* Brairwood, NY: Palomino Press, 1990. Deals with the technological and social changes in the workplace, new hiring criteria; addresses the reader's psychological readiness for the change.

Establishing an objective

Falvey, Jack. *What's Next? Career Strategies After 35*. Charlotteville, VT: Williamson Publishing Co., 1987.

Gerberg, Robert J. *Robert Gerberg's Job Changing System*. Kansas City: Andrews-McMeel, 1986.

Krannich, Ronald L. *Careering & Re-Careering for the 1990's: The Complete Guide to Planning Your Future*. Manassas, VA: Impact Publications, 1989. Discusses trends in the labor force; advice about networking, resume writing, and interviewing.

Morgan, John S. *Getting a Job After 50*. Blue Ridge Summit, PA: TAB Books, 1990.

For workers who are **nearing retirement age** or have already reached it, here are some books that might be useful:

DeCrow, Roger. *Older Americans: New Uses of Mature Ability*. Washington, DC: American Association of Community and Junior Colleges, 1978. Identifies and discusses programs run by community colleges to return older people to the work force through senior employment centers.

Jackson, Beverly. *Young Programs for Older Workers*. New York: Van Nostrand Reinhold, 1980. Describes 69 company personnel policies affecting older workers.

Myers, Albert, and Christopher P. Anderson. *Success Over Sixty*. New York: Summit Books, 1984.

And for people with **disabilities**, these titles could prove helpful:

Bolles, Richard. *What Color Is Your Parachute?* Berkeley, CA: Ten Speed Press, 1993.

Lewis, Adele, and Edith Marks. *Job Hunting for the Disabled*. Woodbury, NY: Barrons, 1983.

Pocket Guide to Federal Help for Individuals with Disabilities. Clearinghouse on the Handicapped, Washington, DC: U.S. Department of Education, 1989. Discusses the many types of federal help for disabled job seekers. Useful and concise, only $1.

For **women and minority groups** in the work force, these titles will be of interest:

Berryman, Sue E. *Routes Into the Mainstream: Career Choices of Women & Minorities*. Columbus, OH: Cts. Educational Training Employment, 1988.

Gutek, Barbara, and Laurie Larwood, eds. *Women's Career Development*. Newbury Park, CA: Sage, 1986.

Higginson, Margaret V., and Thomas L. Quick. *The Ambitious Woman's Guide to a Successful Career*. New York: AMACOM, 1980.

Marino, Kim. *The Resume Guide for Women of the Nineties*. Fort Collins, CO: Tangerine Press, 1990.

Nivens, Beatryce. *The Black Woman's Career Guide*. New York: Anchor Books, 1987.

Zeitz, Baila, Ph.D., and Lorraine Dusky. *The Best Companies for Women*. New York: Simon & Schuster, 1989.

How to Get a Job

**Who's good?
Who's not?**

A listing in this book does not constitute an endorsement of any consulting firm or vocational testing service. Before embarking on a lengthy or expensive series of tests, try to get the opinion of one or more people who have already used the service you're considering. Reputable firms will provide references. You can also contact:

Better Business Bureau of Metropolitan Houston
2707 North Loop West, Suite 900
Houston, TX 77008
Tel.: (713) 868-9500
Contact: Richard McClain

Texas State Attorney General's Office—Consumer Protection
1019 Congress, Suite 1550
Houston, TX 77002
Tel.: (713) 223-5886 ∎

Professional Vocational Analysis

It would be great if there were some psychological test that would confirm without a doubt who you are and precisely what job, career, or field best suits you. Unfortunately, there isn't. Professionals in vocational planning have literally dozens of tests at their disposal designed to assess personality and aptitude for particular careers.

The test most commonly used is probably the Strong-Campbell Interest Inventory (SCII). This multiple-choice test takes about an hour to administer and is scored by machine. The SCII has been around since 1933. The most recent revision, in 1985, made a serious and generally successful attempt to eliminate sex bias.

The SCII offers information about an individual's interests on three different levels. First, the test provides a general statement about the test-taker's interest patterns. These patterns suggest not only promising occupations but also characteristics of the most compatible work environments and personality traits affecting work. Second, the test reports how interested a person is in a specific work activity compared with other men and women. Finally, the occupational scales compare the test-taker with satisfied workers in some 90 different occupations. If you think you'd enjoy being a librarian, for example, you can compare yourself with other librarians and see how similar your likes and dislikes are. The occupational scales indicate how likely you are to be satisfied with the choice of a particular occupation.

Other popular and highly valid career tests include the Myers-Briggs Type Indicator and the 16PF. These tests measure your workstyle and personality and how these might affect your career choice and performance.

Personality/vocational tests come in a variety of formats. Many are multiple choice; some require you to finish incomplete sentences; others are autobiographical questionnaires. No single test should ever be used as

Establishing an objective

an absolute. Personality tests are more important for generating discussion and for providing data that can be used in making judgments.

In the Houston area, vocational guidance and testing are available from a variety of sources. The most comprehensive service is generally provided by private career counselors and career consultants. Their approaches and specialties vary greatly. Some primarily provide testing while others also offer long-term programs that include counseling, resume writing, preparing for the job interview, and developing a job marketing campaign. Fees range from $50 to several thousand dollars.

It's best to find a professional who specializes in the type of vocational help you need. You don't want to spend thousands of dollars on long term psychotherapy when you only need several counseling sessions and tests. On the other hand, if you've had a history of employment problems or are feeling paralyzed in your job search, it is probably well to talk to a career counselor who is also qualified to conduct personal counseling.

The list that follows gives you some idea of what counselors and consultants offer. Telephone these professionals to find out whether their services fit your needs. Although the terms are often used synonymously, there is a difference between a career counselor and consultant. Most professionals use the title *counselor* if they have fulfilled educational and professional requirements determined by the State of Texas to become a Licensed Professional Counselor. The practice of psychology also requires a license in Texas, and many psychologists provide career testing and counseling.

In Texas one can provide career services without a license. Professionals who are not licensed often call themselves career consultants. This field attracts people with a wide variety of backgrounds, education, and levels of competency. That's why it's important to talk to people who have used the service you are considering, and check with the Better Business Bureau to make sure the service is not beset with complaints.

Because career counseling and consulting firms are private, for-profit businesses with high overhead costs, they usually charge more for testing than local universities, community colleges or social service agencies. A more complete discussion of services offered by career consultants is provided in Chapter 6. Also in Chapter 6 is a list of social service agencies, some of which offer vocational testing.

What To Expect from a Career Counselor

What kind of help can you expect from a career counselor that you can't find on your own?

The first thing you'd probably notice is that a counselor really listens to you. They are trained to understand, not to judge. You may find yourself being more candid with a counselor after 30 minutes than you would with a friend you've know for 30 years. The result of this type of interaction is, paradoxically, that you're likely to end up knowing yourself better.

While counselors are trained to understand and support you, they are not there simply to stroke your ego. Your mother or best friend might agree with your plan to change from sales to engineering. A counselor will point out that you've never managed to pass a course in mathematics.

A counselor will understand that career planning is an ongoing, life-long process that manifests itself differently in the various stages of human

How to Get a Job

development that each of us must negotiate. It is a very different thing to hunt for a job at 21, 41, and 61.

Tests aren't the whole answer, but they can be a part of the answer. Counselors know how to interpret tests.

Career counselors aren't locked into outmoded job-search strategies. They can give you ideas on how to make more contacts, write a better resume, and interview with impact. They can spot where your approach needs beefing up more readily than a non-professional.

For most people, a job search is a demanding if not downright stressful time. A counselor can provide both emotional support *and* expert advice.

CAREER COUNSELORS AND CONSULTANTS

Birkman and Associate?
3040 Post Oak Boulevard, Suite 1425
Houston, TX 77056
Tel.: (713) 623-2760
Contact: Joyce Kaufmann
This service employs a method of counseling that involves a 3-4 hour battery of tests in order to process various reports which comprise a manual on the individual. This manual displays the test results concerning personality and interests as well as occupational assessment. Also included is a private consultation of approximately 2 hours. The fee is $400 for the testing and counseling.

David Bissett, Ph.D., and Assoc.
9550 Ella Lee Lane, Suite 2057
Houston, TX 77063
(713) 781-5221
Contact: David Bissett
Offers an extensive personality evaluation in order to discover the individual's personality traits and the possible vocational areas that might be appropriate. The rest of the counseling explores various aspects of the career search such as values clarification, priority setting, interviewing skills, and preparing a resume. The main objective involves both goal setting and job matching (although there is no placement service.) The fee is on a sliding scale, depending on income, with an hour-long initial consultation for $100, in which the number of sessions and individual payments are determined.

Career Clinic
9525 Katy Freeway Suite 210
Houston, TX 77024
Tel.: (713) 465-2456
Contact: Dr. Robert Sarmiento
Offers counseling services in three main areas, including career planning, counseling, and personal marketing. The process involves a battery of tests combined with counseling sessions in order to determine aptitude, interests, and possible career opportunities. The personal marketing aspect consists of particulars such as interviewing skills, pinpointing prospective opportunities, and other facets in the job hunt. There is a free initial consultation, and depending on the program depth, the fee could range from $245 to $495. Individual counseling is $100 an hour.

Center for Continuing Careers
2909 Hillcroft Suite 400
Houston, TX 77057
Tel.: (713) 952-8734

Establishing an objective

Offers a "relational assessment" testing program for unemployed persons. The results are explained in a full day of training so that the participant knows how to use them for his work relationships. The goal is to help give focus and direction to the job search. Fee is $175 per person.

Counseling Services of Houston
1964 West Gray Suite 204
Houston, TX 77019
Tel.: (713) 521-0489
Contact: Rosemary Vienot
Offers a variety of services and a free initial consultation. Services include personality and character testing, interviewing skills and job search techniques, and self- assessment testing. Fees are on a sliding scale and generally range anywhere from $50 to $90.

Rice University Career Services Center
Rice Memorial Center, 2nd floor
Rice University
P..O. Box 1892
Houston, TX 77251
Tel.: (713) 527-4055
Contact: Becky Hayes
Offers a variety of career and personal counseling services. Career courses are offered through the Office of Continuing Studies of Rice University. Individual counseling is available for a $80 per hour fee, and tests are $20 to $30 each. All tests offered here are nationally known, researched, and validated.

Texas Employment Commission Job Search Seminar and Workshop
12455 Beechnut
Houston, TX 77072
Tel.: (713) 530-4300
Contact: Kay Boyd
This service offers free job-search workshops for unemployed persons. During the program, there is a week of classroom-type seminars, in which interviewing techniques, telemarketing skills, and resume writing are discussed. Next, people meet three times a week for a job-search workshop, where, with the help of a counselor, they actually start looking for a job.

Vocational Guidance Service
2600 Southwest Freeway
Houston, TX 77098
(Mail address: P.O.Box 540144, Houston, TX 77254-0144)
Tel.: (713) 659-1800, 831-6863
Contact: Beverly Finn
This group is supported by the United Way, which allows them to offer their services at very affordable rates. Fees are based on a sliding scale and depend on the person's family income or current financial situation. Services include: (a) Career counseling and testing (fees range from $5.00 to $65.00); (b) Placement assistance classes. There is no fee for this service either to the employer or prospective employee. Resume-writing workshop fee is $5.00.

How to Get a Job

Transferring skills from one job to another

After working in Houston for about a year, Sharon decided to make a career change when the urban research center she worked for was faced with financial difficulties.

Having been a music major in college, Sharon was not sure if she had enough useful job skills to transfer into a new career. She became interested in fund-raising at a local university when one of her business contacts mentioned an opening in the development office.

"I volunteered for the annual tele-fund-raising campaign at the university to find out if I could handle development activities. I discovered that I really enjoyed the work. Best of all, many of my skills from the urban research center, especially in communication, writing, and computer literacy, were well-suited for it. I interviewed for the job and got it, with additional help from a recommendation from my business contact." ■

Advice for the Trailing Spouse

In corporate relocation jargon they are "trailing spouses," wives or husbands who move with their spouses who have been transferred. Many may have been uprooted from good jobs in their previous locations. Now, they're forced to go job hunting again in a strange location.

"Often they react with anger and frustration, which only gets in the way of their own job search or career development," says Colin Tipping, a professional counselor and educator who as president of International Relocation Bureau, Inc., conducts relocation stress management workshops and offers spouse counseling services.

"The first thing a trailing spouse should do is deal with any anger and frustration. Acknowledge it, accept it as OK, and express it as openly as possible—if not to your spouse, then to a friend or professional counselor who will listen and understand," advises Tipping. He then offers seven tips:

(1) Let go of attachments to the past, including a previous job or a previous location, and take a good look at what the present has to offer. Forgive your husband or wife for uprooting you and forget that you are a trailing spouse. Reclaim your power and take full responsibility for your own life.

(2) View this move, and this new job search, as an opportunity to think about your life, work, and priorities. Read Marsha Sinetar's book, *Do What You Want and the Money Will Follow.*

(3) Evaluate your work history. Have you really done what you loved to do? Did it make your heart sing? Or were you more attached to status, power, control, image or money?

(4) Think about what kind of work you really want to do and make a list of the possibilities. (Include getting more training, acquiring different skills, etc.)

(5) Be alive and open to the possibilities and opportunities around you.

Establishing an objective

(6) Visualize yourself doing what you love to do, set goals, and create plans that will lead to their achievement.

(7) Go for happiness?

Thinking of Starting Your Own Small Business?

Free information available at the U.S. Small Business Administration offices will answer many of your basic questions about starting a small business. Information packets deal with income tax preparation, loan programs for small businesses, assistance in obtaining government contracts, and solving management and technical problems.

To find out more, attend one of the SBA workshops. Or for personal assistance, call or drop by one of the SBA offices.

Questions are answered by staff members and volunteers in the SCORE (Service Corps of Retired Executives) program. These retired executives draw upon years of experience in helping people start their own business or better manage the one they have. They, in turn, receive a great deal of support and advice from members of ACE (Active Corps of Executives), a group of professionals who volunteer their services. You can find useful information on the ins and outs of becoming an independent contractor, too. Management training programs co-sponsored by the SBA are held all over the area, often at local community colleges.

U.S. Small Business Administration
9301 Southwest Freeway, Suite 550
Houston, TX 7707?
Tel.: (713) 953-6255

Service Corps of Retired Executives (SCORE)
(713) 773-6565
Many people working at SBA are from SCORE and can draw upon years of experience to help people just beginning with their own business.
The Washington Hot Line number is (202) 653-6279.

Writing a Resume That Works

Many people would rather get a root canal than write a resume. We think this aversion usually stems from confusion about the job objective. Once you know the sort of job you're looking for and why you're qualified to fill it, the resume almost writes itself. In fact, we're convinced that the biggest benefit of writing your resume is that it forces you to answer those two questions clearly and succinctly. And once you're armed with answers to questions about your objective and qualifications, you'll be ready to knock 'em dead on the interview.

Keep in mind that *no one ever secured a job offer on the basis of a resume alone.* The way to land a good position is to succeed in the employment interview. *You have to convince a potential employer that you're the best person for the job. No piece of paper will do that for you.*

The resume also goes by the name of *curriculum vita* ("the course of one's life"), or *vita* ("life") for short. These terms are a little misleading, however. A resume cannot possibly tell the story of your life, especially since, as a rule, it shouldn't be more than two pages long. (Academic and scientific *vitae* are the exceptions.) The French word *résumé* means "a summing up." In the American job market, a resume is a concise, written summary of your work

Writing a resume

experience, education, accomplishments, and personal background—the essentials an employer needs to evaluate your qualifications.

A resume is a simple marketing tool. Think of it as your personal ad. It will sometimes get you an interview. But it is often most effective when kept in reserve until *after* you've met an employer in person. Sending a follow-up letter after the interview, along with your resume, reminds the interviewer of that wonderful person he or she met last Thursday.

The Basics of a Good Resume

The resume is nothing for you to agonize over. But since almost every employer will ask you for one at some point in the hiring process, make sure that yours is a good one. Here are four tips to help you:

1. *Be sure your resume is up to date and comprehensive.* At a minimum, it should include your name, address, and phone number; a complete summary of your work experience; and an education profile. (College grads need not include their high school backgrounds.)

2. *Keep the resume concise.* Most employers don't want to read more than two pages, and one page is preferable. Large companies are flooded with literally thousands of resumes every year. In many cases, your resume will be scanned for 10-20 seconds, not read in detail. You must capture the reader's attention quickly. Only then will you get a more careful reading. Describe your experience in short, pithy phrases. Avoid large blocks of copy. Your resume should read more like a chart than a chapter in a textbook. And it should look more like an ad than a legal document.

3. *Keep your resume honest.* Never lie, exaggerate, embellish, or deceive. Tell the truth about your education, accomplishments, and work history. If a deliberate misrepresentation is discovered, you can be summarily dismissed. You needn't account for every single work day that elapsed between jobs, however. If you left one position on October 15 and began the next on January 2, you can minimize the gap by simply listing years worked instead of months.

4. *Your resume should have a professional look.* Whether you type it yourself or have it typed professionally, use a high-quality office typewriter with a plastic ribbon (sometimes called a "carbon" ribbon). Do *not* use a household or office typewriter with a cloth ribbon. Does your resume look sharp enough to go out under your prospective employers' letterheads? If it doesn't, it's probably not sharp enough.

In general, your work experience should include the name, location, and dates of employment of every job you've held since leaving school, plus a summary of your responsibilities and, most important, your accomplishments on each job. If you have an extensive work history, you can present it chronologically. Begin with your present position and work backward to your first job. If you haven't had that many jobs, organize your resume to emphasize the skills you've acquired through experience.

There are no hard and fast rules on what to include in your resume besides work experience and education. There is one school of thought that emphasizes the crucial importance of the job objective. If the employer sees that the candidate is looking for precisely the sort of position that the company wants filled, he will want to consider that candidate more carefully. A personal section containing date of birth, marital status, and so on is optional, but we do not encourage it. We suggest putting down

How to Get a Job

nothing that could have any potential for screening you out. If you have served in the military, you ought to mention that in your resume.

Your salary history and references, however, should not be included in your resume; these should be discussed in person during the interview.

Keep in mind that a resume is a sales tool. Make sure that it illustrates your unique strengths in a style and format *you* can be comfortable with. Indicate any unusual responsibilities you've been given, or examples of how you've saved the company money or helped it grow. Include any special recognition of your ability. For example, if your salary increased substantially within a year or two, you might state the increase in terms of a percentage.

Writing a winning resume

Sioux Campbell, President of Blue Chip Enterprises, a career consulting firm, has helped thousands of anxious job searchers come up with the right resume. She begins her consultation with the assumption that there are generally more candidates than jobs. Accordingly, most employers look to screen rather than hire. This means a resume needs to stand out during a quick scan. "Employers who consider a large number of candidates typically review a resume in about 20 seconds," she says. "You've got to show them that you match their needs during this initial scan to attract more careful consideration."

She considers the job objective to be the thesis of the resume. Everything else is the argument that supports the thesis. Short-term memory is just that—short. But somehow, a good resume will impress whoever scans it with the candidate's strongest selling points. They stick in the reader's mind.

She recommends the following test. Give your resume to several objective reviewers. Allow them 20 seconds. Then ask them what they picked up. Do they readily recall your strongest selling points? If they don't, your resume isn't as effective as it could be. ■

Writing a resume

RESUME FORMAT
NAME

Address   City, State, Zip   Phone

Job Objective: Vital piece of information. Many employers use as screening device or to signal job match; should grab attention and motivate employer to read further.

Employment: Place first the stronger of the two sections, "Employment" or "Education." The more impressive your work history, the more prominently you should display it.

List employment in reverse chronological order, putting the most promotable facts—employer or job title—first.

Give functional description of job if work history is strong and supports job objective.

Skills:
- You may embed these in employment section.
- Put skills section first for career changers.
- Choose skills that are most relevant to job objective.
- Give short statements to support skills.
- Make support statements results oriented.
- Position most marketable skills first.

Education: List in reverse chronological order, putting the most promotable facts—school or degree—first.

Mention any honors or achievements, such as high GPA or Dean's List.

Miscellaneous: Call this section anything applicable: Interests, Activities, Accomplishments, or Achievemnets. Give only information that promotes your candidacy for the position for which you are applying.

References: Available upon request. (Don't waste space on names and addresses. List on a separate sheet.)

Remember: there are no concrete rules in resume preparation. Modify this guide, when necessary, to make the most favorable impression.

How to Get a Job

If your budget permits, consider having your resume typeset professionally or typed on a good-quality personal computer or word processor. Macintosh computers offer a typeface very similar to typesetting and are much less expensive for a high-quality product. This *is* the computer age, and you should have no trouble getting access to computers at most libraries or commercial copy shops. Using a computer or word processor with a laser printer gives you a choice of type faces, such as boldface, italics, and small caps. You can also request that the margins be justified (lined up evenly on the right and left sides, like the margins of a book).

One advantage of typing your resume yourself on a computer is that you can save it on a disk. Then it will be very easy to edit your resume and tailor it for a particular company or position that you have in mind. Some job-search experts suggest you submit a different resume, specifically designed, for each different company or job that you pursue.

No matter what method you use to prepare your resume, be sure to *proofread* it before printing it. A misspelled word or typing error reflects badly on you, even if it's not your fault. Many people in personnel will automatically toss out a resume that bears a blatant typo. Read every word out loud, letter for letter, comma for comma.

Get a friend to go over it for you. Then do it again yourself the next day. Backward.

Do *not* make copies of your resume on a photocopy machine unless it is a top-quality one. Have it printed professionally. The resume you leave behind after an interview or send ahead to obtain an interview may be photocopied several times and copies of copies can be hard to read. You should also avoid such gimmicks as using colored paper (unless it's very light cream or light gray) or using a paper size other than 8 1/2" x 11". Professional photocopy centers will have a good choice of paper stocks with high rag content that are suitable for your resume.

Our purpose here is not to tell you how to write the ideal resume (there *is* no such thing) but rather to provide some general guidelines. The following books are full of all the how-to information you'll need to prepare an effective resume and are available from bookstores or your local library.

BOOKS ON RESUME WRITING

Bostwick, Burdette. *Resume Writing.* New York: John Wiley and Sons, 1985.
Corwin, Leonard. *Your Resume: Key to a Better Job.* New York: Arco, 1988.
Foxman, Loretta D., and Walter L. Polsky. *Resumes That Work: How to Sell Yourself on Paper.* New York: John Wiley and Sons, 1984.
Jackson, Tom. *The Perfect Resume.* New York: Anchor/Doubleday, 1990.
Krannich, Ronald L., and William J. Banis. *High Impact Resumes and Letters.* Career Management Concepts, 1987.
Lewis, Adele. *How to Write a Better Resume.* Woodbury, NY: Barron's Educational Series, 1989.
Nadler, Burton Jay. *Liberal Arts Power: How to Sell It on Your Resume.* Princeton, NJ: Peterson's Guides, 1985.
Parker, Yana. *Damn Good Resume Guidelines.* Berkeley, CA: Ten Speed Press, 1989.
Smith, Michael Holley. *The Resume Writer's Handbook,* 2nd ed. New York: Harper and Row, 1987.

Writing a resume

Should You Hire Someone Else To Write Your Resume?

In general, if you have reasonable writing skills, it's better to prepare your own resume than to ask someone else to do it. If you write your own job history, you'll be better prepared to talk about it in the interview. "Boiler plate" resumes also tend to look and sound alike. On the other hand, a professional resume writer can be objective about your background and serve as a sounding board on what you should and shouldn't include. You might also consider a professional if you have trouble writing in the condensed style required for a good resume.

Here is a list of Houston-area firms that will assist you in preparing your resume. Remember that a listing in this book does not constitute an endorsement. Before engaging a professional writer, ask for a recommendation from someone whose judgment you trust—a personnel director, college placement officer, or a knowledgeable friend. Check with the Better Business Bureau and other consumer advocates listed in Chapter 2 to see if there have been any complaints made about the resume service you are considering.

How to choose a professional

Before engaging a professional to help you write your resume, run through the following checklist of questions.

- **What will it cost?** Some firms charge a set fee. Others charge by the hour. Though many firms will not quote an exact price until they know the details of your situation, you should obtain minimum and maximum costs before you go ahead.
- **What does the price include?** Does the fee cover only writing? Or does it include typesetting? Most firms will charge extra for printing.
- **What happens if you're not satisfied?** Will the writer make changes you request? Will changes or corrections cost extra?
- **How do this writer's fees and experience stack up against others?** It's wise to shop around before you buy writing services, just as you would when purchasing any other service. ■

PROFESSIONAL RESUME PREPARERS

Listed below are some of the largest professional offices in Houston. Many more are listed in the Houston Yellow Pages. Again, we do not specifically recommend any groups.

A Plus Resumes
P. O. Box 55213-5213
Houston, TX 77255-5213
Tel.: (713) 464-6410

How to Get a Job

Unique service, consisting of an interview by telephone after which this company prepares the resume and mails it to the individual. The fee is $40 per resume and inculdes a cover letter. More complex resumes may cost more . Individual may correct the copies and return within 90 days for guaranteed satisfaction.

A-Quality Business Services
5650 Kirby Drive
Houston, TX 77005
Tel.: (713) 666-0007
This company does not write resumes, only types and formats them. The fee is $19.50, which includes 10 copies of the resume on good-quality paper and storage on disk for future updating. Students get a 10 percent discount.

Accent Professional Services
800 Gessner, Suite 1120
Houston, TX 77024
Tel.: (713) 468-1002
Strategic resume preparation, including writing, typing, and formating. The fee is $35 per resume page which includes 4 stationery copies and 1 master. Resumes kept on file for updates.

Best Writing Service
1328 Whispering Pine
Houston, TX 77055
Tel.: (713) 681-8505
Will write and assist with writing, as well as type and format. Fee is $55 for writing and typing. Typing alone is $25. This includes 10 copies of the resume on good stationery.

Image Maker's Ink
6009 Richmond Suite 200
Houston, TX 77057
Tel.: (713) 666-2774
Will write, type, and format resumes. Fee is $35 per resume page. This fee includes typesetting, layout, storage and 25 copies. Extra copies are 30 cents per page. Students receive discount.

Kinko's Copies
1430 San Jacinto
Houston, TX 77002
(713) 654-8161
No writing, just typing and printouts. Computers are provided for those who wish to do their own work. If they do the work, the fee is $25.95 for printout and disk for the first page and $15 for each additional resume page. If you do the work, the fee is $10 per hour use of computer, and $.95 for each printout for the first 10 and $.50 for each after that.

MBA Services
1000 Bay Area Blvd.
Houston, TX 77058
(713) 280-5100
Full service including writing, typing, and formating. Free consultation, no obligation. Fees determined depending on complexity. Guaranteed customer satisfaction. 25 copies of resume with most packages.

The Resume Company
5959 West Loop South Suite 525
Houston, TX 77401

Writing a resume

Tel.: (713) 777-1633
Will write, type, and format your resume. For typing only, fee ranges from $20-$30 per page. For writing and typing, fee ranges from $45-$250, including 10 copies of the resume.

Resume Doctor
808 Travis Street Suite 1532
Houston, TX 77002
Tel.: (713) 654-8865
This service will write, type, and print your resume as well as cover letters. Will keep these on file for future updating. Fee ranges from $25 to $500 and possibly higher.

What NOT To Do with Your Resume Once You Have It Printed

Do not change your resume except to correct an obvious error. Everyone to whom you show the resume will have some suggestion for improving it: "Why didn't you tell 'em that you had a scholarship?" or "Wouldn't this look better in italics?" The time to consider those kinds of questions is *before* you go to the typesetter. Obviously, if you have saved your resume on a floppy disk, it will be easier to revise. Even then, it's probably not worth the trouble to make a lot of nitpicky changes. Remember, there is no such thing as a perfect resume. Except typographically.

Debra N. has been a sales manager in Houston for 20 years. During those years, she has changed jobs seven times, enhancing her career with each move. Debra realized early that using powerful, active verbs to describe her accomplishments made her resume stand out. Here are some sample verbs that job seekers in various career areas might use to help build a more effective resume.

The power of verbs

Management
Controlled
Headed
Implemented

Methods and Controls
Restructured
Cataloged
Verified
Systematized

Public Relations/ Human Relations
Monitored
Handled
Sponsored
Integrated

Creative
Devised
Effected
Originated
Conceived

Advertising/ Promotion
Generated
Created
Tailored
Sparked

Communications
Facilitated
Edited
Consulted
Disseminated

How to Get a Job

Resourcefulness
Rectified
Pioneered
Achieved

Negotiations
Engineered
Mediated
Proposed
Negotiated ■

    A second point to remember: do NOT send out a mass mailing. If you send letters to 700 company presidents, you can expect a response of from 7 to 9 percent—and 80 percent of the responses will be negative. The shotgun approach is expensive; it takes time and costs money for postage and printing. You'll get much better results if you are selective about where you send your resume. We'll discuss this at greater length in Chapter 5. The important thing is to concentrate on known hiring authorities in whom you are interested.

Always Include a Cover Letter

Never, never send your resume without a cover letter. Whether you are answering a want ad or following up an inquiry call or interview, you should always include a letter with your resume. If at all possible, the letter should be addressed to a specific person—the one who's doing the hiring—and not "To whom it may concern." You can generally track the right person down with a few phone calls to the company in question.

    A good cover letter, like a good resume, is brief—usually not more than three or four paragraphs. No paragraph should be longer than three or four sentences. If you've already spoken to the contact person by phone, remind him or her of your conversation in the first paragraph. If you and the person to whom you are writing know someone in common, the first paragraph is the place to mention it. You should also include a hard-hitting sentence about why you're well qualified for the job in question.

    In the next paragraph or two, specify what you could contribute to the company in terms that indicate you've done your homework on the firm and the industry. Finally, either request an interview or tell the reader that you will follow up with a phone call within a week to arrange a mutually convenient meeting.

    Remember that the focus of your job search is to sell yourself as a match to fit an employer's needs. You should emphasize that you match the company's needs throughout all of your communication—your resume, any phone calls, cover letters, and follow-up letters.

Formula for a successful cover letter

Remember to...
- send a resume with every cover letter.
- use high quality, high rag content paper.
- focus and individualize each letter toward a particular company and hand sign it.
- use acceptable business format; letter should be well spaced on the page.
- have someone with a talent for proofing check for grammar, spelling, and formatting mistakes.
- address an individual by name.
- limit your letter to one page.

- prepare and mail many cover letters and resumes together—they are too hard to follow up if they go out separately.
- always mail yourself a letter with the batch of resumes so that you can accurately calculate when they arrive.
- follow up with a phone call. ■

Choosing a Resume Format

There are a number of different methods for composing a quality resume. Every career counselor and resume compiler has his or her own favorite method and style. As the person being represented by the resume, *you* must choose the style and format that best suits and sells you. Many resume books will use different terms for the various styles. We will highlight the three most popular types.

1. *The chronological resume* is the traditional style, most often used in the workplace and job search; that does not mean it is the most effective. Positive aspects of the chronological resume include the traditionalist approach that employers may expect. It also can highlight past positions that you may wish your potential employer to notice. This resume is also very adaptable, with only the reverse chronological order of items as the essential ingredient.

2. *The functional resume* is most common among career changers, people reentering the job market after a lengthy absence, and those wishing to highlight aspects of their experience not related directly to employment. This resume ideally focuses on the many skills one has used at his or her employment and the accomplishments one has achieved. It shows a potential employer that you can do and have done a good job. What it doesn't highlight is where you have done it.

3. *The combination resume* combines the best features of a functional resume and a chronological resume. This allows job seekers to highlight skills and accomplishments while still maintaining the somewhat traditional format of reverse chronological order of positions held and organizations worked for.

Here are some sample resumes and cover letters to help you with your own. The books listed earlier in this chapter will supply many more examples than we have room for here.

SAMPLE CHRONOLOGICAL RESUME

Michael P. Gaeman
2100 Montrose
Houston, TX 77005
(713) 555-0007

WORK EXPERIENCE:	SALES MANAGER. 1987-1992. *Bristol–Myers: Health & Personal Care Division.* Houston, Texas.
	Managed the sales, distribution, shelfing, pricing, and display of all Bristol-Myers health and beauty care products in 50 supermarkets, drug stores, and wholesalers in the Houston area. Intensive on-the-job and education training periods in corporate headquarters and in Dallas and Lubbock.
	CONGRESSIONAL AIDE. 1986-1987. *U.S. Representative William P. Tammany.* Houston, Texas.
	Researched House rules and bills, relayed documents to Washington office, organized news media information, and recorded constituent interest on applicable laws.
	CAMPUS REPRESENTATIVE. School year 1985-1986. *Freebee Corporation of America.* Houston, Texas.
	Organized all on-campus sales of most major credit cards on Houston college campuses. Supervised over 30 campus employees.
EDUCATION:	Rice University, Houston, Texas. B.A., Political Science, May 1987.
	Courses include: Business Law, Applied Probabilty, Statistics, Calculus, Economics, English, Creative Writing, French.
ACTIVITIES:	President, Rugby Spectators Association. **AND HONORS:** Rotary Scholarship for Foreign Study, Stockholm, Sweden.
REFERENCES:	Available upon request.

SAMPLE FUNCTIONAL RESUME

Kristin Lawrence
111 Lexington Street
Anywhere, Texas 77030
(713) 555-1313

CAREER OBJECTIVE
Seeking position in personnel/human resources, or related area.

AREAS OF EXPERTISE

Interpersonal/Communication Skills
- Conducted 20-30 parent-teacher conferences per month
- Counseled individual students as needed
- Supervised and advised one student teacher per semester for three years
- Interviewed applicants for employment; provided supervision and training
- Successfully sold and marketed merchandise to customers

Administrative
- Served as chairperson of community resource system
- Maintained student records (attendance, health, academic)—average 30 students per semester
- Assisted in closing financial transactions in retail store, with average daily receipts of $1,500.00

Planning
- Developed lesson plans for all subjects taught
- Assisted with leadership goals of the school and district
- Planned and developed educational programs for in-service teacher groups

EXPERIENCE

Teacher, fourth grade, Conroe School District, Conroe, TX, 1990–present
Assistant Manager, The Limited, Houston TX, 1987-90 (summers)
Administrative Aide, Shearson Lehman Brothers, Galveston, TX, 1985-87 (summers)

EDUCATION

University of St. Thomas, Houston, TX
B.S., Elementary Education, 1990
G.P.A. 3.7/4.0

Honors/Activities—Dean's List, 3 semesters
Drab Hall Vice-President

Certificate—Teacher, Texas # 007123

SAMPLE COMBINATION RESUME

Susan Rivera
122 Pine Street
Houston, TX 77036
(713) 555-0000

OBJECTIVE:	Software development position, utilizing software engineering skills.
EDUCATION:	University of Houston GPA 3.7/4.0 M.S., Information and Computer Science, 12/90 Washington University (St. Louis) GPA 3.5/4.0 A.B., Mathematics, 5/83
QUALIFICATIONS:	**Career-related projects:** • Designed and implemented multi-tasking operating system for the IBM-PC. • Implemented compiler for Pascal-like language. • Designed menu-based interface for beginning UNIX users. **Languages and operating systems:** • Proficient in **Ada, Modula-2, Pascal, COBOL.** • Working knowledge of IBM-PC hardware and 8088 assembly language. • Experienced in **UNIX, MS-DOS, XENIX,** CP/M operating systems. **Hardware:** IBM-PC (MS-DOS,Xenix), Pyramid 90x (UNIX), Cyber 990 (NOS), Data General MV/10000 (UNIX,AOS/VS)
WORK EXPERIENCE:	Griffin Programming Services, Houston, TX, 10/88–Present • **UNIX Programmer**—Responsible for porting MS-DOS database applications to IBM-PC/AT; running Xenix System V; system administration. Wortham Arts Center, Houston, TX, 11/85–9/88 • **Computer Programmer**—Performed daily disk backup on Burroughs B-1955 machine. Executed database update programs and checks. User assistance. Provided **40% of college expenses** as part-time employee. • From 8/83 to 11/85, held full-time positions as **Box Manager** and **Accountant** for arts organizations in St. Louis and Houston.
REFERENCES:	Furnished upon request.

SAMPLE COVER LETTER

2333 Bering Drive
Houston, TX 77247
January 26, 1993
(713) 555-6886

Ms. Jacqueline Doe
Wide World Publishing Company
1400 Walnut Hill Lane, Suite 250
Houston, TX 77456

Dear Ms. Doe:

As an honors graduate of Houston Baptist University with two years of copy editing and feature writing experience with the *HBU Weekly Herald*, I am confident that I would make a successful editorial assistant with Wide World.

Besides my strong editorial background, I offer considerable business experience. I have held summer jobs in an insurance company, a law firm, and a data processing company. My familiarity with word processing should prove particularly useful to Wide World now that you have become fully automated.

I would like to interview with you as soon as possible and would be happy to check in with your office about an appointment. If you prefer, your office can contact me between the hours of 11 a.m. and 3 p.m. at (713) 555-6886.

Sincerely,

Mary Tyler Baker

How to Get a Job

SAMPLE COVER LETTER

May 15, 1992

2239 Forest Park Boulevard
1500 Rosewood
Bellaire, TX 77444

Mr. Ray Price
Post and Waters
5698 Montrose Boulevard
Houston, TX 77006

Dear Mr. Price:

Your advertisement in the May 13 issue of the *Houston Chronicle* for an experienced accountant seems perfect for someone with my background. My five years of experience in a small accounting firm in Houston has prepared me to move on to a more challenging position in a large and prestigious firm like yours.

As you can see from my resume, my work experience includes not only basic accounting work but also some consulting with a few of our firm's bigger clients. This experience combined with an appetite for hard work, an enthusiastic style, and a desire to succeed makes me a strong candidate for your consideration.

I would appreciate the opportunity to discuss how my background could meet the needs of Post and Waters. I will call you within a week to try to arrange a convenient time to meet.

Sincerely,

Scott Harding
(713) 555-4414

SAMPLE COVER LETTER

December 2, 1992

228 S. Meadowlark Lane
Houston, Texas 77001

Dear Mike:

Just when everything seemed to be going so well at my job, the company gave us a Christmas present that nobody wanted: management announced that half the department will be laid off before the end of the year. Nobody knows yet just which heads are going to roll. But whether or not my name is on the list, I am definitely back in the job market.

I have already lined up a couple of interviews. But knowing how uncertain job hunting can be, I can use all the contacts I can get. You know my record—both from when we worked together at 3-Q and since then. But in case you've forgotten the details, I've enclosed my resume. I know that you often hear of job openings as you wind your way about Houston and environs. I'd certainly appreciate your passing along any leads you think might be worthwhile.

My best to you and Debra for the Holidays.

Cordially,

Lucretia Nichols
(713) 555-1357

Enclosure

How to Get a Job

Seven ways to ruin a cover letter

1. Spell the name of the firm incorrectly.
2. Don't bother to find out the name of the hiring authority. Just send the letter to the president or chairman of the board.
3. If the firm is headed by a woman, be sure to begin your letter, "Dear Sir." Otherwise, just address it, "To Whom It May Concern."
4. Make sure the letter includes a couple of typos and sloppy erasures. Better yet, spill coffee on it first, then mail it.
5. Be sure to provide a phone number that has been disconnected or one at which nobody is ever home.
6. Tell the firm you'll call to set up an appointment in a few days; then don't bother.
7. Call the firm at least three times the day after you mail the letter. Get very angry when they say they haven't heard of you. ■

Researching the Houston Area Job Market

We've said that the key to getting job offers is to convince employers that you match their needs. We'd add that the key to job satisfaction is finding a position whose responsibilities match your interests and abilities. This means you've got to know the job and the company. Once you've figured out what kind of job you want, you need to find out as much as you can about which specific companies might employ you. Your network of personal contacts can be an invaluable source of information about what jobs are available where. But networking can't do it all; at some point, you'll have to do some reading. This chapter fills you in on the directories, newspapers, and magazines you'll need in your search and notes the libraries where you can find them.

Libraries

Public libraries are an invaluable source of career information. Everything from books on resume writing to *Standard and Poor's Register of Corporations, Directors, and Executives* can usually be found in the business and economics sections.

How to Get a Job

Save time by checking with the reference librarians on what is available and where to find it. These staff members will be especially cooperative if you first ask them when their "slow" periods are. These are the times when they can give you their undivided attention.

PUBLIC LIBRARIES

Although no library apart from university career services centers has a job information center, most libraries in Houston have job listings, including the *Harris County Business Guide*, and career information material, such as resume-writing guides. The reference desk at each library will be able to locate these materials. The following libraries, all of which provide job information, are listed by location.

Inner Loop

Central Library
500 McKinney
Houston, TX 77002
Tel.: (713) 236-1313

Carnegie Branch
1050 Quitman
Houston, TX 77009
Tel.: (713) 227-9177

Kashmere Gardens Branch
5411 Pardee
Houston, TX 77026
Tel.: (713) 674-8461

Smith Branch
3624 Scott
Houston, TX 77004
Tel.: (713) 741-6220

Northwest

Collier Branch
6200 Pinemont
Houston, TX 77092
Tel.: (713) 680-1710

West

Frank Branch
6440 West Bellfort
Houston, TX 77035
Tel.: (713) 271-1092

Hillendahl Branch
2436 Gessner
Houston, TX 77080
Tel.: (713) 467-9090

Kendall Branch
14330 Memorial
Houston, TX 77079
Tel.: (713) 497-3590

Southwest

Alief Branch
7979 South Kirkwood
Houston, TX 77072
Tel.: (713) 568-3330

Meyer Branch
5005 West Bellfort
Houston, TX 77035
Tel.: (713) 723-1630

South

Bracewell Branch
10115 Kleckley
Houston, TX 77075
Tel.: (713) 941-3130

Vinson Branch
3100 West Fuqua Road
Houston, TX 77045
Tel.: (713) 433-0356

Researching the job market

UNIVERSITY LIBRARIES AND CAREER SERVICES CENTERS

Local university and community college libraries may also offer resources for job seekers. In Houston many schools have reference libraries that are well equipped with career resource information and job directories that you can use even if you are not an alumnus. Some libraries also offer vocational testing and career guidance, often in conjunction with the school's career planning office. However, these services are often available to alumni only.

The library at the University of Houston-Clear Lake (2700 Bay Area Boulevard, Houston, TX 77058, Tel.: (713) 283-3910) has some job information available in the reference section, though the Counseling and Testing Services Office provides a career resources library that is more extensive and available to the public. The Testing Services Office also provides career counseling for the community.

Rice University (6100 South Main, Houston, TX 77005) also provides community services in career guidance, though their career library is only available to students, alumni, and individuals seeing a counselor. The Rice University Fondren Library's reference center ((713) 527-2504) has some resources that non-alumni may use but not check out.

Other smaller universities such as the University of St. Thomas (3812 Montrose Blvd, Houston, TX 77006) and Texas Southern University (3100 Cleburne, Houston, TX 77004) have some information available in their libraries, and anyone is welcome to use, but not check out, these materials. Both schools also offer career guidance for students and alumni only.

University Business School Libraries

Business School libraries often have a wealth of information concerning local, national, and international businesses. This information is usually available to the public for use within the library but not for checking out. Houston-area universities that house graduate Business Schools and business libraries are:

Rice University
Jones School of Administration
Business Information Center
6100 S. Main Street
Houston, TX 77251
Tel.: (713) 527-8101
An invaluable source of information for people looking for jobs in Houston. In addition to some of the most current national and local directories (all of those listed below are in the library), the BIC has very helpful reference librarians who know almost everything there is to know about finding business information. In addition, the BIC has a computerized listing of firms in the Houston area.

University of Houston, University Park
College of Business
Welcher Hall
4800 Calhoun
Houston, TX 77204
Tel.: (713) 743-2893

How to Get a Job

Directories

When you're beginning your employment research, whether of an entire industry or a specific company, there are four major sources of information with which you should become familiar. All four are available at the Central Library (see above) and the Rice University Business Information Center.

Standard and Poor's Register of Corporations, Directors, and Executives (Standard and Poor's Publishing Co., 25 Broadway, New York, NY 10004) is billed as the "foremost guide to the business community and the executives who run it." This three-volume directory lists more than 45,000 corporations and 70,000 officers, directors, trustees, and other bigwigs.

Each business is assigned a four-digit number called a Standard Industrial Classification (S.I.C.) number, which tells you what product or service the company provides. Listings are indexed by geographic area and also by S.I.C. number, so that it's easy to find all the companies in Houston that produce, say, industrial inorganic chemicals. You can also look up a *particular* company to verify its correct address and phone number, its chief officers (that is, the people you might want to contact for an interview), its products, and, in many cases, its annual sales and number of employees. If you have an appointment with the president of XYZ Corporation, you can consult *Standard and Poor's* to find out where he or she was born and went to college—information that's sure to come in handy in an employment interview. Supplements are published in April, July, and October.

The **Thomas Register of American Manufacturers** and **Thomas Register Catalog File** (Thomas Publishing Co., One Penn Plaza, New York, NY 10119) is published annually. This 16-volume publication is another gold mine of information. You can look up a certain product or service and find out every company that provides it. (Since this is a national publication, you'll have to weed out companies that are not in the Houston area, but that's easy.) You can also look up a particular company to find out about branch offices, capital ratings, company officials, names, addresses, phone numbers, and more. The *Thomas Register* even contains five volumes of company catalogs. Before your appointment with XYZ Corporation, you can bone up on its product line with the *Thomas Register*.

Moody's Complete Corporate Index (Moody's Investor Service, 99 Church St., New York, NY 10007) gives you the equivalent of an encyclopedia entry on more than 20,000 corporations. This is the resource to use when you want really detailed information on a certain company. *Moody's* can tell you about a company's history—when it was founded, what name changes it has undergone, and so on. It provides a fairly lengthy description of a company's business and properties, what subsidiaries it owns, and lots of detailed financial information. Like the directories above, *Moody's* lists officers and directors of companies. It can also tell you the date of the annual meeting and the number of stockholders and employees.

The **Million Dollar Directory** (Dun & Bradstreet, Inc., 3 Sylvan Way, Parsippany, NJ 07054) is a three-volume listing of approximately 120,000 U.S. businesses with a net worth of more than half a million dollars. Listings appear alphabetically, geographically, and by product classification and include key personnel. Professional and consulting organizations such as hospitals and engineering services, credit agencies, and financial institutions other than banks and trust companies are not generally included.

Researching the job market

Printed directories, even those that are regularly and conscientiously revised, go out of date as soon as someone listed in them gets promoted or changes companies. Always double-check a contact whose name you get from a directory or other printed resource, including this one, to make sure he or she is still in the same job. If necessary, call the company's switchboard to confirm the name and title of the person who heads the division or department you're interested in.

The following list contains well over 40 additional directories and guides that may come in handy during your job search.

USEFUL DIRECTORIES

AdWeek Agency Directory
(A/S/M Communications, Inc., 49 E. 21st St., New York, NY 10010)
Lists ad agencies, media and media buying services, key personnel, major accounts.

The Almanac of American Employers: A Guide to America's 500 Most Successful Large Corporations
(Contemporary Books, Inc., 180 North Michigan Ave., Chicago, IL 60601)
Alphabetical profiles of major corporations, including information about benefits, job turnover, and financial stability.

Aviation Telephone Directory
(Directional Media Systems, Inc., 535 W. Lambert Rd., Suite D, Brea, CA 92621)
Suppliers of aviation products and services, airports, and fixed-base operators.

Bacon's Publicity Checker
(Bacon's Publishing Company, 332 S. Michgan Ave., Chicago IL 60604)
Covers over 4,800 trade and consumer magazines, 1,700 daily newspapers, and 8,000 weekly newspapers in the United States and Canada.

Billion Dollar Directory: America's Corporate Families
(Dun and Bradstreet, Inc., 3 Sylvan Way, Parsippany, NJ 07054)
Lists 2,600 United States parent companies and their 24,000 domestic subsidiaries. Organized alphabetically by name of parent company.

Blue Book of Pension Funds (and other investors)
(Dun's Marketing Services, Dun & Bradstreet Corp., 49 Old Bloomfield Rd., Mountain Lakes, NJ 07046)
Companies or groups having at least one defined benefit or defined contribution pension plan with 100 or more plan participants and $1 million or more total assets.

Career Guide: Employment Opportunities Directory
(Dun and Bradstreet, Inc., 3 Sylvan Way, Parsippany, NJ 07054)
Provides accurate, up-to-date information on prospective employers and career opportunities. Employers are listed by location, industry classification, and alphabetical order. Each listing provides the company address, important people, a brief description, hiring practices, and career information. The section entitled "Disciplines Hired Geographically" is useful. This directory is limited to companies with at least 1,000 employees.

College Placement Annual
(College Placement Council, 62 Highland Ave., Bethlehem, PA 18017)

How to Get a Job

Directory of the occupational needs of over 1,200 corporations and government employers. Lists names and titles of recruitment representatives.

Consultants and Consulting Organizations Directory
(Gale Research Co., Book Tower, Detroit, MI 48226)
Contains descriptions of 6,000 firms and individuals involved in consulting; indexed geographically.

Corporate Technology Directory
(Corporate Technology Information Services, 12 Alfred St., Woburn, MA 01801)
Profiles of high-technology corporations, including address, phone, ownership, history, brief description, sales, number of employees, executives, and products. Indexed by company names, geography, technology, and product.

Dictionary of Occupational Titles
(Bureau of Labor Statistics, 441 G St. NW, Washington, DC 20212)
Occupational information on job duties and requirements; describes almost every conceivable job.

Directories in Print
(Gale Research Company, Book Tower, Detroit, MI 48226)
Contains detailed descriptions of all published directories: what they list, who uses them, and who publishes them.

Directory of Texas Manufacturers
(Bureau of Business Research, Graduate School of Business, University of Texas, P.O. Box 7459, Austin, TX 78713)
This publication is organized like *Standard and Poor's*. Companies are listed by geographical location, by product, and in alphabetical order. The SIC code is used for product listings. This is a giant directory and extremely useful if one is interested in manufacturing companies.

Directory of Women-Owned Businesses
(National Association of Women Business Owners, 2000 P St. NW, Suite 511, Washington, DC 20036, free)
Lists women-owned businesses by state; describes products and services.

Employment Opportunities Directory
(Dun's Marketing Services, 1 Penn Plaza, New York, NY 10119)
Designed for those beginning a career; describes job prospects at hundreds of companies.

Encyclopedia of Associations
(Gale Research Co., Book Tower, Detroit, MI 48226)
Lists 14,000 local and national associations, professional clubs, and civic organizations by categories; includes key personnel. Indexed geographically.

Encyclopedia of Business Information Sources
(Gale Research Co., Book Tower, Detroit, MI 48226)
Lists each industry's encyclopedias, handbooks, indexes, almanacs, yearbooks, trade associations, periodicals, directories, computer databases, research centers, and statistical sources.

Engineering, Science and Computer Jobs
(Peterson's Guides, P.O. Box 2123, Princeton, NJ 08543)
Lists specific companies within these industries.

Researching the job market

Everybody's Business
(Doubleday Currency, 666 Fifth Ave., New York, NY 10103)
Candid profiles of 3,000 American manufacturers of well-known brand-name products.

Fairchild's Financial Manual of Retail Stores
(Fairchild Books, Fairchild Publications, Inc., 7 W. 34th St., New York, NY 10001)
Lists 500 publicly held companies in the U.S. and Canada that deal partly or exclusively in retail sales. Arranged alphabetically.

Fairchild's Textile and Apparel Financial Directory
(Fairchild Books, Fairchild Publications, Inc., 7 E. 12th St., New York, NY 10003)
Lists 275 publicly owned textile and apparel corporations. Arranged alphabetically.

Finding a Federal Job Fast
(Impact Publications, 9104-N Manassas Dr., Manassas Park, VA 22111)
Secrets to finding jobs. Helpful in locating job vacancies, marketing oneself, and getting hired.

Finding a Job in the Nonprofit Sector
(The Taft Group, 12300 Twinbrook Parkway, Suite 450, Rockville, MD 20852)
Overview of employment trends, job-hunting tips, and contact and employment-related information for 5000 of largest non-profits in U.S.

Fortune Double 500 Directory
(Time, Inc., 229 West 28th St., New York, NY 10001)
Lists the 500 largest and the 500 second largest industrial corporations, as well as the largest banking, service, financial, and utilities firms in the U.S.

Franchise Opportunities Handbook
(U.S. Government Printing Office, Superintendent of Documents, Washington, DC 20402)
Lists over 1200 franchise companies in the U.S. Includes information on their operation, size, history, capital needed and various forms of assistance available.

Gale Directory of Publications and Broadcast Media
(Gale Research Co., Book Tower, Detroit, MI 48226)
Lists national, local, and trade magazines alphabetically and by state.

Harris County Business Guide
(Business Extension Bureau, 4802 Travis, Houston, TX 77002; (713) 528-5568)
Lists Harris County businesses by business sector (financial, services, etc.) with subheadings under each sector. Indexed at front by company name. Very comprehensive. Each entry contains: name, address, phone, number of employees, and important personnel.

Hispanic Media Guide, USA: Directory of Hispanic Print, Radio & TV Media in the US
(Directories International, Inc., 150 Fifth Ave., Suite 610, New York, NY 10011)
Profiles media outlets serving Hispanics, including information about parent companies, address, and contact. Organized by state.

Hotel and Motel Management—Buyer's Directory I
(Harcourt Brace Jovanovich, Inc., 757 3rd Ave., New York, NY 10017)
Lists about 2,100 companies that supply goods and services to the lodging market; includes separtate sections for hotel chains, related associations, manu-

How to Get a Job

facturers' representatives, franchise and referral organizaitons, consulting firms, personnel agencies, publishers, and schools.

Houston International Business Directory
(Greater Houston Chamber of Commerce, 1100 Milam Building, 25th floor, Houston, TX 77002)
A guide to the "diverse array of firms and organizations in Houston which have multinational dealings—firms represented in other nations, foreign companies with a corporate presence in Houston, Houston firms which facilitate foreign trade, foreign government offices in Houston, and organizations which foster international ties." Has a lot of information but is fairly expensive at $80 (postage and tax included).

The Houston 1000: A Corporate Directory
(Greater Houston Chamber of Commerce, 1100 Milam Building, 25th floor, Houston, TX 77002)
Lists 1,000 "significant" business organizations in the Houston area, including names and titles of key personnel. Listed in alphabetical order; has index of companies by business category. Fairly expensive: $145 (postage and tax included).

International Advertising Association Membership Directory
(IAA, 342 Madison Ave., New York, NY 10173)
Covers 2,700 member advertisers, advertising agencies, media, and other firms involved in advertising. Arranged geographically and by function or service.

International Television Almanac
(Quigley Publishing Company, Inc., 159 W. 53rd St., New York, NY 10019)
Lists television networks, major program producers, major group station owners, cable television companies, distributors, firms serving the industry, equipment manufacturers, casting agencies, literary agencies, advertising and publicity representatives, and television stations.

National Directory of Magazines
(Oxbridge Communications, Inc., 150 Fifth Ave., New York, NY 10011)
Profiles magazines by interest categories; includes key staff names, circulation, and description. Cross-indexed by subject. Indexed alphabetically by title.

National Directory of Newsletters and Reporting Services
(Gale Research Co., Book Tower, Detroit, MI 48226)
Reference guide to national and international information and financial services, association bulletins, and training and educational services.

National Trade & Professional Associations of the United States
(Columbia Books, 1212 New York Ave., Suite 300, Washington, DC 20005)
Alphabetical profiles of associations, including address, phone, affiliations, history, publications, meetings, and annual budget. Indexed by subject, geography, budget and acronym.

Newsletters in Print
(Gale Research, Book Tower, Detroit, MI 48226)
Reference guide to newsletters, financial services, association bulletins.

Occupational Outlook Handbook
(Bureau of Labor Statistics, 441 G St.NW, Washington, DC 20212)
Describes in clear language what people do in their jobs, the training and education they need, earnings, working conditions, and employment outlook.

Researching the job market

O'Dwyer's Directory of Public Relations Firms
(J.R. O'Dwyer & Co., 271 Madison Ave., New York, NY 10016)
Describes 900 public relations firms in the U.S., their key personnel, local offices, and accounts; indexed geographically.

Printing Trades Directory
(A.F. Lewis & Co., Inc., 79 Madison Ave., New York, NY 10016)
Printing plants, bookbinders, typesetters, platemakers, paper merchants and manufacturers, printing machinery manufacturers and dealers, and others serving the graphic arts industry.

QED's Guide to School Districts
(Quality Education Data, 1600 Broadway, 12th Floor, Denver, CO 80202)
Public and private elementary and secondary schools, including basic data and dollars per student, percent minority enrollment, educational specializations of key personnel, VCR units, number of microcomputers, other data.

Reference Book of Corporate Management
(Dun & Bradstreet, Inc., 3 Sylvan Way, Parsippany, NJ 07054)
National directory of 2,400 companies with at least $20 million in sales, listed by name. Also lists biographies of key personnel and directors, including schools attended and past jobs.

Sheldon's Retail Directory
(Phelon, Sheldon & Marsar, 15 Industrial Ave., Fairview, NJ 07022)
Directory of the largest department stores, women's specialty stores, chain stores, and resident buying offices. Geographical listings, plus alphabetical index.

Standard Directory of Advertising Agencies
(Reed Reference Publishers, 121 Chanlonn Rd., New Providence, NJ 07974)
The Red Book of 4,000 advertising agencies and their 60,000 accounts.

Travel Industry Personnel Directory
(Capital Cities Media, 7 W. 34th St., New York, NY 10001)
Lists air and steamship lines, tour operators, bus lines, hotel representatives, foreign and domestic tourist information offices, and travel trade associations

Underwriters' Handbook
(National Underwriter Co., 420 E. 4th St., Cincinnati, OH 45202)
Lists insurance agents, agencies, adjusters, field representatives, consultants, appraisers, audit and inspection services, and related insurance groups and associations.

Who's Who in the Motion Picture Industry and Who's Who in Television
(Packard Publishing Co., 7623 Sunset Blvd., Hollywood, CA 90046)
Names and addresses of hundreds of directors, producers, production companies, and network executives.

Woman's Guide to Career Preparation: Scholarships, Grants and Loans
(Anchor Press, Doubeday Publishing Company, 245 Park Ave., New York, NY 10017)
Lists organizations that provide counseling, scholarships, and other assistance to older women and minority women who are returning to work or seeking a career change.

How to Get a Job

Women Helping Women: A State by State Directory of Services
(Women's Action Alliance, 370 Lexington Ave., New York, NY 10017)
Covers 180 career counseling centers, services for battered women and rape victims, displaced homemaker programs, planned parenthood clinics, skilled trades training centers, women's centers, women's commissions, and women's health services.

A directory for women

The Greater Houston Chamber of Commerce publishes a 41-page directory of women's professional organizations called "Women's Clubs and Organizations." Included are business organizations, useful for networking in a chosen field, health care organizations, and community service groups, among other categories. Many of the community service groups can provide referrals for vocational and personal counseling. The times and locations of each group's meetings are listed for easy reference.

To obtain a copy of the directory, call or write the Greater Houston Chamber of Commerce, 1100 Milam St., Houston, TX, 77002, (713) 658-2409.

Newspapers

Answering want ads is one of several tasks to be done in any job search, and generally among the least productive. According to *Forbes* magazine, only about 10 percent of professional and technical people find their jobs through want ads. Like any other long shot, however, answering want ads sometimes pays off. Be sure to check not only the classified listings but also the larger display ads that appear in the Sunday business sections of the major papers. These ads are usually for upper-level jobs.

Help-wanted listings generally come in two varieties: open advertisements and blind ads. An open ad is one in which the company identifies itself and lists an address. Your best bet is <u>not</u> to send a resume to a company that prints an open ad. Instead, you should try to identify the hiring authority (see Chapter 5) and pull every string you can think of to arrange an interview directly.

The personnel department is in business to screen out applicants. Of the several hundred resumes that an open ad in a major newspaper is likely to attract, the personnel department will probably forward only a handful to the people who are actually doing the hiring. It's better for you to go to those people directly than to try to reach them by sending a piece of paper (your resume) to the personnel department.

Blind ads are run by companies that do not identify themselves because they do not want to acknowledge receipt of resumes. Since you don't know who the companies are, your only option in response to a blind ad is to send a resume. This is among the longest of long shots and usually pays off only if your qualifications are exactly suited to the position that's being advertised. Just remember that if you depend solely on ad responses, you're essentially conducting a passive search, waiting for the mail to arrive or the phone to ring. Passive searchers usually are unemployed a long time.

Newspaper business sections are useful not only for their want ads but also as sources of local business news and news about personnel changes.

Researching the job market

Learn to read between the lines. If an article announces that Big Bucks, Inc. has just acquired a new vice- president, chances are that he or she will be looking for staffers. If the new veep came to Big Bucks from another local company, obviously that company may have at least one vacancy, and possibly several.

MAJOR NEWSPAPERS

The Houston Chronicle
P.O. Box 4260
Houston, TX 77210
Tel.: (713) 220-7211
This newspaper has the largest circulation in Houston. The *Chronicle* has the largest and most diverse employment classified section for the Houston area. Available by subscription or in newsstands.

The Houston Post
P.O. Box 4747
Houston, TX 77210
Tel.: (713) 840-560
The *Post* has a fairly small employment classified section—most advertisers seem to choose The *Chronicle*. However, every Sunday there are always various job and career-related articles. Look for "Employment Weekly" every Sunday in the *Post*. Available by subscription or in newsstands.

The Houston Business Journal
One West Loop South, Suite 650
Houston, TX 77027
Tel.: (713) 688-8811
This is a weekly, small newspaper that covers local business news and regional or national business news as it affects the Houston area. Has a very small classified section; the paper is most useful as a business trends source. Available by subscription or in newsstands.

The Wall Street Journal
2958 Rogerdale
Houston, TX 77042
Tel.: (713) 781-8722
The *Journal* is the nation's leading business newspaper, covering everything from national and international business trends to personnel changes in major corporations. Its classified section usually carries adds for mid- to upper-level management positions. Available by subscription or in newsstands.

How to Get a Job

Sometimes classifieds can bring results

According to statistics, searching classified ads for jobs is usually fruitless. Only 10 percent of all jobs are found by answering newspaper ads. However, in some instances answering classified ads can be useful.

Karen answered an advertisement for a research assistant for a small natural gas research firm. She sent in a resume and cover letter, and in a few days, she had an interview with the company. She did not get the job, but she learned about the industry's characteristics and specifically about job demands in the industry. In addition, the interviewers were impressed with her skills and gave her names to contact for possible future interviews.

So although Karen did not get a job with the specific company, she was able to learn more about the industry she was interested in, and she was put in touch with people who could possibly provide her with a job. ■

LOCAL NEWSPAPERS AND FEATURE MAGAZINES

One of the ways to become more familiar with the Houston community is to read the local feature papers. The ones listed below are fairly popular although not necessarily connected with business.

**Creneau Media Group
(West U, River Oaks, Villages, Bellaire, Downtown, Tanglewood)**
P.O. Box 271961
Houston, TX 77277-1961
Tel.: (713) 880-4611

The Echo
P.O. Box 2705
Humble, TX 77347
Tel.: (713) 446-3733

Houston Metropolitan Magazine
P.O. Box 25386
Houston, TX 77265
Tel.: (713) 524-3000

Houston Press
1800 Bering Drive
Houston, TX 77057
Tel.: (713) 783-7110

Houston Scene Magazine
P.O. Box 19008
Houston, TX 77224
Tel.: (713) 493-6372

La Informacion
6065 Hillcroft
Houston, TX 77081
Tel.: (713) 272-0100

The Leader Newspapers
3500 East T.C. Jester
Houston, TX 77018
Tel.: (713) 686-8494

North Freeway Leader
10939 Airline Drive
Houston, TX 77037
Tel.: (713) 445-1819

Pasadena Citizen
P.O. Box 6192
Pasadena, TX 77506
Tel.: (713) 477-0221

Researching the job market

Public News
1540 West Alabama
Houston, TX 77006
Tel.: (713) 520-1520
This weekly feature newspaper is very popular in the Montrose area of Houston and covers events in the art, music, and literary world. Available at the office on Alabama or at most stores and shops in the Montrose area.

Southern Newspapers
1050 Wilcrest
Houston, TX 77042
Tel.: (713) 266-5481

La Subasta
6100 Hillcroft, Suite 105
Houston, TX 77081
Tel.: (713) 777-1010

The Texas Catholic Herald
1700 San Jacinto
Houston, TX 77002
Tel.: (713) 659-5461

Ultra Magazine
1400 Post Oak Boulevard, Suite 350
Houston, TX 77056-3005
Tel.:(713) 622-1967
Fax: (713) 622-8716

The Village Life
6802 Mapleridge, Suite 6802
Bellaire, TX 77401
Tel.: (713) 668-9293
This small community newspaper is produced for residents of the Medical Center, Rice University, River Oaks, and Braeswood areas of town. Families with children seem to be the target audience. Available by subscription or in small stores in the area.

General Business Magazines

When job hunting, it is useful to be constantly aware of the economy and current business trends. All of the following publications, four of which have Houston offices, provide a general overview of the national business scene.

Business Week
1221 Avenue of the Americas
New York, NY 10020-1001
Tel.: (212) 997-1221

Forbes
2 Shell Plaza, Suite 2325
Houston, TX 77002
Tel.: (713) 228-2272

Fortune
Time Life Building
1271 Avenue of the Americas
New York, NY 10020-1301
Tel.: (212) 586-1212

Money
Time Life Building
1271 Avenue of the Americas
New York, NY 10020-1301
Tel.: (212) 522-1212
Fax: (212) 522-0907

Newsweek
1100 Louisiana, Suite 4775
Houston, TX 77002
Tel.: (713) 951-0170

Time Magazine
1415 Louisiana, Suite 3110
Houston, TX 77002
Tel.: (713) 759-0907

U.S. News and World Report
599 Lexington Avenue
New York, NY 1002-6067
Tel.: (212) 326-5300
Fax: (212) 326-5420

Working Woman
342 Madison Avenue
New York, NY 10173-0008
Tel.: (212) 309-9800
Fax: (212) 503-0746

How to Get a Job

Trade and Special Interest Magazines

To become more familiar with specific industries, it is sometimes helpful to read the publications that address these industries. Listed below are specialized magazines that have editorial offices in Houston, Dallas, or Austin. Many carry local want ads and personnel changes that can be useful to you, as well as news about the industry they serve.

HOUSTON

Daily Court Review
P.O. Box 1889
Houston, TX 77251
Tel.: (713) 528-5437
Tabloid containing sections on law, construction, real estate, and insurance.

Drilling Contractor
P. O. Box 4287
Houston, TX 77210
Tel.: (713) 578-7171
Magazine of the International Assn. of Drilling Contractors, covering technical, economic, and political developments affecting the drilling and production segments of the international petroleum industry.

Gas Digest
11246 South Post Oak
Houston, TX 77035
Tel.: (713) 723-7456
Magazine on gas operations.

Gulf Coast Oil World
Hart Publications, Inc.
3545 Post Oak, Suite 210
Houston, TX 77027
Tel.: (713) 993-9320
Magazine covering onshore and offshore oil and natural gas production, exploration, and transportation in the Gulf States and Gulf of Mexico.

Hydrocarbon Processing
P.O.Box 2608
Houston, TX 77252
Tel.: (713) 529-4301
Magazine about oil refining, petrochemicals, gas, and synfuels.

Northwest Houston Business News
5222 FM 1960 #112
Houston, TX 77069
Tel.: (713) 444-5820
Business news.

Ocean Industry
Gulf Publishing Company
P.O.Box 2608
3301 Allen Parkway
Houston, TX 77252
Tel.: (713) 529-4301

Researching the job market

Magazine covering offshore drilling production and pipeline construction projects.

Ocean Oil Weekly Report
3050 Post Oak Boulevard
Houston, TX 77056
Tel.: (713) 621-9720
Magazine covering offshore oil activities.

Oil, Gas & Petrochemicals Abroad
Gulf Publishing Company
P.O. Box 2608
3301 Allen Parkway
Houston, TX 77252
Tel.: (713) 529-4301
Magazine presenting technical articles for people in the gas and oil business.

Personnel Psychology
745 Haskins Road, Suite A
Bowling Green, Ohio 43402
Tel.: (419) 352-1562
Journal covering empirical research concerning personnel, such as test validation, selection, labor management relations, training, compensation, and reward systems.

Petroleum Engineer International
4545 Post Oak Place Suite 210
Houston, Texas 77027
Tel.: (713) 993-9320
Fax: (713) 840-8585
Trade magazine on drilling for oil and gas, and offshore.

Petroleum Information International
Petroleum Information Corporation
P.O.Box 1702
Houston, TX 77251
Tel.: (713) 961-5660
Covers oil and gas exploration worldwide.

Petroleum Management
7887 San Felipe, Suite 100
Houston, TX 77063
Tel.: (713) 953-0454
Magazine for the petroleum industry.

Pipe Line Industry
P.O.Box 2608
3301 Allen Parkway
Houston, TX 77252
Tel.: (713) 529-4301
Designing, constructing, and operating pipe lines; gas distribution. Also prints international edition.

Pipeline
Oildom Publishing Co. of Texas, Inc.
P. O. Box 2267
Houston, TX 77227

How to Get a Job

Tel.: (713) 622-0676
Magazine on the pipeline trade.

World Oil
Gulf Publishing Co.
P.O. Box 2608
Houston, TX 77252
Tel.: (713) 529-4301
Trade magazine about oil and gas drilling, production, and exploration.

AUSTIN

Food & Service
Texas Restaurant Association
P.O. Box 1429
Austin, TX 78767
Tel.: (512) 472-3666
Restaurant trade magazine.

The Professional Communicator
Women In Communications, Inc.
2101 Wilson Boulevard, Suite 417
Arlington, VA 22201
Tel.: (703) 528-4200
Magazine covering the progress of women in communications.

Texas Architect
Texas Society of Architects
114 West 7th Street, Suite 1400
Austin, TX 78701
Tel.: (512) 478-7386
Magazine for design professionals and their clients.

Texas Banking
Texas Bankers Association
203 West 10th Street
Austin, TX 78701
Tel.: (512) 472-8388
Serves Texas banks and bankers.

Texas Bar Journal
State Bar of Texas
203 West 10th Street
Austin, TX 78701
Tel.: (512) 463-1522
News journal for the legal profession.

Texas Business Review
Bureau of Business Research
P.O.Box 7459
University of Texas at Austin
Austin, TX 78713
Tel.: (512) 471-1616
Newsletter providing commentary on the economic climate of the state.

Texas Dental Journal
Texas Dental Association

Researching the job market

1946 South Interregional Highway
Austin, TX 78704
P.O. Drawer 3358
Austin, TX 78764
Tel.: (512) 443-3675
 Fax: (512) 443-3031
Dental journal.

Texas Insuror
P.O. Box 1663
Austin, Tx. 78767
Tel.: (512) 476-6281
Insurance magazine.

Texas League Savings Account
Texas Savings and Loan League
408 West 14th Street
Austin, TX 78701
Tel.: (512) 474-6235
Magazine serving savings and loan officers.

Texas LP-Gas News
Texas LP Gas Association
P.O. Box 140735
Austin, TX 78714-0735
Tel.: (512) 836-8620
Magazine for LP gas industry.

Texas Nursing
Texas Nurses Association
7600 Burnette Road, Suite 440
Austin, TX 78757-1292
Tel.: (512) 452-0645
Nursing journal.

Texas Oil Marketer
Texas Oil Marketer's Association
701 West 15th Street
Austin, TX 78701
Tel.: (512) 476-9547
Trade oil-marketing journal.

Texas Pharmacy
Texas Pharmaceutical Association
P.O. Box 14709
Austin, TX 78761
Tel.: (512) 836-8350
Magazine featuring industry news and educational articles for practicing pharmacists.

Texas Professional Engineer
Texas Society of Professional Engineers
3501 Manor Road
P.O. Box 2145
Austin, TX 78768
Tel.: (512) 472-9286
Magazine containing profession-related news and features for members of Texas Society of Professional Engineers.

How to Get a Job

The Texas Surveyor
Texas Surveyors Association
400 East Anderson Lane, Suite 340
Austin, TX 78752
Tel.: (512) 834-1275
Magazine that includes technical articles, features, and historical pieces pertinent to surveyors in Texas, Louisiana, and Oklahoma.

TPA Messenger
Texas Press Association
718 West Fifth Street
Austin, TX 78701
Tel.: (512) 477-6755
Magazine on journalism and newspaper publishing.

TSTA Advocate
Texas State Teachers Association
316 West 12th Street
Austin, TX 78701
Educational journal.

DALLAS

Adweek/Southwest
A/S/M Communications, Inc.
2909 Cole Avenue # 220
Dallas, TX 75204
Tel.: (214) 871-9550
Advertising and marketing journal.

Bankers Digest
6440 North Central Expressway, Suite 215
Dallas, TX 75206
Tel.: (214) 373-4544
Texas banking news journal.

Builder Insider
Divibest, Inc.
P.O. Box 191125
Dallas, TX 75219
Tel.: (214) 871-2913
Tabloid for builders, architects, and remodelers.

Daily Commercial Record
706 Main Street
Dallas, TX 75202
Tel.: (214) 741-6366
Newspaper covering business, legal, and real estate interests.

The Insurance Record
Record Publishing Co.
P.O. Box 225770
Dallas, TX 75222
Tel.: (214) 630-0687
Insurance trade magazine.

Journal of Air Law and Commerce
Southern Methodist School of Law

Researching the job market

Dallas, TX 75275
Tel.: (214) 692-2570
Air law and commerce journal.

Legal Assistant Today
Legal Assistant Today, Inc.
6060 North Central Expressway, Suite 670
Dallas, TX 75206-5207
Tel.: (214) 369-6868
Fax: (214) 369-5133
Professional news and information magazine for legal assistants.

Well Servicing
Workover/Well Servicing Publications, Inc.
6060 North Central Expressway, Suite 428
Dallas, TX 75206
Tel.: (214) 692-0771
Oil journal.

Job-Hunt Related Publications

The following newspapers and magazines contain only job listings and job-related information and advice.

AAR/EEO Affirmative Action Register
8356 Olive Boulevard
St. Louis, MO 63132
Tel.: (314) 991-1335
"The only national EEO recruitment publication directed to females, minorities, veterans, and the handicapped." Monthly magazine consists totally of job listings.

Contract Engineer Weekly
CE Publications, Inc.
P.O. Box 97000
Kirkland, WA 98083
Tel.: (206) 823-2222
Weekly magazine of job opportunities for contract engineers.

Federal Jobs Digest
P.O. Box 594
Millwood, NY 10546
Tel.: (914) 762-5111
Elaborate listing of job opportunities with the federal government.

International Employment Hotline
P.O. Box 6170
McLean, VA 22106
Monthly listing of overseas jobs. Provides a resume service for subscribers.

Legal Employment Newsletter
P.O. Box 36601
Grosse Point, MI 48236
Newsletter lists open legal positions, as well as career opportunities in the public-private sector.

National and Federal Legal Employment Report
Federal Reports

How to Get a Job

1010 Vermont Avenue NW, Suite 408
Washington, DC 20005
Tel.: (202) 393-3311
Monthly in-depth listings of attorney and law-related jobs in the federal government and with other public and private employers throughout the U.S.

Opportunities in Non-profit Organizations
ACCESS: Networking in the Public Interest
67 Winthrop Street
Cambridge, MA 02138
Tel.: (617) 495-1000
Monthly listings of non-profit jobs around the country, organized by type of non-profit.

Piloting Careers
Future Aviation Professionals of America
4291-J Memorial Drive
Decatur, GA 30032
Monthly magazine outlines employment opportunities for career pilots.

Developing a Strategy: The ABCs of Networking

Success doesn't just happen, and neither does a successful job search. It's the result of careful planning. Before you rush out to set up your first interview, it's important to come up with a plan. We believe a plan isn't a plan unless it's on paper. Your plan should include researching the job market and systematically contacting potential employers.

This chapter and Chapter 7 will cover specific techniques and tools that you'll find useful in your search. But before we get to them, a few words are in order about your overall approach.

It's Going to Take Some Time

Looking for a new job is no easy task. It's as difficult and time-consuming for a bright young woman with a brand-new MBA as it is for a 50-year-old executive with years of front-line experience. Every once in a while someone lucks out. One of Tom's clients established a record at Camden and Associates by finding a new position in four days. But most people should plan on two to six months of full-time job hunting before they find a position they'll really be happy with.

According to *Forbes* magazine, the older you are and the more you earn, the longer it will take to find what you're looking for—in fact, up to six months for people over 40 earning more than $40,000. People under 40 in the $20,000–$40,000 bracket average two to four months.

Your line of work will also affect the length of your search. Usually, the easier it is to demonstrate tangible bottom-line results, the faster you can line up a job. Lawyers, public relations people, and advertising executives are harder to place than accountants and sales people, according to one top personnel specialist.

Be Good to Yourself

Whether or not you're currently employed, it's important to nurture your ego when you're looking for a new job. Rejection rears its ugly head more often in a job search than at most other times, and self-doubt can be deadly.

Make sure you get regular exercise during your job search to relieve stress. You'll sleep better, feel better, and perhaps even lose a few pounds.

Take care of your diet and watch what you drink. Many people who start to feel sorry for themselves tend to overindulge in food or alcohol. Valium and other such drugs are not as helpful as sharing your progress with your family or a couple of close friends.

Beef up your wardrobe so that you look and feel good during your employment interviews. There's no need to buy an expensive new suit, especially if you're on an austere budget, but a new shirt, blouse, tie, pair of shoes, or hairstyle may be in order.

Maintain a positive outlook. Unemployment is not the end of the world; few people complete a career without losing a job at least once. Keep a sense of humor, too. Every job search has its funny moments. It's OK to joke about your situation and share your sense of humor with your friends and family.

Life goes on despite your job search. Your spouse and kids still need your attention. Try not to take out your anxieties, frustrations, and fears on those close to you. At the very time you need support and affirmation, your friends may prefer to stay at arm's length. You can relieve their embarrassment by being straightforward about your situation and by telling them how they can help you.

Put Yourself on a Schedule

Looking for work is a job in itself. Establish a schedule for your job search and stick to it. You may not be able to control when you land a job or even when you line up a good interview. But you CAN control how you spend each day. If you work hard and systematically, you'll be less likely to give in to self-doubt and depression. You'll also get a good job that much quicker.

If you're unemployed, work full time at your job search—from 8:30 a.m. to 5:30 p.m. five days a week, and from 9:00 a.m. to 12:00 noon on Saturdays. During a job search, there is a temptation to use "extra" time for recreation or to catch up on household tasks. Arranging two or three exploratory interviews will prove a lot more useful to you than washing the car or cleaning out the garage. You can do such tasks at night or on Sundays,

The ABCs of networking

just as you would if you were working. Besides, you ARE working—working hard and systematically to get the best job you can possibly get as quickly as you can get it.

Don't take a vacation during your search. Take it after you accept an offer and before you begin the new job. You might be tempted to "sort things out on the beach." But taking a vacation when you're unemployed isn't as restful as it sounds. You'll spend most of your time worrying about what will happen when the trip is over.

Even if you're currently employed, you should go about your job search seriously and systematically. Establish regular hours, give yourself deadlines, be persistent. If you're scheduling interviews, try to arrange several for one day so that you don't have to take too much time away from your job. You might also arrange interviews for your lunch hour. You can make phone calls during lunch or on your break time. You'd also be surprised at how many people you can reach before and after regular working hours.

Tax deductible job-hunting expenses

A certified public accountant offers the following tips on deducting job-hunting expenses on the income tax form. To qualify for certain deductions, you must hunt for a job in the same field you just left, or in the field that currently employs you. For example, someone who has worked as a public school teacher could not deduct the cost of getting a real estate license and seeking a broker's job.

If you are unemployed or want to switch jobs, expenses can be deducted on the Income Tax Statement of Employee Business Expenses or itemized on Schedule A of Form 1040. Expenses you can deduct include preparing, printing, and mailing resumes; vocational guidance counseling and testing; and travel expenses to and from job interviews. Telephone, postage, and newspaper expenses are also deductible. While seeking work out of town, additional deductions may be allowed for transportation, food, and lodging. ■

Watch Your Expenses

Spend what you have to spend for basic needs such as food, transportation, and housing. But watch major expenditures that could be delayed or not made at all. The kids will still need new shoes, but a $200 dinner party at a fancy place could just as well be changed to turkey sandwiches and beer at home.

Keep track of all expenses that you incur in your job search, such as telephone and printing bills, postage, newspapers, parking, transportation, and meals purchased during the course of interviewing. These may all be tax deductible.

Networking Is the Key to a Successful Job Search

The basic tasks of a job search are fairly simple. Once you've figured out what kind of work you want to do, you need to know which companies might have such jobs and then make contact with the hiring authority. These tasks are also known as researching the job market and generating leads and interviews. Networking, or developing your personal contacts, is a great technique for finding out about the market and industrial trends and is unsurpassed as a way to generate leads and interviews.

Networking is nothing more than asking the people you already know to help you find out about the job market and meet the people who are actually doing the hiring. Each adult you know has access to at least 300 people you do not know. Of course, a lot of them will not be able to do much in the way of helping you find a job. But if you start with, say, 20 or 30 people, and each of them tells you about 3 other people who may be able to help you, you've built a network of 60 to 90 contacts.

Mark S. Granovetter, a Harvard sociologist, reported to *Forbes* magazine that "informal contacts" account for almost 75 percent of all successful job searches. Agencies find about 9 percent of new jobs for professional and technical people, and ads yield, on average, another 10 percent.

How to Start

To begin the networking process, draw up a list of all the possible contacts who can help you gain access to someone who can hire you for the job you want. Naturally, the first sources, the ones at the top of your list, will be people you know personally: friends, colleagues, former clients, relatives, acquaintances, customers, and club and church members. Just about everyone you know, whether or not he or she is employed, can generate contacts for you.

Don't forget to talk with your banker, lawyer, insurance agent, dentist, and other people who provide you with services. It is the nature of their business to know a lot of people who might help you in your search. Leave no stone unturned in your search for contacts. Go through your Christmas card list, alumni club list, and any other list you can think of.

On the average, it may take ten to fifteen contacts to generate one formal interview. It may take five to ten of these formal interviews to generate one solid offer. And it may take five offers before you uncover the exact job situation you've been seeking. You may have to talk to a minimum of 250 people before you get the job you want. The maximum may be several hundred more.

Don't balk at talking to friends, acquaintances, and neighbors about your job search. In reality, you're asking for advice, not charity. Most of the people you'll contact will be willing to help you, if only you tell them *how*.

The ABCs of networking

Here's an example of a networking letter

P.O. Box 1892
Rice University
Houston, TX 77251
(713) 555-3456

April 11, 1993

Dr. Norman Hartman
President
Combined Opinion Research
7000 Louisiana, Suite 101
Houston, TX 77005

Dear Dr. Hartman:

Dr. Obrigon Partito, with whom I have studied these past two years, suggested that you might be able to advise me of opportunities in the field of social and political research in the Houston area.

I am about to graduate from Rice University with a B.A. in History, and I am a member of Phi Beta Kappa. For two of the last three summers, I have worked in the public sector as an intern with Citizens for a Better Government in Houston and with Senator Claghorn in Washington. Last summer I worked as a desk assistant at *Newsweek's* Houston office.

I am eager to begin to work and would appreciate a few minutes of your time to discuss employment possibilities in the field of social and political research. I will be finished with exams on May 24 and would like to arrange a meeting with you shortly thereafter.

I look forward to hearing from you and in any case will be in touch with your office next week.

Sincerely,

Steven Sharp ∎

The Exploratory Interview

If I introduce you to my friend George at a major Houston bank, he will get together with you as a favor to me. When you have your meeting with him, you will make a presentation about what you've done in your work, what you want to do, and you will ask for his advice, ideas, and opinions. That is an exploratory interview. As is true of any employment interview, you must make a successful sales presentation to get what you want. You must convince George that you are a winner and that you deserve his help in your search.

How to Get a Job

The help the interviewer provides is usually in the form of suggestions on how to meet new people or contact certain companies. I introduced you to George. Following your successful meeting, he introduces you to Tom, Dick, and Mary. Each of them provides additional leads. In this way, you spend most of your time interviewing, not staying at home waiting for the phone to ring or the mail to arrive.

A job doesn't have to be vacant in order for you to have a successful meeting with a hiring authority. If you convince an employer that you would make a good addition to his or her staff, the employer might create a job for you where none existed before. In this way, networking taps the "hidden job market." And it's in the "hidden job market" that most of the good jobs are found. Besides, if you make a good impression and stay in touch, one of your contacts might have a hot lead for you two weeks from now.

To make the most of the networking technique, continually brush up on your interviewing skills (we've provided a refresher course in Chapter 7). Remember, even when you're talking with an old friend, you are still conducting an exploratory interview. Don't treat it as casual conversation.

Another term for this initial interview is the "informational interview." This meeting can get you more than additional contacts and news about who's hiring. View it as an opportunity to find out more about the field you're researching. Every time you learn something new, that bit of information becomes grist for formal interviews later on.

Ask each contact to take a look at your resume. Even though they don't have a job to offer you now, they might next month. They also may be able to comment on any gaps in your qualifications. Encourage such frankness. Once you know what your shortcomings are, you'll be in a better position to handle tough questions during formal interviews. You also may be able to rectify professional gaps through study or volunteer work.

Developing Professional Contacts

Friends and acquaintances are the obvious first choice when you're drawing up a list of contacts. But don't forget professional and trade organizations, clubs, and societies—they are valuable sources of contacts, leads, and information. In certain cases, it isn't necessary for you to belong in order to attend a meeting or an annual or monthly lunch, dinner, or cocktail party.

Many such groups also publish newsletters, another valuable source of information about the job market and industry trends. Some professional associations offer placement services to members, in which case it may be worth your while to join officially. At the end of this chapter, we've provided a list of selected organizations that might prove useful for networking purposes.

If you're utterly new to Houston and don't as yet know a soul, your job search will naturally be tougher. But it's not impossible. It just means you have to hustle that much more. Here are some first steps you should take. Start attending the meetings of any professional society or civic organization of which you've been a member in the past. Find a church, temple, or religious organization that you're comfortable with and start attending. Join a special interest group. It could be anything from The Sierra Club to Parents Without Partners.

If you're just out of college (even if you flunked out), work through your alumni association to find out who else in Houston attended your alma

The ABCs of networking

mater. If you were in a fraternity or sorority, use those connections. If you're not a member of any of the groups mentioned above, now's the time to join.

Once you've taken the trouble to show up at a meeting, be friendly. Introduce yourself. Tell people you talk to what your situation is, but don't be pushy. You've come because you're interested in this organization and what it stands for. Volunteer to serve on a committee. You'll get to know a smaller number of people much better, and they'll see you as a responsible, generous person, a person they'll want to help. Do a bang up job on your committee and they'll want to help all the more.

You've already got lots of contacts

Networking paid off for Liz, a young woman eager to make her way in banking or a related industry. She told us why she's glad she took the time to talk with her friends and neighbors about her job search.

"I was having dinner with close friends and telling them about my job search," says Liz. "During the conversation, they mentioned a banker friend they thought might be hiring. As it turned out, the friend didn't have a job for me. But he suggested I come in, meet with him, and discuss some other possibilities. He put me in touch with an independent marketing firm, servicing the publishing industry. The owner of the firm was looking for someone with my exact qualifications. One thing led to another, and pretty soon I had landed exactly the position I wanted." ■

Keeping Yourself Organized

The most difficult part of any job search is getting started. A pocket calendar or engagement diary that divides each work day into hourly segments will make your job much easier. As you start meeting the people who are in a position to hire you, notice that they invariably rely on just such a planner. Do you really want to appear less professional than your interviewers?

You should keep a personal log of calls and contacts. You may want to develop a format that's different from the one shown here. Fine. The point is to keep a written record of every person you contact in your job search and the results of each contact.

Your log (it can be a notebook from the dime store) will help keep you from getting confused and losing track of the details of your search. For example, if you call someone who's out of town until Tuesday, your log can flag this call so it won't fall between the cracks. It may also come in handy for future job searches.

Your log's "disposition" column can act as a reminder of additional sources of help you'll want to investigate. You'll also have a means of timing the correspondence that should follow any interview.

How to Get a Job

CALLS AND CONTACTS

Date	Name & Title	Company	Phone	Disposition
2/10	Chas. Junior, V.P. Sales	Top Parts	277-5500	Interview 2/15
2/10	E. Franklin Sales Manager	Frameco	466-0303	Out of town until 2/17
2/10	L. Duffy Dir. Marketing	Vassar Inc.	826-6112	Out of office. Call in aft.
2/10	P. Lamm Sls. Dir.	Golfco Ent.	386-9100	Busy to 2/28 Call then.
2/10	E. Waixel VP Mktg. & Sales	Half'n'Half Foods	338-1055	Call after 2

If you're unemployed and job hunting full time, schedule yourself for three exploratory interviews a day for the first week. Each of these meetings should result in at least three subsequent leads. Leave the second week open for the appointments you generated during the first. Maintain this pattern as you go along in your search.

We can't emphasize strongly enough how important it is that you put yourself on a job-searching schedule, whether or not you're currently employed. A schedule shouldn't function as a straightjacket, but it ought to serve as a way of organizing your efforts for greatest efficiency. Much of your job-hunting time will be devoted to developing your network of contacts. Still, you should also set aside a certain portion of each week for doing your homework on companies that interest you (see Chapter 4) and for pursuing other means of contacting employers (we'll get to these in a minute).

As you go through your contacts and begin to research the job market, you'll begin to identify certain employers in which you're interested. Keep a list of them. For each one that looks particularly promising, begin a file that contains articles about the company, its annual report, product brochures, personnel policy, and the like. Every so often, check your "potential employer" list against your log to make sure that you're contacting the companies that interest you most.

Go for the Hiring Authority

The object of your job search is to convince the person who has the power to hire you that you ought to be working for him or her. The person you want to talk to is not necessarily the president of the company. It's the person who heads the department that could use your expertise. If you're a salesperson, you probably want to talk with the vice-president of sales or marketing. If you're in data processing, the vice-president of operations is the person you need to see.

How do you find the hiring authority? If you're lucky, someone you know personally will tell you whom to see and introduce you. Otherwise, you'll have to do some homework. Some of the directories listed in Chapter

The ABCs of networking

4 will name department heads for major companies in the Houston area. If you cannot otherwise find out who heads the exact department that interests you, call the company and ask the operator. (It's a good idea to do this anyway since directories go out of date as soon as a department head leaves a job.)

Use an introduction wherever possible when first approaching a company—that's what networking is all about. For those companies that you must approach "cold," use the phone beforehand to arrange a meeting with the hiring authority. Don't assume you can drop in and see a busy executive without an appointment. And don't assume you can get to the hiring authority through the personnel department. If at all possible, you don't want to fill out any personnel forms until you have had a serious interview. The same goes for sending resumes (see Chapter 3). In general, resumes are better left behind, *after* an interview, than sent ahead to generate a meeting.

Telephone Tactics

Cold calls are difficult for most job seekers. Frequently, a receptionist or secretary, sometimes both, stands between you and the hiring authority you want to reach. One way around this is to call about a half-hour after closing. There's a good chance that the secretary will be off to happy hour, and the boss will still be finishing up the XYZ project report. Only now there will be no one to run interference for him or her.

Generally, you're going to have to go through a support staffer, so the first rule is to act courteously and accord him or her the same professional respect you'd like to be accorded yourself. This person is not just a secretary. Often, part of his or her job is to keep unsolicited job hunters out of the boss's hair. You want this intermediary to be your ally, not your adversary. If possible, sell what a wonderfully qualified person you are and how it is to the company's advantage to have you aboard.

If you're not put through to the hiring authority, don't leave your name and expect a return call. Instead, ask when there's a convenient time you might call back, or allow yourself to be put on hold. You can read job-search literature or compose cover letters while you wait. Be sure and keep your target's name and title and the purpose of your call on a card before you, however. You don't want to be at a loss for words when you're finally put through.

Other Tactics for Contacting Employers

Direct contact with the hiring authority—either through a third-party introduction (networking) or by calling for an appointment directly—is far and away the most effective job-hunting method. Your strategy and schedule should reflect that fact, and most of your energy should be devoted to direct contact. It's human nature, however, not to put all your eggs in one basket. You may want to explore other methods of contacting potential employers, but they should take up no more than a quarter of your job-hunting time.

Calling or writing to personnel offices may occasionally be productive, especially when you know that a company is looking for someone with your particular skills. But personnel people, by the nature of their responsibility, tend to screen out rather than welcome newcomers to the company fold. You're always better off going directly to the hiring authority.

How to Get a Job

Consider the case of a company that runs an ad in *The Wall Street Journal*. The ad may bring as many as 600 responses. The head of personnel asks one of the secretaries to separate the resumes into three piles according to education level. The personnel chief automatically eliminates two of the three stacks. He or she then flips through the third and eliminates all but, say, eight resumes. The personnel specialist will call the eight applicants, screen them over the phone, and invite three for a preliminary interview. Of those three, two will be sent to the hiring authority for interviews. That means that 598 applicants never even got a chance to make their case.

Statistically, fewer than one out of four job hunters succeed by going to personnel departments, responding to ads (either open or blind, as described in Chapter 4), or using various employment services. Some do find meaningful work that way, however. We repeat, if you decide to use a method other than networking or direct contact, don't spend more than 25 percent of your job-hunting time on it.

As you might expect, many books have been written on job-hunting strategy and techniques. Here is a list of selected resources.

SELECTED BOOKS ON JOB-HUNTING STRATEGY

Bolles, Richard N. *The Three Boxes of Life and How to Get Out of Them*. Berkeley, CA: Ten Speed Press, 1983.

Bolles, Richard N. *What Color Is Your Parachute?* Berkeley, CA: Ten Speed Press, 1993.

Camden, Thomas M. *The Job Hunter's Final Exam*. Chicago: Surrey Books, 1990.

Davidson, Jeffrey P. *Blow Your Own Horn: How to Market Yourself and Your Career*. New York: American Management Association, 1987.

Figler, Howard. *The Complete Job Search Handbook*. New York: H. Holt & Co., 1988.

Haldane, Bernard. *Career Satisfaction and Success: A Guide to Job Freedom*. New York: AMACOM, 1982.

Half, Robert. *How to Get a Better Job in This Crazy World*. New York: Crown Publishers, 1990.

Hewitt, Linda. *Networking for the Career-Minded Student*. Atlanta, GA: Lenox Publishers, 1985.

Kalt, Meil C., Ph.D., and William B. Helmreich, Ph.D. *Flight Path: How to Get the Job That Launches Your Career After College*. Saint Louis, MO: Fireside Books, 1989. A good starting point; outlines the basic job search clearly and succinctly.

Kleiman, Carol. *Women's Networks*. New York: Ballantine, 1981.

Krannich, Ron, and Caryl Krannich. *Network Your Way to Job & Career Success: the Complete Guide to Creating New Opportunities*. Manassas, VA: Impact Publishers, 1989.

Moses, Bruce E. *How To Market Yourself...Yourself*. New York: Pro-Search, Inc., 1979.

Petras, Kathryn and Ross. *The Only Job Hunting Guide You'll Ever Need*. Las Cruces, NM: Poseidon Press, 1989.

Taggert, Judith, and Associates. *The Job Hunter's Workbook*. Princeton, NJ: Peterson's Guides, 1989. Includes checklists, self-assessment exercises, and worksheets; provides clear, practical advice.

The ABCs of networking

Executive networking

The higher your rung on the corporate ladder, the greater the chances that networking with executives outside your own field will pay off. If you're looking for a top spot in electronics, for instance, don't pass up a chance to discuss your credentials and employment needs with the recruiting executive of an advertising firm. He or she just might have the hidden connection that could land you a great job.

One hiring executive from a large corporation reports: "I network with recruiters from more industries than most people would think, both industries that are related to ours and those that are not. It helps to find out what talent is available. If one of my contacts has someone in a file they don't need and I do, they're happy to tell me about that person. And I work the same way." ■

Networking Groups in the Houston Area

There follows a list of about 100 organized groups, ready-made for networking, forming relationships, and learning inside information about business and commerce in the Houston area. Pick the groups that fit best into your career game plan, and work through them to help you land the job you want.

SELECTED HOUSTON AREA PROFESSIONAL ORGANIZATIONS, TRADE GROUPS, NETWORKS, CLUBS, AND SOCIETIES

Alley Theatre
615 Texas Avenue
Houston, TX 77002
Tel.: (713) 228-9341
Fax: (713) 222-6542
Contact: David Nesmith, House Manager

American Association of University Women
2318 Dorrington, Apartment 8
Houston, TX 77030
Tel.: (713) 681-8085
Contact: Ellen Garland

American Institute of Architects, Houston Chapter
20 Greenway Plaza, Suite 246
Houston, TX 77046-2002
Tel.: (713) 622-2081
Contact : Martha Murphree
Members include architects, intern architects, and persons in related fields. 75 percent of the architects in Houston are members. Monthly meetings and four major events per year. Annual directory and monthly newsletter.

American Institute of Banking
2400 Augusta, Suite 450

How to Get a Job

Houston, TX 77057
Tel.: (713) 785-2400
Executive Director: Lorry Harju

American Insurance Association
2950 North Loop West, Suite 760
Houston, TX 77092
Tel.: (713) 681-6121
Contact: Ronald H. Cobb
The Houston chapter of the National Insurance Society.

American Management Association
7815 Heather Heights Way
Houston, TX 77095
Tel.: (713) 463-8756
Contact: George Evans, Texas Representative

American Marketing Association
P.O. Box 27332
Houston, TX 77227-7332
Tel.: (713) 220-7403
Contact: Joel Schunter
A professional group for people in the marketing industry. National publication is "Marketing News."

American Planning Association
P.O. Box 1562
Houston, TX 77251
Contact: Marlene Gafrick (713) 247-1000
President: Jerry Hiebert (214) 238-4242
The A.P.A. is an association comprised of individuals, professionals, and non-professionals interested in urban development and planned urban environments. Most members are architects, engineers, and planners.

American Society of Civil Engineers
2000 North Loop West, Suite 135
Houston, TX 77018
Tel.: (713) 789-8050
Contact: Steve Neely
President: Martha Juck
Professional and technical group for civil engineers. Meetings are held the third Tuesday of every month from September to June. Publishes monthly newsletter, "Texas Civil Engineer."

American Society of Interior Designers
5120 Woodway, Suite 122
Houston, TX 77056
Tel.: (713) 626-1470
President: Jane Page Crump

American Society of Safety Engineers
700 Waugh Drive
Houston, TX 77019
Tel.: (713) 853-5278
Contact: Jerry Heins, President
Society for safety engineers and other engineers involved in the safety industry on a full or part-time basis. Holds monthly meetings.

The ABCs of networking

American Society of Women Accountants
P.O. Box 2636
Houston, TX 77252
Tel.: (713) 728-5326
Contact: Mary Simpson

American Woman's Society of Certified Public Accountants
P.O. Box 924449
Houston, TX 77292
Tel.: (713) 370-6153
President: Janet Norstrom
Organization of women accountants in Houston.

Art Directors Club of Houston
P.O. Box 271137
Houston, TX 77277
Tel.: (713) 961-3434
Contact: Susan Strickland
An association for artists, art directors, graphic designers, producers, photographers, illustrators, and other people involved in advertising and graphic design. Monthly meetings, including various speakers, and newsletter.

Art League of Houston
1953 Montrose Boulevard
Houston, TX 77006
Tel.: (713) 523-9530
Contact: Kim Veiean
This is a non-profit, visual arts organization. Annual membership meeting, monthly invitations to exhibits, and bimonthly newsletter.

Associated Builders and Contractors of Greater Houston
c/o 2525 West Bellfort, Suite 120
Houston, TX 77054
Tel.: (713) 668-2906
Contact: Mike Gibson
Construction trade association that promotes the "open shop" philosophy. Members are both union and non-union. Monthly dinner meetings and a lot of networking.

Associated General Contractors of America
Houston Chapter
P.O. Box 662
Houston, TX 77001-0662
Tel.: (713) 659-4845
President: Pat Kiley

Association of Consulting Engineers of Metropolitan Houston
2000 North Loop West Suite 135
Houston, TX 77018
Tel.: (713) 680-1595
Fax:(713) 680-1835
President: Cecil Allen

Association of Energy Engineers
c/o 5702 Irish Hill Drive
Houston, TX 77053
Tel.: (713) 869-2894
Contact: Leonard Bachman

How to Get a Job

The members of this organization are people interested in the field of energy management. Meetings are held the second Tuesday of each month.

Automotive Service Association
Houston-Harris County Chapter
8319 Howard Drive
P. O. Box 87171
Houston, TX 77017
Tel.: (713) 643-6008
President: Robert Williams

Buffalo Bayou Coalition
P.O. Box 130725
Houston, TX 77219-0725
Tel.: (713) 880-3369
Contact: Steve Brook
Tel.: (713) 528-7211
Organization for those interested in environmental issues.

Business Artsfund
440 Louisiana, Suite 710
Houston, TX 77002
Tel.: (713) 224-1581
Executive Director: Barbara Kaussman

Business Volunteers for the Arts/Houston
1100 Milam Building, Suite 2725
Houston, TX 77002
Tel.: (713) 658-2483
President: Virginia Lang

Certified Professional Secretary Society of Texas
142 Oyster Creek Drive, Suite 38
Lake Jackson, TX 77566
Contact : Elizabeth Eichelburg
Tel.: (713) 931-4338

Citizens' Environmental Coalition
1413 Westheimer
Houston, TX 77006
Tel.: (713) 880-3369
Contact: Barbara Link
This is a non-profit environmental networking organization that has approximately 50 environmental groups as member organizations. Monthly newsletter, "The Environmental News Exchange."

Cultural Arts Council of Houston
1964 West Gray, Suite 224
Houston, TX 77019
Tel.: (713) 527-9330
Contact: Maurine McCollam
Organization that grants funding money to art groups. Membership is open to the public and to art groups. Annual meeting in June. Publishes bimonthly newsletter called "CACH-up," which includes an arts calendar.

Drywall and Interior Systems Contractors Association
P.O. Box 924555
Houston, TX 77292-4555

The ABCs of networking

Tel.: (713) 690-0604
Fax: (713) 690-0604

Financial Executives Institute, Houston Chapter
P.O. Box 2180
Houston, TX 77252-2180
Tel.: (713) 656-6794
President: Orville Mills, Jr.

Geophysical Society of Houston
7171 Harwin Drive Suite 314
Houston, TX 77036
Tel.: (713) 785-6403
Contact: Margaret Blake
Organization of geophysicists and associates. Has a membership luncheon every month and 3 or 4 social activities throughout the year. Monthly publication, "Geophysicist Society of Houston."

Greater Houston Builders Association
P.O. Box 741189
Houston, TX 77274
Tel.: (713) 776-1445
Contact: Max B. Hoyt
Professional trade organization designed to help builders and associates involved in construction to contend with their problems through collective action. Monthly publication, "Houston Builder"; meet first Tuesday of each month.

Greater Houston Legal Secretaries Association
5525 Airline Drive
Houston, TX 77076
Tel.: (713) 691-6434
President: Laurie Brantley
Contact: Mildred Holeman

Meetings are for meeting people

Laid off during a real estate slump, one enterprising 42-year-old escrow officer decided she would keep her finances flourishing by doing something she enjoyed—gardening. After a few phone calls to friends and former business associates, her newly formed Landscape Redecorating Service was in full bloom.

At the same time, she attended every possible escrow association meeting, dinner, and other professional event. "I set a goal," she recalls, "to contact at least three escrow company owners at each meeting, to let them know I was looking and available. Then I'd drop them a note to give them my phone number in case they wanted to get in touch right away."

About four months after her first dinner meeting, an officer from one of the larger title companies called her for an interview. "He couldn't get me working on that desk fast enough," she remembers. "The $15 I'd spent on that dinner ticket was the best investment I ever made." ■

71

How to Get a Job

Harris County Beer Wholesalers Association
2025 Turning Basin Drive Suite 804
Houston, TX 77021
Tel.: (713) 672-1171
President: Richard Donley

Harris County Medical Society
1133 M.D. Anderson Boulevard Suite 400
Houston, TX 77030
Tel.: (713) 790-1838
Contact: Lisa Conwell
An organization for medical professionals in Harris County.

Houston Advertising Federation
P.O. Box 27592
Houston, TX 77227
Tel.: (713) 522-9591
Contact: Jay Hagins
Organization of people in the advertising and communications industry. The basic goals are to keep people in touch with the latest industry trends and to work with students through internships and scholarships. Monthly newsletter, "HAF-time," and monthly meetings.

Houston Association of Black Journalists
2601 Aibor
Houston, TX 77044
Tel.: (713) 521-0900
Contact: Kijana Weisman
Membership includes anyone from the journalism, advertising, radio, and television industries. Holds monthly meetings.

Houston Association of Legal Secretaries
1100 Louisiana Suite 4200
Houston, TX 77002
Tel.: (713) 752-4371
President: Sue Foley

Houston Association of Life Underwriters
5615 Kirby Drive, Suite 508
Houston, TX 77005
Tel.: (713) 526-5331
President: Bill Sessums

Houston Association of Petroleum Landmen
5353 West Alabama Suite 210
Houston, TX 77056
Tel.: (713) 622-6868
Contact: Mary Livesay
An organization whose purpose is to further the education, knowledge, and interests of petroleum landmen in oil development and exploration. Works to promote effective public relations. Social gatherings and monthly bulletin.

Houston Association of Radio Broadcasters
50 Briar Hollow, Suite 540 East
Houston, TX 77027
Tel.: (713) 621-9401
Contact: Kim Clark
Members are from the commercial radio industry and include 3 university

The ABCs of networking

representatives from communications schools. Quarterly membership meetings and business breakfasts.

Houston Association of School Administrators
3202 Weslayan Suite 212
Houston, TX 77027
Tel.: (713) 622-0652
Fax: (713) 622-4835
Executive Director: Irene Kerr

Houston Ballet Foundation
P.O. Box 130487
Houston, TX 77219-0487
Tel.: (713) 523-6300
Executive Director: Gary Dunning

Houston Bar Association
101 Fannin, Suite 1300
Houston, TX 77002
Tel.: (713) 759-1133
Fax: (713) 759-1710
Contact: Kay Sim
Association for attorneys licensed by the State of Texas. Monthly bulletin and bimonthly magazine.

Houston Board of Realtors
3693 Southwest Freeway
Houston, TX 77027
Tel.: (713) 629-1900
Contact: Yolanda Palacios
Association of people in the real estate industry in the Houston area.

Houston Building Owners and Managers Association
One West Loop South, Suite 708
Houston, TX 77027
Tel.: (713) 961-0086
Fax: (713) 961-2657
President: Frances V. Watts
Chairman: Dave Johnson

Houston Business Council
6161 Savoy Drive, Suite 1030
Houston, TX 77036
Tel.: (713) 974-0286
Society for minority- or women-owned businesses. Orientations are biweekly. Offers a variety of publications.

Houston Business Roundtable
8031 Airport Boulevard, Suite 118
Houston, TX 77061
Tel.: (713) 645-0923
Contact: Art Aamoth
Non-profit trade organization that addresses the concerns of the maintenance and construction industry and promotes cost-effective maintenance.

Houston Civic Arts Association
5305 Bissonnet
Bellaire, TX 77401

How to Get a Job

Tel.: (713) 668-0785
President: Bob Peterson

Houston Contractors Association
3000 Westlayan Suite 230
Houston, TX 77027
Tel.: (713) 871-0784
Vice-President: Royce Hassell

Houston Dental Society
One Greenway Plaza, Suite 110
Houston, TX 77046
Tel.: (713) 961-4337
Contact: Jeannine Jochec
Society for persons in the dental profession in Houston.

Houston Economic Development Council
1100 Milam, Suite 2440
Houston, TX 77002
Tel.: (713) 651-7200
Contact: John Brock
Dedicated to helping businesses utilize the area's resources to meet their specific start-up, expansion, or relocation needs. Source of information and assistance, providing counseling, economic briefings, and data packets, among other things.

Houston Engineering and Scientific Society
3121 Buffalo Speedway
Houston, TX 77098
Tel.: (713) 627-2283
President: Stanley Hruska
Contact: Grace Kantz

Houston Financial Council for Women
9026 Sweet Water
Houston, TX 77037
Tel.: (713) 931-8883
President: Dora Williams

Houston Geological Society
7171 Harwin Suite 314
Houston, TX 77036
Tel.: (713) 785-6402
Contact: Pat Gordon
Society for geologists and associates.

Houston Grand Opera Association
510 Preston Suite 500
Houston, TX 77002
Tel.: (713) 546-0200
Executive Vice-President: Dolores Johnson

Houston International Festival
1100 Louisiana Suite 1275
Houston, TX 77002
Tel.: (713) 654-8808
President: James Austin

The ABCs of networking

Houston Legal Assistants Association
P.O. Box 52266
Houston, TX 77052
Tel.: (713) 580-7722
Fax: (713) 580-7722
Contact: Gayle Brochstein
Association for legal assistants in Houston.

Houston Medical Forum
5511 Austin Suite 101
Houston, TX 77004
Tel.: (713) 529-8677
Contact: James H. Young, Jr., M.D.
A forum for persons involved in the medical profession.

Turning volunteer work into a job

After spending many years working as a volunteer for various organizations, Marian Simon's daughters advised her to "stop giving it away." She decided to look for paid employment. But because she had never held a paid job, Marian was not sure how to begin her job search.

"As a woman in my middle years, I wondered where in the world I would go," says Marian. "I had a good education and a great deal of volunteer experience. I had planned and orchestrated large benefits and had done an inordinate amount of fundraising over the years. I also had done community work in the inner city.

"I talked to some people at a local college. They told me I was well qualified and that I should just go out and look for a job. But I didn't know where 'out' was. Later, career counselors at another local college helped me put together a resume. Then I began to talk to people I knew. I was offered various jobs, none of which thrilled me.

"Then I happened to mention my job search to the president of a hospital where I had done a great deal of volunteer work," says Marian. "He asked me not to take a job until I had talked to him. Later, he hired me as his special assistant, with the charge to 'humanize the hospital.' Over a period of time, I developed a patient representative department.

"When I began the job 11 years ago, I was a one-person operation. As time went on, I added staff. I currently supervise a staff of 9, plus about 25 volunteers. The job of patient representative is now a full-fledged profession. Many women in the field began as volunteers. They knew a lot about the hospital where they were volunteer-

How to Get a Job

ing and thus made the transition into a paid position more easily."

We asked Marian what advice she has for volunteers who want to move into the paid work force. "Go to the career counseling departments of some of the small colleges. Ask them to review your background and tell you what kinds of jobs you may be qualified for. If they suggest that you need additional training, get it. But before you go back to school, investigate the kinds of jobs available in your chosen field. Think about how you can use your volunteer experience in a paid position. Take what you've done and build from it."

In job search lingo, Marian analyzed her volunteer work and identified her functional skills. If you can sell Girl Scout cookies, you can sell other products and services. If you coordinated the fund-raising project for the church building fund, you can coordinate projects for a salary. You just have to convince the hiring authority that your skills are transferable. ■

Houston Personnel Association
P. O. Box 35641
Houston, TX 77235
Tel.: (713) 437-5153
President: Mike Kaan

Houston Restaurant Association
1010 Lamar Suite 1520
Houston, TX 77002
Tel.: (713) 650-3119
Fax: (713) 650-1345
Contact: Bob Feigenbaun
Trade association that represents the food service and hospitality industry as a special interest group. Members range from the smallest companies to the largest chains. Monthly publication, "Houston Restaurant News."

Houston Safe Deposit Association
P.O. Box 920952 Suite 270
Humble, TX 77292-0952
Tel.: (713) 690-2926
Contact: David McGuin

Houston Society of Professional Illustrators
P.O. Box 272011
Houston, TX 77277
Tel.: (713) 723-1373
Contact: James Stevens
Meets the second Wednesday of every month.

Houston Symphony Orchestra
615 Louisiana
Houston, TX 77002

The ABCs of networking

Tel.: (713) 224-4240
Fax: (713) 222-7024
Executive Director: David Wax

Houston Teachers Association
1415 Southmore Boulevard
Houston, TX 77004
Tel.: (713) 528-1968
Contact: Sheryl Saliens
Organization for persons involved in education.

Houston Venture Capitol Association
515 Post Oak Boulevard Suite 310
Houston, TX 77027
Tel.: (713) 621-9444
Contact: Fred Zeidman
The purpose of this organization is to educate the community about the availability of venture capital in Houston. Sponsors an annual venture capital conference.

Independent Electrical Contractors of Houston
4001 Sherwood Lane
Houston, TX 77092
President: Jon Pollock (713) 681-3511
Contact Person: Melene Hunsley (713) 869-1976

Independent Insurance Agents of Houston
952 Echo Lane Suite 310
Houston, TX 77024-2751
Tel.: (713) 973-6171
Fax: (713) 973-7417

Institute of Hispanic Culture
3400 Bissonnet, Suite 135
Houston, TX 77005-2153
Tel.: (713) 666-1492
Contact: Elisabeth Barrett

Institute of International Education
515 Post Oak Boulevard Suite 150
Houston, TX 77027
Tel.: (713) 621-6300
Fax: (713) 621-7958
President: James Faulk

Institute of Management Consultants
3701 Kirby Drive Suite 830
Houston, TX 77098
Tel.: (713) 526-5711
Contact: John Elmer

Institute of Real Estate Management
10700 Richmond Avenue Suite 201
Houston, TX 77042
Tel.: (713) 781-3211
Chief Administrator: Bob Eaton

International Association of Business Communications
1100 West 23rd Street, Suite 200

How to Get a Job

Houston, TX 77008
Tel.: (713) 880-0457

International Association for Financial Planning, Houston Chapter
2200 Post Oak Boulevard, Suite 709
Houston, TX 77056
Tel.: (713) 960-1046
Fax: (713) 960-1254
Executive Director: Charlene Craig

League of Women Voters—Clear Lake Area
15514 Saint Cloud
Houston, TX 77062
Tel.: (713) 474-7963
Contact: Barbara Murry
President: Gail Roache

League of Women Voters—Houston
5373 West Alabama #500
Houston, TX 77056
Tel.: 552-1776
President: Gail Roache

Mechanical Contractors Association of Houston
2401 LaBranch
Houston, TX 77004
Tel.: (713) 686-8606
President: John Morrow
Contact: Robert C. Marshall
Tel.: (713) 659-4926

National Association of Social Workers
810 West 11th Street
Austin, TX 78701
Tel.: (512) 474-1454
Fax: (512) 474-1317

National Electrical Contractors Association
P.O. Box 42949
Bellaire, TX 77242
Tel.: (713) 977-2522
Fax: (713) 977-2923
President: C.W. Henderson

National Institute of Management Acccountants
P.O. Box 1967
Houston, TX 77251
Tel.: (713) 739-5724
President: Jeanne Clark
Contact: May Ramsey
(713) 868-7761

National Organization for Women
P. O. Box 66351
Houston, TX 77266-6351
Tel.: (713) 668-9008

The ABCs of networking

National Society of Fund Raising Executives
10700 Richmond, Suite 207
Houston, TX 77042
Tel.: (713) 266-2800
Fax: (713) 780-4802

Press Club of Houston
P.O. Box 2904
Houston, TX 77252
Tel.: (713) 523-2382
Fax: (713) 523-2382
Contact: Bette Lieber (713) 523-2382

Printing Industries of the Gulf Coast
P.O. Box 130547
Houston, TX 77219
Tel.: (713) 522-2046
Fax: (713) 522-8342
Contact: Don Piercy
A group for businesses in the printing industry.

Professional Accounting Society of Houston
University of Houston, Downtown
101 Main Street, Room 702
Houston, TX 77002
Tel.: (703) 221-1050, Ext. 166
Contact: Virginia Lozana
Student organization at University of Houston. The goal is to familiarize students with business and professional society in Houston. Holds various luncheons and activities with important speakers. Newsletter issued twice a semester.

Professional Secretaries International, Greenspoint Area Chapter
2407 Quiver Lane
Houston, TX 77067
Tel.: (713) 957-5291
Contact Person: Margie Hilliard
President: Cindy Hammer

Professional Secretaries International, Houston Chapter
P.O. Box 53464
Houston, TX 77052-3464
Tel.: (713) 224-4100
President: Karen Carrington
Tel.: (713) 655-8000
An organization of professional secretaries in the Houston area.

How to Get a Job

Internships can lead to permanent relationships

According to an internship program director, internships are unique because they are beneficial to both the employer and the employee. Getting an internship is a good way to really test someone: you (the employee) can figure out whether you really enjoy working in a certain industry, and the employer can decide whether you are perfectly suited for the job.

Internships are not designed to be just another part-time job. An intern is expected to do all the things that an entry-level person would. Productive internships will almost always lead to job offers. In this way, an internship is a great way to get into an industry that you might otherwise find closed to newcomers.

Even if an intern does not decide to stick with the company he or she is working for, a person can gain valuable contacts in an industry, which can be used for networking in future job searches. ■

Public Relations Society of America, Houston Chapter
3272 Westheimer Suite 11
Houston, TX 77098
Tel.: (713) 877-6732
Fax: (713) 922-4634
President: Barbara Langham
Conducts professional seminars, career development activities, and local career placement bureau. Monthly meetings on public relations topics. Local monthly publication called *Prolog*.

Retail Grocers Association of Houston
P.O. Box 7650
Houston, TX 77270
Tel.: (713) 862-3001
Fax: (713) 862-5296
Executive Director: Richard Johnson

Retail Merchants Association of Houston
4201 Fannin
Houston, TX 77004
Tel.: (713) 520-9229
Contact: Maurice J. Aresty
Association for persons in the retail industry in Houston.

Rice Design Alliance
P.O. Box 1892
Houston, TX 77251
Tel.: (713) 524-6297
Fax: (713) 285-5277
Contact: Linda Sylvan
"The Rice Design Alliance is a non-profit educational organization whose purpose is to stimulate greater public awareness of the man-made and natural environments. RDA seeks to involve the general public in issues related to the design of public spaces, parks, offices, etc." Publishes a journal, *Cite*.

The ABCs of networking

Sales & Marketing Executive Society of Houston
719 West Gray
Houston, TX 77019
Tel.: (713) 524-0409
Fax: (713) 524-1861
President: Elroy Forbes
Meets the second Monday of each month.

Society of Industrial and Office Realtors
1300 Post Oak Boulevard Suite 1300
Houston, TX 77056
Tel.: (713) 961-3700
Contact Person: Kelly Parker

Society of Petroleum Engineers
770 South Post Oak Lane, Suite 512
Houston, TX 77056
Tel.: (713) 499-2294
Contact: Bert Nelson
Non-profit trade organization whose purpose is to disseminate technical information about the petroleum industry to its members. Has monthly meetings and publishes *The Journal of Petroleum Engineers.*

Society of Professional Journalists, Houston Chapter
P.O Box 3454
Houston, TX 77253
Contact: Lori Reingold
Society for journalists and journalism students. National newsletter called "The Quill," as well as chapter newsletter.

Society of Women Engineers
P.O.Box 3461
Houston, TX 77253
Tel.: (713) 874-2789
Contact: Cindy Gluth
An organization composed mainly of women who have engineering or technical degrees. The purpose of this group is to promote women in engineering. Monthly newsletter (from August to May) and monthly meetings (except December).

Tax Research Association of Houston and Harris Country
2600 Citadel Plaza Drive, Suite 645
Houston, TX 77008
Tel.: (713) 862-8045
President: George Scott

Texas Accountants and Lawyers for the Arts
1540 Sul Ross
Houston, TX 77006
Tel.: (713) 526-4876
Fax: (713) 526-1299
President: Jay Kolb

Texas Economic & Demographic Association/ Houston Chapter
1100 Milam, 25 Floor
Houston, TX 77002
Tel.: (713) 658-2468
Fax: (713) 658-2429
Contact: Edith Chamber

How to Get a Job

A society primarily for generators and users of economic and demographic data. Members are from business, social sciences, and government. Publishes a resource directory.

Texas Executive Women
P.O. Box 1011
Houston, TX 77251-1011
Tel.: (713) 622-7488
Contact: Karen Pitts
An organization representing professional women in all facets of business. The focus is personal development of individual members as well as community involvement.

Texas Society of Certified Public Accountants
1700 West Loop South, Suite 750
Houston, TX 77027
Tel.: (713) 622-7733
Fax: (713) 622-0522
President: Sheila Root
Director: Nancy A. Rutledge

Texas Society of Professional Engineers, San Jacinto Chapter
3121 Buffalo Speedway
Houston, TX 77098
Tel.: (713) 627-2283
Fax: (713) 627-2289
President: Dr. Roger Eichharn
Tel.: (713) 743-4200

Women Professionals in Government
P.O. Box 61272
Houston, TX 77201
Tel.: (713) 622-7987
Contact: Patti Raben
An organization whose membership includes women from city, county, state, and federal government, METRO, Houston Chamber of Commerce, and others who deal with the public sector. Meetings first Thursday of each month.

Networking for Fun and Profit

To find the best spots in Houston for convivial networking, a pair of young upwardly mobile professionals explored the city's after-work life and found the following:

The "in" places in Houston are always popular for networkers of all types. Some of the "young upwardly mobile professional" types will be found at Savages (2610 Bissonet, 942-0580), Cody's Rooftop Jazz bar & Grill (3400 Montrose, 522-9747), Cafe Adobe (2111 Westheimer, 528-1468), and the River Cafe (3615 Montrose, 529-0088). Capitalizing on the country-western craze, young business professionals flock to the Wild West (10086 Long Point, 465-7121) and Blanco's (3406 W. Alabama, 439-0072). Dave & Buster's (6010 Richmond, 952-2233) provides many an opportunity to swap business cards over the pinball machines. New professionals who want a big network for little money may try the West Alabama Ice House (1919 W. Alabama, 528-0818).

Lawyers and accountants can always be found at the Cattle Guard (2800 Milam, 520-5400). The downtown banking crowd is usually attracted to Chesterfields (1111 Fannin Lower level, 655-1011).

The ABCs of networking

The downtown crowd, including **lawyers, accountants, and consultants**, can be found at La Carafe (813 Congress, 229-9399) and XIT (777 Walker, 228-4400).

Theater people, actors, producers, and stage workers congregate at Birraporetti's (500 Louisiana at Prairie, 224-9494) after performances.

If admitted with a member, the Petroleum Club (800 Bell, 659-1431) can provide conversation with high-level **oil industry** folks.

The cream of the **medical community** mingles at the Doctor's Club (1133 M.D. Anderson Blvd., 790-1414), again, admittance with members only. The rest of the medical community can be found at The Gingerman (5607 Morningside, 526-2770) in the Rice Village.

The **academic community** frequents a number of haunts, including Valhalla (Basement Chemistry Lab, Rice University Campus, 527-3258), Local Charm (1501 Telephone Road, 926-0329), and The Gingerman.

Musicians and those in the music industry relax at Ovations (2536-B Times Blvd., 522-9801) and Rockefellers (3620 Washington, 861-9365).

The **NASA engineers** and other residents of Clear Lake mix at Frenchie's Restaurant (1041 Nasa Road 1, 486-7144), Louie's on the Lake (3813 Nasa Road 1, 326-0551), and J. Larkin's (110 Nasa Road 1, 333-2345).

If you want to rub shoulders with an **international** crowd, try the Richmond Arms (5920 Richmond, 784-7722), the Ale House (2425 W. Alabama, 521-2333), and the Black Labrador Pub (4100 Montrose, 529-1199).

Finally, for those that made it in Houston and have a few years of experience under their belt, the Ritz Carlton Bar (1919 Briar Oaks Lane, 840-7621) and the River Oaks Grill (2630 Westheimer, 520-1738) are popular.

Using Professional Employment Services

Finding a good job is difficult. Your first impulse may be to turn that responsibility over to professional employment services. After all, don't the pros have all the job listings? Unfortunately, they don't.

Yes, it's smart to use every available resource to generate leads and interviews. But professional employment services vary from agencies that specialize in temporary clerical help to executive recruiters who deal primarily with top-management types. Employment agencies, career consultants, and executive recruitment firms differ greatly in the kinds of services they offer and in how—and by whom—they get paid. You can save yourself a lot of time, effort, and possibly money if you're familiar with the different kinds of professional employment services. One handbook that might prove useful is the *Directory of Approved Counseling Services* (American Personnel and Guidance Association, 5201 Leesburg Pike 400, Falls Church, VA 22041).

Using employment services

A listing in this book does not constitute an endorsement of any consulting firm, search firm, or employment agency. Before embarking on a lengthy or expensive series of tests, try to get the opinion of one or more people who have already used the service you're considering. You can also contact:

Better Business Bureau of Metropolitan Houston

Who's good?
Who's not?

2707 North Loop West, Suite 900
Houston, TX 77008
Tel.: (713) 868-9500
Fax: (713) 867-4922
Contact: Richard McClain

Texas State Attorney General's Office—Consumer Protection
1019 Congress, Suite 1550
Houston, TX 77002
Tel.: (713) 223-5886
Fax: (713) 223-5821 ■

Employment Agencies

Employment agencies act as intermediaries in the job market between buyers (companies with jobs open) and sellers (people who want jobs). Agencies are paid for placing people. The fee may be paid by the company, but in some cases it is paid by the worker. Agencies that specialize in restaurant and domestic help, for example, often charge the worker a fee. Usually the placement fee amounts to a certain percentage of the worker's annual salary.

Employment agencies seldom place a candidate in a job that pays more than $50,000 a year. Most employment agencies concentrate on support jobs. Supervisory openings may be listed, too, but employment agencies usually don't handle middle or upper management positions. In the computer field, for example, computer operators, programmers, and perhaps systems analysts could find work through an agency. But directors of data processing or MIS (merchandising information systems) would go to an executive search firm or would job hunt on their own.

A company that's looking for a secretary gains certain advantages by going to a reputable agency. It doesn't have to advertise or screen the hundreds of resumes that would probably pour in from even a small want ad in the Sunday *Chronicle* or *Post*. A good employment agency will send over only qualified applicants for interviews. Referrals are made quickly, and there is no cost to the company until it hires the secretary. For many companies, it's worth it to pay an agency fee to avoid the hassle of prescreening dozens, if not hundreds, of applicants.

The advantage to the agency of a successful placement (besides the fee) is repeat business. After two or three referrals work out well, an employment agency can generally count on receiving future listings of company vacancies.

How to Get a Job

The value to the job seeker of using an employment agency depends on a number of factors, including the quality of the agency, the kind of work you're looking for, how much experience you have, and how broad your network of personal and business contacts is.

In general, an agency's loyalty will be to its source of income. Agencies are more interested in finding you a job than in finding you job satisfaction. Agencies are likely to pressure you to accept a job you don't really want just so they can collect their fee. With few exceptions, an agency probably can't do much more for you than you could do for yourself in an imaginative and energetic job search. (Of course, there's the rub—conducting an imaginative and energetic job search.) If a company has to pay a fee to hire you, you're at a disadvantage compared with applicants who are "free." Also, giving an employment agency your resume could be a serious mistake if you're trying to conduct a confidential job search.

On the other hand, a good agency can help its candidates develop a strategy and prepare for employment interviews. This training can be most valuable to people who are inexperienced in job-hunting techniques. (Of course, you can probably learn job-search strategy and skills more inexpensively by reading the books in our bibliography or attending an adult education class at one of the local colleges.) Agency pros should know the market, screen well, and provide sound advice. A secretary who tries to investigate the Houston market on his or her own will very likely take longer to get the "right" job than someone who uses a quality agency.

Historically, certain employment agencies engaged in practices that can only be called questionable at best, and the field as a whole is trying to polish up a somewhat tarnished image. Stories often appear in the press of unscrupulous firms that charge outrageous up-front fees in exchange for an uninspired resume, a pep talk on job-search strategies, and a list of job openings that are public domain. There are, of course, a number of reputable, highly professional employment agencies. But as in any profession, there are also crooks. It's still a practice in some agencies to advertise non-existent openings to attract applicants for other, less desirable positions.

So much for the pros and cons of employment agencies. If you decide to try one, be sure it's a reputable firm. Ask people in your field to recommend a quality agency, and consult the Better Business Bureau and the Texas Attorney General's Office (listed above) to see if there have been any complaints about the agency you're considering. Most important, *be sure to read the contract thoroughly, including all the fine print, before you sign it.* If you have any questions, or if there's something you don't understand, don't be afraid to ask. It's your right. Make sure you know who is responsible for paying the fee and what the fee is. Remember that *in some cases, an agency's application form is also the contract.*

When you go to an employment agency, treat it the same way you'd treat a job interview. Don't misrepresent yourself, but you want them to think of you as highly marketable. If the agency sees you as very difficult to place, they won't consider you a cost-effective client. If you've paid up-front money, too bad. Even if you haven't, you may have just wasted time better spent conducting your own effective job search.

Here, then, is a selective listing of the Houston area's employment agencies, including their areas of specialty.

Using employment services

EMPLOYMENT AGENCIES

Ackerman Johnson
333 North Sam Houston Parkway, Suite 1210
Houston, TX 77060
Tel.: (713) 999-8875
Fax: (713) 999-7570
Sales and sales management, and engineering/technical.

Administaff, Inc.
19001 Cresant Springs Drive
Kingwood, TX 77339
Tel.: (713) 358-8986
Fax: (713) 358-6492
Employment leasing only.

Administrative Personnel Associates
3355 W. Alabama, Suite 580
Houston, TX 77098
Tel.: (713) 622-1560
Fax: (713) 622-0068
Accounting, data processing, executive secretary, and medical.

Atlantic Technical Services
800 West Belt South, Suite 104
Houston, TX 77042
Tel.: (713) 974-2565
Fax: (713) 974-6153
Placement of contract drafters/ engineers.

Jean William Brown & Associates
5847 San Felipe, Suite 333
Houston, TX 77057
Tel.: (713) 974-7474
Fax: (713) 782-6818
Advertising, public relations, and marketing.

Burnett Personnel Services
9800 Richmond, Suite 800
Houston, TX 77042
Tel.: (713) 977-4777
Fax: (713) 977-7533
Office/clerical, administrative, data processing, and accounting.

Chase Personnel Services
8401 Westheimer, Suite 110
Houston, TX 77063
Tel.: (713) 785-4448
Fax: (713) 785-5247
Professional, clerical, and medical sales.

Clayton Personnel
480 East North Belt, Suite 140
Houston, TX 77060
Tel.: (713) 999-3080
Clerical, secretarial, data processing, word processing, and accounting.

How to Get a Job

Consultants and Designers
10500 Richmond, Suite 217
Houston, TX 77042
Tel.: (713) 784-3696
Oil and gas, structural and technical engineers.

Corporate Consultants Professional Search
4201 W. FM 1960, Suite 230
Houston, TX 77068
Tel.: (713) 580-6480
Sales, administrative, technical, and secretarial.

EDP Computer Services
4600 Post Oak Place, Suite 204
Houston, TX 77027
Tel.: (713) 960-1717
Computer, data processing local and abroad.

General Employment Personnel Consultants
2603 Augusta, Suite 850
Houston, TX 77057
Tel.: (713) 952-0400
Fax: (713) 952-4928
Full services.

Yahne Gibson Personnel
550 Westcott, Suite 560
Houston, TX 77007
Tel.: (713) 869-3600
Fax: (713) 869-6856
Accounting, clerical, and legal.

Houston City Personnel Group
6060 Richmond, Suite 100
Houston, TX 77057
Tel.: (713) 784-0656
Fax: (713) 784-8226
Secretarial and clerical.

Information Search Group
701 N. Post Oak Road, Suite 100
Houston, TX 77024
Tel.: (713) 681-6677
Fax: (713) 681-6690
Computer, data communications, and systems engineers.

Lab Support
1900 West Loop South, Suite 1360
Houston, TX 77027
Tel.: (713) 621-0502
Chemists, scientists, and technical professionals.

Leigh Personnel
2401 Fountain View, Suite 910
Houston, TX 77079
Tel.: (713) 784-4323
Fax: (713) 784-0255
Office and professional.

Using employment services

M. David Lowe Personnel Services
1100 Milam, Suite 2860 (Downtown Office)
Houston, TX 77002
Tel.: (713) 951-9339
Fax: (713) 951-9480
Professional, administrative, and clerical.

M&B Staff Management
P.O. Box 2226
Humble, TX 77347-2226
Tel.: (713) 446-7011
Fax: (713) 446-5237
Employee leasing only.

MetroCareers
P.O. Box 820367
Houston, TX 77282
Tel.: (713) 781-7215
Fax: (713) 975-1459
Full service.

The Morganstern Co.
16800 Imperial Valley Dr., Suite 220
Houston, TX 77060
Tel.: (713) 847-1491
Fax: (713) 820-3864
Management consultants.

New Dimension Designers
P. O. Box 40203
Houston, TX 77240
Tel.: (713) 469-1941
Fax: (713) 469-6221
Engineers, designers, drafters, writers, illustrators, and technicians.

Quinby Personnel
1010 Lamar, Suite 222 (Downtown Office)
Houston, TX 77002
Tel.: (713) 651-1266
Fax: (713) 651-1995
Secretarial and clerical, bookkeeping, and word processing.

Staff Solutions
10303 N.W Freeway, Suite 429
Houston, TX 77092
Tel.: (713) 957-8791
Secretarial, clerical, word processing, and accounting.

Superior Temporaries
P.O. Box 1664
Houston, TX 77251
Tel.: (713) 963-9800
Fax: (713) 963-9700
Full service, local and abroad.

Talent Place
5020 1960West, Suite A-2
Houston, TX 77069

How to Get a Job

Tel.: (713) 893-9191
Acting and print modeling.

Talent Tree Temporaries
9703 Richmond Ave.
Houston, TX 77042
Tel.: (713) 789-1818
Fax: (713) 789-2588
Full service, local and abroad.

Dealing with employment agencies

"After deciding to use an employment agency," according to a career counselor at a Houston university, "the job hunter needs to have a clear idea of what he or she is looking for. A reputable agency will not want to antagonize either their clients (the employers) or the prospective employee. Occasionally, however, an employee is scheduled for an inappropriate interview, resulting in some embarrassment for both the interviewer and the interviewee. Sometimes this is the agency's fault, but many times the person looking for a job does not express his or her interests clearly."

Some advice for people using employment agencies: make sure that the agency knows exactly what you are looking for in your career, such as job description, location, and salary. Also, listen carefully to job and company descriptions when deciding with whom you should interview. The job hunter should be able to sift out interviews that sound inappropriate and to accept those that match their demands. In this way, you can use the time you save to seek additional leads in your job search. ■

Career Consultants

If you open the employment section of the Sunday *Chronicle* or *Post* or the Southwest edition of the *Wall Street Journal,* you'll see several ads for career consultants (also known as career counselors or private outplacement consultants). The ads are generally directed to "executives" earning yearly salaries of anywhere between $20,000 and $300,000. Some ads suggest that the consultants have access to jobs that are not listed elsewhere. Others claim, "We do all the work." Most have branch offices throughout the country.

Career consultants vary greatly in the kind and quality of the services they provide. Some may offer a single service, such as vocational testing or preparing resumes. Others coach every aspect of the job search and stay with you until you accept an offer. The fees vary just as broadly and range from $100 to several thousand dollars. *You*, not your potential employer, pay the fee.

There are many reputable consulting firms in Houston. But as is true of employment agencies, some career consultants have been unethical.

A qualified career consultant can be a real asset to your job search. But *no consultant can get you a job*. Only you can do that. You are the one who will participate in the interview, and you are the one who must convince an employer to hire you. A consultant can help you focus on an objective, develop a resume, research the job market, decide on a strategy, and/or train you in interviewing techniques. But you can't send a consultant to interview in your place. It just doesn't work that way.

Don't retain a career consultant if you think that the fee will buy you a job. The only reason you should consider a consultant is that you've exhausted all the other resources we've suggested here and still feel you need expert and personalized help with one or more aspects of the job search. The key to choosing a career consultant is knowing what you need and verifying that the consultant can provide it.

Check references. A reputable firm will gladly provide them. Check the Better Business Bureau and other resources listed in this chapter. Has anyone lodged a complaint against the firm you're considering? Before you sign anything, ask to meet the consultant who will actually provide the services you want. What are his or her credentials? How long has the consultant been practicing? Who are the firm's corporate clients?

Read the contract carefully before you sign it. Does the contract put the consultant's promises in writing? Which of the consultant's services are not specified in the contract? What does the firm promise? What do *you* have to promise? Are all fees and costs spelled out? What provisions are made for refunds? For how long a time can you use the firm's or consultant's services?

Be sure to do some comparison shopping before you select a consultant. A list of Houston area firms you might want to contact for career counseling is in Chapter 2.

Executive Search Firms

An executive search firm is one that is paid by a company to locate a person with specific qualifications that meet a precisely defined employment need. Most reputable executive search firms belong to an organization called the Association of Executive Recruiting Consultants (AERC). The association publishes a code of ethics for its membership.

A search firm never works on a contingency basis. Only employment agencies do that. The usual fee for a search assignment is 30 percent of the first year's salary of the person to be hired, plus out-of-pocket expenses, which are billed on a monthly basis. During hard times, most companies forgo retaining search firms because it's so expensive.

It's difficult to get an appointment to see a search specialist. Executive search consultants have only their time to sell. If a specialist spends time with you, he or she can't bill that time to a client. If you can use your personal contacts to meet a search professional, however, by all means do so. Executive specialists know the market and can be very helpful in providing advice and leads.

Search firms receive dozens of unsolicited resumes every day. They seldom acknowledge receipt. They keep only a few for future search needs or business development. They really can't afford to file and store them all. Sending your resume to every search firm in the Houston area will be useful only if one firm coincidentally has a search assignment to find someone with *exactly* your background and qualifications. It's a long shot, similar to answering blind want ads.

How to Get a Job

If you're middle or upper management

"Almost any busy business professional can benefit from a management search firm," says Joe Mac Wiggins, Corporate Vice-President for New Business Development with MSI International, a multi-national personnel services company.

"Corporate human resource departments are faced with growing responsibilities in taking care of the people already employed by their companies. Many have little time left over to recruit and hire professionals," says Wiggins. "A management search firm can go straight to the company's top decision makers, the people who have the final say in who gets the job. It's a very time-efficient method."

The management search divisions of MSI International specialize in locating experienced middle and upper managers for Fortune 1,000 companies and other growing businesses.

"A management search firm is not for someone who is changing careers," Wiggins emphasizes. "Unlike employment agencies, where the emphasis is on 'what do you *want* to do?' we look for people with established skills in a given field.

"Males, females, and minorities are equally valuable to the industry. We look for growth-oriented people who are ready to move up, who have good people skills and good communications skills, as well as proven accomplishments and high-level references. If you've got all that going for you," Wiggins concludes, "then we'll be able to assist you in making a job change in a relatively short period of time." ■

EXECUTIVE SEARCH FIRMS

Anderson Bradshaw Associates
1225 North Loop West, Suite 820
Houston, TX 77008
Tel.: (713) 869-6789
Fax: (713) 869-6029
Full service.

Ronnie Boyd & Associates
P.O. Box 22469
Houston, TX 77227
Tel.: (713) 783-5550
Fax: (713) 783-4011
Engineering, oil and gas, local and abroad.

Joseph Chris and Associates
400 East North Belt, Suite 720
Houston, TX 77060

Using employment services

Tel.: (713) 931-8744
Fax: (713) 931-0792
Real estate industry and construction.

Dougan and McKinley
3200 Southwest Freeway, Suite 3300
Houston, TX 77027
Tel.: (713) 432-1800
Fax: (713) 960-0747
Executive and board of directors positions.

The Executive Consulting Group
701 North Post Oak, Suite 610
Houston, TX 77024
Tel.: (713) 686-9500
Fax: (713) 686-9599
Accounting, financial, and legal professionals.

Gulf States Personnel Consultants
650 East North Belt, Suite 224
Houston, TX 77060
Tel.: (713) 999-0051
Fax: (713) 999-1844
Professional and executive recruiting.

Korn Ferry International
1100 Milam Bldg., Suite 3400
Houston, TX 77002
Tel.: (713) 651-1834
Fax: (713) 651-0848
Retainer-based.

Litchfield & Willis
5858 Westheimer, Suite 403
Houston, TX 77057
Tel.: (713) 975-8500
Fax: (713) 975-7660
Banking, industrial, legal, contract basis and executive search.

Loewenstein & Associates
5847 San Felipe, Suite 1250
Houston, TX 77057
Tel.: (713) 952-1840
Fax: (713) 952-4534
Management, sales, local and national executive search.

Management Recruiters of Houston
1360 Post Oak Boulevard, Suite 2110
Houston, TX 77056
Tel.: (713) 850-9850
Fax: (713) 850-1429
Sales, technical, and upper-level administrative.

MetroCareers
P.O. Box 820367
Houston, TX 77282
Tel.: (713) 781-7215

How to Get a Job

Fax: (713) 975-1459
Full service.

Preng & Associates
2925 BriarPark, Suite 1111
Houston, TX 77042
Tel.: (713) 266-2600
Fax: (713) 266-3070
Executive search.

Paul R. Ray & Co.
4801 Woodway, Suite 300 East
Houston, TX 77056
Tel.: (713) 964-2603
Full service.

Richard Wayne and Roberts
24 Greenway Plaza, Suite 1304
Houston, TX 77046
Tel.: (713) 629-6681
Fax: (713) 623-2740
Management consulting.

Russell Reynolds Associates
1000 Louisiana, Suite 4800
Houston, TX 77002
Tel.: (713) 658-1776
Fax: (713) 658-9461
Full service.

Michaels W. Robt and Company
5065 Westheimer, Suite 830
Houston, TX 77056
Tel.: (713) 965-9175
Fax: (713) 965-0509
Full service.

Sales Consultants of Houston
5075 Westheimer, Suite 790
Houston, TX 77056-5606
Tel.: (713) 627-0880
Fax: (713) 622-7285
Sales and sales management.

Search Consultants International
4545 Post Oak Place, Suite 208
Houston, TX 77027
Tel.: (713) 622-9188
Fax: (713) 622-9186
Data processing, engineering, legal, oil and gas.

Texas Search Consultants
11767 Katy Freeway, Suite 430
Houston, TX 77079
Tel.: (713) 497-0600
Fax: (713) 497-6999
Petrochemical industry.

Using employment services

Unlimited Sources
1 Riverway, Suite 1626
Houston, TX 77056
Tel.: (713) 621-4629
Fax: (713) 961-0072
Full service.

John W. Worsham & Associates
2001 Kirby Dr., Suite 505
Houston, TX 77019-6033
Tel.: (713) 522-6505
Accounting, banking, and financial. (Requires prior banking position)

Social Service Agencies

Unlike professional employment agencies, career consultants, and executive search firms, social service agencies are not-for-profit. They offer a wide range of services, from counseling and vocational training to job placement and follow-up—and their services are usually free.

Association for the Advancement of Mexican Americans
204 Clifton
Houston, TX 77011
Tel.: (713) 926-9491
Fax: (713) 926-2672
Offers a service called Educational Talent Search, in which youth, ages 12-21, are helped in choosing schools or careers.

Center for Continuing Careers
2909 Hilcroft, Suite 400
Houston, TX 77057
Tel.: (713) 952-9021
Fax: (713) 952-8829
Trains men and women to market their skills and to improve their self-esteem while unemployed or underemployed. Offers professional testing, career marketing techniques, communications testing, and forty-plus job placement assistance and training.

Covenant House Texas
1111 Lovett
Houston, TX 77006
Tel.: (713) 523-2231
Fax: (713) 523-6904
Covenant House offers a full range of professional services to homeless and runaway youth. These services include vocational and job placement assistance. Contact Ronda Robinson or Tracy McCullough.

Goodwill Industries
5200 Jensen Dr.
P.O. Box 21185
Houston, TX 77026
Tel.: (713) 692-6221
Fax: (713) 692-0923
Offers vocational rehabilitation to disabled people. Services include: vocational counseling and program referral and skills training programs.

Houston Area Urban League
3215 Fannin

How to Get a Job

Houston, TX 77004
Tel.: (713) 526-5127
Fax: (713) 526-8851
Strives to secure equal opportunity for blacks and other minorities. Offers employment development workshops and employment interviews.

Houston Job Training Partnership Council
1919 Smith, Suite 500
Houston, TX 77002
Tel.: (713) 654-1919
Fax: (713) 655-0715
Provides employment training services to economically disadvantaged Houstonians. These services include: employability development training, basic education or GED instruction, vocational classroom training, and on-the-job training.

Lighthouse of Houston
P.O. Box 130435
Houston, TX 77019
Tel.: (713) 527-9561
Fax: (713) 527-8165
Rehabilitation center for the blind and visually handicapped, providing the following services: vocational evaluation, work adjustment and training, career planning, and counseling.

New Directions Club
P.O. Box 92102
Houston, TX 77018
Tel.: (713) 691-0314
Fax: (713) 699-7526
Provides services to ex-offenders on parole, probationers, dischargees, and pretrial diversion clients. Has 90 percent success rate for recidivism. Offers job placement assistance.

Senior Community Service Employment Program
170 Heights Boulevard
Houston, TX 77007
Tel.: (713) 868-3549
Offers temporary work experience for people aged 55 and older, with limited financial resources. The goal is to allow senior citizens to sharpen skills by training and working temporary assignments while looking for permanent employment.

Sheltering Arms
701 North Post Oak, Suite 500
Houston, TX 77024
Tel.: (713) 956-1888
Fax: (713) 956-2079
Provides employment at or near minimum wage for low-income individuals who are 55 or older. Individuals are placed at non-profit part-time jobs (payment is subsidized by Sheltering Arms), with the purpose of being trained for eventual full-time employment.

Shoulder
7655 Bellfort
P.O. Box 4300
Houston, TX 77061
Tel.: (713) 649-7200
Fax: (713) 649-0260

Using employment services

This is a residential facility for chemically addicted persons seeking recovery from their addiction. Offers job training assistance and placement. Contact Jimmetta Scott.

Help for vets

The work of the Vietnam Veterans of America in establishing memorials to Vietnam veterans is well known. But many people do not realize that the group has also established over 100 outreach centers nationwide. The main objective of these centers is to help men and women veterans of the Vietnam War readjust to civilian life.

The centers offer a variety of services. They solicit job listings from both the public and private sectors. Veterans who need additional help are referred to appropriate counseling groups, health agencies, and other organizations.

Vietnam Veterans of America
8100 Washington, Suite 120
Houston, TX 77007
Tel.: (713) 880-8387
Fax: (713) 653-3110 ■

Government and County Agencies

Many employment listings are available through city, state, and federal government offices.

Houston Job Training Program Council
1919 Smith, Suite 500
Houston, TX 77002
Tel.: (713) 654-1919
Fax: (713) 655-0715
A federally funded program which provides job training through a number of agencies; available to qualifying low-income families. A brochure is available listing types of programs, which agencies do what training, and who can qualify (youth or adults).

Texas Employment Commission
P.O. Box 1390
Houston, TX 77251
Tel.: (713) 956-4170
Part of a nationwide system offering free job placement services, an unemployment insurance program, and a variety of programs for special applicants. Complete office listings are in Chapter 8.

How To Succeed In an Interview

If you've read straight through this book, you already know that networking (see Chapter 5) is one of the most important and useful job-hunting techniques around. Networking is nothing more or less than using personal contacts to research the job market and to generate both exploratory and formal job interviews.

Networking and interviewing go hand-in-hand; all the contacts in the world won't do you any good if you don't handle yourself well in an interview. No two interviews are ever identical, except that you always have the same goal in mind: to convince the person to whom you're talking that he or she should help you find a job or hire you personally. An interview is also an exchange of information. But you should never treat it as you would a casual conversation, even if the "interviewer" is an old friend.

Preparing for the Interview—The 5-Minute Resume

Whether you're talking to the housewife next door about her brother-in-law who knows someone you want to meet or going through a final, formal

How to succeed in an interview

interview with a multinational corporation, you are essentially making a sales presentation—in this case, selling yourself. Your goal is to convince the interviewer that you have the ability, experience, personality, maturity, and other characteristics required to do a good job and to enlist the interviewer's help in getting you that job.

In an informal interview you'll be talking first to friends and acquaintances. Most of the people you'll be talking to will *want* to help you. But they need to know who you are, what you've done, what you want to do, and, most important, how they can help you.

To prepare for any interview, first perfect what we like to call the five-minute resume. Start by giving a rough description, not too detailed, of what you're doing now (or did on your last job) so that when you're telling your story, the listener won't be distracted by wondering how it's going to end.

Then go all the way back to the beginning—not of your career, but of your life. Talk about where you were born, where you grew up, what your folks did, whether or not they're still living, what your brothers and sisters do, and so on. Then trace your educational background briefly, and finally, outline your work history from your first job to your latest.

"What!" say many of our clients. "Drag my PARENTS into this? Talk about my crazy BROTHER and the neighborhood where we grew up?"

Yes, indeed. You want to draw the listener into your story, to make him or her interested enough in you to work for you in your search. You want the interviewer to know not only who you are and what you have achieved, but also what you are capable of. You also want to establish things in common with the listener. The more you have in common, the harder your listener will work for you.

Co-author Tom Camden, we are not ashamed to admit, is a master of the five-minute resume. Here's how he would begin a presentation to someone like the neighbor down the street:

"Would it be all right with you if I gave you a broad-brush review of my background? Let you know what I've done, what I'd like to do? That'll give us some time to talk about how I should go about this job search. Maybe I could pick your brain a little about how you can help me. OK?

"Currently, I'm president of Camden and Associates, a consulting firm specializing in corporate outplacement.

"Originally, I'm from Chicago. I'm 57 years old, married, with five kids.

"My father is a security guard at IIT Research Institute; my mother is retired. She used to work for Walgreens—made aspirins, vitamins, and pills. I'm the oldest of four children. My brother John does the traffic 'copter reports for a Chicago radio station. Another brother is also a cop with the Chicago police force. My sister Connie is a consultant for an industrial relations firm.

"I went to parochial schools. When I was fourteen, I left home and went into a monastery. I stayed there until I was nineteen. Then I went to Loyola University, studied psychology, got my degree in '59. I was also commissioned in the infantry.

"I started my graduate work in Gestalt psychology. In 1960 Kennedy called up troops for the Berlin crisis. That included me, so I spent a year on active duty. Following that I came back and continued my graduate work in industrial relations...."

How to Get a Job

Tom took exactly a minute and a half to make this part of his presentation, and he's already given his neighbor several areas in which they may have something in common. He's volunteered enough information, not only to get the neighbor interested in his story, but to let the neighbor form judgments about him.

People don't like to play God, says Tom. Yet it's a fact of life that we constantly form judgments about each other. In an interview—even an exploratory, informal one—you may as well provide enough information to be judged on who you *are*, and not on what someone has to guess about your background. What does it mean to be the oldest of four kids? What can you deduce from Tom's middle-class background?

The typical applicant begins a presentation with something like, "I graduated from school in June, nineteen-whenever, and went to work for so-and-so." Our experience has convinced us that the way to get a job offer is to be *different* from the rest of the applicants. Focus on what makes you unique within the candidate pool. What is different about you? Focus on strengths.

Neither should you spend too much time on your personal history. A minute or two is just about right. That gives you from three to eight minutes to narrate your work history. Most exploratory interviews, and many initial employment interviews, are limited to half an hour. If you can give an oral resume in five to ten minutes, you have roughly twenty minutes left to find out what you want to know (more on that shortly).

How to stand out in a crowd

A senior employment relations representative for one of the nation's largest employers, headquartered in Houston, offers the following tip for standing out in a crowd of interviewees.

"Almost everybody will show up well dressed, with a neatly-typed resume and as professional a manner as he or she can muster. You have to show an employer that you're someone special. Try bringing a backup book with you to every interview, one that contains examples of your work. If you're a secretary, bring some samples of your snazziest typing. If you're a research chemist, perhaps you've published something that you can show or maybe articles have appeared about your work or you can bring along a product that utilizes your research. It all depends on what you do for a living, of course, but use your imagination."

A word about your work history. If you've done the exercises in Chapter 2, or written your own resume, you ought to be able to rattle off every job you've had, from the first to the latest, pretty easily. In the oral resume you especially want to *emphasize your successes and accomplishments* in each job. This will take some practice. We are not accustomed to talking about ourselves positively. From childhood we're conditioned that it's not nice to brag. Well, we are here to tell you that if you *don't* do it in the interview, you *won't* get the offer.

If you're a recent college graduate and don't yet have an impressive employment history, you can emphasize your successes and accomplishments in class and extracurricular activities. Also, you want particularly to emphasize achievements in areas pertinent to the field you hope to enter. You want to highlight those skills that qualify you to fill the position you're seeking. Analyze yourself in terms of your functional skills, such as administrative, writing, analytical. Then talk about those functional skills that match the duties of the job you're going for.

We repeat: *The interview is a sales presentation.* It's the heart of your job search, your effort to market yourself. In an exploratory interview, the listener will be asking, "Should I help this person?" In a formal interview, the employer will be asking, "Should I hire this person?" In either case, the answer will be "yes" only if you make a successful presentation, if you convince the interviewer that you're worth the effort.

So, the first step in preparing for any interview, formal or informal, is to *practice your five-minute resume*. Go through it out loud enough times so that you're comfortable delivering it. Then work with a tape recorder and critique yourself. Try it out on a couple of friends.

When you're preparing for a formal employment interview, *do your homework* on the company. This advice is merely common sense. But it's surprising how many candidates will ask an interviewer, "What does this company do?" Don't be one of them. Before you go in for an employment interview, find out everything you can about the company—its history, organization, products and services, and growth expectations. Get hold of the company's annual report, catalogs, and brochures. Consult your networking contacts, and use the resources suggested in Chapter 4.

Steps to a Successful Interview

Before the Interview
- Self-assessment: identify strengths, goals, skills, etc.
- Research the company.
- Rehearse what you plan to say. Practice answers to common questions.
- Prepare questions to ask employer.

During the Interview
- Make sure you arrive a few minutes early.
- Greet the interviewer by his/her last name; offer a firm handshake and a warm smile.
- Be aware of non-verbal communication. Wait to sit until you are offered a chair. Sit up straight, look alert, speak clearly and forcefully but stay relaxed, make good eye contact, avoid nervous mannerisms, and try to be a good listener as well as a good talker. Smile.
- Follow the interviewer's lead, but try to get the interviewer to describe the position and duties to you fairly early in the interview so that you can then relate your background and skills in context.
- Be specific, concrete, and detailed in your answers. The more information you volunteer, the better the employer gets to know you.
- Offer examples of your work that document your best qualities.
- Answer questions as truthfully and as frankly as you can. Do not appear to be "glossing over" anything. On the other hand, stick to the point and do not over-answer questions. The interviewer may steer

How to Get a Job

the interview into ticklish political or social questions. Answer honestly, trying not to say more than is necessary.

Closing the Interview

- Don't be discouraged if no definite offer is made or specific salary is discussed.
- If you get the impression that the interview is not going well and that you have already been rejected, do not let your discouragement show. Once in a while, an interviewer who is genuinely interested in you may seem to discourage you to test your reaction.
- A typical interviewer comment toward the close of an interview is to ask if you have any questions. Prepare several questions ahead of time, and ask those that weren't covered during the interview.
- At the conclusion of your interview, ask when a hiring decision will be made. Also, thank your interviewer for his or her time and express your interest in the position.

After the Interview

- Take notes on what you feel you could improve upon for your next interview.
- If you are interested in the position, type a brief thank-you letter to the interviewer, indicating your interest.
- If offered the position, one to two weeks is a reasonable amount of time to make a decision. All employment offers deserve a written reply whether or not you accept them.

How to dress

A young friend of ours who wanted to break into investment banking finally landed her first big interview with Charles Schwab & Co. It was fairly easy for her to do her homework on a company of that size. Two days before the interview, however, it suddenly dawned on her that she had no idea how to dress. How did she solve her problem?

"It was pretty easy, actually, and fun, too," says Susan. "All I did was go and hang around outside the office for 15 minutes at lunchtime to see what everybody else was wearing."

However, we recommend that even if the office attire is casual, one should still dress professionally. One career counselor recommends that one should " always dress one step above the attire of those in the office where you are interviewing." ■

What Interviewers Are Looking For

•**General Personality:** Ambition, poise, sincerity, trustworthiness, articulateness, analytical ability, initiative, interest in the firm. (General intelligence is assumed.) Different firms look for different kinds of people—personalities, style, appearance, abilities, and technical skills. Always check

How to succeed in an interview

the job specifications. Don't waste time talking about a job you can't do or for which you don't have the minimum qualifications.

- **Personal Appearance:** A neat, attractive appearance makes a good impression and demonstrates professionalism.
- **Work Experience:** Again, this varies from job to job, so check job specifications. If you've had work experience, be able to articulate the importance of what you did in terms of the job for which you are interviewing and in terms of your own growth or learning. Even if the work experience is unrelated to your field, employers look upon knowledge of the work environment as an asset.
- **Verbal Communication Skills:** The ability to express yourself articulately is very important to most interviewers. This includes the ability to listen effectively, verbalize thoughts clearly, and express yourself confidently.
- **Skills:** The interviewer will evaluate your skills for the job, such as organization, analysis, and research. It is important to emphasize the skills which you feel the employer is seeking and to give specific examples of how you developed them. This is the main reason why it is important to engage in self-assessment prior to the interview.
- **Goals/Motivation:** Employers will assess your ability to articulate your short-term and long-term goals. You should seem ambitious, yet realistic about the training and qualifications needed to advance. You should demonstrate interest in the functional area or industry and a desire to succeed and work hard.
- **Knowledge of the Interviewer's Company and Industry:** At a minimum, you really are expected to have done some homework on the company. Don't waste interview time asking questions you could have found answers for in printed material. Know the firm's position and character relative to others in the same industry. General awareness of media coverage of a firm and its industry is usually expected.

Office decor reveals personality

"You can tell a lot about a company by carefully scrutinizing the office environment during a job interview," says Evan Sullivan. He made a careful study of the decor, layout, and orderliness of several offices the last time he went job hunting.

"Each office has a distinct personality," he says. During his survey he found that a boss's office with soft, comfortable furniture often indicated that the supervisor was easy-going— the type who didn't mind if people lingered to chat. Firmer, more utilitarian chairs could be a tip-off that the person in charge was a no-nonsense type.

Evan used the office decor to determine how he would handle himself in an interview. In an office lined with sports trophies, he inevitably mentioned his football experience. When he noticed during one interview that a manager had a cluttered desk and briefcase, he stressed his organizational skills.

How to Get a Job

> "Use your powers of observation and gut feelings to your advantage in an interview," Sullivan says. We agree wholeheartedly. ■

Handling the Interview

In an exploratory, or informal, interview most of the people you'll talk with will want to help you. But they need to know how. After you've outlined your personal strengths and work history, ask your contact how he or she thinks your experience fits into today's market. What companies should you visit? Specifically, what people should you talk with?

When someone gives you advice or a recommendation to call someone else, do it! Few things are more irritating than to provide free counsel to someone who then ignores it. If your contact suggests that you call Helen Smith, call her!

In a formal employment interview, there are several typical questions you can expect to encounter, though not necessarily in this order:

Tell me about yourself. (This is your cue for the five-minute resume.)

Why do you want to change jobs?

What kind of job are you looking for now?

What are your long-range objectives?

What are your salary requirements?

When could you be available to start here?

Tell me about your present company.

What kind of manager are you?

How would you describe yourself?

What are your strengths and weaknesses?

(In the course of his career, Tom Camden has posed this question to untold numbers of applicants. "They'll list two or three strengths," he says, "and then can't wait to tell me about their weaknesses." Don't be one of those people! Accentuate the positive. Remember, this is a competitive interview.)

Describe your present boss.

To whom can I talk about your performance?

Are you open to relocation?

How long have you been looking for a new job?

Why are you interested in this company? (This is your golden opportunity to show the interviewer that you've done your homework on the company.)

Practice your answers to these questions *before* you go in for the interview. It's probably best not to memorize a verbatim answer, but you should have a clear idea of how you'll respond to all the standard questions. Anticipate other questions you might be asked, and develop answers for them. In general, keep your responses positive. Never volunteer a negative about yourself, another company, or a former employer. Even if you hate your present boss, describe your areas of disagreement in a calm, professional manner. You are selling *yourself,* not downgrading others. It makes

How to succeed in an interview

you appear whiny and petty if you simply complain about the tyrant you work for.

Show interest in the company. Be enthusiastic about the prospect of working for them. You can probably remember how demoralizing it was to be interviewed by someone who seemed disinterested, even bored by your presence. Well, interviewers have feelings too. Even if you're not particularly interested in the company, always conduct the interview as if you were dead set on getting the job.

The interviewer will apply your responses to the questions he or she *really* wants answered.

Does the applicant have the ability to do the job?

Can he or she manage people?

How does he or she relate to people?

What kind of person is this? A leader? A follower?

What strengths does he or she have that we need?

Why the number of job changes so far?

Where is he or she weak?

How did the applicant contribute to present and past companies?

What are his or her ambitions? Are they realistic?

Is he or she too soft or too tough on subordinates?

What is this person's standard of values?

Does he or she have growth potential?

Is there a health problem anywhere?

What is the nature of the "chemistry" between us?

What will the department manager think of this applicant as opposed to the others?

Should this person get an offer?

Getting to know you personally

"Your resume gives a prospective employer the bare-bones facts about your skills and accomplishments. But the interview, eye-to-eye with a company representative, determines whether your personal and professional assets form a nice 'fit' with the company." So says the employment manager of a major telecommunications company.

"In the interview we can measure skill and capability, and we also find out about personality. Skills can be taught, but you're hard pressed to change your personality.

"We always place the most competitive person for the job, and the ability to fit in and get along well with others is as important as knowledge of the job."

This employment manager has a few tips for making the most of your interview. "Prepare yourself psychologically for the interview," he

How to Get a Job

says. "Be there on your best day, if it fits the company's schedule. It's critical to look the part, in your manner and dress. Don't hesitate to ask questions. Be persistent, and don't lie. An experienced interviewer will have you figured out in 15 minutes."

The timing of your application can minimize your having to deal with the stress of rejection, or what the employment manager calls "job-seeking psychosis."

"Many companies hire in high numbers at certain times of the year," he says. "December is the worst month; February and March are better in our industry; then it begins to slow again in October. Find out what the hiring season is for the company you have in mind. This will increase your chances for success." ■

The interview should not be a one-sided affair, however. Questions that you should ask the interviewer are equally important in this exchange of information. For example, you have to know about the job, the company, and the people in your future employment situation. It's necessary to use your judgment to determine how and when to ask questions in an interview. But, without the answers, it will be next to impossible for you to make a sound decision if you receive an offer. Some of the questions you want answered are:

What are the job's responsibilities?

What is the company's recent history? Its current objectives? Its market position? Where are its plants located? What distribution systems does it use?

To whom will I report? What's his or her background?

Why is the job available?

What happened to the previous person who filled the position?

What are the toughest problems I'll have to solve in order to be successful on this particular job?

How much autonomy will I have to get the job done?

How much supervision will I receive to get the job done?

What opportunities are there for training and professional development?

Where does the job lead?

What about travel requirements?

Where is the job located?

Are there any housing, school, or community problems that will develop as a result of this job?

What is the salary range? (Do not raise the question of explicit salary at this point.)

What is the detailed benefit picture?

How to succeed in an interview

What is the company's relocation policy?
When will an offer decision be made?
What references will be required?
When would I have to start?
What is the personality of the company?
Do the job and company fit my plan for what I want to do now?
What's the next step?

During the interview, you should focus first on selling yourself. Next, try to find out as much as you can about the job and the company. The question of explicit salary is one you should never raise. Let this be the interviewing organization's responsibility.

We asked a very successful corporate executive how he would handle an interview in which he was asked to name his main weakness.

"You have to turn tough questions like that one around to your advantage," he replied. "I think I'd tell the employer that my biggest problem is that I'm a workaholic." ■

Sow's ear to silk purse

Some companies administer standardized tests to see if applicants are qualified for certain kinds of work, such as secretarial, data processing, and the like. Many of the libraries listed in Chapter 4 have an impressive number of workbooks to help you prepare for the most common tests. These include study guides for elevator operators, computer programmers, women in the armed forces, law and court stenographers, laboratory aides, supervisory engineers, even mortuary caretakers! Reviews for state board exams for nurses and certified public accountants are also available. ■

Career guides

Following the Interview

Many job seekers experience a kind of euphoria after a good interview. Under the impression that a job offer is imminent, a candidate may discontinue the search. This is a serious mistake. The decision may take weeks, or may not be made at all. On the average, about six weeks elapse between the time a person makes initial contact with a company and receives a final answer. If you let up on the search, you will prolong it. Maintain a constant sense of urgency. Get on with the next interview. Your search isn't over until an offer is accepted and you actually begin the new job. Besides, the next company you interview with might have an even better job.

Always follow up an interview with correspondence. The purpose of the letter is to supplement the sales presentation you made. Thank the interviewer for his or her time and hospitality. Express interest in the position. Then mention up to three additional points to sell yourself further. Or reiterate your primary selling point. Highlight how your specific experience or knowledge is directly applicable to the company's immediate needs. If you forgot to mention something important in the interview, say it now. If possible, try to comment on something the interviewer said. Use that comment to show how your interests and skills perfectly match what they're looking for. Try to establish a date by which a decision will be made.

If you think you could benefit from professional counseling in interviewing skills, consider the resources suggested in Chapter 2 and in Chapter 6. You might also find it helpful to refer to some of the following books:

BOOKS ON INTERVIEWING

Allen, Jeffrey. *How to Turn an Interview Into a Job*. New York: Simon & Schuster, 1988.
Biegelein, J.I. *Make Your Job Interview a Success*. New York: Arco, 1987.
Danna, Jo. *Winning the Job Interview Game: Tips for the High-Tech Era*. Briarwood, NY: Palamino Press, 1986.
Fear, Richard A. *The Evaluation Interview*. 4th ed. New York: McGraw-Hill, 1990.
Goodale, James G. *The Fine Art of Interviewing*. Englewood Cliffs, NJ: Prentice-Hall, 1982.
Grice, Charles R. *Fifteen Tips on Handling Job Interviews*. Orange, CA: Career Publishers, 1981.
Krannich, Caryl R. *Interview for Success*. San Luis Obispo, CA: Impact, 1982.
Marcus, John J. *The Complete Job Interview Handbook*, 2nd ed. New York: Harper & Row, 1988.
Medley, H. Anthony. *Sweaty Palms: The Neglected Art of Being Interviewed*. Berkeley, CA: Ten Speed Press, 1984.
Pell, Arthur R. *How to Sell Yourself in an Interview*. New York: Monarch Press, 1982.
Pettus, Theodore. *One On One—Win the Interview, Win the Job*. New York: Random House, 1981.
Smart, Bradford D. *The Smart Interviewer*. New York: John Wiley & Sons, 1989.
Stewart, Charles J., and William B. Cash. *Interviewing Principles and Practices*. 6th ed. Dubuque, IA: William C. Brown Publishers, 1990.
Yate, Martin John. *Knock 'em Dead with Great Answers to Tough Interview Questions*. Boston: Bob Adams, 1990.

How to succeed in an interview

How to get the most from your references

Don't give a prospective employer a list of your references until they ask for one. Always brief your references before you supply an interviewer with their names and numbers. Tell the references what company you're interviewing with and what the job is. Give them some background on the company and the responsibilities you'll be asked to handle. Provide them with a copy of your resume to refresh their memory on what an outstanding candidate you are. Your references will then be in a position to help *sell* your abilities. Finally, don't abuse your references. If you give their names too often, they may lose enthusiasm for your cause. ■

What To Do If Money Gets Tight

Any job search takes time. One particularly pessimistic career counselor we know suggests you plan to spend about two weeks of search time for every thousand dollars you want to earn per year. (Pity the poor soul who wants to make $60,000!) A more optimistic estimate for a job search is around three to six months, provided the search is conducted full time. Of course, the field you want to enter, your qualifications, and your income requirements all have a big influence on how long things will take.

If you already have a full-time job, it will take you longer to find a new one. But at least you will be receiving a paycheck while you're looking. This chapter is intended for those who are unemployed and facing the prospect of little or no income during the search.

When the financial squeeze is on, the first thing to do is make a thorough review of your liquid assets and short-term liabilities. Ask yourself how much cash you can expect to receive during the next three months from the following sources, plus any others you might come up with:

When money gets tight

Savings
Securities
Silver and gold
Insurance loan possibilities
Second mortgage possibilities
Unemployment compensation
Severance pay
Accrued vacation pay
Personal loan sources (relatives, friends)
Sale of personal property (car, boat, stamp collections, etc.)

Then you should consider exactly what bills absolutely *must* be paid. Don't worry about your total outstanding debt. Many creditors can be stalled or might be willing to make arrangements to forgo principal as long as interest payments are made. Talk to each of your creditors to see if something can be worked out.

The final step is easy—if sometimes painful. You compare the amount of money you have on hand or expect to receive with the amount you know you'll have to spend. The difference tells you exactly what kind of financial shape you're in.

The old adage has it that it's better to be unemployed than underemployed. If you can afford it, it's wise not to take a part-time or temporary job. The more time you spend looking for a good full-time position, the sooner you're likely to succeed. But if the cupboard looks pretty bare, it may be necessary to supplement your income any way legally possible in order to eat during the search.

Try to find part-time or temporary work that leaves you as free as possible to interview during the day. For this reason, many people choose to drive a cab at night or work in a bar or restaurant during the evenings. That kind of job gives you the advantage of flexible hours, but the pay is not always desirable. Commissioned sales positions abound in almost every industry. But if your personality isn't suited to sales work, don't pursue it. You'll find it very frustrating.

Good advice from a bartender

One of our friends, a successful freelance illustrator, spent several years tending bar part-time in various popular Galleria area saloons to support his drawing habit.

"The best places to look for part-time work," he says, "are those where you're already known. Bar owners will rarely hire a bartender who walks in off the street or fresh out of Famous Bartending School's two-week course. That's because it's very easy for bartenders to steal. An owner wants to know someone, to have a sense of a person's character, before he hires a bartender. So if you're looking for part-time work—and this goes for waiters and waitresses, too—spend some time in the place for a couple of weeks. Get to know the people

How to Get a Job

who work there and the regular customers, and become one of the regulars yourself. Learn how the place operates. Every bar or restaurant has its own way of doing things, from handling special orders to taking care of rowdy customers. The more you know about a place, the easier it is to step in when somebody calls in sick or quits."

It's best if you can locate part-time work in your chosen field. The pay is usually more attractive, and you can continue to develop your network of contacts. Many professionals can freelance. An administrative assistant, for example, might be able to find part-time work at a law firm. An accountant might be able to do taxes on a part-time basis and still gain access to new referrals.

Another option for those of you with an entrepreneurial flair is to lease yourself on a contractual basis to employers when you interview with them. Say you're a computer programmer. A company might not have enough computer work to justify hiring someone to fill a full-time position. So you suggest they hire you on a temporary basis until the project is complete. Or offer to come in one day a week because that's all the time it will take. Or suggest that you work on an as needed basis. The advantage to a company is that they don't have to pay you any benefits (except those you're able to negotiate for). The advantage to you is income in your chosen field.

People with technical skills can work themselves into becoming full-time freelancers in just this way. They might even talk an employer OUT of hiring them full time and negotiate contract work in order to maintain the freedom of their self-employed status.

Here are some additional sources to consider when the money is really tight and you need part-time or temporary work.

SELECTED SOURCES FOR PART-TIME AND TEMPORARY WORK

Exclusive Temporaries
806 Main Street, Suite 1001
Houston, TX 77002
Tel.: (713) 228-5700
Fax: (713) 227-2330
Full service.

Health-Care Temporaries
8926 Shervourne, Suite D
Houston, TX 77016
Tel.: (713) 631-7106
Fax: (713) 631-9158
RN, LVN, home health care aid.

Industrial Labor Service
1714 Collingsworth
Houston, TX 77009
Tel.: (713) 224-0202
Fax: (713) 224-6614
Skilled labor, industrial.

When money gets tight

Input Personnel
11777 Katy Freeway, Suite 154
Houston, TX 77079
Tel.: (713) 497-0109
Fax: (713) 497-0166
Word processing only.

Interim Personnel
5177 Richmond Ave., Suite 245
Houston, TX 77056
Tel.: (713) 629-1080
Fax: (713) 629-0010
Full service.

or

Interim Personnel
9525 Katy Freeway, Suite 102
Houston, TX 77024
Tel.: (713) 932-6633
Fax: (713) 932-1199
Clerical, some technical, and some professional

Kelly Services
1100 Milam, Suite 2595
Houston, TX 77002
Tel.: (713) 654-9432
Fax: (713) 752-0319

Olsten Temporary Services
Division of the Olsten Corporation
1000 Louisiana, Suite 1180
Houston, TX 77002
Tel.: (713) 658-1150
Fax: (713) 758-0910
Full service.

Snelling Temporaries
5444 Westheimer, Suite 1430
Houston, TX 77056
Tel.: (713) 621-0066
Fax: (713) 621-8039
Full service.

Staff Solutions
10303 N.W. Freeway, Suite 429
Houston, TX 77092
Tel.: (713) 957-8791
Secretarial, clerical, word processing, accounting.

Western Temporary Service
7324 Southwest Freeway, Suite 220
Houston, TX 77074
Tel.: (713) 771-2831
Full service.

How to Get a Job

Want the inside track? Work as a temporary

Want to get on the inside track in a particular segment of the job market? Want to polish your skills, make contacts, and prove your on-the-job capabilities to the people who do the hiring? Want to make money at the same time?

If so, try temporary employment. That's the advice of the president of a large temporary employment agency.

"If you're not sure exactly what you want to do, working as a temporary is a great way to get exposure to various types of companies," he says. "It can also open the door to a first job.

"Temporary employment gives you the opportunity to be evaluated in an actual work environment where you can put your best foot forward on a daily basis, rather than having to depend on a single 30-minute interview.

"If you come to Houston looking for a job and don't know the city, it's a great way to get into the larger firms," he adds.

Temporary employment companies sometimes provide most of the same benefits you'll find at a regular job, including paid vacations and retirement plans. Some also make group health insurance available.

Another advantage of temporary employment is the free in-house training many such companies offer.

"This is particularly good for someone reentering the job market," he notes. "If you left 15 years ago, you were probably typing on an IBM Selectric. If you come back today to PC-based word-processing and spread-sheet analysis, you've got quite a bit of catching up to do." ■

SELECTED BOOKS ON PART-TIME AND FLEXIBLE EMPLOYMENT

Arden, Lynie. *The Work-at-Home Sourcebook.* Boulder, CO: Live Oak Publications, 1987.
Canape, Charlene. *The Part-Time Solution: The New Strategy for Managing Motherhood.* New York: Harper Collins, 1990.
Hawes, Gene R. *College Board Guide to Going to College While Working: Strategies for Success.* New York: College Entrance Examination Board (distributed by College Board Publications), 1985.
Magid, Renee Y. *When Mothers and Fathers Work: Creative Strategies for Balancing Career and Family.* New York: AMACOM, 1987.
Marsh, DeLoss L. *Retirement Careers: Combining the Best of Work & Leisure.* Williamson, Susan, and Roger Griffith, eds. Charlotte, VT: Williamson Publishing Co., 1991.
O'Hara, Bruce. *Put Work in Its Place.* Victoria, BC, Canada: Work Well, 1988.

When money gets tight

Paradis, Adrain A. *Opportunities in Part-Time and Summer Jobs.* Lincolnwood, IL: VGM Career Horizons, 1987.

Rothberg and Cook. *Part-Time Professional.* Washington, DC: Acropolis Books, 1985.

Federal, State, and Local Government Assistance Programs

If you've exhausted all your resources and can't find part-time or temporary work, you might consider government or private assistance. Many people bristle at the mere mention of "charity" or "welfare." But the help you receive may be needed—and temporary. It's a way of bridging the gap until you land a job. More people take advantage of these sources of assistance than you might imagine. In the case of state and federal aid, your tax dollars have helped to provide the benefits. Your taxes have also paid for the salaries of the people distributing the benefits.

Don't pass judgment on the merits of the following sources until you talk with the professionals who administer their respective programs. Pros can advise you on eligibility and benefits and can also provide you with other ideas and resources.

The responsibilities of the various county departments of family and children's services are identical and are set by the State of Texas. The various county health departments perform similar functions as well, although larger counties with bigger budgets will generally have more elaborate programs.

The county departments of family and children's services administer Medicaid, Food Stamps and Aid to Families with Dependent Children (Welfare) programs. Some counties have funds for limited emergency assistance which can be accessed through Family and Children's services.

The county health departments operate programs for child health, pre-natal and post-partum care, and family planning, as well as immunization, dental health, chronic disease, and environmental health programs. Referals to other clinics are available for aid concerning sexually transmitted diseases (STD)

The following organizations represent some major sources of aid available in the Houston area:

GOVERNMENT AID SOURCES

Harris County Department of Human Resources
9418 Jensen
Houston, TX 77093
Tel.: (713) 696-7900
Fax: (713) 696-7941
Provides financial assistance and services related to financial problems of individuals who have no resources or very limited resources. Grants usually provide food, shelter, and utilities.

Harris County Health Department
2501 Dunstan
Houston, TX 77005
Tel.: (713) 526-1841
Fax: (713) 620-6897
Programs and services listed above.

How to Get a Job

State of Texas Department of Human Services
1349 East 40th Street
Houston, TX 77022
Tel.: (713) 692-3236
Fax: (713) 696-7193
The purpose of this department is to serve and assist the people of Texas by providing income assistance, medical assistance, and social services to persons meeting eligibility.

GETTING UNEMPLOYMENT BENEFITS

You can file for unemployment benefits at any Texas Employment Commission office. To be eligible for benefits, the company you previously worked for must have paid unemployment insurance to the State of Texas, you must register for employment with the TEC, and you must make a realistic job search.

The weekly benefit amount is 1/25th of the highest quarterly wages earned during the claimant's base period, with a maximum of $210 per week. You will need proof of identification, your social security card, and a list of all the companies you have worked for in the last 52 weeks.

If your application is approved, you should receive your first unemployment check in about three weeks. Here are the addresses and phone numbers of a few of the Texas Employment Commision offices in Houston:

Central Downtown Area
Houston Downtown Office
2613 Austin Street
Houston, TX 77004
Tel.: (713) 655-1414

East Houston
Channelview Office
913 Ashland Blvd.
Houston, TX 77530
Tel.: (713) 452-5540

North Houston
West Parker Office
455 W. Parker Road
Houston, TX 77091
Tel.: (713) 699-1788

Northeast Houston
Homestead-Tidwell
P.O. Box 111187
Houston, TX 77293
Tel.: (713) 699-0777

Northwest Houston
Northwest Office
P.O. Box 801801
Houston, TX 77280
Tel.: (713) 890-6982

Pasadena Area
Pasadena Office
3201 Spencer Hwy.
Houston, TX 77504
Tel.: (713) 944-8310

Southeast Houston
South Loop Office
8990 Lakes at 610
Houston, TX 77054
Tel.: (713) 661-3220

Southwest Houston
Southwest Office
12455 Beechnut
Houston, TX 77072
Tel.: (713) 530-4300

Southwest Houston
Rosenberg Office
3926 Ave. H, Suite 6
Houston, TX 77471
Tel.: (713) 342-0696

Spring Branch Area
Spring Branch Office
10125 Emnora
Houston, TX 77280
Tel.: (713) 465-1677

When money gets tight

SELECTED ADDITIONAL SOURCES OF EMERGENCY HELP

American Red Cross
2700 Southwest Freeway
Houston, TX 77098
Tel.: (713) 526-8300
Fax: (713) 526-5871
John McDivitt, General Manager
Offers emergency shelter care and health and safety services.

Interfaith Caring Ministries
P.O. Box 41
League City, TX 77573
Tel.: (713) 332-3881
Maggie Corcoran, Director
Helps people who need food or clothing, money for utility bills, gas to find work, a job, funds for doctor's bills and prescription needs, and legal assistance.

Memorial Assistance Ministries
9501 K Long Point
Houston, TX 77005
Tel.: (713) 468-4516
Guy Wallace, President of the Board
Offers emergency services, including financial assistance, food, and clothing on a limited basis. Has a resale shop that sells low cost, high-quality used clothing and household goods. Profits finance the emergency services.

Salvation Army
1717 Congress Street
Houston, TX 77002
Tel.: (713) 222-8253
Fax: (713) 222-9127
Major Rolan Chambress, Area Commander
Provides an emergency shelter with lodging, food, and other assistance for homeless people. Also has a social services department, where families and individuals can get emergency financial assistance and food supplies.

Traveler's Aid Society of Houston
2630 Westridge
Houston, TX 77054
Tel.: (713) 668-0911
Joan Chellberg, Director
Ofers counseling and assistance for newcomers to the Houston area.

Veterans Administration
2515 Murworth
Houston, TX 77054
Tel.: (713) 664-4664
Ted Myatt, Director
Manages programs for veterans' disability, pension, widow's pension; also provides housing and medical assistance through the Veterans Hospital.

Volunteers of America, Houston
4800 W. 34th, Suite C-54
Houston, TX 77092
Tel.: (713) 956-6310

How to Get a Job

Eliska Cowan, Executive Director
Offers free meals for seniors, low-income housing, and free clothing for children.

Wesley Community Center
1410 Lee Street
Houston, TX 77009
Tel.: (713) 223-8131
Ruth Palmer, Executive Director
Offers emergency food and clothing, counseling, day care, services for single-parent families, and information and referral. Must be low to moderate-income family.

Westheimer Ecumenical Social Ministry
2811 Rodgerdale
Houston, TX 77042
Tel.: (713) 977-9942
Margaret Dudar, Director
This agency provides emergency financial assistance and has a resale shop where clothing and household goods can be purchased for a small fee.

United Way of the Texas Gulf Coast
Tel.: (713) 527-0222
Dr. Judith Craven, President
United Way provides assistance for needs such as food, clothing, and housing, as well as referals to other agencies for help in a vast number of areas, including medical needs and drug abuse.

Telemarketing nets part-time $$$

People who need to earn money while job hunting might consider the telemarketing, or telephone sales, industry. Debbie Schwartz, who has worked as a telemarketing manager, feels that the field offers a variety of challenges and rewards.

"Being a telemarketer is almost like being an actor in a radio play," says Debbie. "Your success depends on how well you control your voice. You also have to be able to receive feedback from people without the benefit of eye contact or body language."

We asked Debbie what telemarketing managers look for in the people they hire. "The crucial element is the person's voice. Telemarketers must speak clearly and have pleasing voices. They also must use standard English grammar. Previous sales experience is a plus, although it's not necessary. Managers also look for people who can handle rejection. A person might get rejected 25 or 30 times before making a sale."

According to Debbie, most telemarketers work in four-hour shifts. "You can't work on the phone for more than four hours without becoming ineffective. Also, many firms operate only in the afternoons and evenings. But some

When money gets tight

firms do have morning hours—those involved in corporate sales, for example."

How much can a telemarketer expect to make?

"Top people can make over $10 per hour," says Debbie. "The average telemarketer makes about $4-$8 per hour. The pay varies depending on whether you are working on a straight commission basis or are being paid a base hourly wage plus commissions."

Debbie suggests investigating a telemarketing firm carefully before accepting a job since there are quite a few fly-by-night operations. But she emphasizes the many benefits of working for a reputable firm: "Telemarketing is a great experience for job hunters. Many of the basic sales techniques that you learn are usable when promoting yourself to a potential employer."

Getting a part-time job in telemarketing requires persistence since managers receive hundreds of calls and applications. "Don't give up," advises Debbie. "Have your sales pitch ready when you call. Sell yourself on the phone in the same way that you would sell a product once you're hired." ■

Where To Turn If Your Confidence Wilts

Recently a bank fired a loan officer who had worked there for more than ten years. The employee was 58 years old, about five-feet, six-inches tall, weighed almost 300 pounds, and did not have a college degree. His written communication skills were negligible. His poor attitude and appearance, lack of enthusiasm, and dismal self-esteem suggested he would be unemployed a long time.

The bank decided to use Tom Camden and Associates' outplacement service to help the person get another job. "There wasn't much we could do about changing his age, education, size, or communication skills," Tom recalls. "But we certainly could—and did—work with him on improving his self-esteem and changing his attitude toward interviewing for new jobs."

After a four-month search, the loan officer succeeded in landing a position that exactly suited his needs. His new job even was located in the neighborhood where he lived. It seemed like a typical success story—until the bank informed Tom Camden about how dissatisfied that person was with the counsel he had received. The man told the bank that they would have been better off paying *him* the consulting fee instead of retaining outside help.

"He was really angry," Tom recalls. "And also full of stress, guilt, fear, anxiety, desire for vengeance, and a host of other emotions."

Such feelings, unfortunately, are not at all unusual. In fact, they're a *normal* part of any job search, particularly for those who have been laid off or fired. That's because rejection, unfortunately, is inevitable in any job search.

If you've read Chapter 5, you know that you may speak with up to 300 people on a formal or informal basis while you're looking for suitable work—and a healthy percentage of those people will be unable or unwilling to help you. Every job seeker must anticipate rejection—it comes with the territory. Being turned down in an interview is a painful experience, and it's normal to feel hurt. The trick is to keep those hurt and angry feelings from clouding your judgment or affecting your behavior.

Dealing with Emotional Stress

If you're beginning to feel your confidence wilt, reread the tips for treating yourself well in Chapter 5. Put yourself on a regular schedule. And stick to it. If you've always worked for others, you're probably used to working within a structured situation. Now you're out of a job, and you've got nobody to give you assignments, no colleagues to provide support, no supervisor to tell you what you're doing right and wrong. This is very stressful for some people. The more stressful you find it, the more important it is for you to create your own structure by working full time in a systematic way to find the right job. In addition to that, make sure you're eating healthy foods and getting enough rest and exercise. Don't punish yourself for being unemployed or losing a job offer.

One of the worst things that can happen in any job search is to let rejection undermine your self-confidence. Like the little boy at the door who asks, "You don't want to buy a magazine, do you?" a person who doesn't feel good about himself will not easily convince an employer that he should be hired. Each new rejection further erodes self-esteem, and the job search stalls or takes a nose dive: "Maybe I *am* a loser. Perhaps I was lucky to have my old job as long as I did. Maybe my sights are set too high. I suppose I should look for something less responsible at a lower salary."

Thoughts such as these cross most people's minds at some time or other in the job search. As we've said, it's normal to feel hurt, angry, and depressed after a series of rejections. It's important, however, to recognize these feelings and learn to work them out in some non-destructive way. It is *not* normal to let such feelings sabotage your job search. Just because you're unemployed or looking for a new job doesn't mean you're a bad or worthless person. The only thing "wrong" with you is that you haven't yet found the offer you want.

When your confidence starts to wilt, turn to a trusted friend or relative. Talk about your feelings frankly. Get mad or sad or vengeful. Then get back to work on your job search. Don't let fear of rejection keep you from making that next call. It may be just the lead you're looking for.

There are no hard and fast rules on when to seek professional counseling and support, but we can offer certain guidelines. If you seriously think you need professional help, you ought to investigate two or three sources. Besides the ones we've listed below, check with your minister, priest, or rabbi. Many clerics are trained counselors, and their help is free.

How to Get a Job

If you feel you have nowhere else to turn, or if you don't want to share your feelings with anyone you know, you should consider psychiatric or psychological counseling. If you're not making calls, not preparing for interviews, or not doing what you know you have to do to get the job you want, you could probably use some counseling.

Everybody feels bad about being rejected. But if you allow those feelings to overwhelm you, or if they're interfering with finding a job, it's probably time to talk with a professional. Another sure sign of emotional problems is waking up most mornings too sick or lethargic from overeating, overdrinking, or abusing some other substance to do what you have to do.

How to Choose a Therapist

Many pschotherapists recommend that you interview several therapists before you enter therapy—even if you have to buy 15 minutes of their time. Ask about cost, credentials, whether your health insurance covers their fees, the type of therapy they practice, the length of time they anticipate would be required to deal with your concerns. The answers to all of these questions are important. But equally important is the sense of rapport you feel. It is vital that you feel comfortable confiding in this person.

There are a number of professions that practice counseling and therapy. A psychiatrist is an M.D. and is able to prescribe medication. A psychologist usually has a Ph.D. or a Master's degree and has gone through an internship or practicum. A clinical social worker has an M.S.W. and has conducted therapy under supervision while in training. There are also psychiatric nurses, pastoral counselors, and guidance counselors.

One of the best ways to find a compatible therapist is to ask your friends. If someone you know well has been helped and swears by a therapist, that's a strong recommendation. There are, unfortunately, a bewildering variety of schools of therapy. Each one has its detractors and its supporters. What worked for your friend might not work for you. Ask your friend how the therapist worked, and try to envision yourself going through a similar process.

The state governing boards for licensure in each of these professions are listed below. However, it is important to keep in mind that in the State of Texas one need not be licensed to offer counseling or help. That makes it much more important that you check out the background of these professionals.

Psychiatrists
Texas State Board of Medical Examiners
P.O. Box 13562
Austin, TX 78711
Tel.: (512) 834-7728
Fax: (512) 834-4597
Directories available by county, listing all medical practictioners; does not provide a separate listing of
psychiatrists.

Psychologists
Texas State Board of Examiners of Professional Psychologists
9101 Burnet Road, Suite 212
Austin, TX 78758
Tel.: (512) 835-2036
Fax: (512) 835-2436

When your confidence wilts

Publishes the *Roster*, a statewide directory of psychologists; available for $10 with a written request.

Counselors
Texas State Board of Examiners of Professional Counselors
1100 West 49th Street
Austin, TX 78756
Tel.: (512) 458-7511
Provides a roster, free of charge, listing all certified professional counselors in Texas.

Social Workers
Texas Department of Human Services
Social Work Certification W-403
P.O. Box 149030
Austin, TX 78714-9030
Tel.: (512) 450-3255
Fax: (512) 450-3848
Provides a statewide directory of social workers.

TELEPHONE CRISIS LINES

If you need help immediately, call any of these numbers.

Alcohol Hotline
Tel.: (713) 777-8021

Alcohol 24-Hour Helpline
Tel.: 1-800-888-9383

Bay Area Crisis Hotline
Tel.: (713) 333-5111

Crisis Hotline of Houston
Tel.: (713) 228-1505

Fort Bend County Women's Center Hotline
Tel.: (713) 342-4357

Houston Area Women's Center
Tel.: (713) 528-5785

Houston Council on Alcoholism & Drug Abuse
Tel.: (713) 520-5502

Information and Crisis Hotline
(713) 337-2469 ext. 5474
For mental health problems.

A Mental Health Referral Service
Tel.: (713) 741-6000

Mental Health and Treatment Hotline
Tel.: (713) 774-6500

Suicide Prevention
Tel.: (713) 285-1505

How to Get a Job

United Way Helpline
Tel.: (713) 688-1800
Links people who need help to locate the appropriate service.

Vocational Guidance Service
Tel.: (713) 659-1800

SELECTED MENTAL HEALTH CENTERS

Alcohol and Drug Help Unit
Sam Houston Memorial Hospital
1615 Hillendahl
Houston, TX 77055
Tel.: (713) 468-4357
24-hour toll-free: 1-800-821-4357
Comprehensive alcohol and drug treatment.

Alcoholics Anonymous
4140 Director's Row, Suite D
Houston, TX 77092
Tel.: (713) 686-6300
Intergroup association.

Alpha Center
Brazosport Memorial Hospital
Lake Jackson, TX 77566
Tel.: (409) 299-2888
Offers an alcohol and drug recovery program. Also addresses mental health problems.

Baywood Hospital
709 Medical Center Boulevard
Webster, TX 77598
Tel.: (713) 332-9550

Calwalder Behavioral Center
Doctors' Hospital
3205 West Davis
Conroe, TX 77304
Tel.: (409) 756-0631 or
1800 Bering Drive
Houston, TX 77057
Assistance for alcoholism and drug addiction. Has inpatient and outpatient services, and employee assistance programs.

Center for Compulsive Behavior
10101 Southwest Freeway, Suite 325
Houston, TX 77074
Tel.: (713) 270-0020
Offers alcohol, drug abuse, eating disorders, and compulsive gambling programs and counseling.

Charter Hospital of Kingwood
2001 Ladbrook Drive
Kingwood, TX 77339
Tel.: (713) 358-2273

When your confidence wilts

Charter Hospital of Sugarland
1550 First Colony Boulevard
Sugarland, TX 77479
Tel.: (713) 980-4000

Five Oaks Residential Treatment Center
1122 Bissonnet
Houston, TX 77005
Tel.: (713) 524-4611

The Gathering Place
P.O. Box 35561
Houston, TX 77235
Tel.: (713) 729-3499

Group Plan Clinic
1775 St. James Place, Suite 120
Houston, TX 77056
Tel.: (713) 871-9707

Houston Guidance Center
3214 Austin
Houston, TX 77004
Tel.: (713) 526-4225

Houston Psychiatric Resources PA
17215 Red Oak Drive, Suite 105
Houston, TX 77090
Tel.: (713) 580-0046

Institute for Living
Mainland Center Hospital
P.O. Box 2756
Texas City, TX 77590
Tel.: (713) 996-5000
Provides biofeedback and consultation services for people suffering from depression or other mental problems. Free assessment.

Laurelwood Hospital
4000 South Wellman
Houston, TX 77381
Tel.: (713) 367-4422

North Brazoria Comprehensive Service Center
4650 Dixie Farm Road
Houston, TX 77581
Center (713) 585-0494
Emergency (713) 331-4502

Post Oak Psychiatric Associates
50 Briar Hollow
Houston, TX 77027
Tel.: (713) 621-6127

Psychiatric Center of Houston
7500 Beechnut, Suite 214
Houston, TX 77074
Tel.: (713) 772-6519

How to Get a Job

The West Oaks System
At Cypress Creek Hospital
17750 Cali
Houston, TX 77090
Tel.: (713) 586-7600

At Ford Bend
4655 Sweetwater Boulevard
Sugarland, TX 77479
Tel.: (713) 980-5300

At Kingwood
3535-A Cedar Knolls
Humble, TX 77090
Tel.: (713) 586-7600

At Willowbrook
9725 Louedd
Houston, TX 77070
Tel.: (713) 469-6395

West Oaks Hospital
6500 Hornwood
Houston, TX 77074
Tel.: (713) 995-0909

Women in Transition

Some Houston psychologists and counseling centers conduct groups for women in transition. These counselors note that it makes a lot of difference whether a transition is chosen or forced upon the woman. A woman who has chosen to go back to school, look for a "real job," or move up the career ladder will probably have fewer problems dealing with identity, self-esteem, and dependency. She has already sorted through her priorities and has a better idea of who she is as an individual. She will, of course, be susceptible to all the difficulties any job seeker must face. But the woman who is widowed or divorced must first struggle with her identity and somehow regain a sense of control over her life.

Support groups are especially helpful for women whose transition has been forced upon them. Together with others who face similar issues, they can more often quickly redefine themselves and regain control over their lives.

One psychologist who went through a midlife transition of her own choosing, has observed that "the biggest obstacle for women in transition is their fear that they lack competence. A big help for such women is to increase their self-confidence one small step at a time. That way, they'll always be meeting challenges but won't feel overwhelmed." Some organizations that can provide help and counseling for women in transition are:

American Association of University Women
2701 Westheimer, #8H
Houston, TX 77098
Tel.: (713) 681-8085

Career Services Center, Rice University
P.O. Box 1892

When your confidence wilts

Houston, TX 77251
Tel.: (713) 527-4055

Chicana Family Center
7524 Avenue E
Houston, TX 77012
Tel.: (713) 923-2316

Houston Area Women's Center
3101 Richmond, Suite 150
Houston, TX 77098
Tel.: (713) 528-2121

Interfaith
4803 San Felipe
Houston, Tx 77056
Tel.: (713) 626-7990

Jewish Family Service
4131 S. Braeswood
Houston, TX 77025
Tel.: (713) 667-9336

National Association of Women Business Owners
6910 Fannin, Suite 265
Houston, TX 77030
Tel.: (713) 796-2834

Options Resource and Career Center
1200 Blalock, Suite 109
Houston, TX 77055
Tel.: (713) 465-1118

Veteran's Center
503 Westheimer
Houston, TX 77006
Tel.: (713) 653-3121

VGS (Vocational Guidance Service)
P.O. Box 540144
Houston, TX 77254-0144
Tel.: (713) 659-1800

Women Empowered
Performance Dynamics Group
10700 North Freeway, Suite 390
Houston, TX 77037
Tel.: (713) 820-6707

What To Do If You Get Fired

Being fired ranks just after the death of someone you love and divorce when it comes to personal traumas. If it should happen to you, *take time to evaluate the bad news before accepting a settlement offer.* If you quickly accept what your employer has to offer, it will be much more difficult to change your situation later. Tell the boss you want some time to think about a settlement. Then go back in a day or two and negotiate.

How to Get a Job

Stay on the payroll as long as you can, even if your pride hurts. Find out if you are eligible for part-time work or consulting jobs to tide you over until you find your new job. You may be able to hang on to insurance and other benefits until you've found new employment.

Try to negotiate a generous severance payment. In the last five years, severance agreements have risen dramatically in some industries. What the company offers at first may not be the maximum. Negotiation doesn't always work, but you certainly ought to try to get the most for your years of service.

Check with your personnel office to make sure you're getting all the benefits to which you are entitled, such as vacation pay and profit sharing. Check your eligibility for unemployment compensation before you accept an offer to resign instead of being terminated.

Don't attack management during your termination interview. It may cost you good references and hurt your chances of finding a new job.

Take advantage of any outplacement assistance that is offered. OK, so maybe the company shouldn't have let you go, and you feel utterly betrayed. Don't reject the company's offer to help. Chances are the outplacement counselor has been hired on a contractual basis and owes the company nothing more than to do his level best to help you find a suitable position.

Risk and Opportunity: Career Transition Issues

Any job search is going to involve risk and opportunity, according to a notable career counselor. If you are autonomous, you are able to view the risk as opportunity and to come up with creative ideas for changing jobs. However, many job searchers begin to lose their sense of independence and control after some setbacks. They start believing that nothing they do will help lift them out of their situation.

An autonomous person is "self-governing" and believes that his actions will have a definite affect on his or her life. One of the most important aspects of finding or changing a job is to keep believing that you can control your life. When this belief begins to falter, many people slip into some of the traps of self-doubt and loss of independence.

Seven key issues that most people confront during a job hunt are:

Self-esteem: Do you feel good about yourself, your daily life, and your future? Are you self-accepting? Do you have a positive self-image?

Self-validation: Do you validate yourself both from without and within? Do you have an inner sense of your own worth? Are you able to learn from the feedback you get from others during the job hunt?

Risk-taking: Are you willing to take the risks needed to get what you want? Are you willing to reveal yourself even in a situation such as a job interview when you're not completely in control?

Sadness or depression: Can you feel sad about loss but still bounce back? Can you learn from failure even as you feel good about success?

Internalized anger: Can you recognize when you feel angry? If you are angry, can you identify which of your needs are not being met? Can you discover effective and appropriate ways to express anger?

Goal setting: Are your goals appropriate to who you are and what you need? Are your goals and expectations realistic in terms of the current job market and your own training and expertise?

When your confidence wilts

Phase of life issues: How have your goals changed over time? Has your self-image changed as you have changed and grown? Are you flexible enough to change as your life changes?

Selecting the Right Job for You

Welcome to the most pleasant chapter of this book. You've figured out what you want to do, developed an acceptable resume, and used your network of contacts and other resources to research the job market and generate all sorts of interviews. If you haven't received a reasonable offer yet, you're close to it.

You have a problem if a company demands an immediate response to a firm offer while you're still investigating other promising leads. The employer making this offer is essentially telling you, "We think you have everything we're looking for, and we want you to start as soon as possible." It is difficult to stall or delay your acceptance just because other promising leads still haven't yielded firm offers. You have to use your best judgment in such a case, but try to delay a final decision until all likely offers are in. Unless you're absolutely desperate, there's no reason to jump at the first offer you receive. One good response to such an offer is to let the company know that you need a little more decision-making time to "be fair to both the company and yourself."

You owe it to both yourself and the people who interviewed you to bring in all outstanding possibilities and *then* make your decision. Tell the employer who made you the offer the truth—that you need more time to review the offer against some others. Agree upon a period of time—five days, two weeks, a month—during which they won't offer the position to anyone else. Obviously, the more time you can get, the better for you, but they may have pressing needs to have someone in place pronto. If the offering company refuses to wait at all, that tells you a great deal about the atmosphere in which you'd be working.

If a company wants you badly enough, they'll wait a reasonable length of time for you to decide. In the meantime, use your offer to "encourage" other companies to reach a decision about your candidacy. We're not suggesting that you play hardball. That probably won't work and might even work against you. But it makes perfect sense to inform other companies who are interested in you that you have an offer. If you're sure you'd rather work for them, say so. But also say that you'll have to accept the first offer if you don't hear from them within the allotted time. Don't lie about your intentions. If you don't intend to accept the first offer, don't say that you do. Otherwise, the second (and perhaps better) company might write you off, assuming that you won't be available by the time they're ready to decide.

A job involves much more than a title and base salary. For any firm offer, be sure you understand what your responsibilities will be, what benefits you'll receive besides salary (insurance, vacation, profit sharing, training, tuition reimbursement, and the like), how much overtime is required (and whether you'll be paid for it), how much travel is involved in the job, who your superior will be, how many people you'll be supervising, and where the position might lead. (Is it a dead-end job or are people in this slot often promoted?) In short, find out anything and everything you need to know to evaluate the offer.

For many positions, especially those requiring several years' experience, it's appropriate to ask for an offer in writing. Such a document should specify the position's title, responsibilities, reporting relationship, compensation, and include a statement of company benefits.

At the very least, before you make a firm decision, be sure to obtain a copy of the company's personnel policy. It will fill you in on such details as the number of paid sick days, overtime and vacation policy, insurance benefits, profit sharing, and the like. These so-called fringe benefits can really add up. It's not a bad idea to try to assign a dollar value to them to help you evaluate the financial pros and cons of each offer.

It seems obvious to us that it's unwise to choose a job exclusively on the basis of salary and benefits. You spend more of your waking hours at work than at any other activity. Don't condemn yourself to working for an impossible boss with colleagues and subordinates you can't stand and doing work that you find boring to accomplish goals you don't believe in.

Finding the Right Culture

Career counselors often warn that you ignore a company's "culture" at your own peril. You can find a position that suits you to a "T" but still be unhappy if you don't fit the culture of the company that hires you. It takes some doing to assess an organization's culture, but it's worth your while.

Some signs are fairly obvious: What do people wear? What is the furniture like? Are office doors kept open or closed? Are there any minorities or women in positions of power? How friendly are people to you? To each

How to Get a Job

other? Does anybody laugh? A very important question to ask—do I feel comfortable here?

There are five aspects of an organization's culture to consider. Try to find out as much as you can about each.

1. What is the relationship between a company and its environment? Does it control its own destiny or must it depend on the mood of an adversarial home office? You probably wouldn't be wise to work for the Department of Defense under a pacifist administration.

2. How does a company view human nature? Good or evil? Changeable or immutable? Answers to these questions determine how employees are treated, how much supervision and control is exerted. How openly will employees communicate? Will there be opportunities for training and development?

3. What are the philosophy and mission of a company? Printed brochures are often good indicators. A good company is clear on what business it's in.

4. How do people relate to each other in a company? Is there a formal flow chart? Are there many vertical levels (the military)? Or is power more evenly and horizontally spread out (some new hi-tech firms)? The more horizontal, the more informal and the easier it is to get things done, generally through relationships.

5. How are decisions made, who makes them, and upon what basis? Facts and reason? Politics? Ideology? Good-old-boy or old-girl network? The whims of an autocrat at the top?

The answers to these questions will determine the working atmosphere for most companies.

Salary Strategy

Before you accept an offer—or bicker over salary—you need to know what other people who fill similar positions are making. The *Occupational Outlook Handbook,* put out by the U.S. Department of Labor every two years, cites salary statistics by field. Probably a better source of information is *The American Almanac of Jobs and Salaries* by John Wright, published by Avon. What you really need to know is what other people with your qualifications and experience are making in Houston for working the job you're considering. Professional societies and associations frequently provide this sort of information. It's one more good reason to belong to one. Probably the best source of all for salary orientation is—you guessed it—your network of contacts.

For advice on how to get the salary you want, we recommend these books:

BOOKS ON SALARY NEGOTIATION

Chapman, Jack. *How to Make $1000 a Minute.* Berkeley, CA: Ten Speed Press, 1987.
Cohen, Herb. *You Can Negotiate Anything.* New York: Bantam Publishing Co., 1982.
Fisher, Roger, and William Ury. *Getting to Yes.* New York: Penguin Books, 1983.
Kennedy, Marilyn Moats. *Gettting the Job You Want & The Money You're Worth.* American College of Executives, 1987.

The right job for you

Kennedy, Marilyn Moats. *Salary Strategies: Everything You Need to Know to Get the Salary You Want.* New York: Rawson Wade, 1982.

Compare the Offers on Paper

You've talked with each employer and taken notes about the responsibilities and compensation being offered. Where possible, you've obtained a job offer in writing. You have also read through the company's personnel policy. Now, make yourself a checklist for comparing the relative merits of each offer. We've provided a sample here, but if another format suits your purposes better, use it. The idea is to list the factors that you consider important in any job, and then assign a rating for how well each offer fills the bill in each particular area.

We've listed some of the factors that we think ought to be considered before you accept any offer. Some may not be relevant to your situation. Others that we've left out may be of great importance to you. So feel free to make any additions, deletions, or changes you want.

Once you've listed your factors, make a column for each job offer you're considering. Assign a rating (say, 1 to 5, with 1 the lowest and 5 the highest) for each factor under each offer. Then, total the scores for each offer.

The offer with the most points is not necessarily the one to accept. The chart doesn't take into account the fact that "responsibilities" may be more important to you than "career path," or that you promised yourself you'd never punch a time clock again. Nevertheless, looking at the pros and cons of each offer in black and white should help you make a much more methodical and logical decision.

Factor	Offer A	Offer B	Offer C
Responsibilities	_____	_____	_____
Company reputation	_____	_____	_____
Salary	_____	_____	_____
Insurance	_____	_____	_____
Paid vacation	_____	_____	_____
Pension	_____	_____	_____
Profit sharing	_____	_____	_____
Tuition reimbursement	_____	_____	_____
On-the-job training	_____	_____	_____
Career path (where can you go from this job?)	_____	_____	_____
Company future	_____	_____	_____
Quality of product	_____	_____	_____

How to Get a Job

or service

Location (housing market, schools, transportation)	_____	_____	_____
Boss(es)	_____	_____	_____
Other workers	_____	_____	_____
Travel	_____	_____	_____
Overtime	_____	_____	_____
Other	_____	_____	_____
_____	_____	_____	_____
_____	_____	_____	_____
TOTAL POINTS	_____	_____	_____

A Final Word

Once you have accepted a job, it's important that you notify each of the people in your log of your new position, company, address, and phone number. Be sure to thank these people; let them know you appreciated their assistance. After all, you never know when you may need to ask them to help you again. You've spent weeks building up a network of professional contacts. *Keep your network alive.*

On each anniversary date of your new job, take the time to run through the self-appraisal process to evaluate your situation and the progress you are making (as measured by increased salary, responsibilities, and abilities). Consider how they compare with the objectives you set at the start of your search. Although you may be completely satisfied in your new assignment, remember that circumstances can change overnight, and you must always be prepared for the unexpected. So make an employment "New Year's Resolution" to weigh every aspect of your job annually and compare the result with what you want and expect from your life's work.

We hope that you have made good use of the job-search techniques outlined in this book. Indeed, we hope that the resulting experiences not only have won you the job you want but—equally important—also have made you a better person. Perhaps the next time you talk to an unemployed person or someone who is employed but seeking a new job, you will look at that person with new insight gained from your own search experiences. We hope you'll gladly share what you've learned about how to get a job in Houston.

The right job for you

Zeroing in on a great place to work

How do you know when you've found a great place to work?

We asked business writer Robert Levering, co-author of *A Great Place to Work: What Makes Some Employers So Good and Some So Bad* and *The 100 Best Companies to Work for In America,* what he considered the key to evaluating a job proposal.

"Before you accept a job," Levering insists, "you ought to ask yourself, 'what kind of relationship am I going to have with the people I work for, with the people I'm going to work with, and with my work itself?'"

When he was tracking down "the 100 best employers in America," the rankings were based on five tangibles: pay, benefits, job security, opportunities for promotion, and ambiance. Now, however, he believes the values that lie behind the perks may be more significant than the perks themselves. Levering states, "You must trust the people you work for, have pride in what you do, and enjoy the people you work with. Simply put, the criteria for a great place to work are trust, pride, and fun.

"Let's face it, a happy marriage isn't defined by a house in the suburbs, two cars in the garage, 2.5 children, and a dog. When you find a great job, it's more than the result of just pay scales, benefits, and a chance to move up."

That doesn't mean that salary range, stock options, or a gourmet corporate cafeteria are irrelevant. Levering explains, "If you feel either you're being cheated or that the company is not paying you as much as it could, that's not just an issue of money. How your employer compensates you for your time tells you about how your employer values you, and that is about trust.

Similarly, pride translates into systems that let people develop their skills. Pride ensures that employees have the tools they need to do their jobs. Pride means workers get credit for their accomplishments. And if your co-workers are relaxed, pleasant to be with, and basically compatible, work is fun. Often that comes down to how much corporate politics permeates the office."

Are companies—other than the 100 best—willing to create a corporate culture based on trust, pride, and fun?

"There are positive signs," Levering says. "Businesses know that the work force has

How to Get a Job

changed. Employees are now highly educated and looking for the best job possible. Employers want to attract and retain the best people, so they want to treat their employees well. A hell of a lot of companies would like to be on the list of the 100 best places to work." ■

Where Houston Works

This chapter contains the names, addresses, and phone numbers of Houston's top 1,500 employers of white-collar workers. The companies are arranged in categories according to the major products and services they manufacture or provide. Where appropriate, entries contain a brief description of the company's business and the name of the personnel director or other contact.

This listing is intended to help you survey the major potential employers in the fields that interest you. It is *selective*, not exhaustive. We have not, for example, listed all the advertising agencies in the city of Houston, as you can find that information in the Yellow Pages. We have simply listed the top 25 or so—that is, the ones with the most jobs.

The purpose of this chapter is to get you started, both looking and thinking. This is the kickoff, not the touchdown. Browse through the whole chapter, and take some time to check out areas that are unfamiliar to you. Many white-collar skills are transferable. People with marketing, data processing, accounting, administrative, secretarial, and other talents are needed in a huge variety of businesses.

Ask yourself in what areas your skills could be marketed. Use your imagination, especially if you're in a so-called specialized field. A dietitian, for instance, might look first under Health Care, or maybe Hotels. But what

How to Get a Job

about Insurance companies, Museums, Banks, or the scores of other places that run their own dining rooms for employees or the public? What about food and consumer magazines? Who makes up all those recipes and tests those products?

The sidebars and interviews that are scattered throughout this chapter are designed to nudge your creativity and suggest additional ideas for your job search. Much more detailed information on Houston's top employers, and other, smaller companies, can be found in the directories and other resources suggested in Chapter 4. We can't stress strongly enough that *you have to do your homework when you're looking for a job,* both to unearth places that might need a person with your particular talents, and to succeed in the interview once you've lined up a meeting with the hiring authority.

A word about hiring authorities: if you've read Chapter 5, you know that the name of the game is to meet the person with the power to hire you, or get as close to that person as you can. You don't want to go to the president or the personnel director if the person who actually makes the decision is the marketing manager or customer service director.

Obviously, we can't list every possible hiring authority in Houston's "top 1,500." If we tried, you'd need a wagon to haul this book around. Besides, printed directories go out of date—even those that are regularly and conscientiously revised. So always double-check a contact whose name you get from a book or magazine, including this one. If necessary, call the company's switchboard to confirm who heads a particular department or division.

Here, then, are Houston's "Top 1,500." Happy hunting!

The Houston area's top 1,500 employers are arranged in the following categories:

Accounting/Auditing
Advertising
Aerospace
Architecture
Banks, Credit Unions, S&Ls
Book and Magazine Publishers
Broadcasting
Chemicals
Computers/Equipment Manufacturers
Computers/Programming and Software
Construction
Drugs and Pharmaceuticals
Educational Institutions
Electronics/Telecommunications
Engineering
Environmental Services
Food/Beverage Producers and Distributers
Foundations
Government Agencies
Health Care
Hotels/Motels
Human Services
Insurance

Where Houston works

Investment Bankers/Stock Brokers
Law Firms
Management Consultants
Media: Newspapers and Magazines
Museums/Art Galleries
Oil, Gas, and Plastics
Paper and Allied Products
Printing
Public Relations
Real Estate Developers and Brokers
Recreation, Sports, and Fitness
Restaurants
Retailers
Travel, Transportation, and Shipping
Utilities

Accounting/Auditing

For networking in the **accounting/auditing industry,** check out the following professional organizations listed in Chapter 5:

PROFESSIONAL ORGANIZATIONS:

American Society of Women Accountants
American Woman's Society of Certified Public Accountants
Professional Accounting Society of Houston
Tax Research Association of Houston and Harris County
Texas Society of Certified Public Accountants

For additional information, you can contact:

American Institute of CPA's
1211 Avenue of the Americas
New York, NY 10036
Tel.: (212) 575-6200
Fax: (212) 575-3846

American Society of Women Accountants
35 East Wacker Drive, Suite 1068
Chicago, IL 60601
Tel.: (312) 726-9030
Fax: (312) 726-4543

Institute of Management Accountants
10 Paragon Drive
Montvale, NJ 07645
Tel.: (201) 573-9000
Fax: (201) 573-8185

National Association of Black Accountants
220 I Street NE, #150
Washington, DC 20002
Tel.: (202) 546-6222
Fax: (202) 547-1041

National Society of Public Accountants
1010 North Fairfax Street
Alexandria, VA 22314
Tel.: (703) 549-6400
Fax: (703) 549-2984

PROFESSIONAL PUBLICATIONS:

Accounting News
The CPA Journal
D & B Reports
Dun's Business Month

Accounting/Auditing

Journal of Accountancy
Managerial Accounting
National Public Accountant

DIRECTORIES:

Accounting/Bookkeeping Service Directory (American Business Directories, Omaha, NE)
Accounting Firms and Practitioners (American Institute of Certified Public Accountants, New York, NY)
American Association of Spanish-Speaking Certified Public Accountants—Membership Directory (American Association of Spanish-Speaking Certified Public Accountants, Washington, DC).
American Institute of Certified Public Accountants —List of Members (American Institute of Certified Public Accountants, New York, NY)
American Women's Society of Certified Public Accountants—Roster (American Women's Society of Certified Public Accountants, Chicago, IL).
National Directory of Certified Public Accountants (Perter Norback Publishing Co., Princeton, NJ)
Who Audits America? (Data Financial Press, Menlo Park, CA)

EMPLOYERS:

Arthur Anderson and Company
711 Louisiana, Suite 1300
Houston, TX 77002
Gene Cooper, Purchasing Officer
Tel.: (713) 237-2323
Fax: (713) 237-2786

Coopers and Lybrand
1100 Louisiana, Suite 4100
Houston, TX 77002
Carroll W. Phillips, Managing Partner
Tel.: (713) 757-5200
Fax: (713) 757-5249

Deloitte and Touche
333 Clay, Suite 2300
Houston, TX 77037
Robert J. Cruikshank, Partner-in-Charge
Tel.: (713) 756-2000
Fax: (713) 756-2005

Ernst and Young
1221 McKinney Suite 2400
Houston, TX 77010
Dennis Purdum, Managing Partner
Tel.: (713) 750-1500
Fax: (713) 750-1501

How to Get a Job

Fitts, Roberts, and Company
6437 High Star
Houston, TX 77074
Larry Tanner, President
Tel.: (713) 774-9761
Fax: (713) 773-6999

Grant Thornton
1200 Smith, Suite 2800
Houston, TX 77002
James P. Hayden, Managing Partner
Tel.: (713) 658-0300
Fax: (713) 655-8741

Harper and Pearson Company
1 Riverway, Suite 1000
Houston, TX 77056
Bruce J. Harper, CEO
Tel.: (713) 622-2310
Fax: (713) 622-5613

Kenneth Leventhal and Company
5 Greenway Plaza, Suite 600
Houston, TX 77046
Richard A. Price, Managing Partner
Tel.: (713) 850-9100
Fax: (713) 871-2093

Mann, Frankfort, Stein and Lipp
12 Greenway Plaza, Suite 800
Houston, TX 77046
Milton Frankfort, Managing Partner
Tel.: (713) 960-1706
Fax: (713) 960-9549

Melton and Melton
10333 Richmond, Suite 500
Houston, TX 77042
R. Talley Melton/H. Palmer Melton, Managing Partners
Tel.: (713) 781-1971
Fax: (713) 781-6780

Moore Stephens, CPA
1100 Milam, Suite 3300
Houston, TX 77006
Frank H. Simonton, Jr., Managing Partner
Tel.: (713) 658-9755
Fax: (713) 658-0298

Pannell, Kerr, Forster
5847 San Felipe, Suite 2300
Houston, TX 77057

Accounting/Auditing

Ron Kaiser, Managing Partner
Tel.: (713) 780-8007
Fax: (713) 784-3360

Peat, Marwick, Main and Company
700 Louisiana
Houston, TX 77002
Terry Strange, Managing Partner
Tel.: (713) 224-4262
Fax: (713) 224-4566

Price Waterhouse
1201 Louisiana, Suite 2900
Houston, TX 77002
Nancy Flesch, Purchasing Officer
Tel.: (713) 654-4100
Fax: (713) 750-4717

Professional Accounting Society
University of Houston, 101 Main Street, Room 104
Houston, TX 77002
Trinidad Perez, President
Tel.: (713) 221-1050

Seidman and Seidman/BDO
1200 Smith, Suite 500
Houston, TX 77002
Mike O'Hare, Managing Partner
Tel.: (713) 659-6551
Fax: (713) 659-3238

Weinstein, Spira and Company
5 Greenway Plaza
Houston, TX 77046
Stanley C. Weinstein/Joel Spira, Managing Partners
Tel.: (713) 622-7000
Fax: (713) 622-9535

White, Petrov & McHone
600 Jefferson, Suite 1100
Houston, TX 77002
Stephen H. Cordill, Jr., President
Tel.: (713) 659-1777
Fax: (713) 658-9606

How to Get a Job

Accounting firms large and small

Richard began his career in public accounting at Deloitte and Touche, one of the country's Big Eight accounting firms. We talked with him about how large and small accounting firms differ.

"Usually, working for a larger firm means learning a specific task," says Richard. "Staffs are larger, so each job is more specialized. You don't usually handle as many components of a job as you would in a smaller firm. You sometimes have more opportunity for hands-on experience in a smaller firm and gain more general management experience.

"Whether you work for a large firm or a small one is really a matter of personal preference and on what career path you wish to embark. I started out with a large public accounting firm for the experience and the opportunity to become certified as a public accountant.

"But regardless of the size of the firm where you began your career, you should remain flexible during your first five years if you wish to advance. If your job is not what you expected, be willing to make a change.

"Also, if you want a manager's position, you may have to move around to gain general managerial experience. Sometimes that will mean a transfer to a department that would not necessarily be your first choice. But if the position rounds out your background, it is usually worth at least a temporary stay." ■

Advertising

For networking in **advertising** and related fields, check out the following professional organizations listed in Chapter 5:

PROFESSIONAL ORGANIZATIONS:

Art Directors Club of Houston
Houston Advertising Federation
Houston Society of Professional Illustrators

For additional information, you can contact:

The Advertising Council
261 Madison Avenue, 11th Floor
New York, NY 10016
Tel.: (212) 922-1500
Fax: (212) 922-1676

American Advertising Federation
1400 K Street NW, Suite 1000
Washington, DC 20005
Tel.: (202) 598-0089
Fax: (202) 598-0159

American Association of Advertising Agencies
666 Third Avenue, 13th Floor
New York, NY 10017
Tel.: (212) 682-2500
Fax: (212) 682-8391

American Marketing Association
250 S. Wacker Drive
Chicago, IL 60606
Tel.: (312) 648-0536

Direct Marketing Association
11 W 42nd Street, 25th Floor
New York, NY 10036
Tel.: (212) 768-7277
Fax: (212) 768-4542

PROFESSIONAL PUBLICATIONS:

Advertising Age
Adweek/Southwest
Direct Marketing Magazine
Journal of Advertising Research
Journal of Marketing Research
Madison Avenue

How to Get a Job

Potentials in Marketing
Product Marketing

DIRECTORIES:

Advertising Career Directory (Career Press, Hawthorne, NJ)
Bradford's Directory of Marketing Research (Bradford's, Fairfax, VA)
International Directory of Market Companies and Services Green Book (American Marketing Association, New York, NY)
International Membership Directory & Market Research Guide (American Marketing Association, Chicago, IL)
Membership Roster (American Marketing Association, Chicago, IL)
Multinational Marketing and Employment Directory (World Trade Academy Press, New York, NY)
Standard Directory of Advertising Agencies (National Register Publishing Co., Skokie, IL)

EMPLOYERS:

Black, Gillock and Langberg
5851 San Felipe, Suite 100
Houston, TX 77057
William Scott Black, President
Tel.: (713) 781-6666
Fax: (713) 781-5097

Campbell, Mithun, Esty, Goodwin, Dannenbaum, Littman, and Wingfield
(C.M.E.G.D.L. & W)
5847 San Felipe
Houston, TX 77057
Jerry Kerr, Chief Executive Officer
Tel.: (713) 266-7676
Fax: (713) 267-7222

Communications Plus
3730 Kirby Drive, Suite 1150
Houston, TX 77098
Karen Kershner, Chief Executive Officer
Tel.: (713) 523-6613
Fax: (713) 522-4002

Eisaman, Johns and Laws Advertising
2121 Sage Road, Suite 200
Houston, TX 77056
Richard J. Westman, Chief Executive Officer
Tel.: (713) 961-4355
Fax: (713) 961-9508

Fellers and Company
P.O. Box 22628
Houston, TX 77227

Advertising

Don Lamm, Chief Executive Officer
Tel.: (713) 621-2680
Fax: (713) 621-3145

Fogarty and Klein
7155 Old Katy Road, Suite 100
Houston, TX 77024
William H. Fogarty/Richard E. Klein, Chief Executive Officers
Tel.: (713) 862-5100
Fax: (713) 869-6560

Harris, Kosmoski and Pinkston
1300 Post Oak Boulevard, Suite 1922
Houston, TX 77056
Edward Harris, Chief Executive Officer
Tel.: (713) 623-8705
Fax: (713) 960-0467

Hinckley and Slade
4 Chelsea Place
Houston, TX 77006
Joe L. Slade, Jr., Chief Executive Officer
Tel.: (713) 520-1515
Fax: (713) 520-7509

McCann-Erickson
1360 Post Oak Boulevard, Suite 1900
Houston, TX 77056
Jim G. Hetherly, Executive Vice President/General Manager
Tel.: (713) 965-0303
Fax: (713) 439-9349

Ogilivy and Mather
1415 Louisiana, Suite 2700
Houston, TX 77002
James S. Hine, Sr., Vice President / Managing Director
Tel.: (713) 659-6688
Fax: (713) 759-0034

Patrick Media Group
1313 West Loop North
Houston, TX 77055
Jerry McCarver, Vice President/General Manager
Tel.: (713) 688-8651
Fax: (713) 956-6277

Penny and Speier
1800 West Loop South, Suite 400
Houston, TX 77027
Charles Lutz, Chief Executive Officer
Tel.: (713) 965-0331
Fax: (713) 961-4128

How to Get a Job

The Quest Business Agency
2900 North Loop West, Suite 1020
Houston, TX 77092
Alan D. Vera, Chief Executive Officer
Tel.: (713) 956-6569
Fax: (713) 956-2593

Rives Smith Baldwin Carlberg
5599 San Felipe Suite 1111
Houston, TX 77056
W. Charles Carlberg, Chief Executive Officer
Tel.: (713) 965-0764
Fax: (713) 965-0135

Sachnowitz Advertising Agency
P.O. Box 130939
Houston, TX 77219
Larry J. Sachnowitz, Chief Executive Officer
Tel.: (713) 521-1010
Fax: (713) 521-0790

Schey Advertising
701 Richmond
Houston, TX 77006
Dick Schey, Chief Executive Officer
Tel.: (713) 522-8300
Fax: (713) 522-7513

Shable, Sawyer and Pitluk
2950 North Loop West, Suite 840
Houston, TX 77092
James R. Shable, Chief Executive Officer
Tel.: (713) 956-9660
Fax: (713) 956-9616

Taylor Smith
2000 West Loop South, Suite 1600
Houston, TX 77027
Larry Taylor, Chief Executive Officer
Tel.: (713) 877-1674
Fax: (713) 877-1674

Trum Advertising
17015 Alcove Lane
Houston, TX 77090
Joseph S. Trum, Chief Executive Officer
Tel.: (713) 444-5184
Fax: (713) 444-6108

Winius-Brandon Advertising
7155 Old Katy Road Suite 100
Houston, TX 77024

Advertising

Art Casper, Chief Executive Officer
Tel.: (713) 862-5100
Fax: (713) 869-6566

How to advertise

Todd, a copywriter for one of the largest advertising firms in Houston, explains: "There are probably three ways to get into an advertising agency: one, get an internship. The pay is pretty low in the position, so you might have to do it while in school or after you've saved some money. Two, start at the company as a secretary. There are many benefits to doing this: you get paid more than an intern, you can get a general overview of the office and the industry, and you have a good possibility of being hired because of the high turnover rate in the industry.

"Third, if you want to work on the creative end of things, put together a portfolio of some of your advertising ideas before your interview. If you don't know much about advertising art or portfolios, try taking a graphics art design class at the local community college or look through some of the advertising awards books (in most libraries).

"Finally, be sure and know something about the industry before you interview, such as what accounts are where and which agency has just won new accounts. Also, decide which part of the organization you want to work for: legal, accounting, traffic, account services, creative, etc. In this way, you can show the employer that you know what you're talking about."■

Aerospace

For additional information, you can contact:

PROFESSIONAL ORGANIZATIONS:

Aerospace Education Foundation
1501 Lee Highway
Arlington, VA 22209

Aerospace Industries Association of America
1250 I Street NW, Suite 1100
Washington, DC 20005-3924
Jane Weeden, Manager of Operations and Personnel
Tel.: (202) 371-8400
Fax: (202) 371-8470

American Institute of Aeronautics and Astronautics
370 L'Enfant Promenade SW
Washington, DC 20024
Tel.: (202) 646-7400
Fax: (202) 646-7508

International Association of Machinists and Aerospace Workers
1300 Connecticut Avenue NW
Washington, DC 20036
Tel.: (202) 857-5200
Fax: (202) 296-1638

National Space Institute
600 Maryland Avenue SW
Washington, DC 20034

PROFESSIONAL PUBLICATIONS:

Aviation Week and Space Technology
Business and Commercial Aviation
Journal of Air Law and Commerce

DIRECTORIES:

Aerospace Industries Association of America—Directory of VTOL Aircraft (Aerospace Industries Association of America, Washington, DC)
Aviation Buyer's Guide (Debora, Shelbyvillle, TN)
Aviation Distributors & Manufacturers Association—Membership Directory (Aviation Distributors & Manufacturers Association, Philadelphia, PA)
Aviation Week & Space Technology, Buyers Guide Issue (McGraw-Hill Publishing Co., New York, NY)

Aerospace

EMPLOYERS:

Astrodetics, Inc.
2951 Marina Bay Drive, Suite 130
League City, TX 77573
Arthur Dennis, President
Tel.: (713) 334-5989
Fax: (713) 334-5812

Bendix Field Engineering Corp.
501 Gemini Avenue
Houston, TX 77058
Glenn Mallery, Purchasing Officer
Tel.: (713) 283-7300
Fax: (713) 480-7522

Boeing Aerospace Operations
P.O. Box 58747
Houston, TX 77258
Walter Nelson, Purchasing Officer
Tel.: (713) 280-2000
Fax: (713) 480-9887

ESCO, Inc.
5310 Glenmont
Houston, TX 77081
Susan Hensley, Personnel Administrator
Tel.: (713) 666-3951
Fax: (713) 666-4025

GE Aerospace
1050 Bay Area Boulevard
Houston, TX 77058
Linda Look, Personnel
Tel.: (713) 488-9005
Fax: (713) 488-1092

Horizon Discovery Group
1910 College Green
Houston, TX 77058
Neal Jackson, President Horizon Engineering
Karen Jackson, President Horizon Discovery Group
Tel.: (713) 280-0132

ILC Space Systems
16665 Space Center Boulevard
Houston, TX 77058
Ronald L. Welch, Vice President of Operations
Tel.: (713) 488-9080
Fax: (713) 488-3646 (Human Resources)

How to Get a Job

Jackson, Bruce D., and Associates
17629 El Camino Real, Suite 207
Houston, TX 77058
Ivy Hooks, President
Tel.: (713) 486-7817
Fax: (713) 486-0115

Johnson Control World Services
P.O. Box 58938
Houston, TX 77258
Frank Adams, Purchasing
Tel.: (713) 483-7906
Fax: (713) 483-4527

Link Flight Simulation Corp.
2224 Bay Area Boulevard
Houston, TX 77058
Pat Cohen, Personnel Director
Tel.: (713) 488-5510
Fax: (713) 280-4083

Loral Space Information Systems
P.O. Box 58487
Houston, TX 77058
Alvin Dailey, Recruiting and Placement Representative
Tel.: (713) 488-1270
Fax: (713) 335-5030

McDonnell Douglas Astronautics Company/Engineering Services
16055 Space Center Boulevard
Houston, TX 77058
Charles A. Jacobson, Vice President/General Manager
Tel.: (713) 280-1500
Fax: (713) 283-1819

Parker-Shane Manufacturing
3815 Hollister
Houston, TX 77080
Donald Swonke, Plant Manager
Tel.: (713) 690-7559
Fax: (713) 690-8441

Rockwell Space Operations Co.
600 Gemini Avenue
Houston, TX 77058
Glynn Lunney, Vice President/General Manager of Houston Operations
Tel.: (713) 282-2000
Fax: (713) 282-4084

Wyle Laboratories Applied Research Division
11001 South Wilcrest

Architecture

Houston, TX 77058
Bruce Duncan, Office Manager
Tel.: (713) 280-8566
Fax: (713) 879-6540

Architecture

For networking in **architecture** and related fields, check out the following professional organizations listed in Chapter 5:

PROFESSIONAL ORGANIZATIONS:

American Institute of Architects, Houston Chapter
American Planning Association
American Society of Interior Designers
Art League of Houston
Cultural Arts Council of Houston
Rice Design Alliance

For additional information, you can contact:

American Institute of Architects
1735 New York Avenue NW
Washington, DC 20006
Tel.: (202) 626-7300
Fax: (202) 626-7420

American Society of Landscape Architects
4401 Connecticut Avenue NW, 5th Floor
Washington, DC 20008
Tel.: (202) 686-2752

Association of Women in Architecture
7440 University Drive
St. Louis, MO 63130

National Organization of Minority Architects
1215 Connecticut Avenue NW
Washington, DC 20036

Society of American Registered Architects
1245 S. Highland Ave.
Lombard, IL 60148
Tel.: (708) 932-4622

PROFESSIONAL PUBLICATIONS:

AIA Journal
Architectural Forum
Architectural Record

How to Get a Job

Builder Insider
Building Design & Construction
Progressive Architecture
Texas Architect

DIRECTORIES:

AIA Membership Directory (American Institute of Architects, New York, NY)
Profile: Firm and Membership Directory (American Institute of Architects, Washington, DC)
Society of American Registered Architects–National Membership Directory (Society of American Registered Architects, Lombard, IL)

EMPLOYERS:

Ray Bailey Architects
P.O. Box 6508
Houston, TX 77265
Ray Bailey/Ray Leiker, Managing Principals
Tel.: (713) 524-2155
Fax: (713) 524-3947

Kenneth Balk and Associates
654 Sam Houston Parkway East, Suite 144
Houston, TX 77060-5990
Ervin Baumeyer, Vice President
Tel.: (713) 931-9920
Fax: (713) 931-8929

Brooks/Collier
3131 Eastside, Suite 100
Houston, TX 77098
Harry Harwood, Partner
Tel.: (713) 520-9990
Fax: (713) 529-5017

Building Services Associates
2626 Richmond, Suite B
Houston, TX 77098
David D. Red, Principal Officer
Tel.: (713) 529-5071
Fax: (713) 529-6877

CRS Sirrine
1177 West Loop South
Houston, TX 77027
Bruce Wilkinson, President/CEO
Tel.: (713) 552-2000
Fax: (713) 623-8051

Architecture

EDI Architecture/Planning
3731 Briarpark Drive, Suite 300
Houston, TX 77042
Victor Mirontschuk/Britten Lee Perkins/Richard Handlen, Managing Principals
Tel.: (713) 789-0395
Fax: (713) 789-7292

Falick/Klein Partnership
8 Greenway Plaza Suite 300
Houston, TX 77046-0801
James Falick FAIA, President and CEO
Tel.: (713) 621-2100
Fax: (713) 621-2178

Gensler and Associates/Architects
700 Louisiana, Suite 900
Houston, TX 77002
Richard Maxwell, Vice President, Managing Principal
Tel.: (713) 228-8050
Fax: (713) 229-9343

House Reh Associates
5847 San Felipe
Houston, TX 77057
Glenn C. House, Jr./Edward M. Reh, Jr., Managing Principals
Tel.: (713) 781-4300
Fax: (713) 781-6904

Index, The Design Firm
5701 Woodway, Suite 200
Houston, TX 77057
Doyle R. Wayman, Managing Principal
Tel.: (713) 977-2594
Fax: (713) 782-9906

Irvine Associates Architects
3 Riverway Suite 1110
Houston, TX 77056
Dennis Irvine, Managing Principal
Tel.: (713) 840-1880
Fax: (713) 840-1891

Bernard Johnson, Inc.
3000 Wilcrest Sutie 200
Houston, TX 77042
Kerri Delgado, Director of Marketing
Tel.: (713) 977-7411
Fax: (713) 977-4781

Kirksey-Meyers Architects
4299 San Felipe, Suite 300

How to Get a Job

Houston, TX 77027
John M. Kirksey, Managing Principal
Tel.: (713) 850-9600
Fax: (713) 850-7308

Llewelyn-Davies Sahni
1990 Post Oak Boulevard., Suite 1200
Houston, TX 77056
Randhir Sahni, Managing Principal
Tel.: (713) 850-1500
Fax: (713) 850-1023

Lloyd, Jones, Fillpot Associates/Architects
802 Lovett Boulevard
Houston, TX 77006
Arthur E. Jones/Bob G. Fillpot, Managing Principals
Tel.: (713) 529-3011
Fax: (713) 529-3011

Lockwood, Andrews, and Newman
1500 Citywest Boulevard, Suite 100
Houston, TX 77042
James Cole, President
Tel.: (713) 266-6900
Fax: (713) 266-2089

Milton McGinty Partnership Architects
601 Sawyer, 3rd Floor
Houston, TX 77007
J. L. Parish/John Milton McGinty, Managing Principals
Tel.: (713) 868-4878

Morris Architects
P.O. Box 22715
Houston, TX 77227
Chris Hudson, Managing Principal
Tel.: (713) 622-1180
Fax: (713) 622-7021

PB-KBB, Inc.
11757 Katy Freeway, Suite 600
Houston, TX 77079
Kermit Allen, Managing Principal
Tel.: (713) 496-5590
Fax: (713) 496-5658

PBR Architects
11 Greenway Plaza, Suite 2210
Houston, TX 77046
Daniel L. Boggio/ Calvin Powitzky, Managing Principals
Tel.: (713) 965-0608
Fax: (713) 961-4571

Architecture

Pierce, Goodwin, Alexander
5555 San Felipe Suite 1000
Houston, TX 77056
Earle S. Alexander, Jr., Managing Principal
Tel.: (713) 622-1444
Fax: (713) 968-9333

RWS Architects
3121 Buffalo Speedway, Suite 304
Houston, TX 77098
Edward R. Richardson, Managing Principal
Tel.: (713) 621-1651
Fax: (713) 621-1677

Sikes, Jennings, Kelly and Brewer
1190 Post Oak Boulevard, Suite 600
Houston, TX 77056
Richard W. Jennings, Managing Principal
Tel.: (713) 629-8600
Fax: (713) 629-0510

Spencer Herolz Architects
4201 Yoakum Road
Houston, TX 77006
J. Gordon Spencer/Robert A. Herolz, Jr., Managing Principals
Tel.: (713) 522-1666
Fax: (713) 522-6260

Tarpley/Lunow Architects
1729 Sunset Boulevard
Houston, TX 77005
Charles Tapley, Managing Principal
Tel.: (713) 522-2776
Fax: (713) 522-6747

Thompson, Nelson and Cardenal
2470 Gray Falls, Suite 150
Houston, TX 77077
Charles Thompson, Phillip E. Nelson, Managing Principals
Tel.: (713) 558-7250
Fax: (713) 558-8609

3/D International
1900 West Loop South, Suite 500
Houston, TX 77027
J. Victor Neuhaus III, Chairman
Tel.: (713) 871-7000
Fax: (713) 871-7174

Watkins, Carter, Hamilton
6575 West Loop South, Suite 300
Bellaire, TX 77401

How to Get a Job

David Watkins/Don Carter/Kirk Hamilton/Robert McKinney, Managing Principals
Tel.: (713) 665-5665
Fax: (713) 665-6213

Ziegler, Cooper
1331 Lamar Suite 1450
Houston, TX 77010
Michael Cooper/R. Scott Ziegler, Managing Principals
Tel.: (713) 654-0000
Fax: (713) 654-1841

Banks, Credit Unions, S&Ls

For networking in **banking** and related fields, check out these professional organizations listed in Chapter 5:

PROFESSIONAL ORGANIZATIONS:

American Institute of Banking
Houston Financial Council for Women
Houston Safe Deposit Association
Houston Venture Capital Association
International Association for Financial Planning, Houston Chapter

For additional information, you can contact:

American Bankers Association
1120 Connecticut Avenue NW
Washington, DC 20036
Tel.: (202) 663-5000
Fax: (202) 828-4544

Bank Marketing Association
1120 Conneticut Avenue NW
Washington, DC 20036
Tel.: (800) 433-9013

Mortgage Bankers Association of America
1125 15th Street NW
Washington, DC 20005
Tel.: (202) 861-6500
Fax: (202) 785-2967

National Association of Bank Women
500 N. Michigan Avenue
Chicago, IL 60611
Tel.: (312) 661-1700

Banking

National Bankers Association (Minority Bankers)
122 C Street NW
Washington, DC 20001
Tel.: (202) 783-3200

Savings and Community Bankers of America
111 E. Wacker Drive
Chicago, IL 60601
Tel.: (312) 644-3100

PROFESSIONAL PUBLICATIONS:

ABA Banking Journal
American Banker
American Business
Bank Marketing Magazine
Bankers Monthly
Banking Law Journal
Banking Magazine
Barron's National Business and Financial Weekly
Boardroom Reports
Business and Society Review
D & B Reports
Savings Institutions
Texas Banking
Texas Business
Texas League Savings Account

DIRECTORIES:

American Bank Directory (McFadden Business Publications, Norcross, GA)
American Banker's Guide to the First 5,000 U. S. Banks (American Banker, New York, NY)
Callahan's Credit Union Directory (Callahan and Associates, Washington, DC)
Money Market Directory (Money Market Directories, Charlottesville, VA)
Moody's Bank and Finance Manual (Moody's Investor Service, New York, NY)
Polk's World Bank Directory, North American ed., (R.L. Polk & Co., Nashville, TN)
The U.S. Savings & Loan Directory (Rand McNally, Chicago, IL)
Western Bank Directory (Western Banker Publications, Inc., San Francisco, CA)

EMPLOYERS, BANKS:

American Bank
1600 Smith
Houston, TX 77001
John Hazard, President
Tel.: (713) 951-7100
Fax: (713) 951-7172

How to Get a Job

Banc One Texas
910 Travis
Houston, TX 77002
Randy Graham, Director of Human Resource
Tel.: (713) 751-6100
Fax: (713) 751-2287

BancTexas Houston, N.A.
8820 Westheimer
Houston, TX 77063
David Weaver, President
Tel.: (713) 781-7171
Fax: (713) 954-2472

Bank of Houston
5115 South Main
Houston, TX 77002
William P. Traylor, President
Tel.: (713) 529-4881
Fax: (713) 529-9131

Bank One Houston
910 Travis
Houston, TX 77002
Randy Graham, Director of Personnel
Tel.: (713) 751-6100
Fax: (713) 751-2287

Charter Bancshares
5200 North Shepherd
Houston, TX 77091
Jill Mueller, Purchasing Officer
Tel.: (713) 692-6121
Fax: (713) 691-7568

Charter National Bank-Colonial
2301 FM 1960 W
Houston, TX 77068
Mark Giles President
Tel.: (713) 440-3100
Fax: (713) 440-4525

Charter National Bank-Houston
5200 North Shepherd
Houston, TX 77018
Richard S. Celli, President
Tel.: (713) 692-6121
Fax: (713) 691-7568

Citizens Bank & Trust Company of Baytown
1300 Rolling Brook
Baytown, TX 77521

Banking

Conrad W. Magouirk, President
Tel.: (713) 427-5771
Fax: (713) 428-8141

Cullen Center Bank & Trust
600 Jefferson
Houston, TX 77002
J. Gordon Muir, Jr., Chairman and CEO
Tel.: (713) 652-7600
Fax: (713) 652-1021

Enterprise Bank Houston
4600 Gulf Freeway
Houston, TX 77023
Howard Tellepsen, Chairman of the Board
Tel.: (713) 923-4600
Fax: (713) 967-7721

Federal Reserve Bank of Dallas, Houston Branch
1701 San Jacinto
Houston, TX 77002
Robert Smith III, Senior Vice President
Tel.: (713) 652-1548
Fax: (713) 652-1526

First City Bancorporation of Texas
1001 Main Street
Houston, TX 77002
Billy Crawley, Purchasing Officer
Tel.: (713) 658-6011
Fax: (713) 658-2340

First City Bank Gulfgate
2900 Woodridge
Houston, TX 77087
Norma Gallaway, CEO
Tel.: (713) 644-5321
Fax: (713) 644-8774

First City Bank of Highland
2900 Weslayan
Houston, TX 77027
Donna Bower, President
Tel.: (713) 627-8000
Fax: (713) 629-3499

First City National Bank of Houston
1111 Fannin
Houston, TX 77002
Mitchell Senger, Executive Vice President
Tel.: (713) 658-6011
Fax: (713) 658-4820

How to Get a Job

First Interstate Bank
1000 Louisiana
Houston, TX 77002
Linnet Dily, President
Tel.: (713) 224-6611
Fax: (713) 250-1888

First Interstate Bank of Texas, N.A.
1000 Louisiana
Houston, TX 77002
Cathy Senninger, Director of Human Resouce
Tel.: (713) 224-6611
Fax: (713) 250-1981

First Interstate Bank–Town and Country
900 Town and Country Lane
Houston, TX 77024
Kim Dees, Vice President
Tel.: (713) 464-9431
Fax: (713) 465-0946

Harrisburg Bank
1001 Broadway
Houston, TX 77012
James W. Allen III, President
Tel.: (713) 923-2801
Fax: (713) 923-1521

Lockwood National Bank of Houston
800 Lockwood Drive
Houston, TX 77020
Paul Jerry, President
Tel.: (713) 674-7661
Fax: (713) 674-1084

Med Center Bank
6631 South Main
Houston, TX 77030
Rober Garrison II, President
Tel.: (713) 790-1976
Fax: (713) 790-9706

Merchants Park Bank
999 North Shepherd Drive
Houston, TX 77008
Anita Stalzup, Cashier
Tel.: (713) 869-0351
Fax: (713) 867-7431

Nations Bank Fannin
1020 Holcomb
Houston, TX 77030

Banking

Trina Fowlkes, President and CEO
Tel.: (713) 790-1000
Fax: (713) 790-7307

Nations Bank Houston
700 Louisiana
Houston, Texas 77002
Elizabeth Rosing, Personnel Director
Tel.: (713) 247-6000
Fax: (713) 247-6152

Post Oak Bank
2200 Post Oak Boulevard
Houston, TX 77056
Joe Bailey, Manager
Tel.: (713) 966-2200
Fax: (713) 966-2292

River Oaks Bank
2001 Kirby Drive
Houston, TX 77019
Charles McMahen, Senior Chairman
Tel.: (713) 526-2211
Fax: (713) 993-8500

Riverway Bank
5 Riverway
Houston, TX 77056
Jack Mayfield, Chairman
Tel.: (713) 552-9000
Fax: (713) 552-9514

South Main Bank
3001 Main
Houston, TX 77002
Vickie Story, Cashier
Tel.: (713) 528-6111
Fax: (713) 528-2103

Sugar Creek National Bank
1 Sugar Creek Boulevard
Sugar Land, TX 77478
Jake Kamin, Chairman
Tel.: (713) 491-2265
Fax: (713) 263-8296

Team Bank
2800 Post Oak Boulevard
Transco Towers, Ground Floor
Houston, TX 77056
Mike Ballasen, Chairman and CEO

How to Get a Job

Tel.: (713) 626-3420
Fax: (713) 993-8793

Texas Commerce Bank, N.A.
712 Main Street
Houston, TX 77002
Marc J. Shapiro, Chairman and CEO
Tel.: (713) 236-4865
Fax: (713) 236-6071

University State Bank
5615 Kirby Drive
Houston, TX 77005
Charles Demny, Senior Vice President and Cashier
Tel.: (713) 526-1211
Fax: (713) 526-9727

EMPLOYERS, CREDIT UNIONS:

Cameron Employees
1000 Silber Road
Houston, TX 77255
D.L. Dorman, President
Tel.: (713) 684-0100
Fax: (713) 684-0126

Communicators Federal
3303 Main Street
Houston, TX 77002
James W. Dodd, President
Tel.: (713) 526-9284
Fax: (713) 529-1564

Educators Community
9100 Westview
Houston, TX 77055
Ron Downing, President
Tel.: (713) 465-3476
Fax: (713) 465-8742

First Educators
4605 Southwest Freeway, Suite 100
Houston, TX 77027
Gary Tuma, President
Tel.: (713) 850-1600
Fax: (713) 621-9231

Houston Police Federal
1600 Memorial Drive
Houston, TX 77007
Ayn Kleiber, President

Banking

Tel.: (713) 237-8700
Fax: (713) 236-8824

Houston Postal
6055 South Loop East
Houston, TX 77087
Samuel Dodson, President
Tel.: (713) 641-6752
Fax: (713) 641-2387

Johnson Space Center Federal
1330 Gemini Avenue
Houston, TX 77058
Becky Lanclos, Director of Personnel
Tel.: (713) 488-7070
Fax: (713) 488-0549

Shell Employees Federal Credit Union
P.O. Box 4511
Houston, TX 77210
William H. Oatis, Jr., President
Tel.: (713) 241-5562

Tenneco Credit Union
1010 Milam Suite 1003
Houston, TX 77002
Rosalie C. Kessler, Manager
Tel.: (713) 757-2733
Fax: (713) 757-2515

EMPLOYERS, SAVINGS & LOANS:

BancPlus Savings Association
3100 South Gessner Drive
Houston, TX 77063
Marie French, Office Manager
Tel.: (713) 972-1091
Fax: (713) 972-1714

Coastal Banc Savings Association
8 Greenway Plaza, Suite 1500
Houston, TX 77046
Manuel J. Mehos, Chairman
Tel.: (713) 623-2600
Fax: (713) 623-0608

First Gibraltar Bank, FSB
13401 North Freeway
Houston, TX 77060
Margaret Tate, Director of Personnel
Tel.: (713) 872-3100

How to Get a Job

Fax: (713) 872-3335
Employment Hotline: (713) 872-3104

Guardian Savings & Loan Association
1220 Augusta
Houston, TX 77057
Robert F. Parker, Chairman
Tel.: (713) 787-3100
Fax: (713) 787-3192

Heights of Texas, FSB
2700 Post Oak Boulevard
Houston, TX 77056
John Bethel, Chairman
Tel.: (713) 552-9787
Fax: (713) 552-9413

United Savings of Texas, FSB
3200 Southwest Freeway
Houston, TX 77098
Paula Shepherd, Director of Human Resources
Tel.: (713) 963-6500
Fax: (713) 965-6883

You have to work to keep banker's hours

An executive vice-president of a major national bank offers the following tricks to succeeding in banking:

"Yes, you work hard. You have to realize that banking is a sales job. A banker is essentially a salesperson in a service business. If you don't like the idea of selling a service—and sometimes being treated like a servant, which is all part of the business—then you really shouldn't be in banking. But some of the people who succeed do very well indeed."

Book and Magazine Publishers

For networking in **book publishing,** check out these professional organizations listed in Chapter 5:

PROFESSIONAL ORGANIZATIONS:

Printing Industries of the Gulf Coast

For additional information, you can contact:

American Booksellers Association
560 White Plains Road
Tarrytown, NY 10591
Tel.: (914) 631-7800

Association of American Publishers
220 East 23rd Street, 2nd Floor
New York, NY 10010
Tel.: (212) 689-8920
Fax: (212) 696-0131

PROFESSIONAL PUBLICATIONS:

American Bookseller
Editor and Publisher
Library Journal
The Professional Communicator
Publishers Weekly
Small Press
TPA Messenger

DIRECTORIES:

American Book Trade Directory (R.R. Bowker, New York, NY)
Literary Market Place (R.R. Bowker, New York, NY)
Publishers Directory (Gale Research Company, Detroit, MI)
Publishers, Distributors and Wholesalers of the United States (R.R. Bowker, New York, NY)

EMPLOYERS:

Cole Publications
10851 Scarsdale, Suite 170
Houston, TX 77089
Rodger Smalley, Regional Director
Tel.: (713) 484-4313
Fax: (713) 484-1054

Corrosion Magazine
P.O. Box 218340

How to Get a Job

Houston, TX 77218
Roula Aboudaher, Managing Editor
Tel.: (713) 492-0535
Fax: (713)

Dame Publications
7800 Bissonnet, Suite 415
Houston, TX 77074
Jan Tiefel, Personnel Director
Tel.: (713) 995-1000
Fax: (713) 995-9637

Duke Publishing
4515 Briar Hollow Place
Houston, TX 77027
Shirley Kirk, Publisher (only resumes)
Tel.: (713) 871-1500

Gulf Publishing Company
3301 Allen Parkway
Houston, TX 77019
Personnel Department
Tel.: (713) 529-4301
Fax: (713) 520-4438

Houston Business Journal
1 West Loop South, Suite 650
Houston, TX 77027
Bill Schadewald, Editor
Tel.: (713) 688-8811
Fax: (713) 963-0482

Houston Metropolitan Magazine
5615 Kirby Drive, Suite 600
Houston, TX 77005
Rose-Ann Bridgers, Manager
Tel.: (713) 524-3000
Fax: (713) 524-8213

Houston Monthly Magazine
1199 Nasa Road
Houston, TX 77058
Personnel Department
Tel.: (713) 480-6618

Informacion
4010 Bluebonnet, Suite 112
Houston, TX 77025
Emilion Sebastian, Manager
(713) 661-9994

Book/Magazine Publishers

Inner-View
P.O. Box 66156
Houston, TX 77266
Kit van Cleave, Editor
(713) 522-9333

Inside Texas Running and Fitness
9514 Bristle Brook
Houston, TX 77083
Personnel Department
Tel.: (713) 498-3208

Ocean Industry
P.O. Box 2608
Houston, TX 77252
Robert Snyder, Managing Editor
Tel.: (713) 529-4301
Fax: (713) 520-4433

Pipeline Magazine/Oildom Publishing
3314 Mercer St.
Houston, TX 77027
Oliver Klinger III, Vice President
(713) 622-0676

Rice University Press
P.O. Box 1892
Houston, TX 77251
Personnel Department
Tel.: (713) 527-6035

Tenneco Publications
203 Briarglen, # 3
Houston, TX 77027
George Lane, President
Tel.: (713) 963-9050
Fax: (713) 623-2773

TransWestern Publishing
12621 Southernwood Suite 100
Houston, TX 77035
Ita Shea, Division Manager
Tel.: (713) 861-6767
Fax: (713) 481-1002

How to Get a Job

Broadcasting

For networking in **broadcasting**, check out these professional organizations listed in Chapter 5:

Houston Association of Radio Broadcasters
Press Club of Houston
Women in Communications

For additional information, you can contact:

PROFESSIONAL ORGANIZATIONS:

American Federation of Television & Radio Artists
260 Madison Avenue
New York, NY 10016
Tel.: (212) 532-0800

Association of Independent TV Stations
1200 18th Street NW
Washington, DC 20036
Tel.: (202) 887-1970

International Radio & Television Society
420 Lexington Avenue
New York, NY 10170
Tel.: (212) 867-6650

National Academy of Television Arts & Sciences
111 W. 57th Street, Room 1020
New York, NY 10019
Tel.: (212) 586-8424

National Association of Broadcasters
1771 N Street CW
Washington, DC 20036
Tel.: (202) 429-5300

National Cable Television Association
1724 Massachusetts Avenue NW
Washington, DC 20036
Tel.: (202) 775-3550

National Radio Broadcasters
2033 M Street NW
Washington, DC 20036

Radio-Television News Directors Association
1000 Connecticut Avenue NW, Suite 615
Washington, DC 20036
Tel.: (202) 659-6510

Broadcasting

Television Information Office
745 Fifth Avenue
New York, NY 10022

Women in Cable
500 N. Michigan Avenue, #1400
Chicago, IL 60611
Tel.: (312) 661-1700

PROFESSIONAL PUBLICATIONS:

Billboard
Broadcasting Communications
Broadcasting Magazine
Cable Age
Cable Marketing
Communications News
Radio World
TV/Radio Age
Television Broadcast
Variety

DIRECTORIES:

Broadcasting Cable Source Book (Broadcasting Publishing Co., Washington, DC)
Broadcasting Yearbook (Broadcasting Publishing Co., Washington, DC)
New York Publicity Outlets (Public Relations Plus, Washington Depot, CT)
Television and Cable Fact Book (Television Digest, Washington, DC)
TV/Radio Age Ten-City Directory (TV Editorial Corp., New York, NY)
Who's Who in Television (Packard House, Beverly Hills, CA)

EMPLOYERS, TELEVISION:

KHOU-TV
Channel 11
1945 Allen Parkway
Houston, TX 77019
Allen Howard, President
Tel.: (713) 526-1111
Fax: (713) 521-4326
CBS affiliated station.

KHTV
Channel 39
7700 Westpark
Houston, TX 77063
Mike Mallernee, Productions Manager
Tel.: (713) 781-3939
Independently owned television station.

How to Get a Job

KPRC-TV
Channel 2
8181 Southwest Freeway
Houston, TX 77051
Lenora Bates, Personnel Manager
Tel.: (713) 771-4631
Fax: (713) 270-9334
NBC affiliated station.

KRIV-TV
Channel 26
3935 Westheimer
Houston, TX 77027
Teresa Adams, Personnel Manager
Tel.: (713) 626-2610
Fax: (713) 623-2982
A Fox television station.

KTRK-TV
Channel 13
3310 Bissonnet
Houston, TX 77005
John Jancar, Personnel Manager
Tel.: (713) 666-0713
Fax: (713) 666-0013
ABC affiliated station.

KTXH-TV
Channel 20
8950 Kirby Drive
Houston, TX 77054
Walter Narr, Productions Manager
Tel.: (713) 661-2020
Fax: (713) 665-3909
Independently owned television station.

KUHT-TV
Channel 8
4513 Cullen Boulevard
Houston, TX 77004
Flor Garcia, Personnel Manager
Tel.: (713) 748-8888
Fax: (713) 749-8216
Houston public broadcasting station.

KXLN-TV
Channel 45
9440 Kirby Drive
Houston, TX 77054
J.A. Trevinl, President
Tel.: (713) 662-4545

Broadcasting

Fax: (713) 668-9054
Pueblo Broadcasting Corporation.

EMPLOYERS, CABLE:

Cable Communications Network
16800 Imperial Valley Drive
Houston, TX 77060
George Gaddie, General Manager
Tel.: (713) 931-6992
Fax: (713) 931-4306

Community Cable Company
13312 Redfish
Houston, TX 77477
Jimmy Newton, Owner
Tel.: (713) 780-4806
Fax: (713) 499-3431

Prime Cable of Harris County
13700 Veterans Memorial Dr.
Houston, TX 77014
Mike Davidson, Personnel Manager
(713) 537-2900

Prime Time Cable
2200 Central Parkway
Houston, TX 77092
Lydia Martin, General Manager
(713) 681-6591

Warner Cable Company
8400 West Tidwell Road
Houston, TX 77040
Pat Berry, Personnel Manager
Tel.: (713) 462-1900
Fax: (713) 668-9054

EMPLOYERS, RADIO:

KACC
Alvin Community College Radio Station
3110 Mustang Rd.
Houston, TX 77511
Cathy Forsythe, General Manage

KIKK AM/FM Radio Station
6306 Gulfton
Houston, TX 77081
Craig Magee, General Manager
Tel.: (713) 772-4433
Fax: (713) 995-7956

How to Get a Job

KILT AM/FM Radio Station
500 Lovett
Houston, TX 77006
Dickie Rosenfeld, General Manager
Tel.: (713) 526-3461
Fax: (713) 526-5458

KKBQ Radio
11 Greenway Plaza
Houston, TX 77046
Don Troutt, General Manager
Tel.: (713) 961-0093
Fax: (713) 963-1293

KLAT Radio La Tremenda
1415 North Loop West
Houston, TX 77006
Gary Stone, General Manager
Tel.: (713) 868-4344
Fax: (713) 868-5947

KMJQ Majic 102 FM
24 East Greenway Plaza
Houston, TX 77046
Monty Lane, General Manager
Tel.: (713) 623-0102
Fax: (713) 622-7369

KODA 99 FM
4810 San Felipe
Houston, TX 77056
Michael Black, Vice President
Tel.: (713) 622-1010
Fax: (713) 622-7369

KPRC Radio
8181 Southwest Freeway
Houston, TX 77051
Tel.: (713) 771-4631

KRBE AM FM
9801 Westheimer
Houston, TX 77042
Nancy Vaeth, General Manager
Tel.: (713) 266-1000
Fax: (713) 954-2344

KTRU Radio
Ley Student Center, 2nd Floor
6100 South Main
Houston, TX 77005
Heidi Bullinga, Director

Tel.: (713) 527-4098
Fax: (713) 527-4093

KUHF
Public Radio Station
3801 Cullen
Houston, TX 77204-0461
John Proffitt, General Manager
Tel.: (713) 743-1806
Fax: (713) 743-1818

Chemicals

For networking in the chemical industry, check out these professional organizations listed in Chapter 5:

PROFESSIONAL ORGANIZATIONS:

Houston Engineering and Scientific Society
Society of Petroleum Engineers

For additional information, you can contact:

American Chemical Society
1155 16th Street NW
Washington, DC 20036
Tel.: (202) 872-4600
Fax: (202) 872-4615

PROFESSIONAL PUBLICATIONS:

Chemical Engineering News
Chemical Marketing Reporter
Chemical Week
Hydrocarbon Processing

DIRECTORIES:

Chem sources—USA (Directories Publishing Company, Ormond Beach, FL)
Chemical & Engineering News—Facts and Figures Issue (American Chemical Society, Washington, DC)
Chemical Industry Directory (Benn Business Information Services Ltd, Tonbridge, Kent, England)
Chemical Industry Yearbook (Chemical Data Services, Sutton, Surrey, England)
Chemical Week—Buyers Guide Issue (McGraw-Hill, New York, NY)

How to Get a Job

Chemical Week—Financial Survey of the 300 largest companies in the U.S. (McGraw-Hill, New York, NY)

Chemicals Directory (American Business Directories, Division American Busisness Lists, Omaha, NE)

EMPLOYERS:

Air Products Manufacturing
1423 Highway 225
Pasadena, TX 77506
Brad Chandler, General Manager
Tel.: (713) 477-6841
Fax: (713) 920-7301

Akzo Chemicals
13000 Baypark Road
Pasadena, TX 77507
Burthold Rodson, Vice President
Tel.: (713) 474-2864

Cain Chemical
5 Greenway Plaza, Suite 2600
Houston, TX 77046
David Mayeux, Personnel
Tel.: (713) 623-7659

Celanese Chemical Company
9502 Bayport Road
Pasadena, TX 77507
Marion A. John, Plant Manager
Tel.: (713) 474-6200
Fax: (713) 474-8095

Dow Chemical, USA
600 Battleground Road
La Porte, TX 77571
H.G. Newton, Site Manager
Tel.: (713) 471-6191
Employment: (713) 978-3300

E.I. DuPont de Nemours
12501 Strang Road
La Porte, TX 77572
Mal Veaux, Plant Manager
Tel.: (713) 471-2771

Ethyl Corporation-Houston Plant
1000 North South Street
Pasadena, TX 77503
Mark Graham, Purchasing Manager
Tel.: (713) 740-1000
Fax: (713) 740-1763

Chemicals

Exxon Chemical Americas
13501 Katy Freeway
Houston, TX 77079
Kent Robertson, President
Tel.: (713) 870-6000
Fax: (713) 870-6661

FMC Corporation Specialty Chemical Division
12000 Bay Area Boulevard
Pasadena, TX 77507
Clinton Hopkins, Resident Manager
Tel.: (713) 474-8705
Fax: (713) 474-8736

W.R. Grace and Company
739 Battleground Road
Deer Park, TX 77536
P.E. Hodskins, Purchasing/Traffic Manager
Tel.: (713) 479-9525
Fax: (713) 479-3608

Hoechst Celanese Corp.
12212 Port Road
Pasadena, TX 77507
John Barth, Director of Personnel
Tel.: (713) 474-6000
Fax: (713) 474-1386

ICI Americas
5757 Underwood Road
Pasadena, TX 77507
Sid Stevens, Director of Personnel
Tel.: (713) 474-5151
Fax: (713) 474-5625

Interox America
3333 Richmond Avenue
Houston, TX 77098
Rene Degrev, Executive Vice President
Tel.: (713) 522-4155
Fax: (713) 524-9032

The Lubrizol Corporation
12801 Bay Area Boulevard
Pasadena, TX 77507
Martin McNeil, Purchasing Manager
Tel.: (713) 479-2851

Lyondell Petrochemical Company
1221 McKinney Suite 1600
Houston, TX 77010
William E. Haynes, Senior Vice President

How to Get a Job

Tel.: (713) 652-7200
Fax: (713) 652-4563(Personnel)

Miles, Inc. (formerly Mobay Synthetics Corporation)
8701 Park Place Boulevard
Houston, TX 77017
Susan Howard, Commercial Services Manager
Tel.: (713) 477-8821
Fax: (713) 477-5666

Nalco Chemical Company
7701 Highway 90-A
Sugar Land, TX 77478
Peter H. Vossos, Regional Purchasing Manager
Tel.: (713) 491-4500
Fax: (713) 263-7849(Personnel)

Pennwalt Corp.
2231 Haden Road
Houston, TX 77015
W.R. Crabtree, Personnel Department
Tel.: (713) 455-1211
Fax: (713) 450-6773

Rohm and Haas of Bayport
13300 Bay Area Boulevard
La Porte, TX 77571
Karen Murphy, Plant Manager
Tel.: (713) 474-4495
Fax: (713) 474-8580

Rohm and Haas of Texas
Highway 225
Deer Park, TX 77536
Jim Waite, Purchasing Officer
Tel.: (713) 476-8100

Texaco Chemical Company
Jefferson Chemical Road
Conroe, TX 77301
B.J. Wells, Purchasing Agent
Tel.: (409) 756-3381

Texas Alkyls
730 Battleground Road
La Porte, TX 77571
C.B. Johnson, Purchasing Agent
Tel.: (713) 479-8411
Fax: (713) 479-7556

Texas Petrochemicals Corp.
8600 Park Place Boulevard

Computers: Equipment

Houston, TX 77017
T.B. Harris, Purchasing Officer
Tel.: (713) 477-9211
Fax: (713) 475-7791

Vista Chemical Company
900 Threadneedle
Houston, TX 77079
Bob Dale, Vice President of Employee Relations
Tel.: (713) 558-3000
Fax: (713) 558-3107

Computers/Equipment Manufacturers

For networking in the **computer industry,** check out this professional organization listed in Chapter 5:

PROFESSIONAL ORGANIZATIONS:

For additional information, you can contact:

ADAPSO–Computer Software and Services Association
1616 N. Ft. Myers
Arlington, VA 22209
Tel.: (703) 522-5055

American Software Users Group
401 North Michigan Avenue
Chicago 60611
Tel.: (312) 644-6610
Fax: (312) 321-6869

Association for Computer Professionals
230 Park Avenue, #460
New York, NY 10169
Tel.: (212) 599-3019

Data Processing Management Association
505 Busse Highway
Park Ridge, IL 60068
Tel.: (708) 825-8124
Fax: (708) 825-1693

IEEE Computer Society
1730 Massachusetts Avenue NW
Washington, DC 20036
Tel.: (202) 371-0101

Independent Computer Consultants Association
933 Gardenview Office Parkway

How to Get a Job

St. Louis, MO 63141
Tel.: (314) 997-4633
Fax: (314) 567-5133

Institute for Certification of Computer Professionals
2200 E. Devon Ave., Suite 268
Des Plaines, IL 60018-4501
Tel.: (708) 299-4227
Fax: (708) 299-4280

National Computer Association
1485 E. Fremont Circle, South
Littleton, CO 80122
Tel.: (303) 797-3559
Fax: (303) 797-3574

Women in Information Processing
Box 39173
Washington, DC 20016
Tel.: (202) 328-6161

PROFESSIONAL PUBLICATIONS:

Byte
Computer Street Journal
ComputerWorld
Data Communicaitons
Datamation
Electronic Business
Electronic News
Information and Word Processing Report
Microtimes
MIS News
PC Week
PC World
Personal Computing

DIRECTORIES:

Computer Lisitng Service's Machinery & Equipment Guide (Wineburg Publications, Skokie, IL)
Computer Peripherals Review (GML Information Services, Lexington, MA)
Computer Review (GML Information Services, Lexington, MA)
Data Processing Equipment Directory (American Business Directories, Omaha, NE)
Data Processing Services Directory (American Business Directories, Omaha, NE)
Data Sources: Hardware and Software Directories (Ziff-Davis, New York, NY)
Design News Electronic Directory (Cahners Publishing Co., Boston, MA)
Directory of Computer Software and Services Companies (ADAPSO, Arlington, VA)
Engineering, Science and Computer Jobs (Peterson's Guides, Princeton, NJ)

Computers: Equipment

ICP Software Directory (International Computer Programs, Indianapolis, IN)
Who's Who in Electronics (Harris Publishing Co., Twinsburg, OH)
Yearbook/Directory (Semiconductor Industry Association, San Jose, CA)

EMPLOYERS:

AMI Systems Division
9000 Southwest Freeway, Suite 400
Houston, TX 77074
Naoma Peterson, Office Manager
Tel.: (713) 777-0106
Fax: (713) 777-1780

Accudata Systems
13700 Veterans Memorial, Suite 280
Houston, TX 77014
Rich Johnson, Owner
Tel.: (713) 440-7220
Fax: (713) 440-4211

Autocad Systems-Cadsys
8830 Interchange
Houston, TX 77054
Jennifer Sheffield, Sales Manager
Tel.: (713) 669-0700
Fax: (713) 668-5514

Bull HN Information Systems
6611 Portwest
Houston, TX 77024
Tom Philippy, District Manager
Tel.: (713) 865-9500
Fax: (713) 865-9563

Community Health Computing
5 Greenway Plaza, Suite 2000
Houston, TX 77046
A. Robinson, Director of Employment
Tel.: (713) 960-1907
Fax: (713) 840-3301

Compaq Computer Corp.
20555 HWY 249
Houston, TX 77070
Eckhard Pfeiffer, President and CEO
Tel.: (713) 370-0670
Fax: (713) 374-1740

Computerland
1400 Post Oak Boulevard
Houston, TX 77056

How to Get a Job

David Wright, Operations Manager
Tel.: (713) 964-4700
Fax: (713) 877-8435

Data General
1900 West Loop South, Suite 1400
Houston, TX 77027
David Stokes, Manager
Tel.: (713) 296-7800
Fax: (713) 296-7829
Send resumes to Human Resources at:
4400 Computer Drive, Westboro, MA 01580
12801 Stemens Freeway, Suite 700, Dallas, TX 75234

Digital Equipment Corp.
2500 City West Boulevard, Suite 1000
Houston, TX 77042
Cathy Brook, Human Resources
Tel.: (713) 953-3500
Fax: (713) 953-3913 (Human Resources)

Heath-Zenith Computers and Electronics
6950 Portwest
Houston, TX 77024
John Averitt, Business Center Manager
Tel.: (800) 777-9108

Hewlett Packard Company
2000 West Loop South
Houston, TX 77027
Jeanie Lambert, Personnel Liason
Tel.: (713) 439-5300
Fax: (713) 439-5495

IBM Federal Systems Division
3700 Bay Area Boulevard
Houston, TX 77058
Anthony J. Macina, General Manager
Tel.: (713) 282-2300
Fax: (713) 282-7183 (Personnel)

Jones Business Systems
6120 West by Northwest Boulevard
Houston, TX 77040
Juanita Kline, Human Resources
Tel.: (713) 895-0600
Fax: (713) 895-93333

MicroMeans, Inc.
5512 Mitchelldale
Houston, TX 77092
Jean Bradshaw, Director of Personnel

Computers: Equipment

Tel.: (713) 688-7888
Fax: (713) 688-5816

NEC Technologies
1225 North Loop West
Houston, TX 77022
Debra Springstone
Tel.: (713) 862-5330
Fax: (713) 862-2170

Network Support Corp.
3701 Kirby Drive, Suite 1110
Houston, TX 77098
Ben McGuire, President
Tel.: (713) 521-1211
Fax: (713) 521-2553

Prime Computer
3200 Wilcrest Drive Suite 100
Houston, TX 77042
Charle Surginery, Manager of Customer Service
Tel.: (713) 974-2691
Fax: (713) 974-0037

Sun Microsystems
12 Greenway Plaza, Suite 1500
Houston, TX 77046
Jack Herzog, District Manager
Tel.: (713) 622-0072
Fax: (713) 622-4694

Telxon
7280 Wynnwood, Suite 220
Houston, TX 77008
Peggy Hall, Director of Personnel
Tel.: (713) 868-5511
Fax: (713) 863-8572

Unisys Corp.
13430 Northwest Freeway
Houston, TX 77040
Joe Moye, General Manager
Tel.: (713) 744-2666
Fax: (713) 744-2586

Wang Laboratories
12 East Greenway Plaza
Houston, TX 77046
Tel.: (713) 965-9925
Fax: (713) 968-7823

How to Get a Job

Send resumes to:
Wang Laboratories
1420 East Rochelle, Suite 200
Irving, TX 75039
Chris Ferguson, Director of Human Resources
Tel.: (214) 432-2300
Fax: (214) 869-0764

Booting up big $$$ in computer sales

Phyllis Daniels competes in the fast lane of a man's world as a computer sales engineer. Her clients are Fortune 500 companies, and her products are communications boards, controllers, and disk and tape subsystems manufactured by a relatively new specialty company.

"It's an emotionally and physically stressful environment, where I constantly have to prove myself," says Phyllis, one of 7 women in a sales force of 60. We asked how she got there and what keeps her successful.

"I use every skill and all the experience I've ever had," said the former teacher and editorial assistant for a steel company's community relations department. "When I decided to go back to school for an associate's degree in computers, I needed a job as well. So I sold cars, and that provided invaluable marketing and people experience, plus communications skills that are absolutely essential in my present business.

"Once I got into computer courses, I realized I couldn't settle for a $20,000 programming job and began laying more plans. And, incidentally, you must prepare yourself for the entry positions in this field. My first job—strictly commission— was with a small systems house, and within a year I was director of marketing with a sales staff of six. I got a total overview of the business so that I could talk from that perspective on my next round of interviews.

"I used a personnel agent who specializes in computer sales to get this position and was very specific with him about my requirements."

Asked to explain her current success, Phyllis responds: "I'd have to say the number one factor is technical expertise—with sales ability second. I read, listen, and pick brains to stay on top of the product and a changing marketplace so that my clients feel that my company has provided a service by sending me. By the way, with little more education than a $20,000 programmer, I'll make at least twice that this year. And the perks are great, too."■

Computers/Programming and Software

(See professional organizations, publications, and directories under "Computers/Equipment Manufacturers.")

EMPLOYERS:

Acad-Plus
9601 Jones Road, Suite 250
Houston, TX 77065
Glenn Seehausen, President
Tel.: (713) 890-3300
Fax: (713) 890-3332

Advanced Computer Services
South Kirkwood Suite 220
Houston, TX 77477
Carl Looney, Manager of Operations
Tel.: (713) 240-2233
Fax: (713) 240-6915

Advanced Image Measurement Systems
3333 West Alabama, Suite 103
Houston, TX 77098
George Batten, President
Tel.: (713) 529-5520

Advantage Data Services
7171 Harwin
Houston, TX 77036
Dennis Herman, Vice President of Sales
Tel.: (713) 784-8494

Advantage Engineering
2141 West Governors Circle, Suite B
Houston, TX 77092
Mike Freeman, Engineering Manager
Tel.: (713) 688-6030
Fax: (713) 680-9825

American Business Networking
14655 Northwest Freeway, Suite 125
Houston, TX 77074
Leone Shaffer, President
Tel.: (713) 895-8877
Fax: (713) 895-8643

Berwick and Associates
6717 Bissonet
Houston, TX 77074
Dick Hiandman, General Manager
Tel.: (713) 779-9663

How to Get a Job

Business Data Center Corporation
P.O. Box 218973
Houston, TX 77218-8973
Baxter Gentry
Tel.: (713) 467-0130

Centennial Computer Systems
8582 Katy Freeway, Suite 100
Houston, TX 77024
Eulalia Nichols, Office Manager
Tel.: (713) 464-8300
Fax: (713) 464-1576

Cimarron Software Services
1830 Nasa Road One
Houston, TX 77058
Edith Hart, Personnel Director
Tel.: (713) 335-5800
Fax: (713) 355-5890

The Coade Engineering Physics Software
12777 Jones Road
Houston, TX 77070
Rex Evans, Owner
Tel.: (713) 890-4566
Fax: (713) 890-3301

Compu-data
417 Columbia
Houston, TX 77007
Wayne Tollett, President
Tel.: (713) 528-2514
Fax: (713) 868-4750

Computer Access Associates
2000 North Loop West, Suite 215
Houston, TX 77018
W. C. Windmeyer, Owner
Tel.: (713) 956-7055
Fax: (713) 956-5314

Computer Systems and Applications
7915 FM 1960 West, Suite 300
Houston, TX 77070
Cliff Taylor, Director of Recruiting
Tel.: (713) 955-1272
Fax: (713) 955-1277

Data Corp.
3200 Southwest Freeway
Houston, TX 77027
Pete Kowalik, Principal

Computers: Software

Tel.: (713) 961-3999
Fax: (713) 961-4438

Henden Computer Management
9301 Southwest Freeway, Suite 625
Houston, TX 77074
Pat Henden, President
Tel.: (713) 988-7127
Fax: (713) 988-7129

Micro Horizons
520 Post Oak Blvd., Suite 520
Houston, TX 77027
William H. Latimer, President
Tel.: (713) 439-7410
Fax: (713) 439-1547

Miramar Computer Consulting
1925 Southwest Freeway, Suite 218
Houston, TX 77098
Paul Goodenough, President
Tel.: (713) 520-5709
Fax: (713) 524-0403

RCL Consulting
4411 Bluebonnet, Suite 108
Stafford, TX 77477
Royce Landman, Owner
Tel.: (713) 240-2777
Fax: (713) 240-0043

Specialty Control Systems
211 E. Parkwood, Suite 109
Houston, TX 77546
Jay Armstrong, President
Tel.: (713) 482-7386
Fax: (713) 482-7847

Synercom Technology
2500 City West Blvd., Suite 1100
Houston, TX 77042
Steve Chutik, Vice President of Human Resources
Tel.: (713) 954-7000
Fax: (713) 785-0880

Systems Application Engineering
3655 Westcenter Dr.
Houston, TX 77042
Debbie Kobas, Manager
Tel.: (713) 783-6020
Fax: (713) 783-3434

How to Get a Job

Texas Electronic Resources
10861 Rockley Rd.
Houston, TX 77099
Al Majek, President
Tel.: (713) 568-5274
Fax: (713) 568-5280

Uni-Komp
7000 Northwest 100, Suite B102
Houston, TX 77092
June Parker, Manager
Tel.: (713) 895-9900
Fax: (713) 895-9914

Unisage, Inc.
9990 Richmond, Suite 105
Houston, TX 77042
Jody Plessala, Payroll Supervisor
Tel.: (713) 266-1405
Fax: (713) 268-7550

Universal Computer Systems
6700 Hollister
Houston, TX 77040
R.T. Brockman, Principal Officer
Tel.: (713) 939-0088
Fax: (713) 744-4501

Vertical Software
3815 Dacoma
Houston, TX 77092
Bob Gemignani, President
Tel.: (713) 680-1993
Fax: (713) 680-9146

Construction

For networking in the **construction industry,** check out these professional organizations listed in Chapter 5:

PROFESSIONAL ORGANIZATIONS:

Associated Builders and Contractors of Greater Houston
Associated General Contractors of America
Drywall and Interior Systems Contractors Association
Greater Houston Builders Association
Houston Business Roundtable
Houston Contractors Association
Independent Electrical Contractors of Houston
Mechanical Contractors Association of Houston
National Electrical Contractors Association

For additional information, you can contact:

Associated General Contractors of America
1957 E Street NW
Washington, DC 20006
Tel.: (202) 393-2040

Construction Industry Manufacturers Association
111 East Wisconsin Avenue, Suite 940
Milwaukee, WI 53202
Tel.: (414) 272-0943

National Association of Home Builders
1201 15th Street NW
Washington, DC 20005
Tel.: (202) 822-0200
Fax: (202) 822-0559

National Association of Minority Contractors
1333 F Street NW, #500
Washington, DC 20004
Tel.: (202) 347-8259

National Association of Women in Construction
327 Adams Street
Fort Worth, TX 76104
Tel.: (817) 877-5551

National Constructor's Association
1730 M Street NW Suite 900
Washington, DC 20036
Tel.: (202) 466-8880
Fax.: (202) 466-7512

How to Get a Job

PROFESSIONAL PUBLICATIONS:

Associated Construction Publications
Builder
Building Design & Construction
Construction Review
Constructor
Engineering News-Record
Pit and Quarry
The Texas Builder
Texas Contractor
Texas Realtor

DIRECTORIES:

Associated Builders & Contractors Membership Directory (Associated Builders & Contractors, Washington, DC)
Blue Book of Major Homebuilders (CMR Associates, Crofton, MD)
Construction Equipment—Construction's Equipment-Owning Giants Issue (Cahners Publishing Company, Des Plaines, IL)
Construction News—Associations Directory Issue (Construction News, Little Rock, AR)
Construction Review—Directory of National Trade Associations, Professional Associations, Professional Societies of the Construction Industries Issue (Construction and Building Products Division, Washington, DC)
Constructor —Directory Issue (Associated General Contractors of America, Washington, DC)
Directory of Construction Associations (Metadata, Inc., New York, NY)
ENR Directory of Contractors (McGraw-Hill, New York, NY)
Guide to Information Sources in the Construction Industry (Construction Products Manufacturers Council, Arlington, VA)

EMPLOYERS:

Basic Constructors
5327 Allen St.
Houston, TX 77007
Edward S. Baxter, President
Tel.: (713) 869-6575
Fax: (713) 869-4733

Becon Construction Company
3000 Post Oak Blvd.
Houston, TX 77056
Cliff Mumm, President
Tel.: (713) 235-1600
Fax: (713) 235-1699

W.S. Bellows Construction Corp.
7272 Pinemont Dr., Suite 200
Houston, TX 77040

Construction

W.S.Bellows, Jr., Chairman of the Board
Tel.: (713) 462-7272
Fax: (713) 690-1229

Belmont Constructors
2400 West Loop South, Suite 550
Houston, TX 77027
John Dillon, Purchasing Officer
Tel.: (713) 621-3223
Fax: (713) 621-1822

Brown and Root
4100 Clinton Dr.
Houston, TX 77020
D.H. Dodd, Vice President
Tel.: (713) 676-3011
Fax: (713) 676-4109

Commercial Drywall
3539 Oak Forest Dr.
Houston, TX 77018
Stan Marek, President
Tel.: (713) 681-9287
Fax: (713) 681-4614

DeJean Construction Company
3602 3rd Ave. North
Texas City, TX 77034
George Pinto , President
Tel.: (713) 486-6576
Fax: (409) 948-3510

Force Corp.
1300 W. Adams
Houston, TX 77571
Sonya Mills, Purchasing Officer
Tel.: (713) 470-0550
Fax: (713) 471-9627

Recruiting Office:
100 W. Main, Suite D
Houston, TX 77571
Jan Page, Personnel Director
Tel.: (713) 471-3144
Fax: (713) 471-1710

Hassell Construction Company
12211 Duncan
Houston, TX 77066
Jim Hassell, President
Tel.: (713) 893-2570
Fax: (713) 580-9170

How to Get a Job

Jalco, Inc.
5148 Lotus St.
Houston, TX 77045
Mr. Lorraine George, President
Tel.: (713) 728-8480
Fax: (713) 729-6553

Linbeck Construction Corp.
3810 W. Alabama
Houston, TX 77027
Leo Linbeck, Jr., Chairman and CEO
Tel.: (713) 621-2350
Fax: (713) 840-7525

Marek Brothers Systems
3539 Oak Forest Dr.
Houston, TX 77018
John Tant, Purchasing Officer
Tel.: (713) 681-2626
Fax: (713) 681-6540

Mundy Companies
11150 S. Wilcrest, Suite 300
Houston, TX 77099
Joe S. Mundy, Chief Operating Officer
Tel.: (713) 530-8711
Fax: (713) 530-8561

E.E. Reed Construction Company
11001 S. Wilcrest, Suite 130
Houston, TX 77009
Kent Rosenberger, Vice President
Tel.: (713) 933-4000
Fax: (713) 933-4852

SAE/Spaw-Glass Construction
13430 Northwest Fwy, Suite 400
Houston, TX 77040
Cecil O. Windsor, President/CEO
Tel.: (713) 895-0505
Fax: (713) 895-7591

Safety Lights Company
6813 Dixie Dr.
Houston, TX 77087
Wayne Hardin, Personnel Director
Tel.: (713) 644-7379
Fax: (713) 644-2649

Safeway Scaffolds Company of Houston
1617 Enid
Houston, TX 77009

Construction

Vicki Land, Purchasing Manager
Tel.: (713) 869-3491
Fax: (713) 869-6541 or (713) 869-3965

South Coast Drywall
1313 Herkimer
Houston, TX 77008
David K. Milam, Sr., President
Tel.: (713) 869-0818
Fax: (713) 869-9528

Tribble & Stephens Company
10610 Haddington Dr.
Houston, TX 77043
Jay Tribble, Chairman
Tel.: (713) 465-8550
Fax: (713) 973-7107

Westheimer Rigging and Heavy Hauling
7001 Easthaven
Houston, TX 77017
Daniel V. McRay, Chairman and CEO
Tel.: (713) 926-4451
Fax: (713) 946-1575

William Brothers Construction Company
3800 Milam
Houston, TX 77006
James D. Pitcock, Jr., President and CEO
Tel.: (713) 522-9821
Fax: (713) 520-5247

Drugs and Pharmaceuticals

For additional information, you can contact:

PROFESSIONAL ORGANIZATIONS:

American Pharmaceutical Association
2215 Constitution Avenue, NW
Washington, DC, 20037
Tel.: (202) 628-4410
Fax: (202) 783-2351

Drug Chemical and Allied Trades Association
2 Roosevelt Avenue
Syosset, NY 11791
Tel.: (516) 496-3317
Fax: (516) 496-2231

National Association of Chain Drugstores
413 North Lee Street
Alexandria, VA 22314
Tel.: (703) 549-3001
Fax: (703) 836-4869

National Association of Retail Druggists
205 Dangerfield Road
Alexandria, VA 22314
Tel.: (703) 683-8200
Fax: (703) 683-3619

Pharmaceutical Manufacturers Association
1100 15th Street NW, Suite 900
Washington, DC 20005
Tel.: (202) 835-3400

PROFESSIONAL PUBLICATIONS:

American Druggist
Cosmetic World
Drug Store News
Drug Topics
Soap/Cosmetics/Chemical Specialties
Texas Pharmacy

DIRECTORIES:

Biotechnology Directory (The Nature Press, New York, NY)
Drug Topics Red Book (Litton Publications, Oradell, NJ)
NACDS Membership Directory (National Association of Chain Drugstores, Arlington, VA)

Drugs/Pharmaceuticals

Pharmaceutical Directory (American Pharmaceutical Association, Washington DC)
Pharmaceutical Manufacturers of the U.S. (Noyes Data Corp., Park Ridge, NJ)

EMPLOYERS:

Bergen Brunswig Corp.
1440 N. Post Oak Rd.
Houston, TX 77055
Troy Jordan, Manager
Tel.: (713) 682-8200
Fax: (713) 682-6946

Bio-Medical Pharmaceutical Manufacturing Corp.
4902 Glenmont
Houston, TX 77081
Tom Loesch, Ph.D., Vice President
Tel.: (713) 668-3081

Braescroft Pharmacy
9730 Hillcroft
Houston, TX 77096
Philip Abramson, Owner
Tel.: (713) 729-1033
Fax: (713) 729-7857

Cynacon
P.O. Box 429
Houston, TX 77469
Rosemary Martinez, Operations Manager
Tel.: (713) 342-3350
Fax: (713) 232-6015
Street Address: 311 Avenue N., Rosenberg, TX 77471

Jack Eckerd Corp.
2061 I-45
Conroe, TX 77385
Phil Paustian, Human Resources Manager
Tel.: (409) 273-1141
Fax: (713) 364-2866

Health Care Supplies
1224 N. Post Oak Road
Houston, TX 77055
Diane Hunt, Manager
Tel.: (713) 682-5515

Matrix Technologies
1000 Louisiana, Suite 600
Houston, TX 77002
Gary Bell, Vice President of Management

How to Get a Job

Michael Trachtenberg, Vice President of Research and Development
Tel.: (713) 655-7867
Fax: (713) 951-0150

Narco Bio-Systems
P.O. Box 143449
Austin, TX 78714-3449
Peggy Edward, Personnel Director
Tel.: (800) 433-5615
Fax: (512) 873-9090

Owen Company Hospital/Pharmacies Management
9800 Centre Parkway, Suite 1100
Houston, TX 77036
Tom Smith, Personnel Director
Tel.: (713) 777-8173
Fax: (713) 777-5417
Alternate Address: P.O. Box 742587, Houston, TX 77274-2587

Spectrum Consumer Products Company
1 Riverway, Suite 1700
Houston, TX 77056
Mark Wilson, President
Tel.: (713) 621-0381
Fax: (713) 622-1937

Summa Rx Laboratories
2525 Ridgmar Blvd.
Fort Worth, TX 76116
Jerry Nelson, President
Tel.: (800) 527-7319
Fax: (817) 325-0807

Educational Institutions

For networking in **education**, check out these professional organizations listed in Chapter 5:

PROFESSIONAL ORGANIZATIONS:

American Association of University Women
Houston Association of School Administrators
Houston Teachers Association
Institute of Hispanic Culture
Institute of International Education

For additional information, you can contact:

American Association of School Administrators
1801 North Moore Streeta
Arlington, VA 22209
Tel.: (703) 528-0700
Fax: (703) 841-1543

American Association of University Women
1111 16th Street NW
Washington, DC 20036
Tel.: (202) 785-7700
Fax: (202) 872-1425

Association of Independent Colleges and Universities
1 DuPont Circle NW Suite 350
Washington, DC 20036
Tel.: (202) 659-2460
Fax: (202) 659-2254

Association of School Business Officials International
1760 Reston Avenue
Reston, VA 22090
Tel.: (703) 478-0405
Fax: (703) 478-0205

National Association of College and University Business Officials
1 DuPont Circle, Suite 500
Washington, DC 20036
Tel.: (202) 861-2500
Fax: (202) 861-2583

National Education Association
1201 16th Street, NW
Washington, DC 20036
Tel.: (202) 833-4000
Fax: (202) 822-7292

How to Get a Job

PROFESSIONAL PUBLICATIONS:

The Chronicle of Higher Education
Education Week
Instructor
School Administrator
Teaching Exceptional Children
Teaching Pre-K-8
Technology and Learning
Today's Catholic Teacher
TSTA Advocate

DIRECTORIES:

Association for School, College and University Staffing—Directory of Membership (Association for School, College and University Staffing, Madison, WI)
Current Openings in Education in U.S.A. (Education Information Service, Newton, MA)
College Placement Annual (College Placement Annual, Bethlehem, PA)
Directory of Educational Asociations (Marquis Publishing Co., Chicago, IL)
Guide to Secondary Schools (College Board, New York, NY)
Peterson's Guide to Independent Secondary Schools (Peterson's Guides, Princeton, NJ)
QED's School Guide (Quality Education Data, Denver, CO)
Texas Higher Education Directory (Association of Texas Colleges and Universities, Arlington, TX)
Texas School Directory (Texas Education Agency, Austin, TX)
There Ought to Be Free Choice (National Coalition of Alternative Community Schools, Glenmoore, PA)
Yearbook of Higher Education (Marquis Publishing Co., Chicago, IL)

COLLEGE AND UNIVERSITY EMPLOYERS:

Alvin Community College
Administrative Office, 3110 Mustang Rd.
Alvin, TX 77511
Lang Windsor, Director of Personnel
Tel.: (713) 331-6111
Fax: (713) 388-4895

Baylor College of Medicine
1 Baylor Plaza, Rm. T-101
Houston, TX 77030
Sherry Williams, Manager of Personnel Services
Tel.: (713) 798-4815

Houston Baptist University
7502 Fondren Rd.
Houston, TX 77074
Don Looser, Vice President

Educational Institutions

Tel.: (713) 774-7661
Fax: (713) 995-3489

Houston Community College System
Leeland Center
2720 Leeland
Houston, TX 77003
Judy Jones, Employment Manager
Tel.: (713) 237-1040
Fax: (713) 864-0471

North Harris Montgomery Community College
Administrative Offices and North Belt Center
250 North Belt East
Houston, TX 77060
Dr. John Pickelman, Manager
Tel.: (713) 591-3500
Fax: (713) 591-3513

Rice University
6100 S. Main
Houston, TX 77005
Caroline Garcia, Director of Human Resources
Tel.: (713) 527-8101
Fax: (713) 285-5100

Texas A & M University at Galveston
P.O. Box 1675
Galveston, TX 77553
Marie Davenport, Personnel Director
Tel.: (409) 740-4428
Fax: (409) 740-4407

Texas Southern University
3100 Cleburne
Houston, TX 77004
Dr. Deanna Burrell, Vice President of Student Affairs
Tel.: (713) 527-7011
Fax: (713) 527-7840

Texas Woman's University
1130 M.D. Anderson Blvd.
Houston, TX 77030
Dr. Kathryn Stream, Executive Director
Tel.: (713) 794-2000
Fax: (713) 794-2320

University of Houston—Clear Lake
2700 Bay Area Blvd.
Houston, TX 77058
Mary Ann Garriguis, Director of Personnel

How to Get a Job

Tel.: (713) 488-7170
Fax: (713) 283-390

University of Houston—Downtown
1 Main St.
Room 925 South
Houston, TX 77002
Geneva Hagedorn, Director of Personnel
Tel.: (713) 221-8060
Fax: (713) 221-8064

University of Houston—University Park
4800 Calhoun
Houston, TX 77204-2770
Carol Parmer, Director of Personnel
Tel.: (713) 743-5770
Fax: (713) 743-5783

University of St. Thomas
3800 Montrose Blvd.
Houston, TX 77006
Joe Elderman, Manager
Tel.: (713) 522-7911
Fax: (713) 525-2125

University of Texas Health Science Center at Houston
7000 Fannin, S50
Houston, TX 77030
Judy Findley, Director of Employment
Tel.: (713) 792-4250
Fax: (713) 794-4576

Wharton County Junior College
911 Boling Highway
Wharton, TX 77488
Dr. Jim Coats, Vice President and Chief Academic Officer
Tel.: (409) 532-4560
Fax: (409) 532-2201

VOCATIONAL AND TECHNICAL SCHOOLS EMPLOYERS:

Bradford School of Business
Cathy Houghston, Director of Education
4669 Southwest Freeway, Suite 300
Houston, TX 77027
Tel.: (713) 629-8940

Center for Advanced Legal Studies
3015 Richmond Ave.
Houston, TX 77098
Doyle Happe, Program Facilitator

Educational Institutions

Tel.: (713) 529-2778
Fax: (713) 523-2715

Computech Career Centers
1010 Waugh Dr.
Houston, TX 77019
Karen Burns, Director
Tel.: (713) 522-1115
Fax: (713) 522-1334

Control Data Institute
2990 Richmond Ave., Suite 600
Houston, TX 77098
Bill Gresham, Director
Tel.: (713) 522-6000
Fax: (713) 522-9244

Hargest Vocational & Technical College
2800 Main St.
Houston, TX 77002
Glensford Craig, Director
Tel.: (713) 524-6882

Southwestern Paralegal Institute
4888 Loop Central Dr., Suite 800
Houston, TX 77081
Janet Covington, Director
Tel.: (713) 666-7600
Fax: (713) 666-2030

Texas School of Business
711 Airtex
Houston, TX 77073
Madeline Burillow, Director
Tel.: (713) 876-2888
Fax: (713) 443-6882

PUBLIC SCHOOL EMPLOYERS:

Aldine Independent School District
14910 Aldine Westfield Rd.
Houston, TX 77032
Nadine Kujawa, Executive Director of Personnel
Tel.: (713) 449-1011
Fax: (713) 449-4911

Alief Independent School District
12302 High Star
Houston, TX 77072
Michelle Willhelm, Superintendent
Tel.: (713) 498- 8110
Fax: (713) 568-5360

How to Get a Job

Alvin Independent School District
Central Administration
301 E. House
Alvin, TX 77511
Stella Ramir, Personnel Secretary
Tel.: (713) 331-3707
Fax: (713) 331-8052

Channelview Independent School District
1403 Sheldon
Channelview, TX 77530
Dr. Larry Curry, Superintendent
Tel.: (713) 452-8008
Fax: (713) 452-8070

Conroe Independent School District
702 N. Thompson
Conroe, TX 77301
Dr. Glenn Smith, Director of Personnel
Tel.: (713) 353-9297
Fax: (409) 539-0504

Cypress-Fairbanks Independent School District
12630 Windfern
Houston, TX 77064
Richard Berry, Superintendent
Tel.: (713) 897-4000
Fax: (713) 469-5759

Danbury Independent School District
P.O. Box 378
Danbury, TX 77534
Brenda Smith, Personnel Director
Tel.: (713) 393-1779
Fax: (713) 922-1219

Deer Park Independent School District
203 Ivy
Deer Park, TX 77536
David Hicks, Assistant Superintendent for Personnel
Tel.: (713) 930-4600
Fax: (713) 930-1945

East Bernard Independent School District
P.O. Box Z
East Bernard, TX 77435
Dr. Nancy McNeil, Superintendent
Tel.: (713) 342-0240
Fax: (409) 335-6085

Fort Bend Independent School District
P.O. Box 1004

Educational Institutions

Sugar Land, TX 77487
Raj Chopra, Superintendent
Tel.: (713) 980-1300
Fax: (713) 980-4644

Friendswood Independent School District
302 Laurel
Friendswood, TX 77546
Fred Nelson, Director of Personnel
Tel.: (713) 482-1267
Fax: (713) 996-5642

Galena Park Independent School District
1601 11th
Galena Park, TX 77547
Dr. Don W. Hooper, Superintendent
Tel.: (713) 672-7491
Fax: (713) 676-2022

Houston Independent School District
3830 Richmond
Houston, TX 77027
Bill Morgan, Assistant Superintendent of Personnel
Tel.: (713) 892-7300
Fax: (713) 892-7316

Katy Independent School District
6301 S. Stadium Lane
Katy, TX 77494
Dr. Hugh Hayes, Superintendent
Tel.: (713) 391-2184
Fax: (713) 391-3432

Klein Independent School District
7200 Spring-Cypress Rd.
Klein, TX 77379
Jim Foreman, Purchasing Officer
Tel.: (713) 376-4180
Fax: (713) 320-0621

Lamar Consolidated Independent School District
3911 Ave. I
Rosenberg, TX 77471
Kathy Graber Raley, Director of Personnel
Tel.: (713) 341-3100
Fax: (713) 341-3598

La Porte Independent School District
724 S. Broadway
La Porte, TX 77571
Richard Hays, Superintendent

How to Get a Job

Tel.: (713) 471-0950
Fax: (713) 471-0838

North Forest Independent School District
P.O. Box 23278
Houston, TX 77228
Dr. Gloria Woods, Director of Personnel
Tel.: (713) 633-1600
Fax: (713) 635-4377

Pasadena Independent School District
1515 Cherrybrook
Pasadena, TX 77502
Rick Schneider, Director of Personnel
Tel.: (713) 920-6901
Fax: (713) 920-4657

Pearland Independent School District
P.O. Box 7
Pearland, TX 77588
Billy Hayes, Director of Personnel
Tel.: (713) 485-3203
Fax: (713) 485-0876

Sheldon Independent School District
8540 C.E. King Parkway
Houston, TX 77044-2099
Michael R. Null, Director of Human Resources
Tel.: (713) 459-7309
Fax: (713) 459-7338

Spring Branch Independent School District
955 Campbell Rd.
Houston, TX 77024
Edna Hamilton, Executive Director
Tel.: (713) 464-1511
Fax: (713) 973-9756

Spring Independent School District
16717 Ella Blvd.
Houston, TX 77090
Stelle Claughton, Director of Personnel
Tel.: (713) 586-1100
Fax: (713) 893-9264

Texas City Independent School District
1401 9th Ave. North
Texas City, TX 77590
Richard Ettredge, Assistant Superintendant of Business
Tel.: (409) 948-2521
Fax: (409) 942-2655

Educational Institutions

Tomball Independent School District
221 W. Main
Tomball, TX 77375
Linda McCarver, Executive Director of Human Resources
Tel.: (713) 351-8243
Fax: (713) 357-3128

PRIVATE SCHOOL EMPLOYERS:

Episcopal High School
4621 Fournace
Bellaire, TX 77401
Reba Phillips, Director of Office Services
Tel.: (713) 660-78404
Fax: (713) 663-5928

Immanuel Lutheran School
306 E 15
Ron Fritsche, Principal
Houston, TX 77008
Tel.: (713) 861-8787

The Kinkaid School
201 Kinkaid School Dr.
Houston, TX 77024
Glenn Ballard, Headmaster
Tel.: (713) 782-1640
Fax: (713) 782-3543

Memorial Lutheran School
5800 Westheimer
Houston, TX 77057
Mr. R.W. Kunz, Headmaster
Tel.: (713) 782-4022
Fax: (713) 782-8064

St. Anne's Catholic Elementary School
1111 S. Cherry
Tomball, TX 77357
Nancy Ruschuber, Principal
Tel.: (713) 351-0093

St. Edward's Catholic Church School
2601 Spring-Stuebner
Spring, TX 77389
Ann Henthorn, Principal
Tel.: (713) 353-4570

St. John's School
2401 Claremont Lane
Houston, TX 77019
Phillips Cannon, Headmaster

How to Get a Job

Tel.: (713) 850-0222
Fax: (713) 622-2309

St. Mark Lutheran School
1515 Hillendahl
Houston, TX 77055
Lowell Goecker, Principal
Tel.: (713) 468-1492
Fax: (713) 468-6735

St. Matthew Lutheran School
5315 Main
Houston, TX 77004
Kim Smolen, Acting Director
Tel.: (713) 526-5733

St. Thomas' Episcopal School
P.O. Box 35096
Houston, TX 77235
Henry L. Walters, Jr., Headmaster
Tel.: (713) 666-3111

St. Thomas High School
4500 Memorial
Houston, TX 77007
Father Albert Gaelens, Principal
Tel.: (713) 864-6348
Fax: (713) 864-5750

Strake Jesuit College Preparatory
8900 Bellaire Blvd.
Houston, TX 77036
Richard Nevle, Principal
Tel.: (713) 774-7651
Fax: (713) 774-6427

Electronics/Telecommunications

For networking in **electronics and telecommunications,** check out these professional organizations listed in Chapter 5:

PROFESSIONAL ORGANIZATIONS:

Association of Records Managers and Administrators
Society for Technical Communication

For additional information, you can contact:

Electronics Industry Association
2001 Pennsylvania Avenue NW
Washington, DC 20006
Tel.: (202) 457-4900
Fax: (202) 457-4985

Institute of Electrical and Electronics Engineers (IEEE)
345 West 47th Street
New York, NY 10017
Tel.: (212) 705-7900
Fax: (212) 752-4929

PROFESSIONAL PUBLICATIONS:

Communications Week
Electronic Business
Electronics
Electronics News
Technology News of America
Telecommunications Report
Telephony

DIRECTORIES:

American Electronics Association Directory (American Electronics Association, Santa Clara, CA)
EIA Trade Directory and Membership List (Electronics Industry Association, Washington, DC)
Electronic Mail (International Resource Development, Norwalk, CT)
Electronic Business—Electronic Business 200 Issue (Cahners Publishing Co., Boston, MA)
Electronic News—Leading Firms Issue (Fairchild Publications, New York, NY)
Electronic Representatives Directory (Harris Publishing Company, Twinsburg, OH)
Society of Telecommunications Consultants—Membership Directory (Society of Telecommunications Consultants, New York, NY).

How to Get a Job

Who's Who in Electronics (Harris Publishing Company, Twinsburg, OH)
U.S. Electronics Industry Directory (Harris Publishing Company, Twinsburg, OH)

EMPLOYERS:

Advanced Telecommunications Corporation
13105 Northwest Fwy.
Houston, TX 77040
Bernie Ebbers, President
Tel.: (713) 690-4200
Fax: (713) 690-4267

Advantage Data Services
914 W. Greens Road, Suite 2A
Houston, TX 77067
Dennis Herman, Vice President of Sales
Tel.: (713) 872-8860

American Teleprocessing Corporation
10681 Haddington Dr.
Houston, TX 77043
Joe Stevens, Vice President of Finance
Tel.: (713) 973-1616
Fax: (713) 973-8321

Arrow Electronics
10899 Kinghurst St.
Houston, TX 77099
Steve Bober, General Manager
Tel.: (713) 530-4700
Fax: (713) 568-8515

A T & T
2777 N. Stemmons Fwy.
Dallas, TX 75207
Personnel Department
Tel.: (800) 331-3449

Bell Cellular
13315 Veterans Memorial Dr.
Houston, TX 77014
Robert Gold, Executive Vice President
Tel.: (713) 586-0606
Fax: (713) 586-9806

Centel Communications Systems, Fisk Division
601 Jefferson, Suite 1000
Houston, TX 77002
John W. Hinkle, Vice President and General Manager
Tel.: (713) 730-4400

Electronics/Telecommunications

Coastal Telephone Company
2100 W. Loop South, Suite 1000
Houston, TX 77027
Marcie Zlotnik, Vice President of Finance
Tel.: (713) 960-0500
Fax: (713) 960-9536

Conference Pros International
10550 W. Off Dr., Suite 102
Houston, TX 77042
Angela Daigle, Operations Manager
Tel.: (713) 781-3377
Fax: (713) 780-5943

Digital Equipment Corporation
2500 City West Blvd., Suite 1000
Houston, TX 77042
Dempsey Wells, Human Resources Consultant
Tel.: (713) 953-3500
Fax: 9713) 953-3547

Executone Information Systems
6970 Portwest Dr., Suite 100
Houston, TX 77024
Tom Maples, District Manager
Tel.: (713) 863-1600
Fax: (713) 863-7350

GTE Mobile Communications
14123 Cicero Rd.
Houston, TX 77095
John Slater, V.P. and General Manager
Tel.: (713) 876-5000
Fax: (713) 872-7177

Houston Electronics Development Corp.
5514 Mitchelldale St.
Houston, TX 77092
Kenny Walker, President
Tel.: (713) 686-3451
Fax: (713) 686-8152

Houston Mobil Communication
3773 Southwest Fwy.
Houstn, TX 77027
Lin Hadley, President
Tel.: (713) 964-5044
Fax: (713) 964-5057

IEPS Electronic
11391 Meadowglen Lane, Suite F
Houston, TX 77082

How to Get a Job

B. Mechanic, President
Tel.: (713) 558-0010
Fax: (713) 558-9738

Intertel
8901 Knight Rd.
Houston, TX 77054
Trudy Simms, Director of Human Resources
Tel.: (713) 748-8700

K-Tec Electronics Corporation
5610 Bonhomme Rd.
Houston, TX 77036
Randy Corporron, President
Tel.: (713) 785-1300
Fax: (713) 954-8484

Kent Electronics Corporation
5600 Bonhomme Rd.
Houston, TX 77036
James Corporron, President
Tel.: (713) 780-7770
Fax: (713) 978-5892

Macha International
11246 S. Post Oak Rd.
Houston, TX 77035
Louis Meharg, Vice President of Engineering
Tel.: (713) 723-5040
Fax: (713) 723-8452

MCI Telecommunications Corporation
201 1 Shell Plaza
Houston, TX 77002
Mel Kimbrell, Senior Manager
Tel.: (713) 237-8892

Mobile Communications Corporation of America
19 Briar Way 100
Houston, TX 77027
Jim Bell, General Manager
Tel.: (713) 963-6400
Fax: (713) 960-7200

Motorola, Inc.
1140 Cypress Station Dr.
Houston, TX 77090
Ken Notter, Trades Manager
Tel.: (713) 637-3600
Fax: (713) 637-3796

Electronics/Telecommunications

NCR Corporation
6808 Hornwood
Houston, TX 77074
Denis Poss, District Administrative Manager
Tel.: (713) 776-4500
Fax: (713) 776-3849

Novell-Accudata Systems
13700 Veterans Memorial, Suite 280
Houston, TX 77014
Rich Johnson, Owner
Tel.: (713) 440-7220
Fax: (713) 440-4211

Offshore Data Services
3200 Wilcrest Dr., Ste 170
Houston, TX 77042
Lloran Sheffer, Owner
Tel.: (713) 781-2713
Fax: (713) 781-9594

Pactel Corporation
9525 Katy Fwy., Suite 103
Houston, TX 77024
Rhonda Reese, General Manager
Tel.: (713) 465-4448
Fax: (713) 935-3044

Paging Products International II
9829 Telephone Rd.
Houston, TX 77075
James L. West, Executive Vice President
Tel.: (713) 991-4930
Fax: (713) 991-4948

Peek Measurement
10335 Landsbury Dr. 300
Houston, TX 77099
John Everhart, Vice President of Marketing
Tel.: (713) 530-0885
Fax: (713) 879-9022

Pronet, Inc.
1416 E. North Belt Dr.
Houston, TX 77032
Suzanne Chadwell, General Manager
Tel.: (713) 987-0787
Fax: (713) 987-0443

Reliability Incorporated
16400 Park Row
Houston, TX 77084

How to Get a Job

Larry Edwards, President
Tel.: (713) 492-0550
Fax: (713) 492-0615

Rolm Company
13100 Northwest Fwy.
Houston, TX 77040
Steve Hauttman, Branch Manager
Tel.: (713) 462-7656
Fax: (713) 939-6818

Shason Microwave Corporation
1120 Nasa Rd. 1, Suite 106
Houston, TX 77058
Mathew Brace, Production Manager
Tel.: (713) 333-1950
Fax: (713) 333-1954

Southwestern Bell Telecommunications
10555 Northwest Fwy.
Houston, TX 77092
Brad Brown, Executive Vice President
Tel.: (713) 957-6000
Fax: (713) 957-6076

Southwestern Bell Telephone Company
3839 W. Alabama, Rm. 140
Houston, TX 77027
Romie Landrum, Director of Personnel
Tel.: (713) 850-5753
Fax: (713) 850 5014

Sprint Communications Company LP
3200 Southwest Fwy.
Houston, TX 77027
Steve Reed, Branch Manager
Tel.: (713) 964-7500
Fax: (713) 964-7555

Sterling Electronics Corporation
4201 Southwest Fwy.
Houston, TX 77027
Leon Webb, Executive Vice President
Tel.: (713) 627-9800
Fax: (713) 629-3939

TRT/FTC Communications
8 E. Greenway Plaza, Suite 930
Houston, TX 77046
Dennis Johnson, Regional Sales Director
Tel.: (713) 528-2640
Fax: (713) 622-9407

Electronics/Telecommunications

U.S. Videotel
5555 San Felipe
Houston, TX 77056
Vicki Angenend, Director of Human Resources
Tel.: (713) 840-9777
Fax: (713) 888-2098

Wang Laboratories
12 East Greenway Plaza
Houston, TX 77046
Tel.: (713) 965-9925
When applying contact: Wang Laboratories in Dallas
Barry Wheeler, Manager
Tel.: (214) 851-7700

Westinghouse Electric Corporation
10510 Harwin Dr.
Houston, TX 77036
Sandra Campbell, General Manager
Tel.: (713) 778-4554
Fax: (713) 778-4434

William Telecommunications Group
1000 Louisiana St.
Houston, TX 77002
David Boatner, Vice President
Tel.: (713) 951-6000
Fax: (713) 951-6053

Xerox Corporation
5151 San Felipe
Houston, TX 77056
John Lyden, Service, or Regina Henry, Sales
Tel.: (713) 961-5755
Fax: (713) 888-6159

How to Get a Job

Engineering

For networking in **engineering,** check out these professional organizations listed in Chapter 5:

PROFESSIONAL ORGANIZATIONS:

American Planning Association
American Society of Civil Engineers
American Society of Safety Engineers
Association of Energy Engineers
Geophysical Society of Houston
Mechanical Contractors Association of Houston
Society of Petroleum Engineers
Society of Women Engineers
Texas Society of Professional Engineers, San Jacinto Chapter

For additional information, you can contact:

American Institute of Plant Engineers
3975 Erie Avenue
Cincinnati, OH 45208
Tel.: (513) 561-6000
Fax: (513) 527-5914

American Society of Civil Engineers
203 N. Wabash Ave.
Chicago, IL 60601
Tel.: (312) 263-1606

American Society of Mechanical Engineers
345 E. 47th St.
New York, NY 10017
(212) 705-7722

Institute of Electrical & Electronics Engineers
345 E. 47th St.
New York, NY 10017
(212) 705-7900

Institute of Industry Engineers
25 Technology Park
Norcross, GA 30092-2901
Tel.: (404) 449-0460
Fax: (404) 263-8532

National Society of Professional Engineers
1420 King St.
Alexandria, VA 22314
Tel.: (703) 684-2810
Fax: (703) 836-4875

Engineering

Society of Women Engineers
345 E. 47th St.
New York, NY 10017

PROFESSIONAL PUBLICATIONS

Building Design and Construction
Chemical Engineering Progress
Civil Engineering
Engineering News Record
Journal of Petroleum Technology
Petroleum Engineer International
Texas Professional Engineer

DIRECTORIES

American Consulting Engineers Council Directory (Amreican Consulting Engineers Council, Washington, DC)
Computers and the Design Professions (American Consulting Engineers Council, Wahington, DC)
Directory of Contract Service Firms (C.E. Publications, Kirkland, WA)
Engineering News-Record—Top 500 Design Firms Issue (McGraw-Hill, New York, NY)
Engineering, Science, and Computer Jobs (Peterson's Guides, Princeton, NJ)
IEEE Directory (Institute of Electrical & Electronics Engineers, New York, NY)
Official Register (American Society of Civil Engineers, New York, NY)
Who's Who in Engineering (Engineering Joint Council, New York, NY)
Who's Who in Technology Today (Research Publications, Woodbridge, CT)

EMPLOYERS:

Allstates Design and Development Company
140 Cypress Station Dr.
Houston, TX 77090
Daniel Batista, Director of Human Resources
Tel.: (713) 444-6000
Fax: (713) 586-6726
Technical Service Division:
4828 Loop Central Dr., Suite 1050
Houston, TX 77081
Tel.: (713) 666-8797
Fax: (713) 666-7989

Barrios Technology
Aerospace Engineering
1331 Gemini Ave.
Houston, TX 77058
Jackie Castro, Purchasing Officer
Tel.: (713) 480-1889
Fax: (713) 283-7900

How to Get a Job

Bechtel, Inc.
3000 Post Oak Blvd.
Houston, TX 77252
Richard Armstrong, Director of Human Resources
Tel.: (713) 235-2000
Fax: (713) 960-9031

Binkley & Barfield, Consulting Engineers
1710 Seamist Dr.
Houston, TX 77008-3189
James A. Binkley, P.E., President
Tel.: (713) 869-3433
Fax: (713) 869-6702

Bovay Engineers
1300 Post Oak Blvd., Suite 300
Houston, TX 77056
Mr. L. N. Maloof, CEO
Tel.: (713) 439-0800
Fax: (713) 964-2860

John Brown
7909 Parkwood Circle Dr.
Houston, TX 77036
Tom Gallatin, Executive Vice President
Tel.: (713) 988-2002
Fax: (713) 772-4673

CDI, Stubbs and Overbeck
Consulting Engineers
12727 Featherwood Dr.
Houston, TX 77034
C.B.Behrens, Senior Vice President
Tel.: (713) 484-7622
Fax: (713) 929-6655

Dow Chemical, USA
400 West Belt South
Houston, TX 77042
Human Resources Department
Tel.: (713) 978-2971
Fax: (713) 978-2783

Ebasco Services
10375 Richmond Ave.
Houston, TX 77042
Charles Siegfried, Manager of Operations
W. W. Owens, Region II Manager
Tel.: (713) 954-2600
Fax: (713) 954-2733

Engineering

Fish Engineering & Construction
1990 Post Oak Blvd.
Houston, TX 77056
J.A. Boyd, President and CEO
Tel.: (713) 621-8300
Fax.: (713) 960-6201

Fluor Daniel
1 Fluor Daniel Dr.
Sugar Land, TX 77478
Steve Bachelor, Manager of Procurement
Tel.: (713) 263-1000
Fax: (713) 263-5111

Ford Aerospace Corporation
Aerospace Engineering
P.O.Box 58487
Houston, TX 77258
C.H. Denny, President, Space Information System Operation
Tel.: (713) 335-1714
Fax: (713) 335-5010

GDS Engineers
2646 South Loop West, Suite 600
Houston, TX 77054
Jim Walters, President
Tel.: (713) 667-9162
Fax: (713) 667-9241

Houston Engineering Center
1 Fluor Dr.
Sugar Land, TX 77478
Stew Heaton, Vice President/General Manager
Tel.: (713) 263-2305
Fax: (713) 263-3276

Jacobs Engineering Group
4848 Loop Central Dr.
Houston, TX 77081
Kurt Aschwege
Tel.: (713) 669-2200
Fax: (713) 668-0857

Johnson Engineering Corporation
Aerospace Engineering
1290 Hercules Dr., Suite 201
Houston, TX 77058
Elaine Moseley, Purchasing Officer
Tel.: (713) 480-8101
Fax: (713) 480-7320

How to Get a Job

M.W. Kellogg
3 Greenway Plaza East
Houston, TX 77046
Ray Waters, Manager of Advertising and Public Relations
Tel.: (713) 960-2160
Fax: (713) 753-5353

Lichter/Jameson and Associates
Consulting Engineers
11111 Brooklet Dr., Suite 100
Houston, TX 77099
Maureen Coleman, Vice President of Human Resources
Tel.: (713) 561-5190
Fax: (713)561-6586

Litwin Engineers and Constructors
1250 W. Sam Houston Pkwy. S.
Houston, TX 77079
Uzi Halevy, President
Tel.: (713) 268-8200
Fax: (713) 268-7499

Lockheed Engineering and Management Services
Aerospace Engineering
2400 NASA Road One
Houston, TX 77058
Charles Jenkins, Purchasing Officer
Tel.: (713) 333-5411
Fax: (713) 333-6100

Lummus Crest
12141 Wickchester
Houston, TX 77079
Ken Watt, Manager of Procurement and Project Controls
Tel.: (713) 531-4000
Fax: (713) 589-3220

Mitre Corporation
1120 NASA Road One
Houston, TX 77058
Jack C. Heberlig, Director of Houston Operations
Tel.: (713) 333-0909
Fax: (713) 333-2813

Walter P. Moore
Consulting Engineers
3131 Eastside, 2nd Floor
Houston, TX 77098
H. Richard Horn, Executive Vice President
Tel.: (713) 630-7300
Fax: (713) 630-7396

Engineering

Professional Service Industries
Consulting Engineers
1714 Memorial Dr.
Houston, TX 77007
Ron Ortwerth, Vice President
Tel.: (713) 224-2047
Fax: (713) 224-8914

Randall Corporation
10255 Richmond Ave.
Houston, TX 77042
Tom Giles, Director/Operations & Manufacturing
Tel.: (713) 461-3400
Fax: (713) 735-6599

S.I.P. Engineering
Chemical Engineering
9920 Gulf Freeway
Houston, TX 77034
Herb Lorfing, Manager of Human Resources
Tel.: (713) 946-9040
Fax: (713) 945-5499

SMC McEver
6363 Richmond Ave., 5th Floor
Houston, TX 77057
Sam Gipson, Vice President of Administration
Tel.: (713) 780-3465
Fax: (713) 780-3572

Stone and Webster Engineering Corporation
330 Barker Cypress
Houston, TX 77095
Norman Horner, Purchasing Officer
Tel.: (713) 492-4000
Fax: (713) 492-4913

Turner, Collie and Braden
Consulting Engineers
5757 Woodway
Houston, TX 77057
James R. Royer, President
Tel.: (713) 780-4100
Fax: (713) 262-2911

Roy F. Weston
Consulting Engineers
5599 San Felipe, Suite 700
Houston, TX 77056
John D. DiFillipo, Jr., Personnel
Tel.: (713) 621-1620
Fax: (713) 621-6959

How to Get a Job

Alternative careers for engineers

There are more kinds of jobs available to engineers than most people would probably guess. For example, Louis received his chemical engineering degree in 1988 and worked for an oil company right after graduating. After a couple of job changes, he began to work for a Houston bank.

"My function at the bank is analogous to a real estate appraiser's function at a mortgage bank. What I do is estimate the value and project the future cash flow of assets such as oil and gas wells, pipelines, and refineries. My advantage is that I have the ability to understand a wide variety of projects as well as look at the business end of the transaction."

When asked if he had any advice for engineers looking for non-engineering kinds of jobs, Louis suggests, "Get your engineering degree and supplement it with as many business courses as possible." Such a well-rounded education increases the opportunities for jobs in a number of fields.■

Environmental Services

For networking in environmental services and related fields, you can contact:

PROFESSIONAL ORGANIZATION:

National Association of Environmental Professionals
815 Second Ave.
New York, NY 10017

PROFESSIONAL PUBLICATIONS:

Environmental Watch
Pollution Engineering
Water Engineering & Management
Water and Wastes Digest

DIRECTORIES:

The Complete Guide to Environmental Careers (The CEIP Fund, Island Press, Washington, DC).
Conservation Directory (National Wildlife Federation, Washington, DC).
Directory of National Environmental Organizations (U.S. Environmental Directories, St. Paul, MN).
EI Environmental Services (Environmental Information Ltd., Bloomington, MN). Lists over 400 waste-handling facilities, 1700 consultants, 470 labs, 700 transportation firms, 375 spill response firms.
Guide to State Environmental Programs (Deborah Hitchcock Jessup, ed., The Bureau of National Affairs, Inc.).
Listing of Awardee Names: Active Awards (Dept. of Energy, Washington, DC). Lists 2,400 companies, organizations, agencies receiving funding from the Department of Energy.
Management of World Wastes—Buyer's Guide Issue (Communication Channels, Inc., Atlanta, GA).
Manufacturer's List (Synergy, New York). Lists 3,000 manufacturers of renewable energy equipment.

EMPLOYERS:

Allwaste Inc.
3040 Post Oak Blvd., Suite 1300
Houston, TX 77056
Julie Caturani, Benefits Coordinator
Tel.: (713) 623-8777
Fax: (713) 622-7845

Baker Hughes
3900 Essex Lane
Houston, TX 77027

How to Get a Job

Shannon Nini, Human Resources Specialist
Tel.: (713) 439-8600
Fax: (713) 439-8782

Enclean Inc.
6750 West Loop South, Suite 1000
Houston, TX 77401
James Turpin, Vice President for Human Resources
Tel.: (713) 661-4777
Fax: (713) 661-0742

Global Marine
777 No. Eldridge Rd.
Houston, TX 77079
Dan Hansen, Manager of Employee Relations
Tel.: (713) 596-5100
Fax: (713) 596-5888

Serv Tech
5200 Cedar Crest Blvd.
Houston, TX 77087
Cheryl Cummings, Manager of Human Resources
Tel.: (713) 644-9974
Fax: (713) 644-0731

Southdown, Inc.
1200 Smith Street, Suite 2400
Houston, TX 77002
Joe Devine, Vice President for Human Resources
Tel.: (713) 650-6200
Fax: (713) 653-8010

Tanknology Environmental
5225 Hollister
Houston, TX 77040
Beth Martin, Payroll Personnel Manager
Tel.: (713) 690-8265
Fax: (713) 895-606

Transamerica Waste
314 North Post Oak Lane
Houston, TX 77024
Tommy Fatjo, Vice President
Tel.: (713) 956-1212
Fax: (713) 956-0262

Food/Beverage Producers and Distributors

For networking in the **food and beverage industry,** check out these professional organizations listed in Chapter 5:

PROFESSIONAL ORGANIZATIONS:

Harris County Beer Wholesalers Association
Houston Restaurant Association
Retail Grocers Association of Houston

For additional information, you can contact:

Dairy and Food Industries Supply Association
6245 Executive Blvd.
Rockville, MD 20852
Tel.: (301) 984-1444

Distilled Spirits Council
12501 I St., NW, Suite 900
Washington, DC 20005
Tel.: (202) 628-3544

Food Marketing Institute
800 Connecticut Ave. NW, Suite 500
Washington, DC 20006
Tel.: (202) 452-8444
Fax: (202) 429-4519

National Association of Beverage Importers
1025 Vermont Ave.
Washington, DC 20005
Tel.: (202) 638-1617
Fax: (202) 638-3122

National Food Distributors Association
401 N. Michigan Ave.
Chicago, IL 60601
Tel.: (312) 644-6610

National Food Processors Association
1401 New York Ave.
Washington, DC 20005

National Frozen Food Association
PO Box 398
Hershey, PA 17033

National Soft Drink Association
1101 16th Street NW
Washington, DC 20036

How to Get a Job

Tel.: (202) 463-6732
Fax: (202) 463-6231

United States Brewers Association
P.O. Box 1435
Topeka, KS 66601

Wine & Spirits Wholesalers of America
1023 15th Street NW, 4th Floor
Washington, DC 20005
Tel.: (202) 371-9792
Fax: 9202) 789-2405

PROFESSIONAL PUBLICATIONS:

Beverage World
Fancy Food
Food and Beverage Marketing
Food Business
Food Industry News
Food Management
Foodservice Product News
Institutional Distribution
Progressive Grocer
Wine Spectator
Wines and Vines

DIRECTORIES:

Beverages Directory (Americn Business Directories, Omaha, NE)
Directory of the Canning, Freezing, Preserving Industries (Judge and Sons, Westminster, MD)
Food Broker's Directory (American Business Directories, Omaha, NE)
Food Engineering's Directory of U.S. Food Plants (Chilton Company, Radnor, PA)
Frozen Food Fact Book and Directory (National Frozen Food Association, Hershey, PA)
Hereld's 5,000: The Directory of Leading U.S. Food, Confectionery and Beverage Trade Lists (Office of Information Products Development and Distribution, International Trade Administration, Department of Commerce, Washington, DC)
National Beverage Marketing Directory (Beverage Marketing Corp., New York, NY)
NFBA Directory (National Food Brokers Association, Washington, DC)
Wholesaler Directory and Buyer's Guide Issue (Dogan Communications, Delray Beach, FL)
Wines &Vines Buyers Guide: Directory of the Wine Industry in North America (The Hiaring Co., San Rafael, CA)

Food/Beverage

EMPLOYERS:

Antone's Import Company
807 Taft
Houston, TX 77019
Josephine A. Antone, President
Tel.: (713) 526-1046
Fax: (713) 526-4179

Coca-Cola Foods
2000 St. James Place
Houston, TX 77056
Timothy J. Haas, President and CEO
Tel.: (713) 888-5000
Fax: (713) 888-5959

Dr. Pepper Bottling Company of Texas
2400 Holly Hall
Houston, TX 77054
Jim Turner, President
Tel.: (713) 799-1024
Fax: (713) 799-7616

Fleming Foods
2525 Minimax Dr.
Houston, TX 77008
Andy Anderson, Purchasing Officer
Tel.: (713) 868-7100
Fax: (713) 868-7108

Frito Lay
16801 Greenspoint Park Dr., Suite 380
Houston, TX 77060
Scott Rude, Area Human Resource Manager
Tel.: (713) 875-0133
Fax: (713) 872-7441

Glazier Food Company
1280 Oliver
Houston, TX 77007
Johnny Johnson, Purchasing
Tel.: (713) 869-6411
Fax: (713) 862-1286

Houston Coca-Cola Bottling Company
2800 Bissonnet
Houston, TX 77005
Cecil E. Green, President and General Manager
Tel.: (713) 664-3451
Fax: (713) 669-3188

How to Get a Job

International Trading Company
3100 Canal St.
Houston, TX 77003
Benjamin Warren, Purchasing
Tel.: (713) 224-5901
Fax: (713) 224-5021

Pepsi South
9300 Laporte Freeway
Houston, TX 77017
Employee Relations
Tel.: (713) 645-4111
Fax: (713) 845-3295

Riviana Foods
2777 Allen Parkway
Houston, TX 77019
Jack Nolingberg, Vice President of Employee Relations
Tel.: (713) 529-3251
Fax: (713) 529-1661

R.J.R. Nabisco
6803 Almeda
Houston, TX 77021
Anthony Muscarello, President
Tel.: (713) 749-0400
Fax: (713) 749-0480

Shasta Beverage
7333 Major
Houston, TX 77061
Tel.: (713) 644-8355
Contact: Personnel Department
26109 Industrial Blvd.
Hayward, CA 94545

Smith Farms
P.O. Box 219
Flatonia, TX 78941
Carl Smith, President
Tel.: (512) 224-4072
Fax: (512) 865-3962

Smith Food Service
3518 East T.C. Jester
Houston, TX 77018
Harry Smith, President
Tel.: (713) 688-3449
Fax: (713) 688-0320

Swiss Chalet Fine Foods
7200 Wynnpark

Food/Beverage

Houston, TX 77008
Max Baumann, Sales Manager
Tel.: (713) 868-9505
Fax: (713) 868-1172

Sysco Food Services
535 Portwall
Houston, TX 77029
Gaynor Richardson, Personnel Supervisor
Tel.: (713) 672-8080
Fax: (713) 672-8483

Tropical Foods
4635 Bellfort
Houston, TX 77051
Stephen James, Manager
Tel.: (713) 734-3565
Fax.: (713) 734-1584

White Swan Food Company
300 Partwall
Houston, TX 77029
Barry Schatmeier, Purchasing Officer
Tel.: (713) 672-2279
Fax: (713) 670-3627

Mouth-watering opportunities in food service management

Kate Williams, manager of a hospital dietary department, sees the food service industry as a growing field with tremendous potential. Hospitals offer a variety of opportunities in food services, according to Kate. Some of the jobs, such as clinical or administrative dietitian, require a college degree in nutrition, but many do not.

"Some employees have experience working at fast-food restaurants," says Kate. "Others just learn on the job. Still others have completed one or two-year programs in food service offered by various colleges."

Besides registered dietitians, Kate's staff includes food service supervisors, who manage the personnel who prepare food; diet technicians, who prepare and implement menus based on information about the patient; diet aides, who perform such tasks as delivering meals to patients; a chef and cooking staff; and a food purchasing agent.

Kate is optimistic about employment prospects in the food service industry as a whole. "There are tremendous opportunities for those with culinary arts skills, as well as for hotel or restaurant food service managers. Opportuni-

How to Get a Job

ties exist in food equipment companies, public and private schools, contract food companies, and food service consulting firms. Right now the possibilities in food marketing are phenomenal.

"The nutritional needs of the growing elderly population," Kate adds, "will also create many new jobs in the food service business as hospitals and other organizations become involved in the field of long-term care." ∎

Foundations

For more information, you can contact:

PROFESSIONAL ORGANIZATIONS:

Council on Foundations
1828 L Street NW, Suite 300
Washington, DC 20036
Tel.: (202) 466-5612
Fax: (202) 785-3926

Foundation Center
79 Fifth Avenue
New York, NY 10003

Independent Sector
1828 L Street NW, Suite 1200
Washington, DC 20036
Tel.: (202) 223-8100
Fax: (202) 457-0609

PROFESSIONAL PUBLICATIONS:

Charities USA
Foundation News
The Humanist

DIRECTORIES:

Corporate Foundation Profiles (Foundation Center, New York, NY)
Corporate Fund Raising Directory (Public Service Materials Center, Hartsdale, NY)
Corporation 500: The Directory of Corporate Philanthropy (Public Management Institute, San Francisco, CA)
Directory—Private Funding for Rural Programs: Foundations and Other Private Sector Resources (National Rural Center, Washington, DC)
Foundation Center National Data Book Profiles (Foundation Center, New York, NY)
Foundation Directory (Foundation Center, New York, NY)
Taft Foundation Reporter (Taft Corporation, Washington, DC)

Foundations

EMPLOYERS:

Bjorksten Research Foundation
9117 Almeda-Genoa Rd.
Houston, TX 77075
Luther L. Yaeger, Vice President
Tel.: (713) 944-9170
Fax: (713) 944-8736

Brown Foundation
P.O. Box 130646
Houston, TX 77219-0646
Katherine B. Dobelman, Executive Director
Tel.: (713) 523-6867
Fax: (713) 523-2917
Mailing Address:
P.O. Box 130646
Houston, TX 77219-0646

Cullen Foundation
601 Jefferson
Houston, TX 77002
Joseph C. Graf, Executive Secretary
Tel.: (713) 651-8835
Fax: (713) 651-8663
Mailing Address:
P.O. Box 1600
Houston, TX 77251

John S. Dunn Research Foundation
3355 W. Alabama, Suite 720
Houston, TX 77098
M. Dow Dunn, President
Tel.: (713) 626-0368

Endowment Fund for the Jewish Community of Houston
5603 S. Braeswood
Houston, TX 77096
Hans Mayer, Executive Director
Tel.: (713) 729-7000
Fax: (713) 721-6232

Fondren Foundation
P.O. Box 2558
Houston, TX 77252
Melanie A. Boone, Assistant Secretary/Treasurer
Tel.: (713) 236-4403
Fax: (713) 546-2119

George and Mary Josephine Hamman Foundation
910 Travis, Suite 1438
Houston, TX 77002

How to Get a Job

C. D. Milby, President
Tel.: (713) 658-8345

Houston Endowment
708 Main St.
Houston, TX 77002
H. Joe Nelson, President
Tel.: (713) 238-8100
Fax: (713) 238-8101

George B. & Irene Lindler Foundation
5036 Tiffany Dr.
Houston, TX 77045
George B. Lindler, Director
Tel.: (713) 433-6724

John P. McGovern Foundation
6969 Brompton
Houston, TX 77025
Dr. John P. McGovern, President
Tel.: (713) 661-4808
Fax: (713) 661-3031

Rockwell Fund
1360 Post Oak Blvd, Suite 780
Houston, TX 77056
Joe M. Green, Jr., President
Tel.: (713) 629-9022
Fax: (713) 629-7702

Strake Foundation
712 Main St.
Houston, TX 77002
George W. Strake, President
Tel.: (713) 546-2400
Fax: (713) 546-2401

Robert A. Welch Foundation
4605 Post Oak Place, Suite 200
Houston, TX 77027
Norbert Dittrich, Executive Manager
Tel.: (713) 961-9884
Fax: (713) 961-5168

Wortham Foundation
2727 Allen Parkway, Suite 2000
Houston, TX 77019
Barbara Snyder, Grants Administrator
Tel.: (713) 526-8849
Fax: (713) 526-7222

Government Agencies

For networking in **government,** check out these professional organizations listed in Chapter 5:

PROFESSIONAL ORGANIZATIONS:

League of Women Voters
National Organization for Women
Women Professionals in Government

For additional information, you can contact:

American Federation of Government Employees
80 F St. NW
Washington, DC 20001
Tel.: (202) 737-8700

American Society for Public Administration
1120 G St. NW, Suite 500
Washington, DC 20005
Tel.: (202) 393-7878
Fax: (202) 638-4952

Civil Service Employees Association
P.O. Box 125, Capital Station
143 Washington Avenue
Albany, NY 12210
Tel.: (518) 434-0191

Council of State Governments
P.O. Box 11910
Iron Works Pike
Lexington, KY 40578
Tel.: (606) 252-2291
Fax: (606) 231-1858

Government Finance Officers Association of U.S. and Canada
180 N. Michigan Ave., Suite 800
Chicago, IL 60601-7401
Tel.: (312) 977-9700
Fax: (312) 977-4806

National Association of Government Employees
2011 Crystal Dr., #206
Arlington, VA 22202

PROFESSIONAL PUBLICATIONS:

The Beacon
Federal Times

How to Get a Job

FedNews
Government Executive
The Municipal Forum
Public Employee Newsletter
Public Management
Public Works Magazine

DIRECTORIES:

Almanac of American Politics (National Journal, Washington, DC)
Braddock's Federal-State-Local Government Directory (Braddock Communications, Alexandria, VA)
Directory of State Officials (Division of Federal-State Relations, Food and Drug Administration, Rockville, MD)
Taylor's Encyclopedia of Government Officials: Federal and State (Political Research, Inc., Dallas, TX)

CITY GOVERNMENT EMPLOYERS:

Alvin, City of
216 W. Sealy
Alvin, TX 77511
Tel.: (713) 388-4200
Fax: (713) 331-7215

Bellaire, City of
7008 S. Rice
Bellaire, TX 77401
Tel.: (713) 662-8222
Fax: (713) 662-8265

Friendswood, City of
109 E. Willowick Ave.
Friendswood, TX 777546
Tel.: (713) 482-3323
Fax: (713) 482-9318

Galena Park, City of
P.O. Box 46
Galena Park, TX 77547
Tel.: (713) 672-2556
Fax: (713) 672-1840

Pasadena, City of
P.O. Box 672
Pasadena, TX 77501
Tel.: (713) 477-1511
Fax: (713) 472-0104

Houston Finance and Administration Department
901 Bagby
Houston, TX 77002

Government

Richard Lewis, Director
Tel.: (713) 247-2087
Fax: (713) 247-1860

Houston Health and Human Services Department
8000 N. Stadium Dr.
Houston, TX 77054
Tel.: (713) 794-9320
Fax: (713) 794-9316

Houston Police Department
500 Jefferson, 15th Floor
Houston, TX 77002
Stephanie Burks, Director
Tel.: (713) 247-1000
Fax: (713) 758-7552

Houston Public Works Department
900 Bagby
Houston, TX 77002
Fred Perrenot, Director
Tel.: (713) 247-2125

Houston Traffic and Transportation Department
500 Jefferson
Houston, TX 77002
Tel.: (713) 658-4300

COUNTY GOVERNMENT EMPLOYERS:

Fort Bend County
P.O. Box 368
Richmond, TX 77406-0368
Roy Cordes, Jr., County Judge
Tel.: (713) 342-3411
Fax: (713) 341-8609

Harris County
1001 Preston, Room 911
Houston, TX 77002
Judge Jon Lindsay, County Judge
Tel.: (713) 755-6666
Fax: (713) 755-8379

Harris County Attorney
2001 Fannin
Houston, TX 77002
Tel.: (713) 755-5800
Fax: (713) 755-6865

Harris County Clerk's Office
1001 Preston

How to Get a Job

Houston, TX 77002
Tel.: (713) 755-6405

Harris County District Attorney's Office
201 Fannin
Houston, TX 77002
Tel.: (713) 755-5800

Harris County District Clerk's Office
301 Fannin, Civil Courts Bldg.
Houston, TX 77002
Tel.: (713) 755-5711

Harris County Sheriff's Department
1301 Franklin
Houston, TX 77002
Employment and Recruiting
Tel.: (713) 221-6000

STATE OF TEXAS EMPLOYERS:

Attorney General's Office
1019 Congress
Houston, TX 77002
Houston Regional Office
Tel.: (713) 223-5886
Fax: (713) 223-5821

Health, State Department of
10500 Forum Place Dr.
Houston, TX 77036
Tel.: (713) 995-1112
Fax: (713) 995-1112

Highways and Public Transportation, State Department of
7721 Washington
Houston, TX 77007
Tel.: (713) 869-4571
Fax: (713) 867-5786

Human Services, Department of
1330 E. 40th
Houston, TX 77022
Tel.: (713) 696-7261
Fax: (713) 696-7193

Public Safety, Department of
10110 Northwest Freeway
Houston, TX 77092
Tel.: (713) 957-6183

Government

Parks and Wildlife Department
State Parks Regional Headquarters #8
105 San Jacinto
LaPorte, TX 77571
Tel: (713) 471-3200
or 1-800-792-1112 for other Texas offices.

Texas Employment Commission
P.O. Box 1390
Houston, TX 77251
Regional Office
Tel.: (713) 956-4170

U.S. GOVERNMENT EMPLOYERS:

Agriculture, Department of
Agriculture Stabilization and Conservation Service, Harris County
P.O. Box 340
Cypress, TX 77429
Tel.: (713) 469-7856

Agriculture, Department of
Food and Nuitrition Service
500 Dallas Avenue, Room 1165
Houston, TX 77002
Tel.: (713) 229-2589
Fax: (713) 229-2231

Army Corps of Engineers
Addicks and Barker Dam
P.O. Box 218747
Houston, TX 77218
Tel.: (713) 497-0740

Commerce, Department of
International Trade Administration
500 Dallas, Suite 1160
Houston, TX 77002
Tel.: (713) 229-2578
Fax: (713) 229-2203

Drug Enforcement Administration
333 West Loop North, Suite 300
Houston, TX 77024
Karen Burnett, Purchasing Officer
Tel.: (713) 681-1771
Fax: (713) 681-1771, ext. 213

Environmental Protection Agency
Field Operations
10625 Fallstone Rd.
Houston, TX 77099

How to Get a Job

Tel.: (713) 983-2100
Fax: (713) 983-2248

Equal Employment Opportunity Commission (EEOC)
1919 Smith, 7th Floor
Houston, TX 77002
Marie Stovall, Administrative Officer
Tel.: (713) 653-3320
Fax: (713) 653-3381

Federal Bureau of Investigation
2500 East T.C. Jester, Room 200
Houston, TX 77008
Michael D. Wilson, Special Agent in Charge
Tel.: (713) 868-2266
Fax: (713) 867-3525

Food and Drug Administration
1445 North Loop West, Suite 420
Houston, TX 77008
Tel.: (713) 220-2322
Fax: (713) 220-2327

Housing and Urban Development
2211 Norfolk, Suite 200
Houston, TX 77098
Tel.: (713) 653-3274
Fax: (713) 653-3305

Internal Revenue Service
1919 Smith
Houston, TX 77002
Tel.: (713) 541-0440

Justice, Department of
U.S. Attorney
440 Louisiana, Suite 900
Houston, TX 77002
Tel.: (713) 238-9400
Fax: (713) 238-9314

Labor, Department of
Employment Standards Administration Office
2320 LaBranch, Room 1007
Houston, TX 77004
Tel.: (713) 750-1800

National Aeronautics and Space Administration
2101 NASA Road One
Houston, TX 77058
Tel.: (713) 483-2135

Health Care

Postal Service
1002 Washington Ave.
Houston, TX 77002
Tel.: (713) 226-3872

U.S. District Court
Clerk, U.S. District Court
P.O. Box 61010
Houston, TX 77208
Tel.: (713) 250-5548

U.S. Small Business Administration
9301 Southwest Freeway, Suite 550
Houston, TX 77074
Tel.: (713) 953-6255
Fax: (713) 953-6280

Veterans Administration
2515 Murworth
Houston, TX 77054
Tel.: (713) 664-4664
No fax.

Health Care

For networking in the **health care industry,** check out these professional organizations listed in Chapter 5:

PROFESSIONAL ORGANIZATIONS:

Harris County Medical Society
Houston Dental Society
Houston Medical Forum

For additional information, you can contact:

American Health Care Association
1201 L Street NW
Washington, DC 20005
Tel.: (202) 842-4444
Fax: (202) 842 3860

American Hospital Association
840 North Lake Shore Drive
Chicago, IL 60611
Tel.: (312) 280-6000
Fax: (312) 280-5979

American Medical Association
515 N. State St.

How to Get a Job

Chicago, Il 60610
Tel.: (312) 464-5000

American Public Health Association
1015 15th Street NW, Suite 300
Washington, DC 20005
Tel.: (202) 789-5600
Fax: (202) 789-5661

National Association of Social Workers
750 1st Street NE
Washington, DC 20002
Tel.: (202) 408-8600

PROFESSIONAL PUBLICATIONS:

ADA News
AHA News
American Journal of Medicine
American Journal of Nursing
Health Care Systems
Hospitals
Modern Healthcare
Modern Hospital
Nations Health
Nursing Outlook
Physician Assistant and Health Practitioner
Texas Dental Journal
Texas Nursing
Texas Optometry
Texas Pharmacy

DIRECTORIES:

American Hospital Association—Guide to the Health Care Field (American Hospital Association, Chicago, IL)
Business/Health Care Coalitions in Profile (Institute for Health Planning, Madison, WI)
Directory of Agencies Serving the Visually Handicapped in the U.S. (American Foundation for the Blind, New York, NY)
Directory of Community Health Centers (National Association of Community Health Centers, Washington, DC)
Directory: Health Systems Agencies, State Health Planning and Development Agencies, Statewide Health Coordinating Councils (Office of Health Planning, Public Health Service, Department of Health and Human Services, Rockville, MD)
Directory of Hospitals (SMG Marketing Group, Chicago, IL)
Saunders Health Care Directory (W.B. Saunders, Philadelphia, PA)

Health Care

EMPLOYERS, HOSPITALS:

AMI Park Plaza Hospital
1313 Hermann
Houston, TX 77004
Paul Craft, Administrator
Tel.: (713) 527-5000
Fax: (713) 527-5982

Bellaire Hospital
5314 Dashwood
Houston, TX 77081
Tom Keefe, Administrator
Tel.: (713) 669-4000
Fax: (713) 668-0259

Columbia Hospital
1917 Ashland
Houston, TX 77008
Micheal Taylor, Director of Human Resources
Tel.: (713) 861-6161
Fax: (713) 861-3592

Diagnostic Center Hospital
6447 Main
Houston, TX 77030
John W. Herndon and William A. Gregory, Administrators
Tel.: (713) 790-0790
Fax: (713) 796-6587

Harris County Hospital District
2525 Hollyhall
Houston, TX 77054
Art Simon, Purchasing Officer
Tel.: (713) 746-5400
Fax: (713) 746-5401

HCA Medical Center Hospital and Women's Hospital of Texas
8081 Greenbriar
Houston, TX 77054
Judy Novak, Administrator
Tel.: (713) 790-8100
Fax: (713) 796-2360

Hermann Hospital
6411 Fannin
Houston, TX 77030
Walter Mischer, Jr., Chairman and CEO
Tel.: (713) 797-4011
Fax: (713) 799-2658

How to Get a Job

Sam Houston Memorial Hospital
1615 Hillendahl
Houston, TX 77055
Tuck Hall, Administrator
Tel.: (713) 468-4311
Fax: (713) 468-7228

Houston Northwest Medical Center
710 FM 1960 West
Houston, TX 77090
J. Barry Shevchuk, Administrator
Tel.: (713) 440-1000
Fax: (713) 440-2474

Houston Veterans Administration Medical Center
20002 Holcombe Blvd.
Houston, TX 77030
Robert F. Stott, Administrator
Tel.: (713) 791-1414
Fax: (713) 794-7218

Humana Hospital—Clear Lake
500 Medical Center Blvd.
Webster, TX 77598
Galen Russell, Administrator
Tel.: (713) 338-3110
Fax : (713) 338-3354

Interim Health Care
10900 Northwest Freeway, Suite 110
Houston, TX 77092
Lynette Ross, Branch Manager
Tel.: (713) 681-7832
Fax: (713) 681-7838

Memorial Healthcare Systems
7737 Southwest Freeway
Houston, TX 77074
Dan S. Wilford, President
Tel.: (713) 776-6992
Fax: (713) 776-5889

Memorial City Medical Center
920 Frostwood
Houston, TX 77024
Robert M. Bryant, Administrator
Tel.: (713) 932-3000
Fax: (713) 827-4096

Memorial Northwest Hospital
1635 North Loop West
Houston, TX 77008

Health Care

Gerald Humphrey, Administrators
Tel.: (713) 867-2000
Fax: (713) 867-2099

Memorial Southeast Hospital
11800 Astoria Blvd.
Houston, TX 77089
Jim Salyer, Administrators
Tel.: (713) 929-6100
Fax: (713) 929-4151

Memorial Southwest Hospital
7600 Beechnut
Houston, TX 77074
Ed Myers, Administrators
Tel.: (713) 776-5000
Fax: (713) 776-5652

Methodist Hospital
6565 Fannin
Houston, TX 77030
A. Frank Smith, Jr., and Larry L. Mathis, Administrators
Tel.: (713) 790-3311
Fax: (713) 790-5929

Northeast Medical Center Hospital
18951 Memorial North
Humble, TX 77338
Fred Mery, Administrator
Tel.: (713) 540-7700
Fax: (713) 540-7846

Northway Healthcare Center
5329 North Freeway
Houston, TX 77022
Debbie Runnels, Administrator
Tel.: (713) 695-5821
Fax: (713) 692-3614

Pasadena Bayshore Medical Center
4000 Spencer Highway
Pasadena, TX 77504
Linda Hischke, Administrator
Tel.: (713) 944-6666

Rosewood General Hospital
9200 Westheimer Rd.
Houston, TX 77063
J.J. Y. Grinney, Administrator
Tel.: (713) 780-7900
Fax: (713) 782-3207

How to Get a Job

Sisters of Charity of the Incarnate Word Health Care Systems
2600 North Loop West
Houston, TX 77092
Larry O. George, Director of Group Purchasing
Tel.: (713) 681-8877
Fax: (713) 681-3462

Spring Branch Memorial Hospital
8850 Long Point Rd.
Houston, TX 77055
Eddie George, CEO
Tel.: (713) 467-6555
Fax: (713) 984-3566

St. Joseph's Hospital
1919 La Branch
Houston, TX 77002
Raymond Khoury, Administrators
Tel.: (713) 757-7552
Fax: (713) 657-7123

St. Luke's Episcopal Hospital
6720 Bertner St.
Houston, TX 77030
Maurice M. Benitez and John A. Burdine, Administrators
Tel.: (713) 791-2011
Fax: (713) 794-6182

Ben Taub General Hospital
1504 Ben Taub Loop
Houston, TX 77030
Mike Bullord, Administrator
Tel.: (713) 793-2000
Fax: (713) 793-2305

Texas Children's Hospital
6621 Fannin St
Houston, TX 77030
Mark A. Wallace, Executive Director and CEO
Tel.: (713) 770-1000
Fax: (713) 770-1005

University of Texas M. D. Anderson Cancer Center
1515 Holcombe Blvd.
Houston, TX 77030
Charles A. LeMaistre, President
Tel.: (713) 792-2121
Fax: (713) 794-5953

Health Care

EMPLOYERS, HMO:

Aetna Health Plans
9494 Southwest Freeway, Suite 350
Houston, TX 77074-1419
Barry Koerpel, Medical Director
Tel.: (713) 776-2887
Fax: (713) 988-5662

CIGNA Healthplan of Texas
1360 S. Post Oak Blvd., Suite 1100
Houston, TX 77056
Dr. Vernon Walters, Medical Director
Tel.: (713) 552-7600
Fax: (713) 552-7699

Metlife Healthcare Network of Texas
5 Post Oak Park, Suite 550
Houston, TX 77027
Dr. Owen Ellington and Dr. George Ogdee, Medical Directors
Tel.: (713) 961-4300
Fax: (713) 961-4431

Prudential Insurance of America
24 Greenway Plaza, Suite 400
Houston, TX 77046
William Hauser, Medical Director
Tel.: (713) 993-9440
Fax: (713) 965-8256

Sanus/New York Life
3800 Buffalo Speedway, #200
Houston, TX 77098
Dr. Gerald Zarin, Medical Director
Tel.: (713) 993-9520
Fax: (713) 963-9417

Travelers Health Network of Texas
2000 Post Oak Blvd., Suite 1650
Houston, TX 77056
David A. Ziegler, Medical Director
Tel.: (713) 623-6936

How to Get a Job

Careers in health care

We spoke with the director of personnel at a local hospital about the hospital industry.

"If you wish to work in the hospital field, it's important to pick a specialty and pursue it as early as possible. Most hospital professions are very specialized and require a great deal of education. Many hospitals recruit right from high school or college if they operate training programs in allied health fields. Right now, physical therapy and nursing are two wide-open fields.

"Once you've been working for a while, I would suggest to anyone, whether in the business or medical end of the hospital industry, that it's a good idea to see if an association or society exists which represents your occupation. The industry is known for its networking, and many associations have placement services. I rarely use an employment agency or place an ad in the paper to fill a position. Trade associations have been more helpful and more effective in filling any opening I might have. Also, for the job hunter, their services are confidential and fairly quick."

Hotels/Motels

For additional information, you can contact:

PROFESSIONAL ORGANIZATIONS:

American Hotel and Motel Association
1201 New York Avenue NW Suite 600
Washington, DC 20005
Tel.: (202) 289-3100
Fax: (202) 289-3199

Hotel Sales & Marketing Association International
1300 L Street, Suite 800
Washington, DC 20005
Tel.: (202) 789-0089
Fax: (202) 789-1725

Meeting Planners International
1950 Stemmins Fwy.
Dallas, TX 75207
Tel.: (214) 746-5222

PROFESSIONAL PUBLICATIONS:

Club Management
Hotel and Motel Management
Hotel and Resort Industry
Lodging Magazine
Meetings and Conventions
Successful Meetings

DIRECTORIES:

Directory of Hotel and Motel Systems (American Hotel and Motel Association, New York, NY)
Hotel and Motel Redbook (American Hotel and Motel Association, New York, NY)
Hotels & Motels Directory (American Business Directories, Omaha, NE)
Membership Directory (Meeting Planners International, Dallas, TX)
Official Hotel and Resort Guide (Murdoch Magazines, News Group Publications, New York, NY)
Resorts Directory (American Business Directories, Omaha, NE)
Southwest Hotel-Motel Review —Buyers Guide Issue (Hotel Review Company, San Antonio, TX)

EMPLOYERS:

Because of the diversity of employment opportunities in any hotel, it is most convenient to contact the general manager (whose name is listed),

How to Get a Job

who can then give you the name of the manager for the department in which you are interested.

Adam's Mark Houston
2900 Briarpark
Houston, TX 77042
Fred Kummer, General Manager
Tel.: (713) 978-7400
Fax: (713) 735-2727

Doubletree Allen Center
400 Dallas
Houston, TX 77002
Harry Greenblatt, General Manager
Tel.: (713) 759-0202
Fax: (713) 759-1166

Doubletree at Post Oak
2001 Post Oak Dr.
Houston, TX 77056
John Lange, General Manager
Tel.: 713) 961-9300
Fax: (713) 623-6685

Four Seasons Houston Center
1300 Lamar
Houston, TX 77010
Francisco Gomez, General Manager
Tel.: (713) 650-1300
Fax: (713) 650-1203

Guest Quarters Suite Hotel-Galleria West
5353 Westheimer
Houston, TX 77056
Steve Chojnacki, General Manager
Tel.: (713) 961-9000
Fax: (713) 877-8835

Holiday Inn Crowne Plaza-Galleria
2222 West Loop South
Houston, TX 77027
Al Stento, General Manager
Tel.: (713) 961-7272
Fax: (713) 961-3327

Holiday Inn Greenway Plaza
2712 Southwest Freeway
Houston, TX 77098
John F. Ribon III, General Manager
Tel.: (713) 523-8448
Fax: (713) 523-8448 x1918

Hotels/Motels

Holiday Inn Houston Downtown
801 Calhoun
Houston, TX 77002
John Mahan, General Manager
Tel.: (713) 659-2222
Fax: (713) 659-8348

Holiday Inn Houston West
14703 Park Row
Houston, TX 77079
Roy McClaney, General Manager
Tel.: (713) 558-5580
Fax: (713) 496-4150

Houston Airport Marriott
Intercontinental Airport
Houston, TX 77032
George Camalier, General Manager
Tel.: (713) 443-2310
Fax: (713) 443-5270

Houston Marriott North at Greenspoint
255 North Sam Houston Pkwy East
Houston, TX 77060
Doug Wiggins, General Manager
Tel.: (713) 875-4000
Fax: (713) 875-6208

Houston Marriott Westside
13210 Katy Freeway
Houston, TX 77079
Carolynn Carr, General Manager
Tel.: (713) 558-8338
Fax: (713) 558-4028

Howard Johnson
6855 Southwest Freeway
Houston, TX 77074
Chung Hung, General Manager
Tel.: (713) 771-0641
Fax: (713) 771-5310

Hyatt Regency Hotel
1200 Louisiana
Houston, TX 77002
Tom Netting, General Manager
Tel.: (713) 654-1234
Fax: (713) 951-0934

L'Hotel Sofitel
425 North Sam Houston Pkwy
Houston, TX 77060

How to Get a Job

Dean Peters, General Manager
Tel.: (713) 445-9000
Fax: (713) 445-9826

J. W. Marriott
5150 Westheimer
Houston, TX 77056
Bob Pittenger, General Manager
Tel.: (713) 961-1500
Fax: (713) 961-5045

Marriott Braeswood
2100 S. Braeswood
Houston, TX 77030
Kyle Ariza, General Manager
Tel.: (713) 797-9000
Fax: (713) 796-2986

Marriott Medical Center
6580 Fannin
Houston, TX 77030
Fuad Savvara, General Manager
Tel.: (713) 796-0080
Fax: (713) 796-2201

Omni Houston Hotel
Four Riverway
Houston, TX 77056
Louis Martinelli, General Manager
Tel.: (713) 871-8181
Fax: (713) 871-8116

Sheraton Astrodome Hotel
8686 Kirby Dr.
Houston, TX 77054
Andy Chapman, Vice President of Operations
Tel.: (713) 748-3221
Fax: (713) 795-8492

Sheraton Crown Hotel & Conference Center
15700 JFK
Houston, TX 77032
Phil Dansby, General Manager
Tel.: (713) 442-5100
Fax: (713) 987-9130

Stouffer Presidente Hotel
6 E. Greenway Plaza
Houston, TX 77046
Hernando Cuellar, General Manager
Tel.: (713) 629-1200
Fax: (713) 629-4706

Hotels/Motels

Westin Galleria/Westin Oaks
5060 W. Alabama
Houston, TX 77056
Barry Sylvester, General Manager
Tel.: (713) 960-8100
Fax: (713) 960-6553

Wyndham Hotel Greenspoint
12400 Greenspoint
Houston, TX 77060
Jack Wagner, General Manager
Tel.: (713) 875-2222
Fax: (713) 875-1652

Hotel management: More than puttin' on the Ritz

With a little more than two years' experience in the hotel business, our friend Kirk landed a job as sales manager for a well-known Houston hotel. We asked him for an overview of the hospitality industry.

"If you want to move up quickly," says Kirk, "this industry is the place to be. It's anything but a dead-end business. Some people stay with the same organization for most of their careers. But I'd say the average is probably around five years with any given company. People are constantly calling and making job offers.

"I studied hotel management and general business. But you can't just walk out of college and into a middle-management position. I started as a receptionist. Then I became a secretary. I don't know anyone who hasn't paid dues for a year or two. If you're interested in food or beverages, you might start out as a dining room assistant. Essentially, you'd be doing the same thing as a secretary—typing up contracts or menus, that sort of thing. You really have to learn the business from the bottom up.

"In sales you move from secretarial work to a full-fledged sales position. I was a sales representative, then was promoted to sales manager. The next step might logically be director of sales or marketing, where I'd be responsible for advertising and marketing strategies, developing budgets, and so on. An equivalent position would be director of food and beverages, the person who's responsible for all the food and drink served in the hotel. After director of sales or food and beverages, you go on to general manager.

How to Get a Job

"I'd say the competition is about average—not nearly as fierce as in the advertising industry, for example. Earning potential is pretty good, too, depending, of course, on the size of the hotel and the city you're in and what kind of company you're working for. You start out pretty low, maybe around $13,000 or $14,000 a year. But each time you move up, you get a hefty raise, or ought to."∎

Human Services

For additional information, you can contact:

PROFESSIONAL ORGANIZATIONS:

Center for Human Services
5530 Wisconsin Avenue
Chevy Chase, MD 20815

National Association of Social Workers
750 1st Street NE
Washington, DC 20002
Tel.: (202) 408-8600

Volunteers of America
3813 N. Causeway Blvd.
Metairie, LA 70002

PROFESSIONAL PUBLICATIONS:

Children and Youth Services Review
The Nonprofit Times
Society

DIRECTORIES:

Community Jobs (Community Careers Resources Center, Washington, DC)
Directory of Agencies (National Association of Social Workers, Washington, DC)
National Directory of Children & Youth Services (Marion Peterson, Longmont, CO)
National Directory of Private Social Agencies (Croner Publications, Queens Village, NY)
National Employment Listing Service for the Criminal Justice System and Social Services (Criminal Justice Center, Sam Houston State University, Huntsville, TX)
Public Welfare Directory (American Public Welfare Association, Washington, DC)

Human Services

Social Service Organizations and Agencies Directory (Gale Research Company, Detroit, MI)
Social Services Organizations (American Business Directories, Omaha, NE)

EMPLOYERS:

American Cancer Society, Texas Division
6301 Richmond
Houston, TX 77057
Barbara Wood, Area Director
Tel.: (713) 266-2877
Fax: (713) 266-4159

American Civil Liberties Union, Greater Houston Chapter (ACLU)
1236 W.Gray
Houston, TX 77009
Helen Gros, Executive Director
Tel.: (713) 524-5925

American Diabetes Association, Texas Affiliate
2211 Norfolk, Suite 614
Houston, TX 77098
Tel.: (713) 523-9673
Fax: (713) 523-4355
Send resumes to Diane Gendel, Regional Director at:
9430 Research Blvd, Echelon II-300
Austin, TX 78759
Tel.: (512) 343-6981

American Heart Association, Houston Division
1415 La Concha
Houston, TX 77054
Beth Wood, Office Manager
Tel.: (713) 797-1812
Fax: (713) 797-1875

American Lung Association
3100 Weslayan, Suite 330
Houston, TX 77027
Nita Pyle, Program Director
Tel.: (713) 968-5800
Fax: (713) 968-5828

Avondale House
3611 Cumming
Houston, TX 77027
Barbara Boyett, Executive Director
Tel.: (713) 993-9544
Fax: (713) 993-0751

How to Get a Job

Better Business Bureau of Metropolitan Houston
2707 North Loop West, Suite 400
Houston, TX 77008
Myrna Phillips, Director of Personnel
Tel.: (713) 868-9500
Fax: (713) 867-4922

Big Brothers and Big Sisters of Houston
3939 Essex Lane
Houston, TX 77027
Frank Ringo, Executive Director
Tel.: (713) 961-5683
Fax: (713) 961-3732

Catholic Charities
3520 Montrose
Houston, TX 77006
Ray Dunleavy, Executive Director
Tel.: (713) 526-4611
Fax: (713) 526-1546

Center for Counseling
2060 North Loop West, Suite 100
Houston, TX 77018
Dr. Tom Billings, Administrator
Tel.: (713) 529-3555
Fax: (713) 957-0320

Center for the Retarded
3550 W. Dallas
Houston, TX 77019
Dr. Bill Walker, Executive Director
Tel.: (713) 528-6371
Fax: (713) 528-0423

Child Abuse Prevention Council
4151 Southwest Freeway, Suite 435
Houston, TX 77027
Rogene G. Calvert, Executive Director
Tel.: (713) 621-6446
Fax: (713) 621-7146

Child Care Council of Greater Houston
7800 Westglen Dr.
Houston, TX 77063
Juanita R. Harang, Executive Director
Tel.: (713) 266-0730
Fax: (713) 266-6586

Christian Community Service Center
3104 Edloe, Suite 203
Houston, TX 77027

Muffin Clark, Executive Director
Tel.: (713) 961-3993

Citizen's Environment Coalition Education Fund
P.O. Box 27579
Houston, TX 77227-7579
Patty Roberson, Director
Tel.: (713) 880-3369
Fax: (713) 880-2003

Clean Houston
2700 Post Oak Blvd., Suite 1728
Houston, TX 77056
Robert Chase, Executive Director
Tel.: (713) 621-7020
Fax: (713) 621-3823

Clean Water Action
3400 Montrose, Suite 303
Houston, TX 77006
Patrick Ball, Director
Maria Furby, Recruiting Officer
Tel.: (713) 528-0381
Fax: (713) 522-1791

Covenant House, Texas
1111 Lovett Blvd.
Houston, TX 77006
Caroline Larson, Executive Director
Janie Patamalai, Director of Personnel
Tel.: (713) 523-2231
Fax: (713) 523-6904

Crisis Intervention of Houston
P.O. Box 130866
Houston, TX 77219
Pat Whitten-Lege, Executive Director
Tel.: (713) 228-1505

DePelchin Children's Center
100 Sandman St.
Houston, TX 77007
Wanda Woody-Roberts, Personnel Director
Tel.: (713) 861-8136

Family Outreach Centers
P.O Box 430725
Houston, TX 77243
Maureen Evans, Manager
Tel.: (713) 465-7192

How to Get a Job

Family Service Center
2707 North Loop West, Suite 1050
Houston, TX 77008
Lloyd Sidwell, Executive Director
Tel.: (713) 861-4849
Fax: (713) 868-2619

Golden Age Hobby House of Houston
2805 Winbern
Houston, TX 77004
Winnie Colley, Executive Director
Tel.: (713) 523-7967

Goodwill Industries of Houston
5200 Jensen Dr.
Houston, TX 77026
Steven P. Lufburrow, President
Tel.: (713) 692-6221
Fax: (713) 692-0923

Greater Houston Convention and Visitors Bureau
3300 Main St.
Houston, TX 77002
Eddie Webster, President
Tel.: (713) 523-5050
Fax: (713) 524-5376

Guadeloupe Area Social Services
326 South Jensen
Houston, TX 77003
Sister Mary Jo May, Director
Tel.: (713) 227-9981
Fax: (713) 225-1242

Harris County Community Development Agency
3100 Timmons Lane, Suite 220
Houston, TX 77027
Bruce Austin, Director
Tel.: (713) 626-5651
Fax: (713) 963-9146

Harris County Department of Adult Probation
49 San Jacinto St.
Houston, TX 77002
Larance Coleman, Director
Tel.: (713) 229-9561
Fax: (713) 229-2426

Harris County Department of Child Protective Services
4040 Milam
Houston, TX 77006

Gene Daniels, Regional Director
Tel.: (713) 526-5701

Harris County Department of Education
6515 Irvington Blvd.
Houston, TX 77022
Betty Griffin, Executive Director
Tel.: (713) 692-6216
Fax: (713) 695-1976

Harris County Department of Juvenile Probation
3540 W. Dallas
Houston, TX 77219
Theresa Ramirez, Director
Tel.: (713) 521-4100
Fax: (713) 521-4148

Harris County Department of Social Services
9418 Jensen
Houston, TX 77093
Charles Leavens, Director
Tel.: (713) 696-7900
Fax: (713) 696-7941

Harris County Domestic Relations Office
49 San Jacinto, 3rd Floor
Houston, TX 77002
Nancy Westerfeld, Chief Administrator
Tel.: (713) 755-6757
Fax: (713) 755-8856

Harris County Housing Authority
3100 Timmons Lane, Suite 330
Houston, TX 77027
Walter L. Jones, Executive Director
Tel.: (713) 626-0917

Harris County Pre-trial Services
301 San Jacinto, Room 408
Houston, TX 77002
Charles Noble, Director
Tel.: (713) 755-5175
Fax: (713) 228-8150

Harris County Public Library
8080 El Rio St.
Houston, TX 77054
Cathy Park, Director
Tel.: (713) 749-9000
Fax: (713) 749-9090

How to Get a Job

Harris County Veterans County Service Office
914 Preston, Room 706
Houston, TX 77002
Hattie Russom, County Vets' Service Officer
Tel.: (713) 755-5243

Hear-Say
2525 Murworth, Suite 202A
Houston, TX 77054
Bea Groginski, Volunteer Coordinator
Tel.: (713) 666-2625

Hope Center for Youth
4115 Yoakum
Houston, TX 77006
David Winship, Executive Director
Tel.: (713) 526-4673
Fax: (713) 526-8108

Housing Authority of the City of Houston
4217 San Felipe
Houston, TX 77027
Joy Fitzgerald, Executive Director
Tel.: (713) 961-1541
Fax: (713) 961-0511

Houston Area Urban League
3215 Fannin
Houston, TX 77004
Sylvia Brooks, President
Tel.: (713) 526-5127
Fax: (713) 526-8851

Houston Area Women's Center
3101 Richmond, Suite 150
Houston, TX 77098
Ellen Cohen, Executive Director
Tel.: (713) 528-6798
Fax: (713) 535-6363

Houston Child Guidance Center
3214 Austin St.
Houston, TX 77004
Susan Blair, Executive Director
Tel.: (713) 526-3232
Fax: (713) 521-0609

Houston Department of Health and Human Services
8000 N. Stadium
Houston, TX 77054
Dr. M. desVignes-Kendrick, Interim Director

Tel.: (713) 794-9311
Fax: (713) 794-9464

Houston Family Association
9327-A, P.O. Box 140
Houston, TX 77024
Pat Wakefield, Director
Tel.: (713) 461-1644

Houston Food Bank
3811 Eastex Freeway
Houston, TX 77026
David Williams, Executive Director
Tel.: (713) 223-3700
Fax: (713) 223-1424

Houston Habitat for Humanity
P.O. Box 270411
Houston, TX 77277
Carl Umland, Acting Executive Director
Tel.: (713) 521-2816
Fax: (713) 521-0251

Houston Hospice
8707 Katy Freeway, Suite 208
Houston, TX 77024
Margaret Caddy, Executive Director
Tel.: (713) 468-2441
Fax: (713) 468-0879

Houston Humane Society
14700 Almeda Rd.
Houston, TX 77053
Sherry Ferguson, Executive Director
Tel.: (713) 433-6421
Fax: (713) 433-4325

Houston Public Library
500 McKinney Ave.
Houston, TX 77002
David Hennington, Director
Tel.: (713) 236-1313

Houston Read Commission
5330 Griggs Rd., #75
Houston, TX 77021
Mona Sosa, Program Services Manager
Tel.: (713) 228-1800
Fax: (713) 845-2560

Houston School for Deaf Children
3636 W. Dallas

How to Get a Job

Houston, TX 77019
Sheryl Jorgensen, Executive Director
Tel.: (713) 523-3633
Fax: (713) 523-8399

Houston Society for the Prevention of Cruelty to Animals
519 Studemont
Houston, TX 77007
Patricia Mercer, Executive Director
Tel.: (713) 869-8227
Fax: (713) 869-5857

Jewish Community Center of Houston, Texas
5601 S. Braeswood Blvd.
Houston, TX 77096
Jerry Wische, Executive Director
Tel.: (713) 729-3200
Fax: (713) 551-7223

Lighthouse of Houston
3530 W. Dallas
Houston, TX 77019
Gibson DuTerroil, President
Tel.: (713) 527-9561
Fax: (713) 527-8165

March of Dimes, Birth Defects Foundation, Texas Gulf Coast Chapter
3000 Wesleyan, Suite 100
Houston, TX 77027
Dianne Bynum, Chapter Director
Tel.: (713) 623-2020
Fax: (713) 964-5417

Muscular Dystrophy Association, Houston/Gulf Coast Chapter
5615 Kirby Dr., Suite 500
Houston, TX 77005
Kim Kaiser, District Director
Tel.: (713) 522-3679
Fax: (713) 522-3588

National Association for the Advancement of Colored People (NAACP)
2002 Wheeler
Houston, TX 77004
Keryl Smith, Executive Director
Tel.: (713) 526-3389
Fax: (713) 630-2699

National Organization for Women (N.O.W.)
P.O. Box 66351
Houston, TX 77266

Kathy Auden, President, Regional Chapter
Tel.: (713) 987-5218

Nation-wide Missing Persons Bureau
3500 Aldine Bender, Box A
Houston, TX 77032
Mildred Stoerner, Founder
Tel.: (713) 449-0355
Fax: (713) 449-4000

Neighborhood Centers
3401 Fannin
Houston, TX 77004
Alvin L. Henry, CEO
Tel.: (713) 236-8377
Fax: (713) 535-2136

New Directions Club
513 Thornton
Houston, TX 77018
Cheryl B. Nolen, Operations Director
Tel.: (713) 691-0314
Fax: (713) 699-7526

Open Door Mission
5803 Harrisburg
Houston, TX 77011
Mac Thornton, Director
Tel.: (713) 921-7520
Fax: (713) 921-4206

Planned Parenthood of Houston and Southeast Texas
3601 Fannin St.
Houston, TX 77004
Peter Durkin, Executive Director
Tel.: (713) 522-6240
Fax: (713) 522-9047

Refugee Services Alliance
5817 Bellaire Blvd.
Houston, TX 77081
Ken Williams, Executive Director
Tel.: (713) 668-8253
Fax: (713) 668-9972

Salvation Army
1717 Congress St.
Houston, TX 77002
Clifford Landress, Executive Assistant to the Area Commander
Tel.: (713) 222-8253
Fax: (713) 222-9127

How to Get a Job

Sheltering Arms
701 N. Post Oak Rd., Suite 500
Houston, TX 77004
Robert Philips, Executive Director
Tel.: (713) 956-1888
Fax: (713) 956-2079

Spina Bifida Association of Texas, Houston Chapter
3003 Yale, Suite 107
Houston, TX 77018
Pat Lyons, President
Tel.: (713) 862-1446

Star of Hope
5013 Calhoun St.
Houston, TX 77004
Randy Tabor, President
Tel.: (713) 748-0700
Fax: (713) 748-5941

State of Texas Department of Human Services
1330 E. 40th St.
Houston, TX 77022
Jess Hall, Personnel Officer
Tel.: (713) 692-3236

The Volunteer Center of the Texas Gulf Coast
3100 Timmons Lane, Suite 100
Houston, TX 77027
Carrie Moffitt, Executive Director
Tel.: (713) 965-0031
Fax: (713) 965-9601

United Way of the Texas Gulf Coast
P.O. Box 924507
Houston, TX 77292
Dr. Judith Craven, President
Tel.: (713) 685-2300
Fax: (713) 956-2868
Physical address:
2200 North Loop West
Houston, TX 77018

Urban Affairs Corporation
2815 Reid St.
Houston, TX 77026
Donna Bryant, Executive Director
Tel.: (713) 692-7036
Fax: (713) 223-4109

VGS, Inc.
2600 Southwest Freeway

Human Services

Houston, TX 77098
Charlie McCarthy, Director of Programs
Tel.: (713) 659-1800
Fax: (713) 535-7168

Volunteers of America, Houston
4800 W. 34th, Suite C54
Houston, TX 77092
Eliska Cowan, CEO
Tel.: (713) 956-6310
Fax: (713) 956-1586

Young Men's Christian Association of the Greater Houston Area (YMCA)
1600 Louisiana
Houston, TX 77002
Betsy Rose, Personnel Coordinator
Tel.: (713) 659-5566
Fax: (713) 659-7240

Young Women's Christian Association of Houston (YWCA)
3621 Willia
Houston, TX 77007
Willie Dean Floyd, Executive Director
Tel.: (713) 868-9922
Fax: (713) 868-5235

Working in the nonprofit world

We asked the director of a local museum what it takes to make it in the nonprofit world.

"Most of the people who enjoy nonprofit work and are successful at it tend to be other-directed. They get satisfaction out of working for a so-called worthy cause. There are very few high paying jobs in the not-for-profit institutions. An executive-level job at a museum, for example, probably pays about half of what a job with similar responsibilities would pay in a profit-making company of the same size.

"One of the fastest-growing specialties within the nonprofit world is fund raising management, probably because nonprofit institutions rely so heavily on grants and contributions." The local chapter of the National Society of Fund Raising Executives [see chapter 5] has several seminars, workshops, and a certification program.■

How to Get a Job

Insurance

For networking in the **insurance** field, check out these professional organizations listed in Chapter 5:

PROFESSIONAL ORGANIZATIONS:

American Insurance Association
Financial Executives Institute, Houston Chapter
Houston Association of Life Underwriters
Independent Insurance Agents of Houston

For additional information, you can contact:

American Council of Life Insurance
1001 Pennsylvania Ave. NW
Washington, DC 20004-2599
Tel.: (202) 624-2000

American Insurance Association
1130 Connecticut Ave. NW
Washington, DC 20036
Tel.: (202) 828-7100

National Association of Independent Insurers
2600 South River Road
Des Plaines, IL 60018
Tel.: (708) 297-7800
Fax: (708) 297-5064

National Association of Life Underwriters
1922 F Street NW
Washington, DC 20006
Tel.: (202) 331-6000
Fax: (202) 331-2171

PROFESSIONAL PUBLICATIONS:

Best's Review
Business Insurance
Independent Agent
Insurance Advocate
The Insurance Record
National Underwriter
Texas Insuror

DIRECTORIES:

Best's Directory of Insurance Agencies (A.M. Best Co., Oldwick, NY)
Best's Review: Property/Casualty Insurance Edition —100 Leading Companies Issue (A.M. Best Company, Oldwick, NY)

Insurance

Business Insurance Directory of Corporate Buyers of Insurance, Benefit Plans and Risk Management Services (Crain Communications, Chicago, IL)

Group Insurance Standard Directory (Dun's Marketing Services, Mountain Lakes, NJ)

Insurance Almanac (Underwriters Publishing Co., Englewood, NJ)

Insurance Field State Insurance Directories (Insurance Field Company, Louisville, KY)

Kirschner's Insurance Directory (Kirschner's Publishing Co., Santa Cruz, CA)

Who's Who in Insurance (Underwriter Printing and Publishing Company, Englewood, NJ)

EMPLOYERS:

Adams and Porter International
510 Bering Dr.
Houston, TX 77057
Hugh Wilson, President
Tel.: (713) 975-7500
Fax: (713) 975-1172

Alexander and Alexander of Texas
5851 San Felipe, Suite 300
Houston, TX 77057
John Howard, Managing Vice President
Tel.: (713) 974-6161
Fax: (713) 972-8708

Allstate Insurance Company
450 Gears Rd., Suite 800
Houston, TX 77067
Tom Rowland, Controller
Tel.: (713) 875-8900
Fax: (713) 875-8934

American General Corp.
2929 Allen Parkway
Houston, TX 77019
Loran Ruhnow, Manager of Purchasing and Support Services
Tel.: (713) 522-1111
Fax: (713) 831-8396

American International Companies
675 Bering
Houston, TX 77057
Human Resources Manager
Tel.: (713) 268-8600

Blue Cross Blue Shield of Texas
4888 Loop Central Dr., Suite 900
Houston, TX 77081
Rogers Colman, President

How to Get a Job

Tel.: (713) 668-0672
Fax: (214) 669-3900

CNA
6565 West Loop South, Suite 300
Bellaire, TX 77401
Catherine Barton, Purchasing Officer
Tel.: (713) 663-5398

Cigna Property and Casualty Companies
1360 Post Oak Blvd., Suite 1200
Houston, TX 77056
Annmarie Steinhilber, Manager
Tel.: (713) 552-7061

Cravens Dargan and Company
1903 Hermann Dr.
Houston, TX 77004
James R. Cravens, Jr., President
Tel.: (713) 525-6100
Fax: (713) 525-6102

Employers Insurance of Texas
2000 Bering Dr., Suite 450
Houston, TX 77057
Larry Manton, District Manager
Tel.: (713) 953-4600
Fax: (713) 953-4858

Fireman's Fund Insurance Company
1616 Voss, Suite 900
Houston, TX 77057
Rosemary Miller, Purchasing Officer
Tel.: (713) 725-2800
Fax: (713) 735-2839

Hartford Insurance Group
450 Gears Rd., Suite 500
Houston, TX 77067
Glenn Damstra, General Manager
Tel.: (713) 874-9600
Fax: (800) 872-4261

Health Economics Corp.
2700 Post Oak Blvd., Suite 1800
Houston, TX 77056
O.D. Harrell, Assistant Vice President
Tel.: (713) 621-9330
Fax: (713) 961-3651

Highlands Insurance Company
10370 Richmond Ave.

Houston, TX 77042-4123
Chuck Lawrence, Personnel Officer
Tel.: (713) 952-9555
Fax: (713) 952-9977

Johnson & Higgins of Texas
333 Clay St., 1400 3 Allen Center
Houston, TX 77002
William J. Keckeisen, Executive Vice President
Tel.: (713) 651-1900
Fax: (713) 651-1261

Liberty Mutual Insurance Company
13201 Northwest Freeway, Suite 400
Houston, TX 77240
Tom Rudder, District Manager
Tel.: (713) 460-4650
Fax: (713) 895-5449

Prudential Capital Corporation
1100 Milam, Suite 3900
Houston, TX 77002
Connie Sullivan, Vice President of Corporate Finance
Tel.: (713) 655-1300
Fax: (713) 658-8338

St. Paul Fire & Marine Insurance Company
2925 Briarpark, Suite 300
Houston, TX 77042-3726
Gary F. Kerrick, General Manager
Tel.: (713) 789-3366
Fax: (713) 789-2801

Travelers Insurance Company
10800 Richmond Ave.
Houston, TX 77042
Tena Bynem, Manager
Tel.: (713) 787-4000
Fax: (713) 787-4247

USF&G Company
13101 Northwest Freeway
Houston, TX 77210
Jim Phipps, Manager
Tel.: (713) 462-2206
Fax: (713) 460-7170

Variable Annuity Life Insurance
2929 Allen Parkway
Houston, TX 77019
Stephen Bickel, President

How to Get a Job

Tel.: (713) 526-5251
Fax: (713) 831-4334

John L. Wortham & Son
2727 Allen Parkway
Houston, TX 77019
A.L. Hahn, Personnel and Purchasing
Tel.: (713) 526-3366
Fax: (713) 526-7018

Investment Bankers/Stock Brokers

For networking in **investment banking,** check out this professional organization listed in Chapter 5:

PROFESSIONAL ORGANIZATION:

Financial Executives Institute, Houston Chapter

For additional information, you can contact:

Association for Investment Management & Research
200 Park Ave.
New York, NY 10166
Tel.: 957-2860

Financial Analysts Federation
5 Boar's Head Lane
P.O. Box 3668
Charlottesville, VA 22903
Tel.: (804) 977-8977

International Association of Financial Planning
2 Concourse Pkwy.
Atlanta, GA 30328
Tel.: (404) 395-1605

Investment Counsel Association of America
20 Exchange Place
New York, NY 10005
Tel.: (212) 344-0999

National Association of Securities Dealers
1735 K Street NW
Washington, DC 20006
Tel.: (202) 728-8000

National Venture Capital Association
1655 N. Fort Myer Dr., #700

Investment/Stock Brokers

Arlington, VA 22209
Tel.: (703) 528-4370

Securities Industry Association
120 Broadway
New York, NY 10271
Tel.: (212) 608-1500

Security Traders Association
1 World Traders Center, #4511
New York, NY 10048
Tel.: (212) 524-0484

PROFESSIONAL PUBLICATIONS:

Commodity Journal
Corporate Finance
Corporate Financing Week
Credit and Financial Management
D&B Reports
Dun's Business Month
Finance, the Magazine of Money and Business
Financial Analysts Journal
Financial Executive
Financial World
Institutional Investor
Investment Dealer's Digest
Northwest Houston Business News
Securities Week
Security Industry and Product News
Stock Market Magazine
Texas Business
Texas Business Review
Wall Street Transcript

DIRECTORIES:

CUSIP Master Directory (Standard & Poors, New York, NY)
Directory of Corporate Financing (Dealer's Digest, New York, NY)
Directory of Registered Investment Advisors (Money Market Directories, Charlottesville, VA)
Dow Jones-Irwin Mutual Fund Yearbook (Dow Jones-Irwin, Homewood, IL)
Harvard Business School Career Guide—Investment Banking (Harvard Business School Press, Cambridge, MA)
Investments & Securities Directory (American Business Directories, Omaha, NE)
Money Market Directory (Money Market Directories, Charlottesville, VA)
New York Stock Exchange Guide (Commerce Clearing House, New York, NY)
Security Dealers of North America (Standard & Poors, New York, NY)
Standard & Poor's Security Dealers of North America (Standard & Poors, New York, NY)

How to Get a Job

Who's Who in the Securities Industry (Economist Publishing Co., New York, NY)

EMPLOYERS:

Advantage Capital
2800 Post Oak Blvd.
Houston, TX 77056
Doug Gehrman, Vice President for Human Resources
Tel.: (713) 993-0500
Fax: (713) 993-4215

Aim Management Group
11 Greenway Plaza, Suite 1919
Houston, TX 77046
Charles T. Bauer, President
Tel.: (713) 626-1919
Fax: (713) 993-9890

American Capital Management and Research
2800 Post Oak Blvd.
Houston, TX 77056
Tel.: (713) 993-0500
Fax: (713) 993-4215

American General Securities
2727 Allen Parkway
Houston, TX 77019
Tel.: (713) 831-3806
Fax: (713) 831-3929

Capstone Financial Services
1100 Milam St., Suite 3500
Houston, TX 77002
Vivian Cox, Office Manager
Tel.: (713) 750-8000
Fax: (713) 750-8057

Cowen & Company
1111 Bagby, Suite 2350
Houston, TX 77002
Shirley Guinn, Personnel Director
Tel.: (713) 652-7100
Fax: (713) 652-7199

Criterion Group
1990 Post Oak Blvd., Suite 1100
Houston, TX 77056-3890
Terry Ellis, President
Tel.: (713) 963-5200
Fax: (713) 963-5235

Investment/Stock Brokers

Dean Witter
3200 Southwest Freeway, Suite 2100
Houston, TX 77027
Don Harris, Branch Manager
Tel.: (713) 965-8700
Fax: (713) 965-8703

Donaldson Lufkin & Jenrette
1301 McKinney, Suite 600
Houston, TX 77010
Peggy Bird, Operations Manager
Tel.: (713) 739-3600

A.G. Edwards & Sons
2000 Post Oak Blvd.
Houston, TX 77056
Diane McCuam, Operations Manager
Tel.: (713) 627-2030
Fax: (713) 621-2767

Eppler Guerin & Turner
2121 Sage Rd., Suite 300
Houston, TX 77056
Tom Bann, Branch Manager
Tel.: (713) 622-0333
Fax: (713) 622-6963

Fayez Sarofim and Company
2 Houston Center, Suite 2907
Houston, TX 77010
Fayez Sarofim, President
Tel.: (713) 654-4484
Fax: (713) 654-8184

First Investors Corp.
6666 Harwin Dr., Suite 570
Houston, TX 77036
William Henderson, Branch Manager
Tel.: (713) 784-3200
Fax: (713) 784-3134

Goldman Sachs & Co.
1000 Louisiana, Suite 550
Houston, TX 77002
H. Scott Caven, Vice President
Tel.: (713) 654-8400

Kemper Financial Services
909 Fannin
Houston, TX 77010
Tel.: (713) 853-2200
Fax: (713) 853-2039

How to Get a Job

Kidder Peabody & Company
1000 Louisiana, Suite 5800
Houston, TX 77002
Thadd Bowman, Branch Manager
Tel.: (713) 751-7600
Fax: (713) 751-7695

KSA Industries/Houston Oilers
6910 Fannin
Houston, TX 77030
K.S. Adams, Jr., President
Tel.: (713) 797-1500

Merrill Lynch Pierce Fenner & Smith
12 E Greenway Plaza, Suite 200
Houston, TX 77046
Beth Warner, Assistant to Resident Life Manager
Tel.: (713) 871-9111
Fax: (713) 993-1561

Murchison Investment Bankers
14550 Torrey Chase Blvd.
Houston, TX 77014
Donna Weaver, Office Manager
Tel.: (713) 440-1234
Fax: (713) 440-4633

Openheimer & Company
333 Clay St., Suite 4700
Houston, TX 77002
Katie Harrison, Manager
Tel.: (713) 650-2000
Fax: (713) 650-2001

Paine Webber
2000 Post Oak Blvd.
Houston, TX 77056
Bernice Forester
Tel.: (713) 871-0901
Fax: (713) 965-8199

Prudential-Bache Securities
1331 Lamar, Suite 1669
Houston, TX 77010
Mel Hawkins, Stock Broker Trainees
Julie Hood, Sales
Sandy Moor, Operations Area
(No phone calls. Send resume and cover letter)

Rauscher Pierce Refsnes
1980 Post Oak Blvd., Suite 100
Houston, TX 77056

Investment/Stock Brokers

Jack Whitley, Manager
Tel.: (713) 626-4910
Fax: (713) 623-9283

Rotan Mosle
P.O. Box 3226
Houston, TX 77253
Doug Oaks, Purchasing Officer
Tel.: (713) 236-3000
Fax: (713) 236-3033

Shearson Lehman Brothers
2500 One Riverway
Houston, TX 77056
Russell Morton, Divisional Director
Tel.: (713) 629-2900
Fax: (713) 629-2923

Smith Barney, Harris Upham & Company
5065 Westheimer, Suite 1200 E
Houston, TX 77056
Carolyn Delano, Branch Manager
Tel.: (713) 960-9669
Fax: (713) 960-0436

Texas First Securities
1360 Post Oak Blvd.
Houston, TX 77056
Missy Buetel, Vice President
Tel.: (713) 993-2000

Underwood, Neuhaus & Company
909 Fannin, Suite 700
Houston, TX 77010
Joe Lowry, Executive Vice President
Tel.: (713) 853-2200
Fax: (713) 853-2203

Variable Annuity Marketing Company
2929 Allen Parkway, Suite 817a
Houston, TX 77019
Tel.: (713) 526-5251
Fax: (713) 831-4334

Westcap Corp.
1301 Fannin St., 23rd Floor
Houston, TX 77002
Ira H. Green, Chairman
Tel.: (713) 651-1111
Fax: (713) 653-5382

How to Get a Job

Woodlands Securities Corp.
1610 Woodstead Ct.
The Woodlands, TX 77380
Tel.: (713) 367-2483
Fax: (713) 298-1182

Law Firms

For networking in the **legal profession,** check out these professional organizations listed in Chapter 5:

PROFESSIONAL ORGANIZATIONS:

Houston Association of Legal Secretaries
Houston Bar Association
Houston Legal Assistants Association

For additional information, you can contact:

American Bar Association
750 North Lake Shore Drive
Chicago, IL 60611
Tel.: (312) 988-5000
Fax: (312) 988-6281

Association of Trial Lawyers of America
1050 31st Street NW
Washington, DC 20007
Tel.: (202) 965-3500

National Bar Association (Minority Attorneys)
1225 11th Street NW
Washington, DC 20001
Tel.: (202) 842-3900

National Association of Bar Executives
750 N. Lake Shore Drive
Chicago, IL 60611
Tel.: (312) 988-5000

National Paralegal Association
P.O. Box 406
Solebury, PA
Tel.: (215) 297-8333

PROFESSIONAL PUBLICATIONS:

ABA Journal
American Lawyer
Banking Law Journal

Law

Criminal Law Bulletin
For the Defense
Law Enforcement Communications
Lawyer's Weekly
Legal Times
The Paralegal
Texas Bar Journal
Trial

DIRECTORIES:

ABA Directory (American Bar Association, Chicago, IL)
Directory of Local Paralegal Clubs (National Paralegal Association, Solebury, PA)
Law & Business Directory of Major U.S. Law Firms (Law & Business, Clifton, NJ)
Martindale-Hubbell Law Directory (Martindale-Hubbell, Summit, NJ)
Now Hiring: Government Jobs for Lawyers (Law Student Division, American Bar Association, Chicago, IL)
United States Bar Directory (Attorneys' National Clearing House, Naples, FL)
Who's Who in American Law (Marquis Who's Who, Chicago, IL)

EMPLOYERS:

Andrews and Kurth
4200 Texas Commerce Tower
Houston, TX 77002
John T. Cabaniss, Managing Chairman
Tel.: (713) 220-4200
Fax: (713) 220-4285

Arnold, White and Durkee
750 Bering Dr., Suite 400
Houston, TX 77057
Peggy McQuade, Manager of Personnel
Tel.: (713) 787-1400
Fax: (713) 789-2679

Baker and Botts
3000 One Shell Plaza
Houston, TX 77002
E.W. Barnett, Managing Partner
Tel.: (713) 229-1234
Fax: (713) 229-1522

Bracewell and Patterson
711 Louisiana, Suite 2900 South Tower Pennzoil Place
Houston, TX 77002-2781
Richard A. Royds, Managing Partner
Tel.: (713) 223-2900
Fax: (713) 221-1212

How to Get a Job

Brown, Parker & Leahy L.L.P.
1200 Smith, Suite 3600
Houston, TX 77002
Timothy R. Brown, Managing Partner
Tel.: (713) 654-8111
Fax: (713) 654-1871

Butler & Binion
1000 Louisiana, Suite 1600
Houston, TX 77002
Doug Badgett, Administrator
Tel.: (713) 237-3111
Fax: (713) 237-3201

Eikenburg and Stiles
1021 Main St., Suite 1100
Houston, TX 77002
John J. Eidenburg, Principal Officer
Tel.: (713) 652-2144
Fax: (713) 655-6986

Fulbright & Jaworski
1301 McKinney, 51st Floor
Houston, TX 77010
Gus Blackshear, Chairman of the Executive Committee
Tel.: (713) 651-5151
Fax: (713) 651-5246

Griggs and Harrison
1301 McKinney, Suite 3200
Houston, TX 77010
W. Garney Griggs, President
Tel.: (713) 651-0600
Fax: (713) 651-1944

Hirsch Glover Robinson & Sheiness
917 Franklin
Houston, TX 77002
Jay Hirsch, Manager
Tel.: (713) 224-8941
Fax: (713) 236-7824

Hutcheson and Grundy
1200 Smith St., Suite 3300
Houston, TX 77002
Jack Carter, Managing Partner
Tel.: (713) 951-2800
Fax: (713) 951-2925

Jackson and Walker
Interfirst Plaza, 1100 Louisiana, Suite 4200
Houston, TX 77002

Law

Managing Committee
Tel.: (713) 652-5100
Fax: (713) 752-4221

Liddell Sapp and Zivley
Texas Commerce Tower, Suite 3400
Houston, TX 77002
Mike Rutledge, Administrative Partner
Tel.: (713) 226-1200
Fax: (713) 223-3717

Lorance and Thompson
303 Jackson Hill, Suite 100
Houston, TX 77007
Ann Aleman, Purchasing Manager
Tel.: (713) 868-5560
Fax: (713) 868-1605

Mayor, Day, Caldwell and Keeton
1900 Nations Bank Center
Houston, TX 77002
Johnathan Day, Managing Partner
Tel.: (713) 225-7000
Fax: (713) 225-7047

Paxson and Bersch
1300 Post Oak Blvd., 23rd Floor
Houston, TX 77056
Office Manager
Tel.: (713) 623-8800
Fax: (713) 993-8451

Porter & Clements
700 Louisiana, Suite 3500
Houston, TX 77002
Nick D. Nicholas, Partner
Tel.: (713) 226-0600
Fax: (713) 228-1331

Sewell and Riggs
333 Clay Ave., Suite 800
Houston, TX 77002
Robert Bramlette, Managing Director
Tel.: (713) 652-8700
Fax: (713) 652-8808

Sheinfield, Maley and Kay
3700 First City Tower
Houston, TX 77002
Sandra S. Gilbert, Administrator
Tel.: (713) 658-8881
Fax: (713) 658-9756

How to Get a Job

Vinson & Elkins, Attorneys at Law
2500 First City Tower, 1001 Fannin St.
Houston, TX 77002-6760
Harry M. Reasoner, Managing Partner
Tel.: (713) 758-2222
Fax: (713) 758-2346

Weil Gotshal and Manges
700 Louisiana, Suite 1600
Houston, TX 77002
B.J. Baker, Managing Partner
Tel.: (713) 546-5000
Fax: (713) 224-0511

Wood, Lucksinger and Epstein
1221 Lamar, Suite 1400
Houston, TX 77010
W.R. Livesay, Jr.
Tel.: (713) 658-1888

Woodard Hall and Primm
7000 Texas Commerce Tower, 600 Travis
Houston, TX 77002
Dennis Villman, Purchasing Officer
Tel.: (713) 221-3800
Fax: (713) 224-3271

Management Consultants

For networking in **management consulting,** check out these professional organizations listed in Chapter 5:

PROFESSIONAL ORGANIZATIONS:

Financial Executives Institute, Houston Chapter
Texas Executive Women

For additional information, you can contact:

ACME-The Association of Management Consulting Firms
230 Park Avenue
New York, NY 10169
Tel.: (212) 949-6571

Institute of Management Consultants
230 Park Avenue
New York, NY 10169
Tel.: (212) 697-8262

National Management Association
2210 Arbor Boulevard
Dayton, OH 45439
Tel.: (513) 294-0421
Fax: (513) 294-2374

Society of Professional Management Consultants
95 Sawyer Road
3 University Park Office, #400
Waltham, MA 02154
Tel.: (617) 894-2547

PROFESSIONAL PUBLICATIONS:

ACME Newsletter
Academy of Management Journal
Academy of Management Review
Administrative Management
Business Quarterly
Consultant News
Harvard Business Review
Management Review
Management Today

DIRECTORIES:

ACME Directory—Directory of Membership and Services (Association of Management Consultants, New York, NY)

How to Get a Job

Business Consultants Directory (American Business Directories, Omaha, NE)
Consultants &Consulting Organizations (Gale Research Co., Detroit, MI)
Directory of Management Consultants (Kennedy & Kennedy, Fitzwilliam, NH)
IMC Directory (Institute of Management Consultants, New York, NY)

EMPLOYERS:

Andersen Consulting
711 Louisiana, Suite 1300
Houston, TX 77002
Randi Mays-Knapp, Recruiting
Tel.: (713) 237-2121
Fax: (713) 237-2786

Benesys
1775 St. James Place, Suite 200
Houston, TX 77056
Shirley Haeckle, Controller
Tel.: (713) 871-0266
Fax: (713) 871-6301

Birkman & Associates
3040 Post Oak Blvd., Suite 1425
Houston, TX 77056
Roger W. Birkman, President
Tel.: (713) 623-2760
Fax: (713) 963-9142

Booz Allen & Hamilton
2525 Bay Area Blvd., Suite 290
Houston, TX 77058
Buddy Lavender, Manager
Tel.: (713) 488-6750
Fax: (713) 488-5618

CCA Southwest
800 Rockmead, Suite 100
Kingwood, TX 77339
Dan McIntyre, Senior Vice President, Development
Tel.: (713) 359-0720
Fax: (713) 359-2696

Coopers & Lybrand
1100 Louisiana, Suite 4100
Houston, TX 77002
Todd Hoffman, Recruiter
Tel.: (713) 757-5200
Fax: (713) 757-5249

Management Consultants

Daugbjerg and Associates
5 Post Oak Park, Suite 2180
Houston, TX 77027
Ray Daugbjerg, President
Tel.: (713) 622-7514
Fax: (713) 622-7512

Econalysis
11707 Ridgewood Circle
Houston, TX 77071
Dennis Giuffre, Consultant
Tel.: (713) 728-3317

Ernst & Young
1221 McKinney, Suite 2400
Houston, TX 77010
Rhonda Eldridge, Recruiting Coordinator
Tel.: (713) 750-1460
Fax: (713) 750-1501

Hay Group
4265 San Felipe, Suite 604
Houston, TX 77027
Dan Fader, General Manager
Tel.: (713) 871-1655

Hewitt Associates
1980 Post Oak Blvd., Suite 1100
Houston, TX 77056
Pete Boerner
Tel.: (713) 871-8919
Fax: (713) 840-9534

King Chapman & Broussard
1100 Milam, Suite 3600
Houston, TX 77002
William Broussard, Vice President
Tel.: (713) 650-6484
Fax: (713) 650-8037

Arthur D. Little
1001 Fannin, Suite 2050
Houston, TX 77002
Mary Fairbrother, Business Manager
Tel.: (713) 650-0335
Fax: (713) 650-6906

Markel Enterprises
2537 S. Gessner, Suite 223
Houston, TX 77063
Charles Yust, President

How to Get a Job

Tel.: (713) 977-8201
Fax: (713) 577-3203

McKinsey & Company
2 Houston Center, Suite 3500
Houston, TX 77010
James Crownover, Manager
Tel.: (713) 650-1299
Fax: (713) 650-1050

William M. Mercer
1221 Lamar, Suite 1200
Houston, TX 77010
Christy Clark, Personnel Administrator
Tel.: (713) 951-0060
Fax: (713) 951-0310

Philbrook Goodale Associates
1200 Post Oak Blvd., Suite 200
Houston, TX 77056
James Goodale, Senior Partner
Tel.: (713) 877-8182

Productivity Enhancements
7322 Southwest Freeway, Suite 1100
Houston, TX 77325
Elijah King, President
Tel.: (713) 683-5752

Ramsey-Sellers Associates
P.O. Box 841159
Houston, TX 77284-1159
Tam Hays, Administrative Manager
Tel.: (713) 859-7771
Fax: (713) 859-7779

Stone & Webster Management Consultants
330 Barker-Cypress Rd.
Houston, TX 77094
Bobbie Deason, Personnel Recruiter
Tel.: (713) 492-4460
Fax: (713) 492-4100

Media: Newspapers and Magazines

For the local trade press and special interest magazines, see Chapter 4. For networking in **media,** check out these professional organizations listed in Chapter 5:

PROFESSIONAL ORGANIZATIONS:

Houston Association of Black Journalists
International Association of Business Communications
Press Club of Houston
Public Relations Society of America, Houston Chapter
Society of Professional Journalists, Houston Chapter
Women in Communications

For additional information, you can contact:

American Newspaper Publishers Association
11600 Sunrise Valley Drive
Reston, VA 22091
Tel.: (703) 648-1000
Fax: (703) 620-4557

Audit Bureau of Circulations
900 North Meacham Road
Schaumburg, IL 60173
Tel.: (708) 605-0909
Fax: (708) 605-0483

Magazine Publishers Association
575 Lexington Avenue Suite 540
New York, NY 10022
Tel.: (212) 752-0055
Fax: (212) 888-4217

National Press Club
529 14th Street NW
Washington, DC 20045
Tel: (202) 622-7500

Suburban Newspapers of America
401 N. Michigan Avenue
Chicago, IL 60611
Tel: (312) 644-6610

PROFESSIONAL PUBLICATIONS:

The Columbia Journalism Review
Editor and Publisher
Folio
The Professional Communicator

How to Get a Job

Suburban Publisher
TPA Messenger
The Writer
Writer's Digest

DIRECTORIES:

Burrelle's Black Media Directory (Burrelle's Media Directories, Livingston, NJ)
Burrelle's Hispanic Media Directory (Burrelle's Media Directories, Livingston, NJ)
Burrelle's Women's Media Directory (Burrelle's Media Directories, Livingston, NJ)
Editor and Publisher International Yearbook (Editor and Publisher, New York, NY)
Folio Magazine—Directory of Magazine Suppliers Issue (Folio Magazine Publishing, New Canaan, CT)
Magazine & Bookseller—Magazine and Paperback Distributors' Directory Issue (North American Publishing Co., New York, NY)
Magazine & Bookseller—Who's Who in the Publishing & Distribution Industry Issue (North American Publishing, New York, NY)
Magazine Industry Market Place (R.R. Bowker, New York, NY)
News Bureaus in the US (Public Relations Publishing, New York, NY)
Standard Rate & Data Service—Print Media Production Data (Standard Rate & Data Service, Wilmette, IL)
Student Guide to Mass Media Internships (Intern Research Group, Boulder, CO)
Who Distributes What and Where: An International Directory of Publishers, Imprints, Working Press of the Nation (National Research Bureau, Chicago, IL)

EMPLOYERS:

Carlyle Communications International
1360 Post Oak Blvd., Suite 2412
Houston, TX 77056
Norma Myers, Manager
Tel.: (713) 622-1967
Fax: (713) 622-8716

Chinese Daily News
9104A Bellaire Blvd.
Houston, TX 77036
Estella Hu, Editor
Tel.: (713) 771-4363
Fax: (713) 270-8222

Cleveland Advocate
107 Hanson
Cleveland, TX 77327
Diana Cole, General Manager
Tel.: (713) 443-7225

Media

Courier Newspaper
100 Avenue A
Conroe, TX 77301
Ken Johnson, Chairman
Tel.: (713) 443-8210
Fax: (409) 756-6676

Creneau Media Group
2009 Lubbock
Houston, TX 77007
Lisa Collins, Office Manager
Tel.: (713) 880-4611
Fax: (713) 880-4644

Daily Court Review
6807 Wynnwood
Houston, TX 77008
Sylvia Valencia, Personnel Director
Tel.: (713) 528-5437
Fax: (713) 869-8887

The Echo
20202 Highway 59 North
Humble, TX 77338
Larry Terry, Editor
Tel.: (713) 446-3733
Fax: (713) 446-0201

Houston Chronicle
P.O. Box 4260
Houston, TX 77210
Ann Turnbach, Personnel Director
Tel.: (713) 220-7171
Fax: (713) 220-6677

Houston Defender
Houston's leading black weekly newspaper.
2626 South Loop West, Suite 250
Houston, TX 77054
Marylyn Marshall, Managing Editor
Tel.: (713) 663-7716
Fax: (713) 663-7116

Houston Metropolitan Magazine
5615 Kirby Dr., Suite 600
Houston, TX 77005
Corina Tiemeyer, General Manager
Tel.: (713) 524-3000
Fax: (713) 524-8213

The Houston Post Company
P.O. Box 4747

How to Get a Job

Houston, TX 77210
Jim Janiga, Personnel Director
Tel.: (713) 840-5600
Fax: (713) 840-6997

Houston Scene Magazine
P.O. Box 19008
Houston, TX 77224
Edwin Dean, Publisher
Tel.: (713) 493-6372

Jewish Herald Voice
3403 Audley
Houston, TX 77098
Jeanne Samuels, Editor
Tel.: (713) 630-0391
Fax: (713) 630-0404

La Informacion
P.O. Box 20726
Houston, TX 77225
Personnel Department
Tel.: (713) 272-0100
Fax: (713) 272-0011

Leader Newspaper
3500 East T.C. Jester, Suite A
Houston, TX 77018
Renee Walker, Personnel
Tel.: (713) 686-8494
Fax: (713) 686-0970

North Freeway Leader
10939 Airline Dr.
Houston, TX 77037
Bob White, Editor
Tel.: (713) 445-1819
Fax: (713) 686-0970

Pasadena Citizen
102 S. Shaver
Pasadena, TX 77506
David Holgate, Manager
Tel.: (713) 477-0221
Fax: (713) 477-9090

Southern Newspapers
1050 Wilcrest
Houston, TX 77042
Personnel Department
Tel.: (713) 266-5481
Fax: (713) 266-1847

Media

La Subasta
6100 Hillcroft
Houston, TX 77081
Orlando Budini, Editor and Publisher
Tel.: (713) 777-1010
Fax: (713) 271-7523

The Texas Catholic Herald
1700 San Jacinto
Houston, TX 77002
Marion Zientek, Editor
Tel.: (713) 659-5461
Fax: (713) 759-9151

Getting the scoop on a newspaper career

Jeff Canning was a high school student when he began working part time for a local suburban newspaper chain. He enjoyed the work so much that he returned to the chain after serving in the armed services. Today, Canning serves as senior news editor for the chain. We asked him about his career path in the news business.

"I've done everything from cub reporter to working the copy desk to serving as the chief of the metro desk," says Canning. "Now I'm the senior news editor. The important thing is that each time I made a move, I became more valuable to the company or any company that might have wanted to hire me."

Canning offers the following advice to people who want to break into the news business. "I always tell young people who express an interest in the business to do two things: first, get some writing samples together—anything to show you can handle the English language. Second, try to gain some work experience. College newspapers, local weekly suburban newspapers, and local feature magazines are sometimes understaffed and willing to give newcomers a try.

"When you begin looking for a full-time job, hit every publication in the area. It's a good idea to send your resume to the news editor instead of the managing editor or editor-in-chief. The latter are certainly good choices, but if a paper has a senior news editor, he or she may not receive as much mail as other editors on staff. News editors will usually forward resumes to the proper people, along with a personal note.

"After you've been working for at least a

How to Get a Job

year, you can consider moving around. Most newspapers like to see two to three years experience in one area, and some require as much as five to seven years experience. Keep that in mind if you get tired of covering a beat you don't really like. You have to pay your dues. When you are ready to move, you can check trade journals such as *Editor and Publisher*, although they list primarily entry-level positions. Your contacts and word of mouth will get you the jobs you really want. So make networking one of your priorities right from the beginning." ■

Museums/Art Galleries

For networking among **museums and art galleries,** check out these professional organizations listed in Chapter 5:

PROFESSIONAL ORGANIZATIONS:

Alley Theatre
Art League of Houston
Business Artsfund
Business Volunteers for the Arts/Houston
Cultural Arts Council of Houston
Houston Civic Arts Association
Houston Grand Opera Association
Houston International Festival
Houston Symphony Orchestra
Texas Accountants and Lawyers for the Arts

For additional information, you can contact:

American Association of Museums
1225 I Street NW, Suite 200
Washington, DC 20005
Tel.: (202) 289-1818
Fax: (202) 289-6578

American Federation of Arts
41 East 65th Street
New York, NY 10021
Tel.: (212) 988-7700
Fax: (212) 861-2487

Arts and Business Council
130 East 40th Street
New York, NY 10016

Museums/Art Galleries

National Assembly of Local Arts Agencies
1420 K Street, NW
Washington, DC 20005
(202) 371-2830

National Assembly of State Arts Agencies
1010 Vermont Avenue, NW
Washington, DC 20005
(202) 347-6352

PROFESSIONAL PUBLICATIONS:

ArtCom
Art Direction
Art Forum
Artweek
Art World
Curator
Inner-view
Museum News

DIRECTORIES:

American Art Directory (Jacques Cattell Press, New York, NY)
Directory for the Arts (Center for Arts Information, New York, NY)
Historic Exploring Science: Guide to Contemporary Museums of Science and Technology (Association of Science-Technology Centers, Washington, DC)
National Arts Guide (National Arts Guide, Chicago, IL)
National Arts Jobbank (Western States Arts Foundation, Santa Fe, NM)
NASAA Directory (National Assembly of State Art Agencies, Washington, DC)
Official Museum Directory (American Association of Museums, Washington, DC)
Texas Museum Directory (Texas Historical Commission, Austin, TX)

EMPLOYERS:

Antique Car Museum
505 North Loop West
Houston, TX 77008
Stephanie Tomfohrde, Schedule Coordinator
Tel.: (713) 868-2243

Art Works
12280 Westheimer, Suite 400
Houston, TX 77077
Theo Smith, President
Tel.: (713) 497-7703

How to Get a Job

Artigiani Galleries
2421 S. Shepherd
Houston, TX 77019
Mark Lincoln, Owner
Tel.: (713) 521-1213

Black Heritage Gallery
5408 Almeda Rd.
Houston, TX 77004
Robbie Lee, Personnel Director
Tel.: (713) 529-7900
Fax: (713) 942-9580

Children's Museum
1500 Binz
Houston, TX 77004
Jane Jerry, Director
Tel.: (713) 522-1138
Fax: (713) 522-5747

Collins Lowell Gallery
2903 Saint St.
Houston, TX 77027
L. Collins, President
Tel.: (713) 622-6962
Fax: (713) 871-9930

Confederate Museum
2740 FM 359
Richmond, TX 77469
JoElla Morris, President
Tel.: (713) 342-8787

Contemporary Arts Museum
5216 Montrose
Houston, TX 77006
Mike Reed, Director of Personnel
Tel.: (713) 526-0773
Fax: (713) 526-6749

Dean Day Gallery
1724 Post Oak Blvd.
Houston, TX 77056
Ms. Dean Day, Owner
Tel.: (713) 963-9963

Fort Bend County Museum
500 Houston St., Box 251
Richmond, TX 77469
Michael Moore, Director
Tel.: (713) 342-6478

Museums/Art Galleries

Harris County Heritage Society
1100 Bagby
Houston, TX 77002
Linda Woodberry, Business Manager
Tel.: (713) 655-1912
Fax: (713) 655-7527

Horizon Galleries
Town and Country Center, East Suite 200
Houston, TX 77024
Chris Colaneri, Manager
Tel.: (713) 973-7777
Fax: (713) 973-0725

Houston Center for Photography
1441 W. Alabama
Houston, TX 77006
Jean Caslin, Director
Tel.: (713) 529-4755
Fax: (713) 529-9248

Houston Museum of Natural Science
1 Hermann Circle Dr., Hermann Park
Houston, TX 77030
Linda Piersol, Assistant Controller
Tel.: (713) 639-4614
Fax: (713) 523-4125

Meredith Long Galleries
2323 San Felipe
Houston, TX 77019
Meredith Long, President
Tel.: (713) 523-6671
Fax: (713) 523-2355

Menil Collection
1515 Sulross
Houston, TX 77006
Paul Winkler, Director
Tel.: (713) 525-9400
Fax: (713) 525-9444

Museum of Fine Arts/Houston
P.O. Box 6826
Houston, TX 77265
Donna Fleming, Personnel Director
Tel.: (713) 526-1361
Fax: (713) 639-7595

Railroad Museum of the Gulf Coast, Chapter NRHS
7390 Mesa Dr.
Houston, TX 77028

How to Get a Job

Carl Green, Manager
Tel.: (713) 631-6612

C.G. Rein Galleries
1700 Bissonnet St.
Houston, TX 77005
Gina Alderman, Manager
Tel.: (713) 526-4916

Gerhard Wurzer Galleries
5701 Memorial
Houston, TX 77007
Gerhard Wurzer, Director
Tel.: (713) 863-1933
Fax: (713) 869-9466

Oil, Gas, and Plastics

For networking in the **oil, gas, and plastics industry,** check out these professional organizations listed in Chapter 5:

PROFESSIONAL ORGANIZATIONS:

Geophysical Society of Houston
Houston Association of Petroleum Landmen
Houston Geological Society
Society of Petroleum Evaluation Engineers

For additional information, you can contact:

American Gas Association
1515 Wilson Boulevard
Arlington, VA 22209
Tel.: (703) 841-8400
Fax: (703) 841-8406

American Petroleum Institute
1201 Main Street, Suite 2535
Dallas, TX 75202
Tel.: (214) 748-3841

Clean Energy Research Institute
University of Miami
219 McArthur Bldg., Box 248294
Coral Gables, FL 33124
Tel.: (305) 284-4666

Society of the Plastics Industry
1275 K Street, NW, Suite 400

Oil/Gas/Plastics

Washington, DC 20005
Tel.: (202) 371-5200

PROFESSIONAL PUBLICATIONS

Drilling Contractor
Drilling—The Wellsite Magazine
Gas Digest
Gulf Coast Oil World
Hydrocarbon Processing
Modern Plastics
National Petroleum News
Ocean Industry
Ocean Oil Weekly Report
Oil and Gas Digest
Oil and Gas Journal
Petroleum Engineer International
Petroleum Information International
Petroleum Management
Petroleum Marketer
Pipeline
Pipeline Industry
Plastics World
Texas LP-Gas News
Texas Oil Marketer
Well Servicing
World Oil

DIRECTORIES:

Brown's Directory of North American & International Gas Companies (Energy Publications, Dallas, TX)
Energy Job Finder (Mainstream Access, New York, NY)
Gulf Coast Oil Directory (Resource Publications Division, Spearhead Publications, Houston, TX)
Modern Plastics, encyclopedia issue (McGraw Hill, New York, NY)
National Petroleum News—Buyer's Guide Issue (Hunter Publishing, Des Plaines, IL)
Offshore Contractors and Equipment Worldwide Directory (PennWell Publishing, Tulsa, OK)
Oil Directory of Texas (R. W. Byram and Co., Austin, TX)
Oil and Gas Directory (Geophysical Directory, Houston, TX)
Petroleum Supply Annual (Office of Oil & Gas, Energy Information Administration, Department of Energy, Washington, DC)
Plastics World Plastics Directory (Cahners, Newton, MA)
Southwest Oil World —Drilling Contractors Directory Issue (Hart Publications, Denver, CO)
U.S.A. Oil Industry Directory (PennWell Publishing, Tulsa, OK)
Whole World Oil Directory (National Register Publishing, Wilmette, IL)

How to Get a Job

EXPLORATION AND DEVELOPMENT:

Adams Resources and Energy
6910 Fannin
Houston, TX 77030
K.S. Adams, Jr., Chairman, CEO, President
Tel.: (713) 797-9966
Fax: (713) 795-4495

Agip Petroleum Company
2950 North Loop West, Suite 300
Houston, TX 77092
Georgio Pescenti, Executive Vice President
Tel.: (713) 688-6281
Fax: (713) 688-1853

Amoco Production Company
501 Westlake Park Blvd.
Houston, TX 77079
Ross Rogers, Purchasing Officer
Tel.: (713) 556-2000
Fax: (713) 556-4144

Anadarko Petroleum Company
17001 Northchase Dr.
Houston, TX 77060
Robert J. Allison, Jr., Chairman
Tel.: (713) 875-1101
Fax: (713) 874-3385

Ashland Exploration
14701 St. Mary's Lane, Suite 200
Houston, TX 77079
Tom Wilkinson, President
Tel.: (713) 531-2900
Fax: (713) 870-7328

BHP Petroleum (Americas)
5847 San Felipe, Suite 3600
Houston, TX 77057
Wayne D. Adams, Materials Coordinator
Tel.: (713) 780-5000
Fax: (713) 780-5086

Cabot Energy Corporation
550 Westlake Park Blvd., Suite 170
Houston, TX 77079
Boyd D. Taylor, President
Tel.: (713) 589-4600

Coastal Corp.
9 Greenway Plaza

Oil/Gas/Plastics

Houston, TX 77046
John Castennien, Director of Procurement
Tel.: (713) 877-1400
Fax: (713) 877-3136

Columbia Gas Development Corp.
1 Riverway
Houston, TX 77056
J.P. Bornman, Jr., President
Tel.: (713) 871-3400
Fax: (713) 871-3683

Elf Exploration
1000 Louisiana, Suite 3800
Houston, TX 77002
Jean-Paul Giraudet, President
Tel.: (713) 658-9811
Fax: (713) 650-1189

Exxon Production Research Company
3120 Buffalo Speedway
Houston, TX 77098
William Snow, Employee Relations Manager
Tel.: (713) 965-4222
Fax: (713) 966-6026

Marathon Oil Company
5555 San Felipe
Houston, TX 77056
Personnel Director
Tel.: (713) 629-6600

Meridian Oil
2919 Allen Parkway, Suite 1100
Houston, TX 77019
Don Clayton, Principal Officer
Tel.: (713) 831-1600

Mitchell Energy and Development Corp.
2001 Timberloch Place
The Woodlands, TX 77380
George P. Mitchell, Chairman and President
Tel.: (713) 377-5500
Fax: (713) 377-6910

Mobil Exploration and Producing, US
12450 Greenspoint Dr.
Houston, TX 77060
George Bourgeois, Personnel Director
Tel.: (713) 775-2000
Fax: (713) 775-4000

How to Get a Job

Mosbacher Energy Company and Mosbacher Management Company
712 Main St., Suite 2200
Houston, TX 77002
Robert Mosbacher, Chairman and CEO
Tel.: (713) 546-2500
Fax: (713) 546-2595

Oxy USA
5 Greenway Plaza, Suite 2400
Houston, TX 77046
Robert W. Brewer, Executive Vice President
Tel.: (713) 840-4100
Fax: (713) 840-4179

Pennzoil Company
Pennzoil Place, 700 Milam
Houston, TX 77002
Personnel Department
Tel.: (713) 546-4000

Phillips Petroleum Company
6330 West Loop South
Bellaire, TX 77401
Connie Brown, Personnel Director
Tel.: (713) 669-3666

Pogo Producing Company
5 Greenway Plaza, Suite 2700
Houston, TX 77046
Paul van Wagenen, President
Tel.: (713) 297-5000
Fax: (713) 297-5100

Sandefer Oil and Gas
First City Tower, 1001 Fannin, Suite 2300
Houston, TX 77002
Personnel Department
Tel.: (713) 753-9200
Fax: (713) 753-9230

Shell Oil Company
900 Louisiana
Houston, TX 77002
Personnel Department
Tel.: (713) 241-6161

Shell Western E & P
200 N. Dairy Ashford
Houston, TX 77079
Wanda Hopkins, Personnel Director

Oil/Gas/Plastics

Tel.: (713) 870-2121
Fax: (713) 870-2897

Sonat Exploration Company
4 Greenway Plaza
Houston, TX 77046
Donald G. Russell, Chairman and CEO
Tel.: (713) 940-4000
Fax: (713) 840-4944

Total Minatome
909 Fannin, Suite 2000
Houston, TX 77010
John Folnk, President and CEO
Tel.: (713) 739-3000
Fax: (713) 739-316

Transco Energy Company
2800 Post Oak Blvd.
Houston, TX 77056
John DesBarres, President and CEO
Tel.: (713) 439-2000
Fax: (713) 439-2440

Union Texas Petroleum
1330 Post Oak Blvd.
Houston, TX 77056
Keith Wiggins, Personnel Officer
Tel.: (713) 623-6544
Fax: (713) 968-2771

Zapata Corporation
600 Travis
Houston, TX 77002
Jim Porter, Personnel Director
Tel.: (713) 226-6500
Fax: (713) 226-6084

OIL AND GAS MARKETING:

Amerada Hess Corp.
1201 Louisiana, Suite 700
Houston, TX 77002
Clyde Crouch, Administrative Officer
Tel.: (713) 658-9770
Fax: (713) 752-5658

Anadrill-Schlumberger
200 Macco Blvd.
Sugar Land, TX 77478
Tom Bake, President

How to Get a Job

Tel.: (713) 240-4949
Fax: (713) 928-4433

Conoco, Inc.
600 N. Dairy Ashford
Houston, TX 77079
Constantine Nicandros, President and CEO
Tel.: (713) 293-1000
Fax: (713) 293-1440

Exxon Company, USA
800 Bell
Houston, TX 77002
Public Affairs Department
Tel.: (713) 656-3636
Fax: (713) 656-3291

Howell Corporation
1010 Lamar, Suite 1800
Houston, TX 77002
Paul N. Howell, Chairman and CEO
Tel.: (713) 658-4000
Fax: (713) 658-4007

Mobil Oil
12450 Greenspoint Dr.
Houston, TX 77060
George Bourgeois, Personnel Director
Tel.: (713) 775-2000
Fax: (713) 775-4000

Triangle Refineries
2211 Norfolk, Suite 1100
Houston, TX 77098
Ray A. Freels, President
Tel.: (713) 638-4700
Fax: (713) 638-4829

OIL AND GAS PRODUCTION:

Adams Resources Exploration Corp.
6910 Fannin
Houston, TX 77030
Jay Grimes, Personnel Manager
Tel.: (713) 797-9966
Fax: (713) 795-4495

American Exploration
1331 Lamar, Suite 900
Houston, TX 77010
Niki Sessions, Manager of Human Resources

Oil/Gas/Plastics

Tel.: (713) 756-6000
Fax: (713) 756-6001

Amoco Production Company
P501 Westlake Park Blvd.
Houston, TX 77079
Terry Stevens, Employment Coordinator
Tel.: (713) 556-2000
Fax: (713) 556-4225

Atlantic Richfield Company
15375 Memorial Dr.
Houston, TX 77079
Bill Goodman, Employer Relations Manager
Tel.: (713) 584-6000
Fax: (713) 584-3268

BHP Petroleum
5847 San Felipe, Suite 3600
Houston, TX 77057
Dennis Loughridge, Manager
Tel.: (713) 780-5000
Fax: (713) 780-5329

The George R. Brown Partnership
4700 First City Tower, 1001 Fannin
Houston, TX 77002-7608
Patrick Yerian, Comptroller
Tel.: (713) 652-4901
Fax: (713) 655-1541

Chevron
1301 McKinney
Houston, TX 77010
Sharon McKinney, Personnel Director
Tel.: (713) 754-2000
Fax: (713) 754-2016

Citation Oil and Gas Corporation
8223 Willow Place South, Suite 250
Houston, TX 77070
Louise Day, Office Manager
Tel.: (713) 469-9664
Fax: (713) 469-0168

Coastal Corps
9 Greenway Plaza
Houston, TX 77046
Lloyd Healy, Director of Employment
Tel.: (713) 877-1400
Fax: (713) 877-3639

How to Get a Job

Davis Bros. Oil Producers
1100 Milam, Suite 2200
Houston, TX 77002
Elena Jayne, Personnel Manager
Tel.: (713) 224-8224
Fax: (713) 659-8070

Enron Corp.
1400 Smith St.
Houston, TX 77002
Kenneth L. Lay, Chairman and CEO
Tel.: (713) 853-6161
Fax: (713) 853-3129

Exxon Company USA
800 Bell
Houston, TX 77002
Jay Rouse, Human Resources Manager
Tel.: (713) 656-3636

Marathon Oil Company
5555 San Felipe
Houston, TX 77056
Greg Larson, Human Resources Manager
Tel.: (713) 629-6600
Fax: (713) 296-2755

Occidental Oil and Gas
1980 Post Oak Blvd.
Houston, TX 77056
Tel.: (713) 840-4100
Personnel Office
P.O. Box 300
Tulsa, OK 74102
Fax: (918) 561-4663

Pacific Enterprises Oil Company
3040 Post Oak Blvd, Suite 600
Houston, TX 77056
Tom Walton, Regional Operations Manager
Tel.: (713) 960-1040
Fax: (713) 968-6945

Pennzoil Company
700 Milam
Houston, TX 77002
Jeannette Flake, Director of Human Resources
Tel.: (713) 546-4000
Fax: (713) 546-6589

Phillips Petroleum Company
6330 West Loop South

Oil/Gas/Plastics

Bellaire, TX 77401
Connie Brown, Employee Relations Representative
Tel.: (713) 669-3666

Quintana Petroleum Corp.
601 Jefferson
Houston, TX 77002
Wil Lunn, Human Resources Manager
Tel.: (713) 651-8600
Fax: (713) 651-8663

Texaco, Inc.
1 Allen Center
Houston, TX 77002
Ann Steinmetz, Employee Relations Representative
Tel.: (713) 666-8000

OILFIELD EQUIPMENT, SUPPLIES, SERVICES:

Atlas Wireline Services
10011 Meadowglen
Houston, TX 77042
Karen Krochenski, Personnel Director
Tel.: (713) 972-4000
Fax: (713) 972-5796

Baker Hughes
3900 Essex Lane, Suite 1200
Houston, TX 77027
Shannon Nini, Human Resources Manager
Tel.: (713) 439-8600
Fax: (713) 439-8782

Baker Oil Tools
9100 Emmott Rd.
Houston, TX 77040
Donna Paparazzo, Personnel Director
Tel.: (713) 466-1322
Fax: (713) 466-2675

Baker Performance Chemicals
3920 Essex Lane
Houston, TX 77027
R.O. Sterns, Purchasing Manager
Tel.: (713) 599-7400
Fax: (713) 599-7444

Bowen Tools
2400 Crockett
Houston, TX 77007
Pat Ferraro, Director of Purchasing

How to Get a Job

Tel.: (713) 869-6711
Fax: (713) 868-8861

Camco
7030 Ardmore
Houston, TX 77054
Terry Woodall, Personnel Director
Tel.: (713) 747-4000
Fax: (713) 747-6751

Cameron Iron Works, USA
13013 Northwest Freeway
Houston, TX 77040
D. Bounds, Director of Procurement
Tel.: (713) 939-2211
Fax: (713) 939-2354

Core Laboratories: A Division of Western Atlas International
5295 Hollister Rd.
Houston, TX 77040
Freddi Manni, District Manager
Tel.: (713) 460-9600
Fax: (713) 690-5770

Dia-Long Company
3330 Old Spanish Trail
Houston, TX 77021
C.G. Halloway, President
Tel.: (713) 747-2100
Fax: (713) 747-4834

Dow Chemical USA
400 Sam Houston Parkway South
Houston, TX 77042
Human Resources Department
Tel.: (713) 978-2971
Fax: (713) 978-2749

Dowell Schlumberger
1155 N. Dairy Ashford, Suite 600
Houston, TX 77079
Harry Love, Personnel Director
Tel.: (713) 556-7700
Fax: (713) 556-7201

Dresser Industries
3 Greenway Plaza,
Houston, TX 77002
George Chapman, Facilities & Services
Tel.: (713) 297-2000
Fax: (713) 297-2954

Oil/Gas/Plastics

Drill-Quip
13550 Hempstead Highway
Houston, TX 77040
Gary D. Smith, Director
Tel.: (713) 939-7711
Fax: (713) 939-8063

EnerServ Products
8223 Willow Place South, Suite 190
Houston, TX 77070
Kent D. Manby, Executive Vice President
Tel.: (713) 955-3500
Fax: (713) 955-3525

Global Marine
777 N. Eldridge
Houston, TX 77079
C.R. Luigs, Chairman, CEO, and President
Tel.: (713) 596-5100
Fax: (713) 531-1260

Halliburton Logging Services
2135 Highway 6 South
Houston, TX 77242
David Otte, Personnel Director
Tel.: (713) 496-8100
Fax: (713) 496-8886

Halliburton Services
1415 Louisiana, Suite 2300
Houston, TX 77002
Mark Awalt, Sales Manager
Tel.: (713) 652-6000
Fax: (713) 652-6066

Homco International
4710 Bellaire Blvd., Suite 200
Bellaire, TX 77401
Albert McBride, Purchasing Officer
Tel.: (713) 663-6444
Fax: (713) 663-5586

Hydril Company
3300 North Belt East
Houston, TX 77032
John Van Riper, Purchasing Officer
Tel.: (713) 449-2000

International Tool and Supply Company
1776 Yorktown, Suite 700
Houston, TX 77056
Manager of Personnel Services

How to Get a Job

Tel.: (713) 961-8000
Fax: (713) 961-7020

National Oilwell
5555 San Felipe
Houston, TX 77056
Tom Duessel, Personnel Director
Tel.: (713) 960-5100
Fax: (713) 960-5428

Oilfield Rental Service Company
950 McCarty Dr.
Houston, TX 77029
Glenn Harper, Purchasing Officer
Tel.: (713) 672-1601
Fax: (713) 672-0821

Oteco Equipment Company
2828 Trout St.
Houston, TX 77093
Dick Bullis, Purchasing Officer
Tel.: (713) 695-3693
Fax: (713) 695-3520

Otis Engineering Company
5177 Richmond, Suite 1295
Houston, TX 77056
Mike Gist, Regional Manager
Tel.: (713) 993-0773
Fax: (713) 993-0061

Petrolite Equipment & Instruments Group
5455 Old Spanish Trail
Houston, TX 77023
Carol Ware, Personnel Director
Tel.: (713) 926-7431
Fax: (713) 926-1162

Pool Company
10375 Richmond
Houston, TX 77042
Frank LaBrenz, Personnel Director
Tel.: (713) 954-3000
Fax: (713) 954-3244

Reed Tool Company
6501 Navigation
Houston, TX 77011
Charles Branch, Personnel Director
Tel.: (713) 924-5200
Fax: (713) 924-5112

Oil/Gas/Plastics

Sanbzik Rock Tools
P.O. Box 40402
Houston, TX 77240-0402
Dan Parsons, Purchasing Manager
Tel.: (713) 460-6200
Fax: (713) 460-6229

Smith International
16740 Hardy
Houston, TX 77032
Joe Sizemore, Personnel Director
Tel.: (713) 443-3370
Fax: (713) 233-5997

Tuboscope Vetco International
2835 Holmes Rd.
Houston, TX 77051
Mimi Ballanfant, Personnel Director
Tel.: (713) 799-5100
Fax: (713) 799-5561

VAM PTS
19210 Hardy Rd.
Houston, TX 77073
Dolly Smith, Personnel Director
Tel.: (713) 821-5510
Fax: (713) 821-7760

Vetco Pipeline Services
1600 Brittmoore Rd.
Houston, TX 77043
Roger Schultz, Personnel Director
Tel.: (713) 461-6112
Fax: (713) 461-6112 (send)

Weatherford International
1360 Post Oak Blvd., Suite 1000
Houston, TX 77056
Kathy Hutto, Director of Personnel
Tel.: (713) 439-9400
Fax: (713) 621-0994

Wilson Downhole Service
911 Hardy
Houston, TX 77020
Terry Theiss, Personnel Director
Tel.: (713) 237-3952
Fax: (713) 237-8217

Wilson Industries
1301 Conti
Houston, TX 77002

How to Get a Job

Ann Gray, Personnel Director
Tel.: (713) 237-3700
Fax: (713) 237-3345

PLASTICS:

Amicon Plastics
8500 Commerce Park, Suite 110
Houston, TX 77036
Ron Annis, Personnel Director
Tel.: (713) 661-1337
Fax: (713) 988-0500

Brummerhop's Plast-Tech
1203 Missouri
Houston, TX 77587
Jeff Brummerhop, General Manager
Tel.: (713) 941-2121
Fax: (713) 941-2134

Butler Professional Service Group
808 S. Main
Highlands, TX 77562
Malcolm Butler, Owner
Tel.: (713) 426-4556
Fax: (713) 426-4559

Custom Rubber Products
2625 Bennington
Houston, TX 77293
Delma Knox, Personnel Director
Tel.: (713) 691-2211

Plasteco, Inc.
12600 Wallaceville
Houston, TX 77013
Paul Ultis, General Manager
Tel.: (713) 453-8696
Fax: (713) 453-8372

Plastic Fabricators
6830 Lindbergh
Houston, TX 77087
Nancy Stevens, Personnel Director
Tel.: (713) 645-4271

Resins International
270 Shea Place
Houston, TX 77002-1034
Management Offices
Tel.: (713) 229-0360
Fax: (713) 229-0361

Tex-Trude, Inc.
2001 Sheldon Rd.
Houston, TX 77530
Don Lueken, Office Manager
Tel.: (713) 452-5961
Fax: (713) 452-5581

Paper and Allied Products

For additional information, you can contact:

PROFESSIONAL ORGANIZATIONS:

American Paper Institute
260 Madison Avenue
New York, NY 10016
Tel.: (212) 340-6000
Fax: (212) 689-2628

Paper Industry Management Association
2400 East Oakton Street
Arlington Heights, IL 60005
Tel.: (708) 956-0250
Fax: (708) 956-0520

Technical Association of the Pulp and Paper Industry
P.O. Box 105113
Atlanta, GA 30348
Tel.: (404) 446-1400
Fax: (404) 446-6947

PROFESSIONAL PUBLICATIONS:

Fiber Market News
Good Packaging Magazine
Packaging
Paper Age
Paper Sales
Prima Magazine
Pulp and Paper
TAPPI Journal

DIRECTORIES:

Directory of the Forest Products Industry (Miller Freeman, San Francisco, CA)
Fibre Market News—Directory of Paper Stock Dealers Issue (Market News Publishing, New York, NY)
Lockwood's Directory of Pulp, Paper & Allied Trades (Miller Freeman, San Francisco, CA)

How to Get a Job

Paper Industry Management Association—Membership Directory (Paper Industry Management Association, Arlington Heights, IL)
Paper Year Book (Harcourt Brace Jovanovich, Cleveland, OH)
Post's Pulp and Paper Directory (Miller Freeman, San Francisco, CA)
PPI International Pulp & Paper Directory (Miller Freeman, San Francisco, CA)
Pulp & Paper—North American Industry Factbook (Miller Freeman, San Francisco, CA)
TAPPI Directory (Technical Association of the Pulp and Paper, Packaging and Converting Industries, Atlanta, GA)

EMPLOYERS:

Apollo Paper Company
2514 Fairway Park Dr.
Houston, TX 77092
Nick Nicholson, President
Tel: (713) 688-6961
Fax: (713) 688-0101

Arvey Paper and Office Products
2201 Taylor
Houston, TX 77007
Steve Jones, Assistant Manager
Tel: (713) 861-9153
Fax: (713) 864-8083

Associated Diazo Products
3706 Drexel
Houston, TX 77027
Glenn Hansche, President
Tel: (713) 622-1062
Fax: (713) 622-2702

BMP Paper and Printing
8303 Kempwood
Houston, TX 77055
Rita Bucklew, Treasurer
Tel: (713) 228-9191
Fax: (713) 465-3337

Bosworth Papers
6550 Long Point, Suite 200
Houston, TX 77055
Thomas Jordan, Owner
Tel: (713) 683-8888
Fax: (713) 683-6213

Brawner Paper Company
5702 Armour Dr.
Houston, TX 77020
Rod Keith, Personnel Director

Paper

Tel: (713) 675-6584
Fax: (713) 673-6923

Butler Paper Company
8042 Katy Frwy
Houston, TX 77024
Rebecca Strawmyer, Office Manager
Tel: (713) 956-9941
Fax: (713) 681-8207

Cascade Impex Company
6825 Fulton
Houston, TX 77022
Ray Lalji, Owner
Tel: (713) 691-5296
Fax: (713) 691-5299

Century Paper
4902 Gulf Freeway
Houston, TX 77023
Harvey Glanzrockm, Area Vice President and CEO
Tel: (713) 928-5171
Fax: (713) 921-0913

Champion International Corporation, Sheldon Mill
11611 5th St.
Sheldon, TX 77044
Paul Riehle, Vice President of Operations
Tel: (713) 456-8780
Fax: (713) 456-6430

Gulf Coast Paper Company
437 Commerce Ave.
Houston, TX 77531
Ed Walker, Branch Manger
Tel: (713) 880-9619
Fax: (713) 265-7622

Gulf Systems
7720 FM 1960 East
Humble, TX 77346
Don Kyser, Warehouse Manager
Brenda Marshall, Office Manger
Tel: (713) 225-0088
Fax: (713) 852-1590

International Services Plus
3801 Lockwood Dr.
Houston, TX 77026
Betty Demas, Assistant Manager
Tel: (713) 672-0518
Fax: (713) 672-6722

How to Get a Job

Jake's Egg and Distributing Co.
939 West 18
Houston, TX 77008
Leonard Bench, President
Tel: (713) 868-1301
Fax: (713) 868-4326

Micro-Ware Paper Co.
1330 Sherwood Forest, Suite 301
Houston, TX 77043
Joyce Eades, Office Manager
Tel: (713) 464-7433
Fax: (713) 464-3772

Monarch Paper Company
4414 Hollister
Houston, TX 77040
Charles White, President
Tel: (713) 744-5700
Fax: (713) 939-0821

Nationwide Papers
10300 North Loop East
Houston, TX 77029
Charles Dieeter, Operations Credit Manager
Tel: (713) 672-9557
Fax: (713) 672-0955

Palmer Paper Co.
8019 Kempwood
Houston, TX 77055
Landis Kamas, Accounting Manager
Tel: (713) 683-0200
Fax: (713) 683-5042

Paper Plus
8930 Clarkcrest
Houston, TX 77063
Ty Foster, Manager
Tel: (713) 785-1292

Pollock Paper Distributors
3502 Yale
Houston, TX 77018
Karen Baker, Operations Manager
Tel.: (713) 861-4571
Fax: (713) 868-1435

Scott Paper Co.
140 Cypress Station, Suite 125
Houston, TX 77090
Wade Bartlett, District Manager

Paper

Tel: (713) 580-0566
Fax: (713) 580-0550

Simpson Pasadena Paper Company
P.O. Box 872
Pasadena, TX 77501
Al Adam, Purchasing Officer
Tel: (713) 475-6200
Fax: (713) 475-6205

Three Star Supply
7541 Dillon
Houston, TX 77061
Steve Horn, Executive Vice President
Tel: (713) 643-0075
Fax: (713) 644-3605

Union Camp Corp., School Supply and Stationery Division
3851 Yale
Houston, TX 77018
Johnnie Armstrong, Personnel Assistant
Tel: (713) 692-3511
Fax: (713) 692-0680

How to Get a Job

Printing

For networking in the **printing industry,** check out this professional organization listed in Chapter 5:

PROFESSIONAL ORGANIZATION:

Printing Industries of the Gulf Coast

For additional information, you can contact:

National Association of Printers and Lithographers
780 Palisade Avenue
Teaneck, NJ 07666
Tel.: (201) 342-0700
Fax: (201) 692-0286

Printing Industries of America
100 Daningerfield Road
Alexandria, VA 22314
Tel.: (703) 519-8100

Technical Association of the Graphic Arts
P.O. Box 9887
Rochester, NY 14623-0887
Tel: (716) 272-0557
Fax: (716) 475-2250

PROFESSIONAL PUBLICATIONS:

American Printer
Graphic Arts Monthly
Print
Print Industries of the Gulf Coast
Printing News

DIRECTORIES:

Adweek Portfolio (A/S/M Communications, New York, NY)
Directory of Typographic Services (National Composition Association, Arlington VA)
Graphic Arts Green Book (A. F. Lewis & Co., Hinsdale, IL)
National Association of Quick Printers -Roster (National Association of Quick Printers, Chicago,   IL)
Press Magazine —Buyers' Index Issue (B&B Publishing, Denver CO)
Printers Directory (American Business Directories, Omaha, NE)
Printing Impressions —Top 500 General Printers Issue (North American Publishing, Philadelphia, PA)
Printing Trades Blue Book (A. F. Lewis & Co., Hinsdale, IL)
Who's Who in Screen Printing (Equipment and Tool Institute, Alexandria, VA)

Printing

EMPLOYERS:

AdPlex
500 Century Plaza Dr., Suite 100
Houston, TX 77073
Galen Walters, President
Tel: (713) 874-0500
Fax: (713) 821-8654

Bowne of Houston
1200 Oliver
Houston, TX 77007
William Jupp, President
Tel: (713) 869-9181
Fax: (713) 869-7705

Brandt & Lawson
815 Live Oak
Houston, TX 77003
David Hart, President
Tel: (713) 227-5173
Fax: (713) 227-4803

Cargill Printing & Stationery
2910 McKinney
Houston, TX 77003
George Alexander, President
Tel: (713) 223-0123
Fax: (713) 223-2305

Champagne Fine Printing & Lithographic
1130 Silber Rd.
Houston, TX 77055
Bill Hill, President
Tel: (713) 681-9999
Fax: (713) 681-8769

Clarke & Courts
2521 Fairway Park Dr., Suite 420
Houston, TX 77092
John Gilliam, Personnel Director
Tel: (713) 528-4185
Fax: (713) 956-0563

Corporate Services
3303 West 12th St.
Houston, TX 77008
Frank Jolly, President
Tel: (713) 461-2080
Fax: (713) 861-0161

How to Get a Job

Diversified Lithographics
2127 Harland
Houston, TX 77055
Mario Mesa, Production Superintendent
Tel: (713) 681-9229
Fax: (713) 681-3948
Mailing address:
P.O. Box 55970
Houston, TX 77255-5970

R.R. Donnelley Financial, Houston
1015 S. Shepherd
Houston, TX 77019
Barbara Schetter, General Manager
Tel: (713) 630-1000
Fax: (713) 630-0082

Falcon Fast Print
6400 Westpark, Suite 220
Houston, TX 77057
Mae Hoffman, Manager
Tel: (713) 977-2555
Fax: (713) 977-1188

Formcraft
10401 Stella Link
Houston, TX 77025
Frank Blumenfeld, President
Tel: (713) 660-6010
Fax: (713) 660-8974

Grover Printing Company
5829 Beverly Hill
Houston, TX 77057
Kent Winton, President
Tel: (713) 780-4141
Fax: (713) 952-8687

Gulf Printing Company
2210 W. Dallas
Houston, TX 77019
Dick Boerger, President
Tel: (713) 529-4201
Fax: (713) 525-4283

Haywood Graphics
2022 Pech Rd.
Houston, TX 77055
Patrick Haywood, President
Tel: (713) 464-2658
Fax: (713) 464-5669

Printing

International Mailing Systems
904 Hutchins
Houston, TX 77003
Norm Pegram, CEO, Partner
Tel: (713) 222-8871
Fax: (713) 222-0334

Kwik-Kopy Corporation
1 Kwik Kopy Lane
Houston, TX 77429
F.C. (Bud) Hadfield, Chairman
Tel: (713) 373-3535
Fax: (713) 373-4450

Pasadena Citizen
102 S. Shaver
Houston, TX 77506
Mark Singletary, Publisher
Tel: (713) 477-0221
Fax: (713) 477-9090

Premier Company
3484 W. 11th St.
Houston, TX 77008
William Justice, President
Tel: (713) 868-6300
Fax: (713) 868-4520

Quick Tick International
9494 Kirby
Houston, TX 77054
Don Andrews, President
Tel: (713) 669-1900
Fax: (713) 669-1569

Ridgway's
5711 Hillcroft
Houston, TX 77036
Yandell Rogers, Jr., President
Tel: (713) 782-8580
Fax: (713) 952-4618

Riverside Press
7400 Pinemont
Houston, TX 77040
Robert D. Lane, President
Tel: (713) 462-2700
Fax: (713) 462-6188

Screen Graphics
6450 Bingle
Houston, TX 77092

How to Get a Job

Peter Carey, President
Tel: (713) 690-6666
Fax: (713) 690-7317

Space Age Laminating & Bindery Company
3400 White Oak Dr.
Houston, TX 77077
Shelly Nesloney, President
Tel: (713) 868-1471
Fax: (713): 868-4821

TriStar Webb Graphics
4010 Airline Dr.
Houston, TX 77002
Sue Kelso, Purchasing Officer
Tel: (713) 691-0001
Fax: (713) 691-5013

Western Lithograph
4335 Directors Row
Houston, TX 77092
John Bobbit, President
Tel: (713) 681-2100
Fax: (713) 681-2150

Wetmore & Company
1645 West Sam Houston Parkway North
Houston, TX 77043
Lisette Robalin, Purchasing Officer
Tel: (713) 468-7175
Fax: (713) 468-8021

Charles P. Young, Houston
1616 McGowen
Houston, TX 77004
Joe Davis, CEO and President
Tel: (713) 652-2100
Fax: (713) 650-1982

Xerox Reproduction Center
1614 Fannin
Houston, TX 77002
Doug Durham, Center Manager
Tel: (713) 651-3090
Fax: (713) 651-1302

Public Relations

For networking in **public relations,** check out these professional organizations listed in Chapter 5:

PROFESSIONAL ORGANIZATIONS:

American Marketing Association
International Association of Business Communicators
Public Relations Society of America, Houston Chapter

For additional information, you can contact:

Public Relations Society of America
33 Irving Place, 3rd Floor
New York, NY 10003
Tel.: (212) 995-2230
Fax: (212) 995-0757

Women Executives in Public Relations
P.O. Box 781, Murray Hill Station
New York, NY 10156
(212) 721-9661

PROFESSIONAL PUBLICATIONS:

O'Dwyer's Newsletter
Public Relations Journal
Public Relations Review
Publicist
PR News
PR Reporter

DIRECTORIES:

Bacon's Publicity Checker (Bacon's Publishing Co., Chicago, IL)
Directory of Personal Image Consultants (Image Industry Publications, Staten Island, NY)
Directory of Public Affairs Officers (Public Affairs Council, Washington, DC)
International Association of Business Communicators—IABC Membership and Services Directory (International Association of Business Communicators, San Francisco, CA)
National School Public Relations Association—Directory (National School Public Relations Association, Arlington, VA)
O'Dwyer's Directory of Corporate Communications (J.R. O'Dwyer Co., New York, NY)
O'Dwyer's Directory of Public Relations Firms (J.R. O'Dwyer Co., New York, NY)
Public Relations Journal—Directory Issue (Public Relations Society of America, New York, NY)

How to Get a Job

EMPLOYERS:

Mel Anderson Communications
6901 Corporate Dr., Suite 201
Houston, TX 77036
Mel Anderson, Jr., CEO
Tel.: (713) 981-4390

A.R. Busse & Associates
8602 Oakford
Houston, TX 77024
Alvin R. Busse, CEO
Tel.: (713) 626-1144
Fax: (713) 626-1144

Bernstein & Associates
4600 Post Oak Place, Suite 200
Houston, TX 77027
Patricia Bernstein, President
Tel.: (713) 961-4881
Fax: (713) 961-4941

Brown, Nelson & Associates
6200 Savoy, Suite 250
Houston, TX 77036
Guy E. Brown and George Nelson, CEOs
Tel.: (713) 784-6200
Fax: (713) 784-6356

Churchill Group
5851 San Felipe, Suite 200
Houston, TX 77057
Mirrel Kephart, President
Tel.: (713) 781-0020
Fax: (713) 781-0062

de la Garza & Associates
24 Greenway Plaza, Suite 1303
Houston, TX 77046
Henry A. de la Garza, CEO
Tel.: (713) 622-8818
Fax: (713) 622-443

Daniel J. Edelman of Texas
1 Greenway Plaza, Suite 700
Houston, TX 77046
James O. Cox III, Executive Vice President and General Manager
Tel.: (713) 623-2666
Fax: (713) 622-2142

Susan Farb Public Relations
7500 San Felipe, Suite 475

Public Relations

Houston, TX 77063
Susan Farb Morris, CEO
Tel.: (713) 978-7377
Fax: (713) 978-6460

Goldstein Communications
2400 Agusta, Suite 350
Houston, TX 77057
Gerry and Joanne Goldstein, CEOs
Tel.: (713) 266-0043
Fax: (713) 266-9034

Quest Business Agency
2900 North Loop West, Suite 1020
Houston, TX 77092
Alan D. Vera, CEO
Tel.: (713) 956-6569

Read-Poland Associates
5177 Richmond Ave.
Houston, TX 77056
Hank Moore, CEO
Tel.: (713) 622-5040
Fax: (713) 622-7658

Schey Public Relations
701 Richmond Ave.
Houston, TX 77006
Dick Schey, CEO
Tel.: (713) 522-7705
Fax: (713) 552-7513

The Tate Agency
5615 Kirby, Suite 440
Houston, TX 77005
Karen Tate, CEOs
Tel.: (713) 526-2292
Fax: (713) 526-2348

Vollmer Public Relations
712 Main, Suite 2900
Houston, TX 77002
Helen Vollmer and Allen Caudle, CEOs
Tel.: (713) 546-2230
Fax: (713) 546-2231

Wright Marketing Communications
50 Briar Hollow Lane, Suite 300
Houston, TX 77027
Thomas A. Wright, CEO
Tel.: (713) 840-0840
Fax: (713) 840-9329

How to Get a Job

Contacts and volunteer experience pay off in P.R.

Nancy is a public relations professional at a large P.R. firm in Houston. When she graduated from college in 1981, there were not very many jobs other than teaching available for women in Texas. She worked as a Pan Am flight attendant for a little while until she got married.

After 11 years of raising children, Nancy decided she wanted to get back into the work force. In her volunteer experiences, she had frequently worked in the area of publicity and thought that she could apply her skills to a real job.

An old friend of hers from school told Nancy about a job as assistant sports information director at her alma mater. Having always been interested in public relations and in writing, Nancy applied for the job and, despite having been out of the work force for 11 years, was hired. Her various volunteer activities had taught her valuable skills, and keeping in touch with old friends had given her useful contacts.

Nancy changed jobs a few times, each time gaining new experience and contacts, and finally ended up with a good position at a large firm.

Real Estate Developers and Brokers

For netwoking in the **real estate industry,** check out these professional organizations listed in Chapter 5:

PROFESSIONAL ORGANIZATIONS:

Houston Board of Realtors
Houston Building Owners and Managers Association
Institute of Real Estate Management
Society of Industrial and Office Realtors

For additional information, you can contact:

International Real Estate Institute
8383 E. Evans Road
Scottsdale, AZ 85260
Tel: (602) 998-8267

National Association of Realtors
430 North Michigan Avenue, Suite 500
Chicago, IL 60611
Tel.: (312) 329-8292
Fax: (312) 329-8882

National Network of Commercial Real Estate Women
808 17th Street NW, #3200
Washington, DC 20006
Tel.: (202) 223-9669

PROFESSIONAL PUBLICATIONS:

Daily Commercial Record
Real Estate News
Realty and Building
Texas Realtor

DIRECTORIES:

American Real Estate Guide (LL & IL Publishing, Marhasset, NY)
American Society of Real Estate Counselors Directory (ASREC, Chicago, IL)
Commercial-Investment Real Estate Council-Roster of CCIM Designeees (Realtors National Marketing Institute, Chicago, IL)
Directory of Certified Residential Brokers (Retail National Marketing Institute, Chicago, IL)
Houston Office Development (Houston Chamber of Commerce, Houston, TX)
National Association of Real Estate Investment Trusts—Directory of Members (National Association of Real Estate Investment Trusts, Washington, DC)

How to Get a Job

National Real Estate Investor—Directory Issue (Communication Channels, Atlanta, GA)
National Roster of Realtors (Stanats Communications, Cedar Rapids, IA)
Society of Industrial Realtors—Directory (Society of Industrial Realtors, Washington, DC)
Who's Who in Creative Real Estate (Who's Who in Creative Real Estate, Glendale, CA)
Who's Who in Real Estate (Grey House Publishing, Sharon, CT)

EMPLOYERS:

Alliance Commercial
16808 El Camino Real, Suite 130
Houston, TX 77058
Lyle Anderson, President
Tel.: (713) 480-9600
Fax: (713) 480-9939

Ameritec Realty
4710 Bellaire, Suite 120
Bellaire, TX 77401
Julia Nicastro, Purchasing Officer
Tel.: (713) 668-4447
Fax: (713) 668-8822

Appelt, Womack, Ricks & Herder
4910 One Shell Plaza
Houston, TX 77002
Bruce L. Womack, President
Tel.: (713) 222-2111
Fax: (713) 222-1118

Asset Plus Corporation
1800 Bering Dr., Suite 320
Houston, TX 77057
Pat Young, Office Manager
Tel.: (713) 782-5800
Fax: (713) 268-5111

Bering Realty Corporation
2221 S. Voss Rd.
Houston, TX 77057
Conrad Bering, Jr., President
Tel.: (713) 782-8482
Fax: (713) 952-9832

Boyd, Page & Associates
2700 Post Oak Blvd., Suite 300
Houston, TX 77056
Candice Asch, Office Manager
Tel.: (713) 877-8400
Fax: (713) 877-1019

Real Estate

CD Commercial Real Estate Services
2500 West Loop South, Suite 100
Houston, TX 77027
Kenneth Sandstad, Regional Manager
Tel.: (713) 840-6500
Fax: (713) 960-8583

Century Development
1980 Post Oak Blvd., Suite 1200
Houston, TX 77056
Shirley McGuyer, Executive Assistant to the Chairman
Tel.: (713) 621-9500
Fax: (713) 621-1441

Clarion Properties
3 Riverway, Suite 670
Houston, TX 77056
Kathy Ealm, Office Manager
Tel.: (713) 963-0963
Fax: (713) 963-8019

Coldwell Banker Residential Real Estate Services
60601 S. Braeswood
Houston, TX 77096
Judy Dowty, Personnel
Tel.: 772-7800
Fax: 541-3327

Commercial Real Estate Associates
3200 Southwest Freeway, Suite 1100
Houston, TX 77027
Penny Davis, Personnel Administrator
Tel.: (713) 650-8500
Fax: (713) 961-5621

Covington & Rutledge
7500 San Felipe, Suite 990
Houston, TX 77063
Tel.: (713) 974-7600
Fax: (713) 974-2007

Cushman Realty Corp.
2800 Post Oak Blvd., Suite 5300
Houston, TX 77056
Linda Ray, Office Manager
Tel.: (713) 877-1700
Fax: (713) 877-1965

Cushman & Wakefield of Texas
1300 Post Oak Blvd., Suite 1300
Houston, TX 77056
M.J. Gilbert, Branch Administrator

How to Get a Job

Tel.: (713) 961-3700
Fax: (713) 961-4221

Friendswood Development Company
233 Benmar
Houston, TX 77060
John E. Walsh, Jr., President
Tel.: (713) 875-7700
Fax: (713) 875-7717

Fuller Commercial Brokerage Company
4615 Southwest Freeway, Suite 755
Houston, TX 77027
Dennis Swoboda, President and CEO
Tel.: (713) 850-8400
Fax: (713) 850-0412

Fuller-Wallace, Realtors
13739 Southwest Freeway
Sugarland, TX 77478
Joyce Wallace, Owner
Tel.: (713) 491-6051
Fax: (713) 491-0010

Mac Haik Realty
11757 Katy Freeway, Suite 1500
Houston, TX 77079
Mac Haik, President
Tel.: (713) 496-7788
Fax: (713) 596-6444

Helmsley-Spear of Texas
5898 Burgoyne
Houston, TX 77057
Samuel Koret, Vice Preaident
Tel.: (713) 783-6000
Fax: (713) 783-3262

Hines Interests Limited Partnership
2800 Post Oak Blvd.
Houston, TX 77056-6118
Martha Carlin, Purchasing Manager
Tel.: (713) 621-8000
Fax: (713) 966-2051

Horizon Realty Group
3845 FM 1960 West, Suite 110
Houston, TX 77068
Dennis Patillo, President
Tel.: (713) 537-9500
Fax: (713) 893-5049

Real Estate

Jones Lang Wootton
1201 Louisiana, Suite 3210
Houston, TX 77002
Office Manager
Tel.: (713) 651-9800
Fax: (713) 750-0601

K2 Realty
131 Brooks, Suite 100
Sugarland, TX 77478
Melvin Knesek, Owner/Broker
Tel.: (713) 491-5880
Fax: (713) 491-5723

Laguarta & Company
2737 Buffalo Speedway
Houston, TX 77098
James Krimmel, Comptroller
Tel.: (713) 622-2200
Fax: (713) 622-5628

Lewis Partners
4299 San Felipe
Houston, TX 77027
Shelly Hilton, Office Manager
Tel.: (713) 871-9494
Fax: (713) 871-9493

Linkous, Farris & Potter
3050 Post Oak Blvd., Suite 150
Houston, TX 77056
Estelle Potter, Vice President
Tel.: (713) 629-0500
Fax: (713) 629-0504

Henry S. Miller/Grubb & Ellis
1360 Post Oak Blvd., 9th Floor
Houston, TX 77056
Ann Jacobs, Office Manager
Tel.: (713) 626-8888
Fax: (713) 599-5113

Mischer Corporation
2727 North Loop West, Suite 200
Houston, TX 77008
Walter M. Mischer, Sr., Chairman of the Board
Tel.: (713) 869-7800
Fax: (713) 864-0526

Moody Rambin Interests
5858 Westheimer, Suite 404
Houston, TX 77057

How to Get a Job

Rhonda Huss, Senior Property Manager
Tel.: (713) 952-0562
Fax: (713) 952-2177

Paragon Group
5851 San Felipe, Suite 880
Houston, TX 77057
Doug Knaus, General Manager
Tel.: (713) 975-6880
Fax: (713) 975-8777

Realty Executives
14780 Memorial Dr.
Houston, TX 77079
Bill Winchell, Jr., General Manager
Tel: (713) 496-7500
Fax: (713) 496-0387

Tanglewood Corporation
1661 Tanglewood
Houston, TX 77056
William James Miller, President and CEO
Tel.: (713) 622-8100
Fax: (713) 961-2958

Tenneco Realty
1010 Milam
Houston, TX 77002
Michael Walsh, CEO
Tel.: (713) 757-2131
Fax: (713) 757-4395

Trammel Crow Company
1800 West Loop South, Suite 600
Houston, TX 77027
Matt Khourie, President
Tel.: (713) 626-8600
Fax: (713) 623-4236

Transwestern Property Company
6671 Southwest Freeway, Suite 200
Houston, TX 77074
Jerry Taylor, Senior Vice President of Property Management
Tel.: (713) 270-7700
Fax: (713) 270-6285

Trione & Gordon
1900 West Loop South, Suite 1200
Houston, TX 77027
Deborah Rammelt, Office Manager
Tel.: (713) 961-5009
Fax: (713) 961-5000

Real Estate

Weingarten Realty Investors
2600 Citadel Plaza, Suite 300
Houston, TX 77008
Judy Barn, Director of Human Resources
Tel.: (713) 866-6000
Fax: (713) 866-6049

Woodlands Corporation
2201 Timberloch Place
The Woodlands, TX 77380
Roger L. Galatas, President
Tel.: (713) 377-5700
Fax: (713) 377-6910

Zann Commercial Brokerage
2525 Bay Area Blvd., Suite 160
Houston, TX 77058
Bob Zannelli, President
Tel.: (713) 280-8088
Fax: (713) 280-0815

Location, location, location...

Bob Billingsley is a partner in a local firm that leases office space in downtown Houston. We talked with him recently about getting started in commercial real estate.

"Leasing commercial real estate in Houston is a very tough business," says Billingsley. "You don't make any money during your first year or two in the business. There's a very high attrition rate. But if you stick with it, you can make more money than your peers in other fields ever dreamed of. Six-figure incomes are not uncommon among people who have been in the business only five years.

"At our firm, we don't hire people right out of school; we look for people with some experience in the business world and in real estate. But many of the larger firms will hire recent grads and train them. In fact, some large firms have formal training programs. If you're a young person just starting out, I'd suggest getting a job with a bigger firm. Then be like a blotter—soak up everything they can teach you. After a few years, reevaluate your position with the company. The problem with the bigger firms is that they sometimes tend to ignore you once they've trained you. In a smaller firm, the senior people see more of a relationship between your success and the overall success of the company. Also, there's a lot of competition within a large firm. It's easy to get lost in the shuffle."

How to Get a Job

We asked Billingsley what qualifications are needed to succeed in commercial real estate. "You have to be tough, because you'll face a certain amount of rejection. You have to be hungry, because this is an extremely competitive business. A college degree is helpful, but it isn't required. This business is basically sales—getting out and seeing people, convincing them that your skills and knowledge are up to snuff. When you're just starting out, it's also very important to have a mentor in the company."■

Recreation, Sports, and Fitness

For additional information you can contact:

PROFESSIONAL ORGANIZATIONS:

Aerobics & Fitness Association of America
15250 Ventura Blvd., #310
Sherman Oaks, CA 91403
Tel.: (818) 905-0040

National Association of Sporting Goods Wholesalers
P.O. Box 11344
Chicago, IL 60611
Tel.: (312) 565-0233

National Recreation & Parks Association
2775 S. Quincy St., Suite 300
Arlington, VA 22206
Tel.: (703) 820-4940

National Sporting Goods Association
1699 Wall Street
Mt. Prospect, IL 60056
Tel.: (708) 439-4000
Fax: (708) 439-0011

PROFESSIONAL PUBLICATIONS:

American Fitness
Athletic Business
Parks and Recreation
Sporting Goods Dealer
Sporting Goods Trade

DIRECTORIES:

Directory of Information Sources in Health, Physical Education and Recreation
(ERIC Clearinghouse on Teacher Education, Washington, DC)

Recreation/Sports/Fitness

Health Clubs Directory (American Business Directories, Omaha, NE)
New American Guide to Athletics, Sports, and Recreation (New American Library, New York, NY)
Parks and Recreation Buyer's Guide (National Recreation and Parks Association, Alexandria, VA)
Salesman's Guide to Sporting Goods Buyers (Salesman's Guides, New York, NY)
Sporting Goods Directory (Sporting Goods Dealer, St. Louis, MO)
Sports Administration Guide and Directory (National Sports Marketing Bureau, New York, NY)

EMPLOYERS:

American Athletic Club
2927 Allen Parkway
Houston, TX 77019
Judy Best, Director
Tel: (713) 831-2582

Bayou Park Club
4400 Memorial Dr.
Houston, TX 77007
Kim Banes, Manager
Tel: (713) 880-9330

Body Fit
14360 Bellaire, #124
Houston, TX 77083
Lou Ann Welsh, Director
Tel: (713) 568-3488

Charlie Fitness Club and Hotel
9009 Boone Rd.
Houston, TX 77099
Jim Austin, General Manager
Tel: (713) 530-0000
Fax: (713) 530-3701

Costas Gym
12084 Veterans Memorial Dr.
Houston, TX 77067
Mark R. Costa, Owner
Tel: (713) 537-7300

Gold's Gym
11222 Richmond, #150
Houston, TX 77082
Rick Zimmer, Director
Tel: (713) 493-9075
Fax: (713) 493-9763

How to Get a Job

Houston Metropolitan Racquet Club
One Allen Center
Houston, TX 77002
Sammy Giammalva, Director
Tel: (713) 652-0700
Fax: (713) 655-1013

Houstonian Club
111 N. Post Oak Lane
Houston, TX 77024
Joe Russo, Director
Tel: (713) 680-2626
Fax: (713) 680-2992

Institute for Preventive Medicine Health & Fitness Center
6560 Fannin
Houston, TX 77030
Judy Henry, Manager
Tel: (713) 790-6450
Fax: (713) 790-4699

Kingwood Athletic Club
806 Russell Palmer Rd.
Kingwood, TX 77339
Todd Danielson, General Manager
Tel: (713) 358-7765
Fax: (713) 358-4580

Memorial Athletic Club
14690 Memorial Dr.
Houston, TX 77079
David J. Cardone, Director
Tel: (713) 497-7570
Fax: (713) 497-1827

Powerhouse Gym
9538 Richmond
Houston, TX 77063
Joe DaMare, Director
Tel: (713) 952-7697

President & First Lady Health & Racquet Clubs
7255 Clarewood
Houston, TX 77036
Tracy Cantlon, Manager
Tel: (713) 771-8395
Fax: (713) 701-0269

Sir James Athletic Club
6136 Highway 6 North
Houston, TX 77084

Recreation/Sports/Fitness

Jim Gatto, Director
Tel: (713) 463-6815

Stone's Fitness Center
2424 Falcon Pass
Houston, TX 77062
Bobby Grimes, Director
Tel: (713) 488-3155

Sugar Land Athletic Club
9920 Highway 90A
Sugar Land, TX 77478
Mary Poitevinp, General Manager
Tel: (713) 242-7500

Texas Club
Texas Commerce Center
601 Travis St.
Houston, TX 77002
Tim McNutt, Director
Tel: (713) 227-7000
Fax: (713) 227-2701

Texas Lady-Texan Spas
142 FM 1960 East
Houston, TX 77073
Roger Wittenberns, President
Tel: (713) 367-8880
Fax: (713) 871-7709

Woodlands Athletic Center
11111 Winterberry Place
The Woodlands, TX 77380
John Phillips, Director
Tel: (713) 363-9500

World Gym
5080 Richmond
Houston, TX 77056
Denise Barnette, General Manager
Tel: (713) 963-9644

YMCA of the Greater Houston Area
1600 Louisiana
Houston, TX 77002
Bill Phillips, Director
Tel: (713) 659-5566
Fax: (713) 659-7240

How to Get a Job

Restaurants

For networking in the **restaurant industry,** check out this professional organization listed in Chapter 5:

PROFESSIONAL ORGANIZATION:

Houston Restaurant Association

For additional information, you can contact:

Council on Hotel, Restaurant, and Institutional Education
20 Henderson Building
University Park, PA 16802
Tel.: (814) 865-1736

National Restaurant Association
1200 17th Street NW
Washington, DC 20036
Tel.: (202) 331-5900
Fax: (202) 331-2429

PROFESSIONAL PUBLICATIONS:

Beverage Media
Fast Service/Family Restaurant
Food & Service
Food & Wine
Food Industry Newsletter
Food Management
Foodservice Product News
Nation's Restaurant News
Restaurant Hospitality
Restaurants and Institutions
Signature Magazine

DIRECTORIES:

Directory of Chain Restaurant Operators (Business Guides, New York, NY)
Directory of Hotel and Restaurant Management Programs (Holiday Inn University, Olive Branch, MS)
Restaurants (American Business Directories, Omaha, NE)
Restaurant Hospitality—Hospitality 500 Issue (Penton/IPC, Columbus, OH)
Restaurants and Institutions—Annual 400 Issue (Cahners Publishing Co., Des Plaines, IL)
Restaurants and Institutions–Annual Job Surveys, Aug. issue (Cahners Publishing Co., Des Plaines, IL)
Taverns Directory (American Business Directories, Omaha, NE)

AREA RESTAURANTS:

Birraporetti's
1997 W. Gray
Houston, TX 77019
Matt Morgan, General Manager
Tel.: (713) 529-9292
Fax: (713) 529-7232

Bistro-Vino
819 W. Alabama
Houston, TX 77006
Mohammad Bayegan, Owner
Tel.: (713) 526-5500
Fax: (713) 526-7170

Bombay Palace
3901 Westheimer
Houston, TX 77027
Ajoy Bhattacharya, General Manager
Tel.: (713) 960-8472
Fax: (713) 963-8061

Brennan's, Houston
3300 Smith
Houston, TX 77006
Alex Brennan-Martin, Owner
Tel.: (713) 522-9711
Fax: (713) 522-9142

Carraba's Italian Restaurant
3115 Kirby
Houston, TX 77098
Suzanne Kish, General Manager
Tel.: (713) 522-3131
Fax: (713) 522-1526

Cattle Guard Restaurant and Bar
1010 N. Hwy 6
Houston, TX 77079
Mike Bastion, General Manager
Tel.: (713) 439-5094

Flying Dutchman Restaurant and Oyster Bar
505 Second
Kemah, TX, 77565
Glenn Davis, General Manager
Tel.: (713) 334-7575
Fax: (713) 334-3708

Great Greek
80 Woodlake Square

How to Get a Job

Houston, TX 77063
Vasili Magaziz, Manager
Tel.: (713) 783-5100
Fax: (713) 783-0219

Hartz Chicken
14409 Cornerstone Village Dr.
Houston, TX 77014
George Samaras, President
Tel.: (713) 583-0020
Fax: (713) 580-3752

Houlihan's Old Place
1800 S. Post Oak Blvd.
Houston, TX 77056
Gary Wallerman, President
Tel.: (713) 621-1740
Fax: (713) 621-1749

House of Pies
3112 Kirby
Houston, TX 77098
Gilbert Saenz, General Manager
Tel.: (713) 528-3816
Fax: (713) 529-6730

Hunan Dragon
3111 S. Shepherd
Houston, TX 77098
Phong Ranguy, Manager
Tel.: (713) 523-9087

Kettle Restaurants
3131 Argonne
Houston, TX 77098
Harry L. Chambers, President
Tel.: (713) 524-3464
Fax: (713) 524-7956

Michaelangelo's
307 Westheimer
Houston, TX 77006
Abbas Hussein, Manager
Tel.: (713) 524-7836

Ninfa's Mexican Restaurant
214 N. Nagle
Houston, TX 77003
Frolian Hernandez, Chief Operating Officer
Tel.: (713) 228-6906
Fax: (713) 228-0135

Restaurants

Old Heidelberg
1810 Fountain View
Houston, TX 77057
Anne Marie Buett, General Manager
Tel.: (713) 781-3581

On the Border Cafe
4608 Westheimer
Houston, TX 77027
Jim Disbrow, General Manager
Tel.: (713) 961-4494
Fax: (713) 993-0750

Pappas Company
642 Yale
Houston, TX 77007
Harris Pappas, President
Tel.: (713) 869-0151
Fax: (713) 869-4932

Pappasito's Cantina
6445 Richmond
Houston, TX 77057
Jim Cossey, General Manager
Tel.: (713) 784-5253
Fax: (713) 789-2118

Ragin' Cajun Seafood and Po-Boys
4302 Richmond Ave.
Houston, TX 77027
Frank Messina, Owner
Tel.: (713) 623-6321
Fax: (713) 621-7274

Tony Roma's Restaurant
6360 Richmond Ave.
Houston, TX 77057
John Covington, General Manager
Tel.: (713) 952-7427
Fax: (713) 952-0587

Stables Steak House
7325 S. Main
Houston, TX 77030
Jay Mulvey, Owner
Tel.: (713) 795-5900

Star Pizza
2111 Norfolk
Houston, TX 77098
Ted Curry, Manager
Tel.: (713) 523-0800

How to Get a Job

Subway
3518 S. Shepherd
Houston, TX 77098
Richard Nickerson, Owner
Tel.: (713) 529-9345

Taj Majal
8328 Gulf Freeway
Houston, TX 77017
D. Prabhakarrao, Manager
Tel.: (713) 649-2818

Tokyo Gardens Japanese Restaurant
4701 Westheimer
Houston, TX 77027
Glen Gondo, Manager
Tel.: (713) 622-7886
Fax: (713) 622-0626

FAST FOOD CHAINS:

Beck's Prime
1980 Post Oak Blvd.
Houston, TX 77056
Mike Gieszler, General
Tel.: (713) 961-3570
Fax: (713) 961-0133
3 Houston-area locations.

Burger King
12404 Park Central Dr., Suite 250
Dallas, TX 75251
Craig Bushey, Operations Vice President
Tel.: (214) 934-7969
Fax: (214) 934-7970
62 Houston-area locations.

Dairy Queen
1915 Aldine Bender
Houston, TX 77032
Tel.: (713) 442-3484
Larnell Leverett, District Manager
32 Houston-area locations.

Domino's Pizza
Area franchise:
9894 Bissonet, Suite 420
Houston, TX 77036
Gene Cassell, Area Supervisor
Tel.: (713) 771-5558
Fax: (713) 771-5666

Restaurants

Corporate headquarters:
13355 Noel Rd., Suite 455
One Galleria Tower
Dallas, TX 75240-6612
Brad Webb, Corporate Operations Director
Tel.: (214) 392-3030
Fax: (214) 458-2192
73 Houston-area locations.

Jack-in-the-Box
5005 Mitchelldale
Houston, TX 77092
Jim Beckham, Regional Manager
Tel.: (713) 683-3999
Fax: (713) 681-3796
100 Houston-area locations.

Kentucky Fried Chicken
363 N. Sam Houston Pkwy E.
Houston, TX 77060
Tom Burres, Director of Operations
Tel.: (713) 820-5595
70 Houston-area locations.

Long John Silvers Seafood Shoppes
5121 Antoine
Houston, TX 77092
Tel.: (713) 681-2039
or for national headquarters: 1-800-342-3669
40 Houston-area locations.

McDonald's Restaurants
3707 FM 1960 W.
Houston, TX 77068
Starr Holland, Office Manager
Tel.: (713) 580-3322
Fax: (713) 587-7366
145 Houston-area locations.

Mr. Gatti's
4502 N. Hwy 6
Houston, TX 77084
David Darrow, District Manager
Tel.: (713) 680-9191
16 Houston-area locations.

Popeye's
7100 Regency Square Blvd., Suite 118
Houston, TX 77036
Ms. Eddie King, Director of Operations
Tel.: (713) 781-2169

How to Get a Job

Fax: (713) 783-6678
47 Houston-area locations.

Taco Bell
Regional office:
2300 Valley View Ln., Suite 400
Irving, TX 75062
Craig Barton, Zone Manager of Human Resources
Tel.: (713) 488-0326
Tel.: (214) 258-2200
Fax: (214) 258-2248
68 Houston-area locations.

Two Pesos
10777 Westheimer
Houston, TX 77042
Don Hill, District Manager
Tel.: (713) 781-0067
Fax: (713) 781-3016
17 Houston-area locations.

Wendy's Old Fashioned Hamburgers
5500 Northwest Central
Houston, TX 77092
Jan Vasko, Human Resources
Tel.: (713) 939-8100
Fax: (713) 939-7745
52 Houston-area locations.

Whataburger Restaurants
1900 North Loop West
Houston, TX 77018
Bud Shaw, Regional Supervisor
Tel.: (713) 685-5300
Fax: (713) 680-8660
74 Houston-area locations.

Retailers

For networking in the **retail industry,** check out these professional organizations listed in Chapter 5:

PROFESSIONAL ORGANIZATIONS:

American Marketing Association
Retail Merchants Association of Houston
Sales & Marketing Executive Society of Houston

For additional information, you can contact:

General Merchandise Distributors Council
1275 Lake Plaza Drive
Colorado Springs, CO 80906
Tel.: (719) 576-4260
Fax: (719) 576-2661

National Association of Chain Drug Stores
413 N. Lee Street
P.O. Box 1417-D49
Alexandria, VA 22314
Tel.: (703) 549-3001

National Association of Convenience Stores
1605 King Street
Alexandria, VA 22314
Tel.: (703) 684-3600

National Association of Wholesaler Distributors
1725 K Street, NW Suite 710
Washington, DC 20006-1401
Tel.: (202) 872-0885
Fax: (202) 785-0586

National Grocers Association
1825 Samuel Morse Drive
Reston, VA 22090
Tel.: (703) 437-5300

National Retail Federation
100 West 31st Street
New York, NY 10036
Tel.: (212) 244-8780
Fax: (212) 629-0942

National Retail Hardware Association
5822 W. 74th St.
Indianapolis, IN 46278
Tel.: (317) 290-0338

How to Get a Job

PROFESSIONAL PUBLICATIONS:

Adweek/Southwest
Chain Store Age
College Store Executive
Merchandising
National Grocer
Pharmacy Weekly
Store Planning
Stores
Women's Wear Daily

DIRECTORIES:

Chain Drug Stores Membership Directory (National Association of Chain Drug Stores, Alexandria, VA)
Chain Store Age General Merchandise Edition—Top 100 Chains Issue (Lebhar-Friedman, New York, NY)
Convenience Stores Membership Directory (National Association of Convenience Stores, Alexandria, VA)
Dealerscope Merchandising—National Buyer's Guide Issue (North American Publishing, Philadelphia, PA)
Department Store Sales (Fairchild Books, New York, NY)
Directory of General Merchandise/Variety Chains & Specialty Stores (Business Guides, New York, NY)
Discount Store News—Top Chains Issue (Lebhar-Friedman, New York, NY)
Factory Outlet World (Murray Shor, Suffern, NY)
National Mall Monitor—Retail Tenant Directory (National Mall Monitor, Clearwater, FL)
Nationwide Directory—Mass Market Merchandisers (Salesman's Guides, New York, NY)
Salesman's Guide Nationwide Directory: Major Mass Market Merchandisers (Salesman's Guides, New York, NY)
Sheldon's Retail Directory of the U.S. and Canada (PS&M, Inc., Fairview, NJ)
Stores—Top 100 Issue (National Retail Merchants Association, New York, NY)

BUSINESS RETAILERS:

A&E Product Company
4235 Richmond Ave.
Houston, TX 77027
C.A. Gremillion, President
Tel.: (713) 621-0022
Fax: (713) 621-2537

Business Equipment of Houston
2525 W. Bellfort, Suite 105
Houston, TX 77054
Tom Hardy, President

Retailers

Tel.: (713) 661-4000
Fax: (713) 661-4831

Cole, W.B., Supply
1001 Allen-Genoa Rd.
South Houston, TX 77587
Bill Lipscome, Owner
Tel.: (713) 944-2345
Fax: (713) 944-5207

Danka Business Systems
1291 N. Post Oak, Suite 130
Houston, TX 77055
Tom Frederick, Manager
Tel.: (713) 799-8888
Fax: (713) 688-2382

Design Services
P.O. Box 4285
Houston, TX 77024
Cathy Johnson, Vice President
Tel.: (713) 868-6589
Fax: (713) 861-9821

Eastman Kodak Company
16945 N. Chase Dr., Suite 1800
Houston, TX 77060
Mike Walsh, Regional Manager
Tel.: (713) 874-6800
Fax: (713) 874-6897

Finger's Office Furniture
4001 Gulf Freeway
Houston, TX 77003
Jim Kohnert, Vice President
Tel.: (713) 225-1371
Fax: (713) 221-4467

Global Services
2902 W. 12th St.
Houston, TX 77008
Steve Eifert, President
Tel.: (713) 864-8777
Fax: (713) 864-1900

Konica Business Machines
10161 Harwin, Suite 117
Houston, TX 77036
Johnny Williams, Division-Branch Manager
Tel.: (713) 995-0643
Fax: (713) 995-9834

How to Get a Job

Joyce Office Products
580 N. Shepherd
Houston, TX 77007
Tom Kirkpatrick, President
Tel.: (713) 868-3600
Fax: (713) 868-2516

Malloy's Cash Register Company
2101 Polk
Houston, TX 77003
Eugene Malloy, Chairman
Tel.: (713) 224-9528
Fax: (713) 224-4915

McCoy
611 W. 38th St.
Houston, TX 77018
Thad Minyard, President
Tel.: (713) 697-2417
Fax: (713) 691-6757

Minolta Business Systems
2872 Antoine
Houston, TX 77092
Werner Godosar, Manager
Tel.: (713) 686-9727
Fax: (713) 686-2008

Office Depot
10217 Katy Freeway
Houston, TX 77024
Paul Weardon, Manager
Tel.: (713) 467-7807
Fax: (713) 467-6935

Pitney-Bowes
4200 Westheimer, Suite 101
Houston, TX 77027
Pete Roberts, Director of Sales
Tel.: (713) 622-4681
Fax: (713) 622-8638

Richards, S.P., Company
1246 Silber
Houston, TX 77055
Bill Wyrick, Manager
Tel.: (713) 688-4485
Fax: (713) 684-5035

CONSUMER GOODS RETAILERS:

Bank, Joseph A., Clothiers
2030 W. Gray
Houston, TX 77019
Randy Corbitt, Manager
Tel.: (713) 523-7077

Beall's Department Store
347 Greenspoint Mall
Houston, TX 77060
Rusty Sparks, Manager
Tel.: (713) 875-4444

Blair Uniforms
5960 South Loop East
Houston, TX 77033
Richard Silen, Vice President
Tel.: (713) 733-1345
Fax: (713) 733-2746

Britt's Department Store
315 Northline Mall
Houston, TX 77022
Nelson Rockwell, Manager
Tel.: (713) 692-6111

Brooks Brothers
1200 McKinney, Suite 105
Houston, TX 77010
Harold Jones, Manager
Tel.: (713) 659-4000
Fax: (713) 752-0718

Business Micro Graphics Corp.
3730 Dacoma
Houston, TX 77092
Karen Roselle, Manager
Tel.: (713) 957-0800
Fax: (713) 957-4858

Craig's Ready to Wear
5631 Braxton
Houston, TX 77036
Mary Bell, Payroll
Tel.: (713) 780-4883
Fax: (713) 780-3768

Dillard's
4925 Westheimer
Houston, TX 77056
Dorothy Hines, Personnel Director

How to Get a Job

Tel.: (713) 622-1200
Fax: (713) 622-2641

Dilly Uniform Company
2327 Commerce
Houston, TX 77002
Charles Christenson, Owner
Tel.: (713) 228-0418
Fax: (713) 228-3465

Everitt-Buelow Company
2315 Post Oak Blvd.
Houston, TX 77056
Randy Griegsby, Manager
Tel.: (713) 622-4710

Foley's
1110 Main
Houston, TX 77001
Don Andrus, Chairman
Tel.: (713) 651-6098
Fax: (713) 651-6937

Foot Action
216 Gulf Gate Mall, 7100 Gulf Freeway
Houston, TX 77087
Jim Powell, District Manager
Tel.: (713) 649-8235
Fax: (713) 643-1467

Front Row
6632 Southwest Frwy.
Houston, TX 77074
Austin Wicke, Manager
Tel.: (713) 667-4647
Fax: (713) 785-1769

Isabell Gerhart
1554 W. Gray
Houston, TX 77019
Bob Brubaker, Manager
Tel.: (713) 526-6600
Fax: (713) 526-8227

K-Mart Discount Store
Tel.: (713) 771-3656
Fax: (313) 643-1000
36 Houston area locations.

Loehmann's, Inc.
7455 Southwest Freeway
Houston, TX 77074

Retailers

Ted Heine, Manager
Tel.: (713) 777-0164
No fax.

Lord & Taylor
5061 Westheimer
Houston, TX 77056
Jill McCleary, Manager
Tel.: (713) 627-8100
Fax: (713) 627-8100 ext. 500

Macy's
20131 Highway 59, Suite 4000
Humble, TX 77338
Harry Hadland, Manager
Tel.: (713) 280-5600
Fax: (713) 540-0900
5 other Houston area locations

Marshall Field's
10609 Town & Country Lane
Houston, TX 77024
Alison Hay, Manager
Tel.: (713) 827-2700
Fax: (713) 827-6573

Marshall's
9401 Katy Freeway
Houston, TX 77024
Tel.: (713) 465-8065
7 other Houston area locations

Mervyn's
1408 Baybrook Mall Dr.
Houston, TX 77020
Joe Martinez, Manager
Tel.: (713) 280-8800
Fax: (713) 280-8800 (transfer)

Miller's Outpost
5015 Westheimer, Suite 2012
Houston, TX 77056
Maria Schendor, Manager
Tel.: (713) 850-1533

Montgomery Ward & Company
500 Northline Mall
Houston, TX 77022
Ray Strauss, Manager
Tel.: (713) 691-8700
Fax: (713) 691-8722

How to Get a Job

Neiman Marcus
10615 Town & Country Way
Houston, TX 77024
Ken Gaston, Manager
Tel.: (713) 984-2100

Norton-Ditto Company
910 Travis
Houston, TX 77002
Tim Brown, Manager
Tel.: (713) 688-9800
Fax: (713) 655-9806

Palais Royal
10201 S. Main
Houston, TX 77025
Bernard Fuchs, President'
Tel.: (713) 667-5601
Fax: (713) 669-2709

J.C. Penney Co.
202 Sharpstown Center
Houston, TX 77005
Tel.: (713) 774-7400
6 other Houston area locations

Walter Pye's
438 Meyerland Plaza Mall
Houston, TX 77096
H. Walter Pye, Jr., Owner
Tel.: (713) 664-5501
Fax: (713) 664-9706

Sakowitz Furs
5026 Westheimer
Houston, TX 77056
Woody Nassar, Manager
Tel.: (713) 622-7947
Fax: (713) 622-7954

Saks Fifth Avenue
1800 Post Oak Blvd.
Houston, TX 77056
Bob Pike, Manager
Tel.: (713) 627-0500
Fax: (713) 622-7341

Sears Roebuck & Company
4201 S. Main
Houston, TX 77002
Tel.: (713) 527-2301
9 other Houston area locations

Retailers

Sears Surplus Store
11732 1/2 Eastex Freeway
Houston, TX 77039
Tel.: (713) 442-5345
4 other Houston area locations

Target Stores
12001 East Freeway
Houston, TX 77029
Joe Dodd, Manager
Tel.: (713) 451-2111
14 other Houston area locations

Tootsie's
4045 Westheimer
Houston, TX 77027
Tel.: (713) 629-9990

Wal-Mart Discount Cities
1705 Fry Rd.
Katy, TX 77449
Tel.: (713) 578-7007
15 other Houston area locations

Weiner's Stores
6005 Westview Dr.
Houston, TX 77055
L.J. Kleypass, Personnel
Tel.: (713) 688-1331
Fax: (713) 688-6976
48 other Houston area locations

Woolworth, F.W., Company
3902 Shepherd Dr. North
Houston, TX 77018
Tel.: (713) 697-3537
7 other Houston area locations

Wormser Hat Stores
816 Travis
Houston, TX 77002
Verlin Smith, Owner
Tel.: (713) 222-9371

How to Get a Job

Getting the scoop on success

Our friend Trudy was 20 years old and desperate for a job when she saw an ad in the paper for a scooper at a newly opened ice cream parlor. Having spent a high-school summer working in a soda shop, she applied for—and got—the job.

"When I started," Trudy recalls, "I was the only person working there full time during the day—besides the manager. I made $5 an hour. Whether she did it deliberately or not, the manager sort of tutored me in a lot of the things she did—how to make deposits, how to order, that sort of thing. I guess she was sort of lazy because I did most of her chores.

"I had been there four months when the manager quit without notice. The owner, who had been out of town, returned the next day in a panic. He made me assistant manager—by default, I guess, because I was the only one who had any idea how to run the place. He placed an ad for a manager right away, and applications just poured in. Meanwhile, he showed me a few more things I needed to know.

"Anyway, after a week went by, the owner told me to ignore the resumes that were coming in—even those from people with 20 years' experience. He made me the manager—at a salary of $22,000 a year."

Why Trudy?

"I worked really hard, right from the beginning. I was always on time, and I never called in sick. All the other kids there were just trying to earn money for college. I was trying to make a living. I told the manager I wanted to work 40 hours a week, and I would get really upset if I worked only 39.

"The experienced people who applied for the job weren't willing to do the grunt work. They wouldn't scoop when things got busy, and they didn't want to deal with unloading 120 tubs of ice cream. All they wanted to do was paper work.

"I don't plan to be doing this the rest of my life, but as long as I'm doing it, I want to do it well. I think we have the best quality ice cream, and that's important to me. We're also one of the most successful places in the city, and I'm happy for the part I play in it."

Travel, Transportation, Shipping

For additional information, you can contact:

PROFESSIONAL ORGANIZATIONS:

Airline Pilots Association
1625 Massachusetts Ave., NW
Washington, DC 20036
Tel.: (703) 689-2270

American Society of Travel Agents
1101 King Street
Alexandria, VA 22314
Tel.: (703) 739-2782

American Trucking Association
2200 Mill Road
Alexandria, VA 22314
Tel.: (703) 838-0230

Association of American Railroads
50 F Street NW
Washington, DC 20001
Tel.: (202) 639-2100

Institute of Transportation Engineers
525 School Street, SW Suite 410
Washington, DC 20024
Tel.: (202) 554-8050
Fax: (202) 863-5486

Travel Industry Association of America
1133 21st Street NW, 8th Floor
Washington, DC 20036-3357

United States Tour Operators Association
211 E. 51st Street, Suite 12-B
New York, NY 10022
Tel.: (212) 944-5727

PROFESSIONAL PUBLICATIONS:

Air Travel Journal
AOPA Pilot
ASTA Travel News
Aviation Week and Space Technology
Business and Commercial Aviation
Commercial Car Journal
Tours and Resorts
Traffic Management

How to Get a Job

Transport 2000
Transportation & Distribution
Travel Agent
Trux

DIRECTORIES:

American Society of Travel Agents—Membership Roster (American Society of Travel Agents, Washington, DC)
Aviation Directory (E.A. Brennan Co., Garden Grove, CA)
Institue of Certified Travel Agents—Directory (Institute of Certified Travel Agents, Wellesley, MA)
Moody's Transportation Manual (Moody's Investor Service, New York, NY)
TIA International Travel News Directory (Travel Industry Association of America, Washington, DC)
Travel Industry Personnel Directory (Travel Agent Magazine, New York, NY)

TRANSPORTATION AND SHIPPING:

ABC Moving & Storage
2601 Southwest Freeway
Houston, TX 77098
Roger Harrison, Manager
Tel.: (713) 526-2341
Fax: (713) 526-8654

Airborne Express
16220 Air Center Blvd.
Houston, TX 77032
Joe Manz, Manager
Tel.: (713) 443-8510
Fax: (713) 821-3764

American Airlines
363 N. Sam Houston Pkwy East, Suite 1200
Houston, TX 77060-2408
Ernie Weiskerger, Manager
Tel.: (713) 878-0000
Fax: (713) 878-0011

Arrow Trucking Company
435 S. Sheldon
Channelview, TX 77530
Powell Craker, Manager
Tel.: (713) 457-5672
Fax: (713) 457-5178

Bludworth Bond Shipyard
8114 Hockley
Houston, TX 77012
Monty Bludworth, Personnel

Travel/Transportation/Shipping

Tel.: (713) 923-2001
Fax: (713) 921-6161

British Airways
1100 Milam, Suite 250
Houston, TX 77037
Division Manager
Tel.: (800) 247-9297

Central Freight Lines
5800 Mesa
Houston, TX 77028
Linda Bowligny, Personnel Manager
Tel.: (713) 635-4100
Fax: (713) 635-1045

Chemical Leaman Tank
1700 Central St.
Houston, TX 77017
Karen Carter, Terminal Manager
Tel.: (713) 928-3131
Fax: (713) 928-2717

Consolidated Freight Ways
7345 Roundhouse
Houston, TX 77078
Chuck Penter, Division Manager—South Texas Division
Tel.: (713) 635-9394

Continental Airlines
174321 J.F. Kennedy Blvd.
Houston, TX 77032
Ed Digangi, Director of Reservations
Tel.: (713) 821-2100
Fax: (713) 230-3347
2929 Allen Parkway, 9th Floor
Houston, TX 77019
William Crouch, Director of Employment
Tel.: (713) 834-500

Danner's
7130 Navigation
Houston, TX 77011
Jim Maxcey, Vice President
Tel.: (713) 923-2651
Fax: (713) 923-2159

Delta Airlines
7800 Airport Blvd.
Houston, TX 77061
Tel.: (713) 448-3000
Headquarters:

How to Get a Job

Delta Airlines Inc.
1030 Delta Blvd.
Hartsfield-Atlanta International Airport
Atlanta, Georgia 30320
Boyd McBurnett, Manager of Employment Administration
Tel.: (404) 715-2600
Fax: (404) 714-1400

DHL Worldwide Courier Express
2350 North Belt East, Suite 1000
Houston, TX 77032
Cathy Bell, Human Resources Specialist
Tel.: (713) 442-8818
Fax: (713) 442-0295

DSI Transports
2401 Battleground Rd.
Deer Park, TX 77536
Tom Caskey, Manager
Tel.: (713) 478-1000
Fax: (713) 479-2005

Federal Express
4702 Travis
Houston, TX 77002
Bob Hanlon, Senior Manager
Tel.: (713) 522-5826
Fax: (713) 520-1549

Five Star Transportation
7814 Miller Rd., Suite 3
Houston, TX 77049
Dora Garcia, Personnel Director
Tel.: (713) 452-3191
Fax: (713) 452-4300

Garrett General Aviation
17250 Chanute Rd.
Houston, TX 77032
Al Jamail, Human Resources Manager
Tel.: (713) 443-7300
Fax: (713) 821-5185

Hi-Port Industries
409 E. Wallisville Rd.
Highlands, TX 77562
Cary Stockdale, Vice President of Human Resources
Tel.: (713) 426-5561
Fax: (713) 426-6394

Hot Shot Delivery
701 Shepherd

Travel/Transportation/Shipping

Houston, TX 77007
Richard Dana, Manager
Tel.: (713) 869-7575
Fax: (713) 862-6354

Houston Belt & Terminal Railway
501 Crawford, Suite 202
Houston, TX 77002
T.M. Stone, Personnel
Tel.: (713) 222-1133

Intercontinental Airport
16930 J.F.K. Blvd.
Houston, TX 77032
John Ferguson, Manager
Tel.: (713) 230-3100
Fax: (713) 230-2874

Kerr Steamship Company
2 Northpoint
Houston, TX 77060
Marta Blogett, Personnel Director
Tel.: (713) 931-2500
Fax: (713) 931-1569

Loomis Armored
103 N. Jackson
Houston, TX 77002
Bill Hasty, Manager
Tel.: (713) 224-6058
Fax: (713) 220-8022

Martin Gas Transport
10850 I-10 East
Baytown, TX 77520
David Seamore, Manager
Tel.: (713) 383-3445
Fax: (713) 383-7262

Matlack
2700 Appelt Dr.
Houston, TX 77015
Bud Wylie, Manager
Tel.: (713) 457-3957

Merchants Fast Motor Lines
5880 Kelley
Houston, TX 77026
Lisa Blankenship, Personnel Manager
Tel.: (713) 631-1333
Fax: (713) 636-6511

How to Get a Job

Metropolitan Transit Authority of Harris County
1201 Louisiana
Houston, TX 77002
Gwendolyn M. Simpson, Director of Human Resources
Tel.: (713) 739-4000
Fax: (713) 739-4925

Mission Petroleum Company
8450 Mosley
Houston, TX 77075
Tom Loop, Personnel
Tel.: (713) 943-8250
Fax: (800) 467-3988

Patterson Truck Lines
539 S. Sheldon Rd.
Channelview, TX 77530
Paula Fpurgeon, Personnel
Tel.: (713) 452-5443
Fax: (713) 452-3293

Port of Houston Authority
111 East Loop North
Houston, TX 77029
Melanie Sherman, Personnel
Tel.: (713) 670-2476
Fax: (713) 670-2479

Port Terminal Railroad Association
501 Crawford, Suite 423
Houston, TX 77002
Terry Stone, Personnel Director
Tel.: (713) 546-3339
Fax: (713) 546-3349

Roadway Express
5703 Britmoore
Houston, TX 77041
Jerry Fielder, Manager
Tel.: (713) 466-9909
Fax: (713) 896-1702

Southern Pacific Transportation Company
913 Franklin
Houston, TX 77002
Linda Woodard, Personnel
Tel.: (713) 223-6338

Southwest Airlines Company
Houston Hobby Airport
7910 Airport Boulevard
Houston, TX 77061

Travel/Transportation/Shipping

Frank Martinio, Superviser
Tel.: (713) 641-0674
Fax: (713) 640-1040

Southwestern Barge Fleet
18310 Market Channelview
Channelview, TX 77530
Harold Lee, Manager
Tel.: (713) 452-5857
Fax: (713) 860-3215

Strachan Shipping Company
10050 Northwest Freeway
Houston, TX 77092
Bill Homburg, Personnel
Tel.: (713) 683-3500
Fax: (713) 683-0595

Tex-Pack Express of Houston
4301 East Park
Houston, TX 77028
Derrick Monroe, Manager/Personnel
Tel.: (713) 674-6883
Fax: (713) 674-2861

Union Pacific
2802 Moy
Houston, TX 77007
W.F. Poppe, Manager
Tel.: (713) 864-3686

Utility Fuels
11 East Greenway Plaza, Suite 800
Houston, TX 77046
Lee Webb, Personnel Director
Tel.: (713) 888-4500
Fax: (713) 888-4606

TRAVEL EMPLOYERS:

AAA Travel
3000 Southwest Freeway
Houston, TX 77098
Joyce Bashner, Office Manager
Tel.: (713) 524-1851
Fax: (713) 522-4159

Accent on Travel
1018 North Highway 288
Angleton, TX 77515
Leah Tigner, Owner

How to Get a Job

Tel.: (800) 966-4762
Fax: (409) 849-2045

Ace Travel House
6910 Fannin, Suite 200
Houston, TX 77030
Jeff Cole, General Manager
Tel.: (713) 797-9444
Fax: (713) 797-1295

The All Season Travel Group
3 Riverway, Suite 1000
Houston, TX 77056
Alexander N.R. Shreders, Vice President of Operations
Tel.: (713) 622-8700
Fax: (713) 622-7704

American Express Travel Office
2503 River Oaks
Houston, TX 77019
Sheila Benoit, Manager
Tel.: (713) 527-8226
Fax: (713) 284-1390
4 other Houston area locations

Apple Travel
2471 South Braeswood
Houston, TX 77030
Henry M. Rosenblum, Owner
Tel.: (713) 661-0000
Fax: (713) 661-4025

Atlas Travel
3411 Montrose Boulevard
Houston, TX 77006
Barbara Provence
Tel.: (713) 527-4555
Fax: (713) 527-9619

Thomas Cook Travel, USA
2000 West Loop South, Suite 650
Houston, TX 77027
Gena Carlo, Office Manager
Tel.: (713) 871-3900
Fax: (713) 871-3912

Duckett's Custom Travel
12158 Greenspoint Drive
Houston, TX 77060
Cheryl S. Duckett, Owner
Tel.: (713) 875-9340
Fax: (713) 875-5345

Travel/Transportation/Shipping

Group Incentive Travel
15425 North Freeway, Suite 130
Houston, TX 77090
Brad Bogle, Manager
Tel.: (713) 873-8640
Fax: (713) 876-4428

Lifeco American Express
2901 Wilcrest, Suite 600
Houston, TX 77042
Terry Gordon, Manager
Tel.: (713) 954-7500
Fax: (713) 954-7733

Neiman-Marcus Travel Service
2600 S. Post Oak Blvd.
Houston, TX 77056
Nancy Edwards, Manager
Tel.: (713) 993-9402
Fax: (713) 960-1337

Oaks Travel Corp.
3100 Wilcrest, Suite 360
Houston, TX 77042
Tori Thompson, Corporate Director
Tel.: (713) 975-1999
Fax: (713) 789-5834

Sunbelt Travel
5858 Westheimer, Suite 101
Houston, TX 77057
David Neely, Manager
Tel.: (713) 978-6300
Fax: (713) 978-5031

Supertravel
500 Dallas, Suite P75
Houston, TX 77002
Marlene Lothian, Office Manager
Tel.: (713) 655-0140
Fax: (713) 655-0167

Ultra Travel
4550 Post Oak Place Drive, Suite 128
Houston, TX 77027
Fran Gahagan-Will, Owner
Tel.: (713) 963-0369
Fax: (713) 963-0553

Vacation Travel Services
9821 Katy Freeway, Suite 170
Houston, TX 77024

How to Get a Job

Barbara Briggs, Owner
Tel.: (713) 932-7698
Fax: (713) 932-9080

Windsor Travel Corp.
600 Travis, Suite 2075
Houston, TX 77002
Jim Schwartz, Owner
Tel.: (713) 228-1111
Fax: (713) 227-8294

Woodlake Travel Services
2513 South Gessner
Houston, TX 77063
Bettie H. Bernstein, Owner
Tel.: (713) 789-7500
Fax: (713) 789-2951

Utilities

For additional information, you can contact:

PROFESSIONAL ORGANIZATIONS:

American Public Gas Association
P.O. Box 1426
Vienna, VA 22183
Tel.: (703) 281-2910

American Public Power Association
2301 M Street NW
Washington, DC 20037-1484
Tel.: (202) 296-9800

National Utility Contractor's Association
1235 Jefferson Davis Highway
Arlington, VA 22202
Tel.: (703) 486-2100
Fax: (703) 979-8628

North American Telecommunications Association
2000 M Street NW
Washington, DC 20036
Tel.: (202) 296-9800
Fax: (202) 296-4993

United States Telephone Association
900 19th Street NW
Washington, DC 20006
Tel.: (202) 835-3100
Fax: (202) 835-3248

Utilities

Utilities Telecommunications Council
1150 17th Street NW, Suite 1000
Washington, DC 20036
Tel.: (202) 872-0030
Fax: (202) 872-1331

PROFESSIONAL PUBLICATIONS:

Communications Daily
Electric Light and Power
Electrical World
Public Power
Public Utilities
Telecommunications Reports
Telephony

DIRECTORIES:

Brown's Directory of North American Gas Companies, (Harcourt Brace Jovanovich, Cleveland, OH)
Electric Companies (American Business Directories, Omaha, NE)
Electric-Utility Solar-Energy Activities (Electric Power Research Institute, Palo Alto, CA)
Electrical World Directory of Electric Utilities (McGraw-Hill, New York, NY)
International Directory of Nuclear Utilities (Lotte Ltd., Lakewood, CO)
Moody's Public Utility Manual (Moody's Investor Service, New York, NY)
Power Engineering -New Generating Plants Issue (Technical Publishing Co., Barrington, IL)
Sourcebook (North American Telephone Association, Washington, DC)
Telephone Engineer & Management Directory (Harcourt Brace Jovanovich, Geneva, IL)

EMPLOYERS:

AT&T
6310 Telephone Road
Houston, TX 77087
Tel.: (713) 645-3318
Fax: (713) 645-2174
Send resumes in care of Linda Matello to:
2777 Stemmons Freeway, Suite 1425, Dallas, TX 75207
Long distance telecommunications services.

Ace Telephone
600 Kendrick, Suite A14
Houston, TX 77060
Cheryl Harris, Office Manager
Tel.: (713) 999-7755
Fax: (713) 999-7125
Sale and service of telephone equipment.

How to Get a Job

Am-Tex Corp.
1505 South Highway 6, Suite 210
Houston, TX 77077
Karen Hays, Personnel Director
Tel.: (713) 589-6000
Fax: (713) 589-2023
Development and maintenance of water and waste water systems for commercial and residential disticts.

Boyer
9318-A Reid Lake
Houston, TX 77064
Linda Boyer, Vice President
Tel.: (713) 466-5395
Fax: (713) 466-8198
Underground electrical, sewer, and excavation work.

Columbia Gulf Transmission
2603 Augusta Drive
Houston, TX 77057
Margaret Brown, Director of Personnel
Tel.: (713) 267-4100
Fax: (713) 267-4110
Natural gas transportation company.

Entex Gas Co.
1600 Smith
Houston, TX 77002
Howard Bell, President and CEO
Tel.: (713) 654-5100
Fax: (713) 654-5916
Natural gas distribution company servicing Montgomery and Walker Counties.

Gulf States Utilities Company
9425 Pinecroft Drive
Conroe, TX 77380
Joseph Donnelly, President
Tel.: (713) 367-6472
Fax: (409) 760-7054
Electrical service supplier for the Conroe area.

Harris County Fresh Water Supply—District 6
117 Tower
Channelview, TX 77530
Steve Early, District Superintendent
Tel.: (713) 452-2232
No fax.
Groundwater and sewage servicer for the Channelview area.

Hays Utility Service Corp.
2200 Sciaaca Road

Utilities

Spring, TX 77373
Linda Reeves, General Manager
Tel.: (713) 353-9756
Fax: (713) 353-6105
Water and sewer service supplier for north and west Houston, and southern Montgomery County.

Houston Industries
4400 Post Oak Parkway
Houston, TX 77027
Don D. Jordan, President and CEO
Tel.: (713) 629-3000
Fax: (713) 629-3129
Public holding company for utility, finance, communications and development companies.

Houston Lighting and Power
611 Walker
Houston, TX 77002
Larry B. Horrigan, Vice President, Purchasing & Materials Management
Tel.: (713) 228-9211
Fax: (713) 623-3587
Electric utility service for the Greater Houston/Galveston Metropolitan area.

Southwestern Bell Telephone Company
Employment Office
P.O. Box 1530
Houston, TX 77002
Sharon Harrell, Manager—Non-Management Staffing
Tel.: (713) 850-5750 (Job Hotline)
Tel.: (713) 850-5717
Local and long distance phone services.

TEBCO Services
9103 Shoal Creek
Houston, TX 77064
Ken Love, Field Service Manager
Tel.: (713) 955-0555
Fax: (713) 955-0666
Water utility management company for districts within Harris and Montgomery Counties.

Transco Energy Company
2800 Post Oak Boulevard
Houston, TX 77056
Glenna Pierpont, Personnel Administrator
Tel.: (713) 439-2000
Fax: (713) 439-2440
Oil, coal, and natural gas pipeline production company.

Employers Index

A

A&E Product Company, 338
AAA Travel, 353
ABC Moving & Storage, 348
Acad-Plus, 185
Accent on Travel, 353
Accudata Systems, 181
Ace Telephone, 357
Ace Travel House, 354
Adams and Porter International, 263
Adam's Mark Houston, 246
Adams Resources and Energy, 292
Adams Resources Exploration Corp., 296
AdPlex, 311
Advanced Computer Services, 185
Advanced Image Measurement Systems, 185
Advanced Telecommunications Corporation, 208
Advantage Capital, 268
Advantage Data Services, 185, 208
Advantage Engineering, 185
Aetna Health Plans, 243
Agip Petroleum Company, 292
Agriculture, Department of, 235
Aim Management Group, 268
Air Products Manufacturing, 176
Airborne Express, 348
Akzo Chemicals, 176
Aldine Independent School District, 201
Alexander and Alexander of Texas, 263
Alief Independent School District, 201
Alliance Commercial, 320
All Season Travel Group, The, 354
Allstate Insurance Company, 263
Allstates Design and Development Company, 215
Allwaste Inc., 221
Alvin, City of, 232
Alvin Community College, 198
Alvin Independent School District, 202
Am-Tex Corp., 358
Amerada Hess Corp., 295
American Airlines, 348
American Athletic Club, 327
American Bank, 159
American Business Networking, 185
American Cancer Society, Texas Division, 251
American Capital Management and Research, 268
American Civil Liberties Union, Greater Houston Cha, 251
American Diabetes Association, Texas Affiliate, 251
American Exploration, 296
American Express Travel Office, 354
American General Corp., 263
American General Securities, 268
American Heart Association, Houston Division, 251
American International Companies, 263
American Lung Association, 251
American Teleprocessing Corporation, 208
Ameritec Realty, 320
AMI Park Plaza Hospital, 239
AMI Systems Division, 181
Amicon Plastics, 304
Amoco Production Company, 292, 297
Anadarko Petroleum Company, 292
Anadrill-Schlumberger, 295
Andersen Consulting, 278
Anderson, Arthur, and Company, 141
Anderson, Mel, Communication, 316
Andrews and Kurth, 273
Antique Car Museum, 287
Antone's Import Company, 225
Apollo Paper Company, 306
Appelt, Womack, Ricks & Herder, 320
Apple Travel, 354
Army Corps of Engineers, 235
Arnold, White and Durkee, 273
Arrow Electronics, 208
Arrow Trucking Company, 348
Art Works, 287
Arthur D. Little, 279
Artigiani Galleries, 288
Arvey Paper and Office Products, 306
Ashland Exploration, 292
Asset Plus Corporation, 320
Associated Diazo Products, 306
Astrodetics, Inc., 151
AT&T, 208, 357
Atlantic Richfield Company, 297
Atlas Travel, 354
Atlas Wireline Services, 299
Attorney General's Office, 234
Autocad Systems-Cadsys, 181
Avondale House, 251

Employers Index

B

Bailey, Ray, Architects, 154
Baker and Botts, 273
Baker Hughes, 221, 299
Baker Oil Tools, 299
Baker Performance Chemicals, 299
Balk, Kenneth, and Associates, 154
Banc One Texas, 160
BancPlus Savings Association, 165
BancTexas Houston, N.A., 160
Bank, Joseph A., Clothiers, 341
Bank of Houston, 160
Bank One Houston, 160
Barrios Technology, 215
Basic Constructors, 190
Baylor College of Medicine, 198
Bayou Park Club, 327
Beall's Department Store, 341
Bechtel, Inc., 216
Beck's Prime, 334
Becon Construction Company, 190
Bell Cellular, 208
Bellaire, City of, 232
Bellaire Hospital, 239
Bellows, W.S., Construction Corp., 190
Belmont Constructors, 191
Ben Taub General Hospital, 242
Bendix Field Engineering Corp., 151
Benesys, 278
Bergen Brunswig Corp., 195
Bering Realty Corporation, 320
Bernstein & Associates, 316
Berwick and Associates, 185
Better Business Bureau of Metropolitan Houston, 252
BHP Petroleum, 297
BHP Petroleum (Americas), 292
Big Brothers and Big Sisters of Houston, 252
Binkley & Barfield, Consulting Engineers, 216
Bio-Medical Pharmaceutical Manufacturing Corp., 195
Birkman & Associates, 278
Birraporetti's, 331
Bistro-Vino, 331
Bjorksten Research Foundation, 229
Black, Gillock and Langberg, 146
Black Heritage Gallery, 288
Blair Uniforms, 341
Bludworth Bond Shipyard, 348
Blue Cross Blue Shield of Texas, 263
BMP Paper and Printing, 306
Body Fit, 327
Boeing Aerospace Operations, 151
Bombay Palace, 331
Booz Allen & Hamilton, 278
Bosworth Papers, 306
Bovay Engineers, 216
Bowen Tools, 299
Bowne of Houston, 311
Boyd, Page & Associates, 320
Boyer, 358
Bracewell and Patterson, 273
Bradford School of Business, 200
Braescroft Pharmacy, 195
Brandt & Lawson, 311
Brawner Paper Company, 306
Brennan's, Houston, 331
British Airways, 349
Britt's Department Store, 341
Brooks Brothers, 341
Brooks/Collier, 154
Brown and Root, 191
Brown Foundation, 229
Brown, George R., Partnership, The, 297
Brown, John, 216
Brown, Nelson & Associates, 316
Brown, Parker & Leahy L.L.P., 274
Brummerhop's Plast-Tech, 304
Building Services Associates, 154
Bull HN Information Systems, 181
Burger King, 334
Business Data Center Corporation, 186
Business Equipment of Houston, 338
Business Micro Graphics Corp., 341
Busse, A.R., & Associates, 316
Butler & Binion, 274
Butler Paper Company, 307
Butler Professional Service Group, 304

C

Cable Communications Network, 173
Cabot Energy Corporation, 292
Cain Chemical, 176
Camco, 300
Cameron Employees, 164
Cameron Iron Works, USA, 300
Campbell, Mithun, Esty, Goodwin, Dannenbaum, Littma, 146
Capstone Financial Services, 268
Cargill Printing & Stationery, 311
Carlyle Communications International, 282
Carraba's Italian Restaurant, 331
Cascade Impex Company, 307
Catholic Charities, 252
Cattle Guard Restaurant and Bar, 331
CCA Southwest, 278

How to Get a Job

CD Commercial Real Estate Services, 321
CDI, Stubbs and Overbeck, 216
Celanese Chemical Company, 176
Centel Communications Systems, Fisk Division, 208
Centennial Computer Systems, 186
Center for Advanced Legal Studies, 200
Center for Counseling, 252
Center for the Retarded, 252
Central Freight Lines, 349
Century Development, 321
Century Paper, 307
Champagne Fine Printing & Lithographic, 311
Champion International Corporation, Sheldon Mill, 307
Channelview Independent School District, 202
Charlie Fitness Club and Hotel, 327
Charter Bancshares, 160
Charter National Bank-Colonial, 160
Charter National Bank-Houston, 160
Chemical Leaman Tank, 349
Chevron, 297
Child Abuse Prevention Council, 252
Child Care Council of Greater Houston, 252
Children's Museum, 288
Chinese Daily News, 282
Christian Community Service Center, 252
Churchill Group, 316
CIGNA Healthplan of Texas, 243
Cigna Property and Casualty Companies, 264
Cimarron Software Services, 186
Citation Oil and Gas Corporation, 297
Citizens Bank & Trust Company of Baytown, 160
Citizen's Environment Coalition Education Fund, 253
Clarion Properties, 321
Clarke & Courts, 311
Clean Houston, 253
Clean Water Action, 253
Cleveland Advocate, 282
CNA, 264
Coade Engineering Physics Software, The, 186
Coastal Banc Savings Association, 165
Coastal Corp., 292
Coastal Corps, 297
Coastal Telephone Company, 209
Coca-Cola Foods, 225
Coldwell Banker Residential Real Estate Services, 321

Cole Publications, 167
Cole, W.B., Supply, 339
Collins Lowell Gallery, 288
Columbia Gas Development Corp., 293
Columbia Gulf Transmission, 358
Columbia Hospital, 239
Commerce, Department of, 235
Commercial Drywall, 191
Commercial Real Estate Associates, 321
Communications Plus, 146
Communicators Federal, 164
Community Cable Company, 173
Community Health Computing, 181
Compaq Computer Corp., 181
Compu-data, 186
Computech Career Centers, 201
Computer Access Associates, 186
Computer Systems and Applications, 186
Computerland, 181
Confederate Museum, 288
Conference Pros International, 209
Conoco, Inc., 296
Conroe Independent School District, 202
Consolidated Freight Ways, 349
Contemporary Arts Museum, 288
Continental Airlines, 349
Control Data Institute, 201
Cook, Thomas, Travel, USA, 354
Coopers & Lybrand, 278
Coopers and Lybrand, 141
Core Laboratories, A Division of Western Atlas International, 300
Corporate Services, 311
Corrosion Magazine, 167
Costas Gym, 327
Courier Newspaper, 283
Covenant House, Texas, 253
Covington & Rutledge, 321
Cowen & Company, 268
Craig's Ready to Wear, 341
Cravens Dargan and Company, 264
Creneau Media Group, 283
Crisis Intervention of Houston, 253
Criterion Group, 268
CRS Sirrine, 154
Cullen Center Bank & Trust, 161
Cullen Foundation, 229
Cushman & Wakefield of Texas, 321
Cushman Realty Corp., 321
Custom Rubber Products, 304
Cynacon, 195
Cypress-Fairbanks Independent School District, 202

Employers Index

D

Daily Court Review, 283
Dairy Queen, 334
Dame Publications, 168
Danbury Independent School District, 202
Danka Business Systems, 339
Danner's, 349
Data Corp., 186
Data General, 182
Daugbjerg and Associates, 279
Davis Bros. Oil Producers, 298
Day, Dean, Gallery, 288
de la Garza & Associates, 316
Dean Witter, 269
Deer Park Independent School District, 202
DeJean Construction Company, 191
Deloitte and Touche, 141
Delta Airlines, 349
DePelchin Children's Center, 253
Design Services, 339
DHL Worldwide Courier Express, 350
Dia-Long Company, 300
Diagnostic Center Hospital, 239
Digital Equipment Corp., 182
Digital Equipment Corporation, 209
Dillard's, 341
Dilly Uniform Company, 342
Diversified Lithographics, 312
Domino's Pizza, 334
Donaldson Lufkin & Jenrette, 269
Donnelley, R.R., Financial, Houston, 312
Doubletree Allen Center, 246
Doubletree at Post Oak, 246
Dow Chemical USA, 300
Dow Chemical, USA, 176, 216
Dowell Schlumberger, 300
Dr. Pepper Bottling Company of Texas, 225
Dresser Industries, 300
Drill-Quip, 301
Drug Enforcement Administration, 235
DSI Transports, 350
Duckett's Custom Travel, 354
Duke Publishing, 168
Dunn, John S., Research Foundation, 229
DuPont de Nemours, 176

E

East Bernard Independent School District, 202
Eastman Kodak Company, 339
Ebasco Services, 216
Echo, The, 283
Eckerd, Jack, Corp., 195
Econalysis, 279
Edelman, Daniel J., of Texas, 316
EDI Architecture/Planning, 155
Educators Community, 164
Edwards, A.G., & Sons, 269
Eikenburg and Stiles, 274
Eisaman, Johns and Laws Advertising, 146
Elf Exploration, 293
Employers Insurance of Texas, 264
Enclean Inc., 222
Endowment Fund for the Jewish Community of Houston, 229
EnerServ Products, 301
Enron Corp., 298
Enterprise Bank Houston, 161
Entex Gas Co., 358
Environmental Protection Agency, 235
Episcopal High School, 205
Eppler Guerin & Turner, 269
Equal Employment Opportunity Commission (EEOC), 236
Ernst & Young, 279
Ernst and Young, 141
ESCO, Inc., 151
Ethyl Corporation-Houston Plant, 176
Everitt-Buelow Company, 342
Executone Information Systems, 209
Exxon Chemical Americas, 177
Exxon Company USA, 296, 298
Exxon Production Research Company, 293

F

Falcon Fast Print, 312
Falick/Klein Partnership, 155
Family Outreach Centers, 253
Family Service Center, 254
Farb, Susan, Public Relations, 316
Federal Bureau of Investigation, 236
Federal Express, 350
Federal Reserve Bank of Dallas, Houston Branch, 161
Fellers and Company, 146
Finger's Office Furniture, 339
Fireman's Fund Insurance Company, 264
First City Bancorporation of Texas, 161
First City Bank Gulfgate, 161
First City Bank of Highland, 161
First City National Bank of Houston, 161

How to Get a Job

First Educators, 164
First Gibraltar Bank, FSB, 165
First Interstate Bank, 162
First Interstate Bank of Texas, N.A., 162
First Interstate Bank–Town and Country, 162
First Investors Corp., 269
Fish Engineering & Construction, 217
Fitts, Roberts, and Company, 142
Five Star Transportation, 350
Fleming Foods, 225
Fluor Daniel, 217
Flying Dutchman Restaurant and Oyster Bar, 331
FMC Corporation Specialty Chemical Division, 177
Fogarty and Klein, 147
Foley's, 342
Fondren Foundation, 229
Food and Drug Administration, 236
Foot Action, 342
Force Corp., 191
Ford Aerospace Corporation, 217
Formcraft, 312
Fort Bend County, 233
Fort Bend County Museum, 288
Fort Bend Independent School District, 202
Four Seasons Houston Center, 246
Friendswood, City of, 232
Friendswood Development Company, 322
Friendswood Independent School District, 203
Frito Lay, 225
Front Row, 342
Fulbright & Jaworski, 274
Fuller Commercial Brokerage Company, 322
Fuller-Wallace, Realtors, 322

G

Galena Park, City of, 232
Galena Park Independent School District, 203
Garrett General Aviation, 350
GDS Engineers, 217
GE Aerospace, 151
Gensler and Associates/Architects, 155
Gerhart, Isabell, 342
Glazier Food Company, 225
Global Marine, 222, 301
Global Services, 339
Golden Age Hobby House of Houston, 254
Goldman Sachs & Co., 269
Gold's Gym, 327
Goldstein Communications, 317
Goodwill Industries of Houston, 254
Grace, W.R., and Company, 177
Grant Thornton, 142
Great Greek, 331
Greater Houston Convention and Visitors Bureau, 254
Griggs and Harrison, 274
Group Incentive Travel, 355
Grover Printing Company, 312
GTE Mobile Communications, 209
Guadeloupe Area Social Services, 254
Guardian Savings & Loan Association, 166
Guest Quarters Suite Hotel–Galleria West, 246
Gulf Coast Paper Company, 307
Gulf Printing Company, 312
Gulf Publishing Company, 168
Gulf States Utilities Company, 358
Gulf Systems, 307

H

Haik, Mac, Realty, 322
Halliburton Logging Services, 301
Halliburton Services, 301
Hamman, George and Mary Josephine, Foundation, 229
Hargest Vocational & Technical College, 201
Harper and Pearson Company, 142
Harris County, 233
Harris County Attorney, 233
Harris County Clerk's Office, 233
Harris County Community Development Agency, 254
Harris County Department of Adult Probation, 254
Harris County Department of Child Protective Servic, 254
Harris County Department of Education, 255
Harris County Department of Juvenile Probation, 255
Harris County Department of Social Services, 255
Harris County District Attorney's Office, 234
Harris County District Clerk's Office, 234
Harris County Domestic Relations Office, 255
Harris County Fresh Water Supply—District 6, 358
Harris County Heritage Society, 289
Harris County Hospital District, 239

Employers Index

Harris County Housing Authority, 255
Harris County Pre-trial Services, 255
Harris County Public Library, 255
Harris County Sheriff's Department, 234
Harris County Veterans County Service Office, 256
Harris, Kosmoski and Pinkston, 147
Harrisburg Bank, 162
Hartford Insurance Group, 264
Hartz Chicken, 332
Hassell Construction Company, 191
Hay Group, 279
Hays Utility Service Corp., 358
Haywood Graphics, 312
HCA Medical Center Hospital and Women's Hospital of, 239
Health Care Supplies, 195
Health Economics Corp., 264
Health, State Department of, 234
Hear-Say, 256
Heath-Zenith Computers and Electronics, 182
Heights of Texas, FSB, 166
Helmsley-Spear of Texas, 322
Henden Computer Management, 187
Hermann Hospital, 239
Hewitt Associates, 279
Hewlett Packard Company, 182
Hi-Port Industries, 350
Highlands Insurance Company, 264
Highways and Public Transportation, State Departmen, 234
Hinckley and Slade, 147
Hines Interests Limited Partnership, 322
Hirsch Glover Robinson & Sheiness, 274
Hoechst Celanese Corp., 177
Holiday Inn Crowne Plaza-Galleria, 246
Holiday Inn Greenway Plaza, 246
Holiday Inn Houston Downtown, 247
Holiday Inn Houston West, 247
Homco International, 301
Hope Center for Youth, 256
Horizon Discovery Group, 151
Horizon Galleries, 289
Horizon Realty Group, 322
Hot Shot Delivery, 350
Houlihan's Old Place, 332
House of Pies, 332
House Reh Associates, 155
Housing and Urban Development, 236
Housing Authority of the City of Houston, 256
Houston Airport Marriott, 247

Houston Area Urban League, 256
Houston Area Women's Center, 256
Houston Baptist University, 198
Houston Belt & Terminal Railway, 351
Houston Business Journal, 168
Houston Center for Photography, 289
Houston Child Guidance Center, 256
Houston Chronicle, 283
Houston Coca-Cola Bottling Company, 225
Houston Community College System, 199
Houston Defender, 283
Houston Department of Health and Human Services, 256
Houston Electronics Development Corp., 209
Houston Endowment, 230
Houston Engineering Center, 217
Houston Family Association, 257
Houston Finance and Administration Department, 232
Houston Food Bank, 257
Houston Habitat for Humanity, 257
Houston Health and Human Services Department, 233
Houston Hospice, 257
Houston Humane Society, 257
Houston Independent School District, 203
Houston Industries, 359
Houston Lighting and Power, 359
Houston Marriott North at Greenspoint, 247
Houston Marriott Westside, 247
Houston Metropolitan Magazine, 168, 283
Houston Metropolitan Racquet Club, 328
Houston Mobil Communication, 209
Houston Monthly Magazine, 168
Houston Museum of Natural Science, 289
Houston Northwest Medical Center, 240
Houston Police Department, 233
Houston Police Federal, 164
Houston Post Company, The, 283
Houston Postal, 165
Houston Public Library, 257
Houston Public Works Department, 233
Houston Read Commission, 257
Houston Scene Magazine, 284
Houston School for Deaf Children, 257
Houston Society for the Prevention of Cruelty to Animals, 258

How to Get a Job

Houston Traffic and Transportation Department, 233
Houston Veterans Administration Medical Center, 240
Houstonian Club, 328
Howard Johnson, 247
Howell Corporation, 296
Human Services, Department of, 234
Humana Hospital—Clear Lake, 240
Hunan Dragon, 332
Hutcheson and Grundy, 274
Hyatt Regency Hotel, 247
Hydril Company, 301

I

IBM Federal Systems Division, 182
ICI Americas, 177
IEPS Electronic, 209
ILC Space Systems, 151
Immanuel Lutheran School, 205
Index, The Design Firm, 155
Informacion, 168
Informacion, La, 284
Inner-View, 169
Inside Texas Running and Fitness, 169
Institute for Preventive Medicine Health & Fitness, 328
Intercontinental Airport, 351
Interim Health Care, 240
Internal Revenue Service, 236
International Mailing Systems, 313
International Services Plus, 307
International Tool and Supply Company, 301
International Trading Company, 226
Interox America, 177
Intertel, 210
Irvine Associates Architects, 155

J

Jack-in-the-Box, 335
Jackson and Walker, 274
Jackson, Bruce D., and Associates, 152
Jacobs Engineering Group, 217
Jake's Egg and Distributing Co., 308
Jalco, Inc., 192
Jewish Community Center of Houston, Texas, 258
Jewish Herald Voice, 284
Johnson & Higgins of Texas, 265
Johnson, Bernard, Inc., 155
Johnson Control World Services, 152
Johnson Engineering Corporation, 217
Johnson Space Center Federal, 165
Jones Business Systems, 182
Jones Lang Wootton, 323
Joyce Office Products, 340
Justice, Department of, 236

K

K-Mart Discount Store, 342
K-Tec Electronics Corporation, 210
K2 Realty, 323
KACC, 173
Katy Independent School District, 203
Kellogg, M.W, 218
Kemper Financial Services, 269
Kent Electronics Corporation, 210
Kentucky Fried Chicken, 335
Kerr Steamship Company, 351
Kettle Restaurants, 332
KHOU-TV, 171
KHTV, 171
Kidder Peabody & Company, 270
KIKK AM/FM Radio Station, 173
KILT AM/FM Radio Station, 174
King Chapman & Broussard, 279
Kingwood Athletic Club, 328
Kinkaid School, The, 205
Kirksey-Meyers Architects, 155
KKBQ Radio, 174
KLAT Radio La Tremenda, 174
Klein Independent School District, 203
KMJQ Majic, 102 FM, 174
KODA 99 FM, 174
Konica Business Machines, 339
KPRC Radio, 174
KPRC-TV, 172
KRBE AM FM, 174
KRIV-TV, 172
KSA Industries/Houston Oilers, 270
KTRK-TV, 172
KTRU Radio, 174
KTXH-TV, 172
KUHF, 175
KUHT-TV, 172
Kwik-Kopy Corporation, 313
KXLN-TV, 172

L

La Porte Independent School District, 203
Labor, Department of, 236
Laguarta & Company, 323
Lamar Consolidated Independent School District, 203
Leader Newspaper, 284
Leventhal, Kenneth, and Company, 142
Lewis Partners, 323

Employers Index

L'Hotel Sofitel, 247
Liberty Mutual Insurance Company, 265
Lichter/Jameson and Associates, 218
Liddell Sapp and Zivley, 275
Lifeco American Express, 355
Lighthouse of Houston, 258
Linbeck Construction Corp., 192
Lindler, George B. & Irene, Foundation, 230
Link Flight Simulation Corp., 152
Linkous, Farris & Potter, 323
Litwin Engineers and Constructors, 218
Llewelyn-Davies Sahni, 156
Lloyd, Jones, Fillpot Associates/ Architects, 156
Lockheed Engineering and Management Services, 218
Lockwood, Andrews, and Newman, 156
Lockwood National Bank of Houston, 162
Loehmann's, Inc., 342
Long John Silvers Seafood Shoppes, 335
Long, Meredith, Galleries, 289
Loomis Armored, 351
Loral Space Information Systems, 152
Lorance and Thompson, 275
Lord & Taylor, 343
Lubrizol Corporation, The, 177
Lummus Crest, 218
Lyondell Petrochemical Company, 177

M

Macha International, 210
Macy's, 343
Malloy's Cash Register Company, 340
Mann, Frankfort, Stein and Lipp, 142
Marathon Oil Company, 293, 298
March of Dimes, Birth Defects Foundation, Texas Gul, 258
Marek Brothers Systems, 192
Markel Enterprises, 279
Marriott Braeswood, 248
Marriott, J. W., 248
Marriott Medical Center, 248
Marshall Field's, 343
Marshall's, 343
Martin Gas Transport, 351
Matlack, 351
Matrix Technologies, 195
Mayor, Day, Caldwell and Keeton, 275
McCann-Erickson, 147
McCoy, 340

McDonald's Restaurants, 335
McDonnell Douglas Astronautics Company/Engineering, 152
McGovern, John P., Foundation, 230
MCI Telecommunications Corporation, 210
McKinsey & Company, 280
Med Center Bank, 162
Melton and Melton, 142
Memorial Athletic Club, 328
Memorial City Medical Center, 240
Memorial Healthcare Systems, 240
Memorial Lutheran School, 205
Memorial Northwest Hospital, 240
Memorial Southeast Hospital, 241
Memorial Southwest Hospital, 241
Menil Collection, 289
Mercer, William M., 280
Merchants Fast Motor Lines, 351
Merchants Park Bank, 162
Meridian Oil, 293
Merrill Lynch Pierce Fenner & Smith, 270
Mervyn's, 343
Methodist Hospital, 241
Metlife Healthcare Network of Texas, 243
Metropolitan Transit Authority of Harris County, 352
Michaelangelo's, 332
Micro Horizons, 187
Micro-Ware Paper Co., 308
MicroMeans, Inc., 182
Miles, Inc. (formerly Mobay Synthetics Corporation), 178
Miller/Grubb & Ellis, Henry S., 323
Miller's Outpost, 343
Milton McGinty Partnership Architects, 156
Minolta Business Systems, 340
Miramar Computer Consulting, 187
Mischer Corporation, 323
Mission Petroleum Company, 352
Mitchell Energy and Development Corp., 293
Mitre Corporation, 218
Mobil Exploration and Producing, US, 293
Mobil Oil, 296
Mobile Communications Corporation of America, 210
Monarch Paper Company, 308
Montgomery Ward & Company, 343
Moody Rambin Interests, 323
Moore Stephens, CPA, 142
Moore, Walter P., 218
Morris Architects, 156

How to Get a Job

Mosbacher Energy Company and Mosbacher Management C, 294
Motorola, Inc., 210
Mr. Gatti's, 335
Mundy Companies, 192
Murchison Investment Bankers, 270
Muscular Dystrophy Association, Houston/Gulf Coast, 258
Museum of Fine Arts/Houston, 289

N

Nalco Chemical Company, 178
Narco Bio-Systems, 196
Nation-wide Missing Persons Bureau, 259
National Aeronautics and Space Administration, 236
National Association for the Advancement of Colored, 258
National Oilwell, 302
National Organization for Women (N.O.W.), 258
Nations Bank Fannin, 162
Nations Bank Houston, 163
Nationwide Papers, 308
NCR Corporation, 211
NEC Technologies, 183
Neighborhood Centers, 259
Neiman Marcus, 344
Neiman-Marcus Travel Service, 355
Network Support Corp., 183
New Directions Club, 259
Ninfa's Mexican Restaurant, 332
North Forest Independent School District, 204
North Freeway Leader, 284
North Harris Montgomery Community College, 199
Northeast Medical Center Hospital, 241
Northway Healthcare Center, 241
Norton-Ditto Company, 344
Novell-Accudata Systems, 211

O

Oaks Travel Corp., 355
Occidental Oil and Gas, 298
Ocean Industry, 169
Office Depot, 340
Offshore Data Services, 211
Ogilivy and Mather, 147
Oilfield Rental Service Company, 302
Old Heidelberg, 333
Omni Houston Hotel, 248
On the Border Cafe, 333
Open Door Mission, 259

Openheimer & Company, 270
Oteco Equipment Company, 302
Otis Engineering Company, 302
Owen Company Hospital/Pharmacies Management, 196
Oxy USA, 294

P

Pacific Enterprises Oil Company, 298
Pactel Corporation, 211
Paging Products International II, 211
Paine Webber, 270
Palais Royal, 344
Palmer Paper Co., 308
Pannell, Kerr, Forster, 142
Paper Plus, 308
Pappas Company, 333
Pappasito's Cantina, 333
Paragon Group, 324
Parker-Shane Manufacturing, 152
Parks and Wildlife Department, 235
Pasadena Bayshore Medical Center, 241
Pasadena Citizen, 284, 313
Pasadena, City of, 232
Pasadena Independent School District, 204
Patrick Media Group, 147
Patterson Truck Lines, 352
Paxson and Bersch, 275
PB-KBB, Inc., 156
PBR Architects, 156
Pearland Independent School District, 204
Peat, Marwick, Main and Company, 143
Peek Measurement, 211
Pennwalt Corp., 178
Penny and Speier, 147
Penney, J.C., Co., 344
Pennzoil Company, 294, 298
Pepsi South, 226
Petrolite Equipment & Instruments Group, 302
Philbrook Goodale Associates, 280
Phillips Petroleum Company, 294, 298
Pierce, Goodwin, Alexander, 157
Pipeline Magazine/Oildom Publishing, 169
Pitney-Bowes, 340
Planned Parenthood of Houston and Southeast Texas, 259
Plasteco, Inc., 304
Plastic Fabricators, 304
Pogo Producing Company, 294
Pollock Paper Distributors, 308

Employers Index

Pool Company, 302
Popeye's, 335
Port of Houston Authority, 352
Port Terminal Railroad Association, 352
Porter & Clements, 275
Post Oak Bank, 163
Powerhouse Gym, 328
Premier Company, 313
President & First Lady Health & Racquet Clubs, 328
Price Waterhouse, 143
Prime Cable of Harris County, 173
Prime Computer, 183
Prime Time Cable, 173
Productivity Enhancements, 280
Professional Accounting Society, 143
Professional Service Industries, 219
Pronet, Inc., 211
Prudential Capital Corporation, 265
Prudential Insurance of America, 243
Prudential-Bache Securities, 270
Public Safety, Department of, 234
Pye's, Walter, 344

Q

Quest Business Agency, 317
Quest Business Agency, The, 148
Quick Tick International, 313
Quintana Petroleum Corp., 299

R

R.J.R. Nabisco, 226
Ragin' Cajun Seafood and Po-Boys, 333
Railroad Museum of the Gulf Coast, Chapter NRHS, 289
Ramsey-Sellers Associates, 280
Randall Corporation, 219
Rauscher Pierce Refsnes, 270
RCL Consulting, 187
Read-Poland Associates, 317
Realty Executives, 324
Reed, E.E., Construction Company, 192
Reed Tool Company, 302
Refugee Services Alliance, 259
Rein, C.G., Galleries, 290
Reliability Incorporated, 211
Resins International, 304
Rice University, 199
Rice University Press, 169
Richards, S.P., Company, 340
Ridgway's, 313
River Oaks Bank, 163
Riverside Press, 313

Riverway Bank, 163
Rives Smith Baldwin Carlberg, 148
Riviana Foods, 226
Roadway Express, 352
Rockwell Fund, 230
Rockwell Space Operations Co., 152
Rohm and Haas of Bayport, 178
Rohm and Haas of Texas, 178
Rolm Company, 212
Roma's Restaurant, Tony, 333
Rosewood General Hospital, 241
Rotan Mosle, 271
RWS Architects, 157

S

S.I.P. Engineering, 219
Sachnowitz Advertising Agency, 148
SAE/Spaw-Glass Construction, 192
Safety Lights Company, 192
Safeway Scaffolds Company of Houston, 192
Sakowitz Furs, 344
Saks Fifth Avenue, 344
Salvation Army, 259
Sam Houston Memorial Hospital, 240
Sanbzik Rock Tools, 303
Sandefer Oil and Gas, 294
Sanus/New York Life, 243
Sarofim, Fayez, and Company, 269
Schey Advertising, 148
Schey Public Relations, 317
Scott Paper Co., 308
Screen Graphics, 313
Sears Roebuck & Company, 344
Sears Surplus Store, 345
Seidman and Seidman/BDO, 143
Serv Tech, 222
Sewell and Riggs, 275
Shable, Sawyer and Pitluk, 148
Shason Microwave Corporation, 212
Shasta Beverage, 226
Shearson Lehman Brothers, 271
Sheinfield, Maley and Kay, 275
Sheldon Independent School District, 204
Shell Employees Federal Credit Union, 165
Shell Oil Company, 294
Shell Western E & P, 294
Sheltering Arms, 260
Sheraton Astrodome Hotel, 248
Sheraton Crown Hotel & Conference Center, 248
Sikes, Jennings, Kelly and Brewer, 157
Simpson Pasadena Paper Company, 309
Sir James Athletic Club, 328

How to Get a Job

Sisters of Charity of the Incarnate Word Health Car, 242
SMC McEver, 219
Smith Barney, Harris Upham & Company, 271
Smith Farms, 226
Smith Food Service, 226
Smith International, 303
Sonat Exploration Company, 295
South Coast Drywall, 193
South Main Bank, 163
Southdown, Inc., 222
Southern Newspapers, 284
Southern Pacific Transportation Company, 352
Southwest Airlines Company, 352
Southwestern Barge Fleet, 353
Southwestern Bell Telecommunications, 212
Southwestern Bell Telephone Company, 212, 359
Southwestern Paralegal Institute, 201
Space Age Laminating & Bindery Company, 314
Specialty Control Systems, 187
Spectrum Consumer Products Company, 196
Spencer Herolz Architects, 157
Spina Bifida Association of Texas, Houston Chapter, 260
Spring Branch Independent School District, 204
Spring Branch Memorial Hospital, 242
Spring Independent School District, 204
Sprint Communications Company LP, 212
St. Anne's Catholic Elementary School, 205
St. Edward's Catholic Church School, 205
St. John's School, 205
St. Joseph's Hospital, 242
St. Luke's Episcopal Hospital, 242
St. Mark Lutheran School, 206
St. Matthew Lutheran School, 206
St. Paul Fire & Marine Insurance Company, 265
St. Thomas' Episcopal School, 206
St. Thomas High School, 206
Stables Steak House, 333
Star of Hope, 260
Star Pizza, 333
State of Texas Department of Human Services, 260
Sterling Electronics Corporation, 212
Stone & Webster Management Consultants, 280
Stone and Webster Engineering Corporation, 219
Stone's Fitness Center, 329
Stouffer Presidente Hotel, 248
Strachan Shipping Company, 353
Strake Foundation, 230
Strake Jesuit College Preparatory, 206
Subasta, La, 285
Subway, 334
Sugar Creek National Bank, 163
Sugar Land Athletic Club, 329
Summa Rx Laboratories, 196
Sun Microsystems, 183
Sunbelt Travel, 355
Supertravel, 355
Swiss Chalet Fine Foods, 226
Synercom Technology, 187
Sysco Food Services, 227
Systems Application Engineering, 187

T

Taco Bell, 336
Taj Majal, 334
Tanglewood Corporation, 324
Tanknology Environmental, 222
Target Stores, 345
Tarpley/Lunow Architects, 157
Tate, The, Agency, 317
Taylor Smith, 148
Team Bank, 163
TEBCO Services, 359
Telxon, 183
Tenneco Credit Union, 165
Tenneco Publications, 169
Tenneco Realty, 324
Tex-Pack Express of Houston, 353
Tex-Trude, Inc., 305
Texaco Chemical Company, 178
Texaco, Inc., 299
Texas A & M University at Galveston, 199
Texas Alkyls, 178
Texas Catholic Herald, The, 285
Texas Children's Hospital, 242
Texas City Independent School District, 204
Texas Club, 329
Texas Commerce Bank, N.A., 164
Texas Electronic Resources, 188
Texas Employment Commission, 235
Texas First Securities, 271
Texas Lady-Texan Spas, 329
Texas Petrochemicals Corp., 178
Texas School of Business, 201
Texas Southern University, 199
Texas Woman's University, 199
Thompson, Nelson and Cardenal, 157

370

Employers Index

3/D International, 157
Three Star Supply, 309
Tokyo Gardens Japanese Restaurant, 334
Tomball Independent School District, 205
Tootsie's, 345
Total Minatome, 295
Trammel Crow Company, 324
Transamerica Waste, 222
Transco Energy Company, 295, 359
Transwestern Property Company, 324
TransWestern Publishing, 169
Travelers Health Network of Texas, 243
Travelers Insurance Company, 265
Triangle Refineries, 296
Tribble & Stephens Company, 193
Trione & Gordon, 324
TriStar Webb Graphics, 314
Tropical Foods, 227
TRT/FTC Communications, 212
Trum Advertising, 148
Tuboscope Vetco International, 303
Turner, Collie and Braden, 219
Two Pesos, 336

U

U.S. District Court, 237
U.S. Small Business Administration, 237
U.S. Videotel, 213
Ultra Travel, 355
Underwood, Neuhaus & Company, 271
Uni-Komp, 188
Union Camp Corp., School Supply and Stationery Divi, 309
Union Pacific, 353
Union Texas Petroleum, 295
Unisage, Inc., 188
Unisys Corp., 183
United Savings of Texas, FSB, 166
United Way of the Texas Gulf Coast, 260
Universal Computer Systems, 188
University of Houston—Clear Lake, 199
University of Houston—Downtown, 200
University of Houston—University Park, 200
University of St. Thomas, 200
University of Texas Health Science Center at Houston, 200
University of Texas M. D. Anderson Cancer Center, 242

University State Bank, 164
Urban Affairs Corporation, 260
USF&G Company, 265
Utility Fuels, 353

V

Vacation Travel Services, 355
VAM PTS, 303
Variable Annuity Life Insurance, 265
Variable Annuity Marketing Company, 271
Vertical Software, 188
Vetco Pipeline Services, 303
Veterans Administration, 237
VGS, Inc., 260
Vinson & Elkins, Attorneys at Law, 276
Vista Chemical Company, 179
Vollmer Public Relations, 317
Volunteer Center of the Texas Gulf Coast, The, 260
Volunteers of America, Houston, 261

W

Wal-Mart Discount Cities, 345
Wang Laboratories, 183, 213
Warner Cable Company, 173
Watkins, Carter, Hamilton, 157
Weatherford International, 303
Weil Gotshal and Manges, 276
Weiner's Stores, 345
Weingarten Realty Investors, 325
Weinstein, Spira and Company, 143
Welch, Robert A., Foundation, 230
Wendy's Old Fashioned Hamburgers, 336
Westcap Corp., 271
Western Lithograph, 314
Westheimer Rigging and Heavy Hauling, 193
Westin Galleria/Westin Oaks, 249
Westinghouse Electric Corporation, 213
Weston, Roy F., 219
Wetmore & Company, 314
Wharton County Junior College, 200
Whataburger Restaurants, 336
White, Petrov & McHone, 143
White Swan, 309
White Swan Food Company, 227
William Brothers Construction Company, 193
William Telecommunications Group, 213
Wilson Downhole Service, 303
Wilson Industries, 303

How to Get a Job

Windsor Travel Corp., 356
Winius-Brandon Advertising, 148
Wood, Lucksinger and Epstein, 276
Woodard Hall and Primm, 276
Woodlake Travel Services, 356
Woodlands Athletic Center, 329
Woodlands Corporation, 325
Woodlands Securities Corp., 272
Woolworth, F.W., Company, 345
World Gym, 329
Wormser Hat Stores, 345
Wortham Foundation, 230
Wortham, John L., & Son, 266
Wright Marketing Communications, 317
Wurzer, Gerhard, Galleries, 290
Wyle Laboratories Applied Research Division, 152
Wyndham Hotel Greenspoint, 249

X

Xerox Corporation, 213
Xerox Reproduction Center, 314

Y

YMCA of the Greater Houston Area, 329
Young, Charles P., Houston, 314
Young Men's Christian Association of the Greater Ho, 261
Young Women's Christian Association of Houston (YWC, 261

Z

Zann Commercial Brokerage, 325
Zapata Corporation, 295
Ziegler, Cooper, 158

General Index

A

Accounting/Auditing: selected firms; professional groups, professional magazines, and directories, 140-143

Advertising: selected agencies; professional groups, professional magazines, and directories, 145-149

Aerospace: selected firms; professional groups, publications, and directories, 150-153

Aid, 115-118

Architecture: selected firms; professional groups, professional magazines, and directories, 153-158

Art Galleries: *see Museums/Art Galleries*

Associations: *see Information Resources for listing of local Network Groups*

Auditing: *see Accounting*

B

Banks/Credit Unions/S&Ls: selected institutions; professional groups, professional magazines, and directories, 159-166

Beverage Industry: *see Food/Beverage*

Book/Magazine Publishers: selected firms; professional groups, professional magazines, and directories, 167-169

Books: *see Resource Books*

Broadcasting: selected firms and TV, cable, and radio stations; professional groups, trade magazines, and directories, 170-175

C

Career Analysis: *see Vocational Testing*

Career Consultants, 15-17, 90-91

Career Objectives, how to establish, 9-11

Career Transition Issues, 128

Chambers of Commerce, 4-7

Charitable Organizations, 117

Chemical Industry: selected companies; trade groups, trade magazines, and directories, 175-179

Colleges, list of local: *see Educational Institutions*

Computer Industry: selected equipment manufacturers and programming and software companies; trade groups, trade magazines, and directories: 179-184 (equipment manufacturers); 185-188 (programming and software)

Consultants, Career: *see Career Consultants*

Consultants, Vocational:
how to choose, 15, 90-91
local listing, 16-17

Construction: selected firms; professional groups, professional magazines, directories, 189-193

Consumer Protection Agencies, 14

Counseling, Career, 15-17, 90-91

Counseling, Psychological:
as support during job search, 121-126

Cover Letter: *see also Resume*
preparation of, 28, 36
sample formats, 33-35

Crisis Centers, 123

D

Data Processing: *see Computer Industry*

Day Care Centers, 7

Department Stores: *see Retailers*

Directories, 40-46 *(see also under employment categories)*

Disabled Workers: *see Handicapped Workers*

Drugs and Pharmaceuticals: selected manufacturers; trade groups, trade magazines, and directories, 194-196

E

Educational Institutions: selected schools, universities, colleges; professional groups, professional magazines, and directories, 197-206

Economic Outlook for Houston area, 3

Electronics/Telecommunications: selected firms; trade groups, trade magazines, and directories, 207-213

373

Employers Index, 360
Employment Agencies:
  listing of local agencies, 87-90
  pros and cons of using, 85-86
Employment Services, *see Chapter 6 and the following:*
  government, 96-97
  social service agencies, 95-96
  veterans, 97
Engineering: selected firms; professional groups, professional magazines, and directories, 214-220
Environmental Services:
  selected firms, professional groups, and publications, 221-222
Executive Search Firms:
  listing of local firms, 92-95
  pros and cons of using, 91

F

Financial Assistance Programs, 115-116
Financial Management: *see Chapter 8*
  during job search, 59, 110-112
Fired: *see Chapter 9*
  coping with being fired, 121, 127
Fitness: *see Recreation/Sports/Fitness*
Food/Beverage Industry: selected food and beverage producers and distributors; trade groups, trade magazines, and directories, 223-227
Foundations: selected institutions; professional groups, publications, and directories, 228-230

G

Government Agencies: selected federal, state, and local agencies; professional groups, professional magazines, and directories, 231-237
Government Assistance Programs, 115-116
Government Employment Resources, 97
Guidance, Vocational, 15-17, 90-91; *see also Chapter 2*

H

Handicapped Workers:
  resource books, 13
Health Care: selected health care facilities; professional groups, professional magazines, and directories, 237-243
Hotels/Motels: selected firms; professional groups, professional magazines, and directories, 245-249
Human Services: selected providers; professional groups, professional magazines, and directories, 250-261

I

Information Resources (*see also Resource Books*):
  career resource facilities, 15-17, 39
  Chambers of Commerce, 4-7
  directories, 40-46
  job-hunting strategy books, 12-13, 66
  job listings, 55-56
  libraries, 37-39
  libraries, university, 39
  magazines, feature, 48
  magazines, general, 49
  magazines, trade and special interest, 50-55
  network groups (listing of local), 67-82
  newspapers, 46-49
  small business, 19
  visitor and relocation information, 4, 7-8
  women, 13, 45, 46, 126
Insurance Industry: selected underwriters and brokers; professional groups, professional magazines, and directories, 262-266
Internships, 80
Interviewing:
  books on, 108
  exploratory, or informal, 61, 98-100
  follow-up correspondence, 108
  formal, 104-107
  how to succeed in, *see Chapter 7*
  personal history in, 98-100
  techniques and strategies, 101-107, *also see Chapter 7*
  work history in, 100

374

General Index

Investment Bankers/Stock Brokers: selected investment bankers and stock brokers; professional groups, professional magazines, and directories, 266-272

J

Job Market:
  local trends, 3-4
  researching the job market, *see Chapter 4*
Job Offer:
  evaluation of, 133-136
Job Search :
  conducting while employed versus unemployed, 110
  handling finances during, 59, 110-112
  how to cope, 57-59, 110-111, 128
  length of, 57, 110
  listings, 55-56
  when to conduct, 9

L

Law Firms: selected law firms; professional groups, professional magazines, and directories, 272-276
Libraries, 37-39

M

Magazines: *see under Information Resources*
Management Consultants: selected firms; professional groups, professional magazines, and directories, 277-280
Media, Newspapers and Magazines: major publications; professional groups, professional magazines, and directories, 281-285
Mental Health Centers, 124-126
Mid-Life Career Change: *see Resource Books*
Museums/Art Galleries: selected institutions; professional groups, magazines, directories, 286-290

N,O

Networking (*see Chapter 5*):
  as key to job search success, 60
  contacts (how to locate), 60-63
  executive, 67
  exploratory interviews, 61, 98-100
  function of, 60
  hiring authority (how to contact), 64-66
  local networks, 67-82
  organization and recordkeeping, 63-64
  sample letter, 61
  telephone networking, 65
Newspapers:
  listing of local newspapers, 46-49
  want-ads and how to answer, 48, 66
Oil, Gas, and Plastics: selected firms; professional groups, publications, and directories, 290-304
Organizations, Professional, 67-82 (*see also under employment categories*)

P

Paper and Allied Products: selected companies; trade groups, trade magazines, and directories, 305-309
Part-Time Employment, 112-114
Personnel Department, 66
Pharmaceuticals: *see Drugs and Pharmaceuticals*
Plastics: *see Oil, Gas, and Plastics*
Printing Industry: selected firms; trade groups trade magazines, and directories, 310-314
Psychological Counseling, 121-126
Public Relations: selected firms; professional groups, publications, and directories, 315-318

R

Radio Stations: *see Broadcasting*
Real Estate: selected firms; professional groups, professional magazines, and directories, 319-325
Recreation/Sports/Fitness: selected providers; professional groups, professional magazines, and directories, 326-329
References, Use of, 109
Relocation, 4, 18

Resource Books:
  on career planning, 12-13
  for college students, 12
  for handicapped workers, 13
  on interviewing, 108
  on job-hunting strategy, 12-13, 66
  for mid-life career change, 12
  for resume preparation, 24
  for retirement years, 13
  on salary negotiation, 132
  for vocational analysis, 12-13
  for women, 13, 45-46
Restaurant Industry: selected restaurants; professional groups, professional magazines, and directories, 330-336
Resume: *see Chapter 3; see also Cover Letter*
  distribution of, 28
  function of, 20
  preparation of, 21-24, 29
  professional resume preparers, 25-27
  resource books on, 24
  sample formats, 23, 30-32
  screening done by employer, 66
Retailers: selected retailers; professional groups, professional magazines, and directories, 337-345

S

Salary Negotiation, 132
  resource books on, 132
Service Corps of Retired Executives (SCORE), 19
Small Business Administration assistance, 19
Social Service Agencies, 117-118
Sports: *see Recreation/Sports/Fitness*
Spouse Employment, 18
Stock Brokers: *see Investment Bankers/Stock Brokers*

T

Tax Deductible Expenses, 59
Telecommunications: *see Electronics/Telecommunications*
Telemarketing, 118
Telephone Networking, 65
Television: *see Broadcasting*
Temporary Employment: *see Part-Time Employment*
Testing, Vocational, 14, 39, 95
Trade Magazines, 50-55

Trade Organizations, 67-82, *see also under employment categories*
Transportation in Houston area, 7-8
Travel, Transportation, Shipping: selected firms; trade groups, trade magazines, and directories, 347-356

U,V

Unemployment Benefits, 116
Universities: *see Educational Institutions*
Utilities: area companies; trade groups, trade magazines, and directories, 356-359
Veteran's Centers, 97
Vocational Consultants: *see Consultants, Vocational*
Vocational Objective:
  how to develop, *see Chapter 2*
  self-appraisal exercise, 10-11
Vocational Testing:
  types of assessment tests, 14
  where offered, 16-17, 39, 95
Volunteer Work, possibility of it leading to employment, 75, 318

W

Want-ads, 48, 66
"Watering Holes" for Networking, 82
Women:
  career resource centers, 126-127
  resource books for, 13, 45-46